For Jerome Mazzaro

Library of Congress Cataloging in Publication D

Phillips, Robert S
    The confessional poets.

    (Crosscurrents/modern critiques)
    Bibliography: p.
    1.   American poetry—20th century—History and
criticism. I. Title.
PS323.5.P5   811'.5'409   73–8970
ISBN 0–8093–0642–5

Copyright © 1973 by Southern Illinois University Press
All rights reserved
Printed in the United States of America
Designed by Andor Braun

POETRY EXPLICATION

Grateful acknowledgment is made to the following publishers and agents
for their permission to use quotations that appear in this volume.

STANLEY KUNITZ: From "A Choice of Weapons" from *Selected Poems
1928–1958* by Stanley Kunitz. Copyright © 1956 by Stanley Kunitz.
Reprinted by permission of Atlantic-Little, Brown.
ROBERT LOWELL: *Life Studies*, copyright © 1956, 1959 by Robert
Lowell; *For the Union Dead*, copyright © 1956, 1960, 1961, 1962,
1963, 1964 by Robert Lowell; *Notebook*, copyright © 1967, 1968,
1969, 1970 by Robert Lowell. Reprinted with the permission of

iv

The Confessional Poets

Robert Phillips

WITH A PREFACE BY

Harry T. Moore

SOUTHERN ILLINOIS UNIVERSITY PRESS
Carbondale and Edwardsville

FEFFER & SIMONS, INC.
London and Amsterdam

Crosscurrents / MODERN CRITIQUES

Harry T. Moore, *General Editor*

Parts of this book appeared in different form in several publications. They are reprinted here with permission and with thanks to the editors of those journals.

"Snodgrass and the Sad Hospital of the World," *University of Windsor Review*, 4, No. 2 (Spring 1969).

"The Bleeding Rose and the Blooming Mouth: The Love Poems of Anne Sexton," *Modern Poetry Studies*, 1, No. 1 (June 1970).

"John Berryman's Literary Offenses" (under the title "Balling the Muse," copyright © 1971 by the University of Northern Iowa) *North American Review*, 257, No. 4 (Winter 1971–72).

"The Dark Funnel: A Reading of Sylvia Plath," *Modern Poetry Studies*, 3, No. 2 (Fall 1972).

Material included in chapter 4 was published as "Grimm Tales," *Modern Poetry Studies*, 3, No. 4 (1972).

I would be remiss if I did not acknowledge the support of my friend, Erica Jong, who in a dark time helped these eyes to see. The late William Van O'Connor encouraged this book. And once again my beloved wife, Judith Bloomingdale, has helped beyond the possibilities of acknowledgment.

Contents

Preface

The lyric poem is, by definition, personal. But the confessional poem is more intensely so. As Robert Phillips points out in the present book, we can trace confessional poetry as far back as Sappho, comparatively early in the ancient world, as well as to Catullus, a later poet of classic times; Mr. Phillips also mentions Whitman. There is of course Lawrence in our own century: has any poet ever written anything more nakedly confessional than "Look! We Have Come Through" (1917)?

Recently in America an entire group of verse makers has appeared, virtually members of a "school"; and it is these writers whom Mr. Phillips (along with M. L. Rosenthal) calls the confessional poets. Some of them were influenced by Robert Lowell, whom they in turn influenced to a certain extent. It is the working out of these relationships and the analysis of various poems by these men and women that make the present book so attractively interesting a critical study.

As it points out, the confessional poetry of today substantially began in 1959 when Robert Lowell published his Life Studies, though Lowell's vision may be partly traceable to those of some earlier writers, such as Baudelaire and Rilke, whose verses he translated as what he called "imitations." And, as Mr. Phillips notes, the late Theodore Roethke, one of the poets this volume deals with specifically, had written in the confessional vein back in 1948, with The Lost Son, although he "did not greatly influence other poets, at least not until years later." Besides Lowell and Roethke, the author deals with Anne Sexton, W. D. Snodgrass, John Berryman, and Sylvia Plath, the last two suicides like Hart Crane.

Besides her poetry, Sylvia Plath wrote a confessional novel, The Bell Jar, which Mr. Phillips also treats. Indeed, he gives us the fullest picture yet drawn of Lowell and Sylvia Plath in terms of their confessional lyrics, accentuating the burden of family upon their lives, in the case of Plath even stressing the suggestions of unconscious incest buried in the poetry. But Mr. Phillips's thorough investigation of the work of these and other contemporary "confessionalists" in no way spoils it; indeed, his explication shows some of them as all the more effective as poets.

Indeed, he displays not only gifts as an examiner of these poets, but also a talent for equalizing criticism. He is particularly incisive in looking at the last two volumes by John Berryman, whom he finds committing "offenses" against the confessional genre. Mr. Phillips on various occasions shows that he doesn't beamishly accept all confessional writings, but this balancing element in his critical approach makes his praise all the more valuable when he bestows it. He gives us a fine summary of a movement and of the writings of those who are a part of it; and, as previously indicated, his evaluations of them are very useful.

He expresses regret that he cannot deal with even more poets and indicates that the space limitations of this series make his wish to do so impossible. Regrettably, the series has to keep its volumes at a certain length, or below, because of current printing costs; we want to maintain these books within a certain price-range, particularly so that students can purchase them. The publishers join Mr. Phillips in lamenting these space limitations, for he suggests that he would have liked to discuss other poets, including, for their later confessional work, Stanley Kunitz (whom he does deal with in passing) and Karl Shapiro. But what Robert Phillips has given us in this book is of unquestionable value for modern criticism and modern poetry.

HARRY T. MOORE

Southern Illinois University
March 21, 1973

Introduction

This study is, so far as I know, the first book-length attempt at examining what has come to be a major development in American literature in the second half of the twentieth century—i.e., the "confessional" poem, the "confessional" poet. A short view was taken by M. L. Rosenthal, in the second chapter of his *The New Poets* (1967). But whereas books of confessional poetry continue to multiply, books of criticism about them are curiously absent.

Yet it could be argued that we are living in a great Age of Autobiography. We no longer believe in the general truths about human nature, only the subjective ones. *Let me tell you about my wound . . . Let me tell you about my scars and deformities . . .* our writers cry out. Not only poems, but the novel (*Herzog; Portnoy's Complaint*) and journalism (Norman Mailer's *The Prisoner of Sex;* Merle Miller's *On Being Different*) are all part of this current autobiographical frenzy. All these are writers who assume that objectivity is impossible, and who in their writing are determined, come what may, to "let it all hang out." And it must be conceded that the poets have far outdistanced their prose cousins in accomplishment and recognition.

While I offer, in my opening pages, a leisurely and informal definition of just what constitutes a confessional poem, it should be said at the outset that such poetry rarely conforms to the *Webster's New Collegiate Dictionary* definition of poetry as "The embodiment in appropriate language of beautiful or high thought . . ." The subjects of confessional poetry are rarely beautiful; the language is frequently less so. To appreciate it the reader must first accept the view that there are no inherently poetic or unpoetic materials—only sensibilities which render materials into poetry. He must agree with Wallace Stevens, who felt nothing too mundane to provide a base for poetic construction. By divining resemblances or analogies, Stevens said, "one may find intimations of immortality in an object on the mantelpiece; and these intimations are as real in the mind in which they occur as the mantelpiece itself." The reader should also embrace William Carlos Williams's belief that the *materia poetica* is anything "seen, smelt, touched, apprehended, and understood to be what it is— the flesh of a constantly repeated permanence."

Williams and Stevens, of course, were not confessional poets. The difference between their type of poetry and that which is the subject of this study should be apparent in the first chapter. Yet they are just two of a host of American poets in the first five decades of this century whose attitudes toward poetic material made possible the achievement of confessional poetry. The change in point of view began with Walt Whitman. Today his followers push this attitude to the extreme. One could be facetious and say that a Father Complex and the willingness to write openly about it is a necessary criterion for becoming a confessional poet—since the reader will encounter here such poets as Sylvia Plath, John Berryman, Theodore Roethke, and Robert Lowell, all of whom appear obsessed by father love / hatred or by the necessity for father atonement, as is Stanley Kunitz. But this would be no more accurate than to say that a confessional poet is one whose father's name was Otto (a forename shared by both the elder Roethke and the elder Plath). Another common theme is mental illness. To those readers who would turn their backs upon such poetry, thinking it too nakedly embarrassing, and calling the poems mad and the poets madmen, I would gently remind them of the Cheshire Cat's reply to Alice when she protested, "But I don't want to go among mad people!" The cat's famous response was, of course, "Oh, you can't help that . . . we're all mad. I'm mad, you're mad."

Exactly. In this post-Christian, post-Kennedy, post-pill America, that which in former times passed as insanity of sorts is now often enough the norm. As E. M. Forster proclaimed in *Howards End*: "What are the facts? We are all mad more or less, you know, in these times." Only the outcry of the most anguished is strong enough to be heard above the riots at home and the war abroad, the constant uncertainty of the self. It was also Wallace Stevens who said, "As life grows more terrible, its literature grows more terrible." Anne Sexton would agree, telling her countrymen "one can't build little white picket fences to keep nightmares out." Because the world has changed, the men and women writing today write a changed poetry. Multiple marriages and miscarriages, war atrocities and suicides can now be seen as just as valid subjects for the poet as, say, an imperfect rose or a perfect lady. There are, after all, more police sirens than nightingales heard in our cities; more garbage disposals than Grecian urns in our homes; more smokestacks than yew trees on the horizon. As the editors of a recent college poetry anthology have said, "too much of the world we know would be excluded and the poet would become a half-man if his songs did not include pain, anguish, and ugliness, as well as pleasure, delight, and beauty."

Perhaps the new poet focuses too exclusively upon the pain, anguish, and ugliness of life at the expense of its pleasure, delight, and beauty. Some manage to embrace all experience—notably Theodore Roethke, whose books cover a wide range of mood and styles, including nonsense verse. But for the most part those under discussion have made anguish their focal point; and if one agrees that we not only live in the best of times but, in some ways, the worst of times, to read their work carefully is to attain a heightened perception of the way we really live here and now. Seen in this manner the confessional poets are not, in their choice of subjects, "sicker" than the rest of us—they merely hold back less.

I have concentrated on poets whose confessional books have been issued since 1959 (with the exception of Roethke, whose *The Lost Son* precedes that date). Primarily I have commented on the subject of the poets' work, rather than the form. For an introductory book, I felt that what a poet has to say is more important than how he says it. With the truly seminal books of the movement—*Life Studies, Heart's Needle, The Lost Son,* as well as with Mrs. Sexton's *Love Poems*—I have attempted a poem-by-poem textual explication in the manner of "A Reader's Guide to . . ." Less important books receive less detailed treatment and are discussed thematically. Wherever interviews or personal comments by the poets were available to illuminate their work, I have quoted from them. I have also cross-referenced the poets' subjects and symbols when possible. The critical methods I employ vary from poet to poet; this is not a thesis book in which the critic tries to make each poet's work "prove" a given point. Only in my last chapter, on Sylvia Plath, for instance, have I attempted a psychoanalytical approach based on known biographical facts. In the instance of Plath, a plethora of memoirs and solid biographical material have already been made available, making such an approach possible and, hopefully, fruitful. Finally, I have attempted to guide, to appraise, and to point to what are new avenues of creation open to the poet writing today.

The size of books in the Crosscurrents series prevents the inclusion of discussion of some poets, young and older, who perhaps belong in this company. Some critics will doubtless miss a discussion of Allen Ginsberg. Surely Ginsberg has been, if nothing else, at times nakedly confessional. His sole motivation seems to be to strip himself bare, as he has done, literally, on the stage during at least one poetry reading. But to stand unclothed, to confess all, is not necessarily to create art. The most boring old drunk on the barstool can strip and confess. Not that Ginsberg is ever exactly boring. But creating the poem as a work of art seems to interest him not at all. Rather than perfect the poem, he prefers to leave it to be "*discovered* in the mind and in the process of writing it out on the page as notes, transcriptions."

I refrain from a chapter on Ginsberg, but not for reasons of poetics but rather of content. "Howl," the poem which made Ginsberg infamous, and the rest of the pieces in the volume appearing under that title, are more universal public wails than personal. There and elsewhere Ginsberg wears the mantle of Whitman and Lindsay: both of whom he has acknowledged in print as mentors. And though I have called Whitman an important precursor of confessional poetry, no one save Ginsberg has used him directly as a model. Moreover, Ginsberg's *Howl* (1956) and *Kaddish* (1961) seem to have influenced no other poet in the confessional school the way that Lowell's *Life Studies* and Snodgrass's *Heart's Needle* have done. While Ginsberg's candor has been admired, it has not been imitated; the lack of form in his long-line narratives with their sloppy diction, syntax, and rhythms has been found unsatisfactory if not inferior. For all his/her emotional compulsions, every poet discussed in this volume is a consummate craftsman. It is as if the well-made poem in itself brings order to the poet's life. Ginsberg alone confronts chaos with chaos. His poems are not hewn, but spewn, and the reader is left with a feeling of satiation rather than satisfaction.

Ginsberg, who preaches better than he practices, has made a vital distinction between confessional and non-confessional poetry in his *Paris Review* interview, in which he states the difference as that which one would tell one's friends and what one would tell one's Muse. The problem of the confessional poet, Ginsberg says, is to break down that distinction, to approach the Muse as frankly as one talks with one's friends: "It's the ability to commit to writing, to *write*, the same way that you . . . are!" Ginsberg advocates a literature free of the hypocrisy which pre-supposes that formal literature must be different in subject, in diction, and even in organization, from our quotidian inspired lives. To Ginsberg, confessional poetry is born of "the self-confidence of someone who knows that he's really alive, and that his existence is just as good as any other subject matter." [1] To this I would merely add that no genuine art is *merely* autobiographical, as Ginsberg's own work reveals. The aesthetic process must transform motifs without demolishing their bearing.

Unlike the omission of Ginsberg, I genuinely regret exclusion of a chapter, eliminated for reasons of length, on the development of Stanley Kunitz. Kunitz was late in joining the movement: *The Testing-Tree*, his confessional testament, was not published until twelve years after *Life Studies*. Some may not consider him part of the movement yet. But I maintain Kunitz has always been favorably disposed toward highly personal poetry. One of his early poems, "A Choice of Weapons," must be read as a defense of the confessional mode: ". . . do not pity those whose motives bleed / Even while strolling in a former garden. / Observe that tears are bullets when they harden; / The triggered poem's no water-pistol toy, / But shoots its course, and is a source of joy."

While looking favorably upon confessional poetry, Kunitz erected in his earlier books such barriers of rhetoric one was often uncertain concerning the poet's attitude toward his subject. But with *The Testing-Tree* Kunitz abandoned gnarled obscurities in favor of simple, direct, trustful confessional statements; he here openly, admirably explored the mythic father / son theme embedded in his early books. Interested readers are referred to my discussion of that volume as published in *North American Review*, 257, No. 1 (Spring 1971–72).

Others who might have been included in this book are Denise Levertov, Maxine Kumin, Adrienne Rich, John Logan, Jerome Mazzaro, William Heyen, Barbara Harr, Randall Jarrell, and Karl Shapiro (the later books). So might Delmore Schwartz, whose fiction and early poetry were important precursors of today's confessional literature: "High in the summer branches the poet sang. / His throat ached, and he could sing no more."

ROBERT PHILLIPS

Falmouth, Massachusetts, 1969—
Düsseldorf, Germany 1972

The Confessional Poets

1

The Confessional Mode in Modern American Poetry

"The poets? The poets lie too much," Nietzsche said. Since 1959, however, there have been a number of American poets determined not to lie in verse. Whatever the cost in public exposure or private anguish, their subjects are most often themselves and always the things they most intimately know. The emotions that they portray are always true to their own feelings. And the opinions they express are born of deep personal conviction, not currency of literary fashion. The work of these poets has been called "confessional." As a genre, "confessional poetry" has become a potent force in the literary history of the post-Eisenhower years. One need only recall the numerous Pulitzer Prizes and National Book Awards for Poetry won by its leading practitioners since 1959: Lowell, Kunitz, Jarrell, Roethke, Sexton, Snodgrass, Kumin, and Berryman have all been recipients, some several times each, for volumes which fall within our definition.

The critic M. L. Rosenthal takes at least partial credit for naming "The Confessional Poets." Writing of the first time he had used the phrase, in his review of that seminal book, Robert Lowell's *Life Studies* (in 1959), Rosenthal states, "The term 'confessional poetry' came naturally to my mind . . . Whoever invented it, it was a term both helpful and too limited, and very possibly the conception of a confessional school has by now done a certain amount of damage." [1]

Another poet-critic, Hayden Carruth, has independently found the term "confessional" to be damaging, feeling it "implied that Lowell was engaged in public breast-beating, a kind of refreshing new psycho-exotic pastime, or in a shallow exercise of 'self-expression,' long ago discredited; whereas in fact his aim was far more serious than that." [2]

What both men fail to realize is not only that the "conception of a confessional school" did not spring full panoplied from the brain of M. L. Rosenthal; but also that Robert Lowell's poetry did not initiate it. Lowell in fact would be the first to admit that his writing stems from a tradition rather than an innovation: in his volume of translations he has written what he chooses to call "imitations" of confessional poems by Rilke, Baudelaire, others.

There have always been confessional poets. That is, there have always been confessional artists, some of whom happen to be poets. Even the cavemen, drawing on walls the images of animals they had to kill, were in their way confessional artists. If they drew the image of the animal truly enough, they believed, it would insure a successful slaying. "The arrow or ax delivered the final blow, but the beast was really done in by his depiction, the rendering of him by the hunter, whose real weapon was his art." [3]

All confessional art, whether poetry or not, is a means of killing the beasts which are within us, those dreadful dragons of dreams and experiences that must be hunted down, cornered, and exposed in order to be destroyed. But the therapeutic value of confessional poetry did not achieve official recognition until the early 1970's, when several universities began giving formal training in "poetry therapy," under the assumption that the poem of an inhibited, repressed person may tell his doctor more than a revelation of his dreams.[4] This obviously has been the experience of Anne Sexton, who says in her *Paris Review* interview, "my doctors tell me that I understand something in a poem that I haven't integrated into my life. In fact, I may be concealing it from myself, while I was revealing it to the readers. The poetry is often more advanced, in terms of my unconscious, than I am. Poetry, after all, milks the unconscious." [5] Which is why, we suppose, that we are always told that "Confession is good for the soul." This need to confess is as old as man, and its manifestations as old as the cave paintings. To aver that "confessional poetry" began with Robert Lowell is to claim that architecture began with Frank Lloyd Wright. Even Sappho in the sixth century B.C. wrote, "I confess / I love that / which caresses / me." [6] And Catullus, more than two thousand years ago, confided, "I hate and love. / And if you ask me why, / I have no answer, but I discern, / can feel, my senses rooted in eternal torture." [7]

This sense of eternal torture is one of the motivating forces behind any confessional art. That is why St. Augustine, with his acute sensitivity to the conflicts and problems of the inner life, must be considered an important progenitor of confessional literature. (There is evidence that at least one modern poet has consciously patterned his book after Augustine: see Chapter 5 on John Berryman. The difference between Augustine's autobiographical confession, with his concern for the self and his intense awareness of evil, and today's confessions, lies in the way he resolved his existential dilemmas. Augustine employed Christian metaphysics, whereas today's poets by and large resort to existential methods.) An Augustinian awareness of human nature and a sense of eternal torture also permeates that great "poem," Jean Jacques Rousseau's *Confessions*—one of the frankest self-revelations ever offered the public, and one written two hundred years ago (1781–88). It was followed by the numerous "confessions" of nineteenth-century Romantics, De Quincey, Musset, Chateaubriand, and certainly the Wordsworth of *The Prelude*.

More recently, America's Walt Whitman, ever confessional, declares in one of his Calamus poems: "As I pass O Manhattan, your frequent and swift flash of eyes offering me love, / Offering response to my own—these repay me, / Lovers, continual lovers, only repay me." Whitman may have been America's first blatantly confessional poet. Certainly if Robert Lowell is the father of the current group, Whitman is the great-grandfather. At least three moderns have acknowledged him as such. Allen Ginsberg, in his "A Supermarket in California," pays tribute to Whitman and calls him the "lonely old courage teacher." It was Whitman who taught courage to many moderns—the courage to write about what they are and where they have been. John Berryman, in *The Dream Songs*, makes several allusions to "the great Walt," and states that a Whitman was one of five books he took to Ireland. And Theodore Roethke invokes the good grey poet with these words: "Be with me, Whitman, maker of catalogues: / For the world invades me again."

Yet the role of confessional poet is not a popular view assigned to Whitman by certain academics. Sculley Bradley, for instance, has said that Whitman's references to Self were really "socialized" references, as in, for instance, the "I" of old ballads. Professor Bradley states that Whitman assumed for himself "only what all others could have on their own terms assumed." [8] But it was Whitman who wrote, "I am the man, I suffered, I was there." Where is the socialization in that kind of naked statement? This is not T. S. Eliot, hiding behind the mask of Tiresias, in his statement, "I, Tiresias, have suffered all . . . ," a comparison about which more will be said shortly.

Sappho, Catullus, Augustine, Rousseau, Rilke, Baudelaire, Whitman, countless others through the ages have written with the Self as primary subject, the Self treated with the utmost frankness and lack of restraint. It is well to remember that, at the least, confessional poetry can be traced as far back as Sir Thomas Wyatt, which is pretty far; and that Pope's famous *Epistle to Arbuthnot* is a worthy example of the genre, as is Wordsworth's *Prelude* and Byron's *Don Juan*. The confessional mode, then, has always been with us. It merely has not until recently been officially "named." It is that writing which is highly subjective, which is in direct opposition to that other school of which Auden and Eliot are modern members—writers who consciously strove all but to obliterate their own concrete personalities in their poems. It is poetry written in opposition to, or reaction from, the Eliotic aesthetic which influenced several generations of poets, and which can best be summarized in Old Possum's statement, "Poetry is not a turning loose of emotion, but an escape from emotion; it is not the expression of personality, but an escape from personality." [9]

In refusing to don the Eliotic mantle of reticence, these new confessional poets give to the public those outpourings previously reserved for the Father Confessor or the analyst. For nearly fifteen hundred years the priest and church gave relief to the morally isolated and disturbed. When the Church proved incapable of maintaining her leadership in intellectual circles, creative people in particular turned to analysts for self-understanding. Yet even this form of confession became, for some, as morally crippling as that to the priest. Thus many have turned to the more Protestant form of individual confession on the printed page—getting it all out in the open, with no second party between them and the "sinful" thoughts or deeds which estrange them from themselves and others.

If Lowell did not start this revival of the confessional mode in America, it must be conceded that it was not prevalent and imitated until the end of the 1950s, when he broke from the Catholic themes and constipated language of his early work to parade forth the adulteries, arrests, divorces, and breakdowns which constitute his *Life Studies*. (Roethke's *The Lost Son*, for instance, appeared as early as 1948, but did not greatly influence other poets, at least not until years later.) Until Lowell's volume, the exceedingly tidy "academic" poem was king: the witty, Audenesque poem which could open with an allusion to Ares and close with a reference to the *New Yorker*—as in fact Auden's own "Under Which Lyre" actually does. When such poems were not "witty" they were deliberately obscure.

Life Studies was the first postwar book, written as self-therapy and breaking through to the personal, which reached a wide audience. Its influence upon other poets was profound. Just as all short stories are said to have come out from Gogol's "Overcoat," so all modern American confessional poetry seems influenced by Lowell's direct, easily understood volume. *Life Studies* was the antithesis of all that was witty or obscure. It struck an hitherto lost chord whose echoes reverberate even today. Books which in effect begin where Lowell left off, as well as blatant imitations by writers who add nothing of their own, continue to appear in America. (English poets, on the other hand, were not especially influenced, except perhaps for Ted Hughes, and we must remember that he was the husband of Sylvia Plath, an American Lowell student.)

Chronologically Lowell was perhaps not the first to acknowledge in the confessional mode a vision which was representative of our time, a vision which could be therapeutic and life-enhancing. We have mentioned Roethke's *The Lost Son*. But the credit might rest more with W. D. Snodgrass. Lowell has said as much: "He [Snodgrass] did these things before I did, though he's younger than I am and had been my student. He may have influenced me, though people have suggested the opposite." [10] And Anne Sexton, the reigning high-priestess of the confessional school, also credits Snodgrass with showing her how to dare to be true: "W. D. Snodgrass showed me in the first place . . ." [11] When asked if her study with Lowell didn't really mark the beginning of her confessional poems, she has said, "At that time Lowell had not revealed what he was doing." [12] Elsewhere she states she had sent Lowell the poems of her own *To Bedlam and Part Way Back* the year before *Life Studies* appeared. [13]

So Snodgrass must indeed be recognized as a cofounder of the school, and perhaps Mrs. Sexton as a third. Snodgrass's first and best book, *Heart's Needle*, was published in 1959, the same year as *Life Studies*. (Mrs. Sexton's first volume, the above-mentioned *To Bedlam and Part Way Back*, was published a year later. In all probability the personal poems Snodgrass and Sexton submitted to Lowell did show the older poet how to remove the mask and articulate his life in art. It is interesting to conjecture what effect, if any, the work of Sylvia Plath had upon Lowell as well. Together with Anne Sexton she regularly visited Lowell's poetry classes at Boston University during 1958–59, the year prior to *Life Studies*.) A fascinating short literary history might be written tracing the interrelations of this group from Boston to Iowa City to London. Anne Sexton, for instance, made a pilgrimage to the Antioch Writers' Conference to meet and learn from Snodgrass. In Plath's case, Lowell has hastened to deny the influence: "Somehow none of it sank very deep into my awareness. I sensed her abashment and distinction, and never guessed her later appalling and triumphant fulfillment." [14] Sexton, on the other hand, does not mind saying she learned from Plath's later work, *Ariel*—particularly from Plath's daring to write "hate poems." [15]

However influenced, Lowell remains the one spiritual father of the family. Significantly, that is the name Mrs. Sexton gives Lowell in her own prose reminiscence of the Boston class: "We tried, each one in his own manner; sometimes letting our own poems come up, as for a butcher, as for a lover. Both went on. We kept as quiet as possible *in view of the father*" (italics mine).[16] One certainly can find in Plath's work, as well as in Mrs. Sexton's, an affinity for the Lowell of *Life Studies* and beyond. The other great influence upon the later poets is Theodore Roethke, with his preoccupation with Self, his openness of metaphor, and his fierce concentration on intensely personal themes. Mrs. Sexton was not kidding when she wrote to Miss Plath, "if you're not careful, Sylvia, you will out-Roethke Roethke." [17] In a few poems, such as "Mushrooms" and "Poppies in July," and the radio play "Three Women," she did. (Compare her plea, "Leaves and petals attend me. I am ready," with Roethke's "Worm, be with me. This is my hard time.") Plath also shared with Roethke a gift for Keats's "negative capability"—a personal identification with the "personality" of the poetic subject, be it a stone or a saint.

What specifically are the characteristics of the new poetry? Generally it consists of balanced narrative poems with unbalanced or afflicted protagonists. These are poems which ask rather than answer questions. They employ irony and understatement as a means of attaining artistic detachment—as in Lowell's line, "My mind's not right," from "Skunk Hour."

The confessional poets chiefly employ the Self as sole

poetic symbol. They are artists whose total mythology is the lost self. (One of Roethke's books is titled *The Lost Son*; Jarrell published both *Losses* and *The Lost World*.) A confessional poem is surely not a mere recitation of losses or facts. Nor should the facts displayed be taken for literal truth. Nevertheless, as its name implies, confessional poetry springs from the need to confess. Each poem is in some way a declaration of dependence. Or of guilt. Or of anguish and suffering. Thus, the writing of each such poem is an ego-centered, though not an egocentric, act; its goal is self-therapy and a certain purgation. In her third book Mrs. Sexton declares, "Everyone has left me / except my muse, / *that good nurse*" (italics are hers). The epigraph from a letter by Kafka which she appends to her second volume is definitive: "A book should serve as the axe for the frozen sea within us."

A true confessional poet places few barriers, if any, between his self and direct expression of that self, however painful that expression may prove. That is how he differs from all nonconfessional poets such as Eliot and Pound, writers who valued privacy and sought expression through the adoption of *personae* (Eliot's Prufrock, Pound's Mauberly), or through the use of an objective correlative. When Eliot wrote in his now-famous Hamlet essay, "The only way of expressing emotion in the form of art is by finding an 'objective correlative,' in other words, a set of objects, a situation, a chain of events which shall be the formula of that *particular* emotion; such that when the external facts, which must terminate in sensory experience, are given, the emotion is immediately evoked . . . ," he was setting himself against most poetry we would term confessional.[18] Because the latter mode dispenses with a symbol or formula for an emotion and gives the naked emotion direct, personally rather than impersonally. (There are exceptions. Snodgrass manages to combine objective correlatives with subjective confessions very skillfully, as with the flowers in "Leaving the Motel" and the moon in "Partial Eclipse." In most modern confessional poetry, however, if there are correlatives, they are subjective rather than objective ones.)

Moreover, confessional poetry is an expression of personality rather than an escape from it.

When Coleridge was hurt into writing about his dope addiction, he set up an elaborate screen between himself and public exposure. The hallucinatory vision of the writhing snakes was offered as a vision of the ancient mariner's, not of Coleridge's, and was supposed to be the result of the mariner's excessive guilt upon having killed the albatross, rather than of Coleridge's guilt over addiction and family estrangement. Today, Robert Lowell and Allen Ginsberg eschew *personae* altogether and write directly of hallucinatory experiences.

There are, then, no restrictions on subject matter. One writes as freely about one's hernia as about one's "hyacinth girl." The themes are more often than not domestic or intimate ones dealing with hitherto "unpoetic" material. Witness the titles of some of the movement's most celebrated poems: "Meditation in Hydrotherapy" and "Lines Upon Leaving a Sanitarium" (Roethke); "Face Lift" and "Thalidomide" and "Contusion" (Plath); "The Operation" and "The Men's Room in the College Chapel" (Snodgrass); "Viewing the Body" (S. S. Gardons); "In the Baggage Room at Greyhound" and "Mescaline" (Ginsberg); "Menstruation at Forty," "In Celebration of My Uterus," and "Ballad of the Lonely Masturbator" (Sexton).

Obviously the confessional is an antielegant mode whose candor extends even to the language in which the poems are cast. The language of the confessional poem is that of ordinary speech, whether in blank verse or free, rhymed or no. "Daddy, Daddy, you bastard, I'm through" Sylvia Plath shouts, and through this realistic, idiomatic language the poet gets closer to the realities of American life. These are days, surely, when the hyper-elegant language of an Anthony Hecht or a Richard Wilbur or a John Hollander seems superfluous or anachronistic. On a day, say, when we have assassinated another of our political leaders. Or bombed another civilian village in Vietnam.

However, in their pursuit of ordinary language most of the confessional poets do not go so far as Ginsberg, whose

Howl was initially seized by U.S. Customs and the San Francisco police and became the subject of a lengthy court trial before being judged not obscene. But even when they employ more genteel language, the direct approach of these contemporary poets may shock. To the reader startled, for instance, by Anne Sexton's unconventional love poems, we would refer him to Sappho, who wrote, "Why am I crying? / Am I still sad / because of my lost maidenhead?" [19] Sappho outsextons Sexton.

Openness of language leads to openness of emotion. For decades American poets seemed afraid of emotion. Now their work is suffused with it. This surely marks a new direction in modern American poetry, a return to the less-traveled way of Whitman. For prior to *Life Studies*, in which Lowell abandoned his reserve and passionately cried out, "Grandpa! Have me, hold me, cherish me!" our age had been like the Augustan Age of Queen Anne—one afraid, even ashamed of emotion. Generations of poets had censored their feelings, filtering them through screens of "tough" language. One even prided himself upon being a "tough-minded lyricist," though, as John Hall Wheelock once ruefully inquired, just what one was supposed to be tough about was difficult to determine.

The apotheosis of this dry aesthetic was achieved in the poetry of John Crowe Ransom, that supremely "objective" poet in whose work death itself is described euphemistically as "a brown study"; at its worst, death is merely "vexacious." Ransom and his imitators in the *Kenyon Review* crowd used wit, archness, and euphony to achieve perspective and combat sentimentality. Their "modernist" techniques worked, surely, but at the cost of producing a dehumanized art. The confessional poets, at the risk of all else, return that which is uniquely human to poetry. Rather than fearing emotion, they make it their stock-in-trade.

This is not to say that confessional poems are wild, unchecked emotional outbursts. Few are. There is a considerable amount of understatement to be found in the best work of the school. Not understatement to the point of self-consciousness and artifice, as in some of Ransom and Tate.

But a toning-down, a holding-back, as if the mere recitation of the horrors of modern life were strong amplification. It is not sufficient to have the courage to speak out; one must also know when to hold back. As Louise Bogan pointed out in her review of *Life Studies*, to write almost exclusively of oneself and one's setting—naming names and places—presents awesome problems of tact and tone. The best confessional poets acknowledge this difficulty, and write accordingly.

Part of this "holding back" by the poet ultimately derives from his intentional holding of facts in check, and often eliminates as well as embellishes the truth. While a confessional poem is one which mythologizes the poet's personal life, it has its elements of fancy like any other. It does not constitute, certainly, a mere recitation of fact for fact's sake, nor should the "facts" recited be mistaken for literal truth. If they were, one would be positive that Anne Sexton had a brother killed in the war (she hadn't) and that Jerome Mazzaro has a twin sister who is a nun (equally untrue). On a psychological or symbolic level, of course, it may be true to each of the two poets' natures that a part of Mrs. Sexton (Jung's *animus*) died during the war, or that an element of Mr. Mazzaro's makeup is an *anima* which aspires to high spirituality. (Jung's terms refer to the personification of the feminine nature of a man's unconscious and the masculine nature of a woman's; these manifest themselves most typically in the form of figures in dreams and fantasies. Therefore, we should not be at all surprised to find imaginary brothers, sisters, dream girls, dream lovers, in poetry of the most matter-of-fact kind.) [20] Indeed, Mrs. Sexton has spoken of writing, on occasion, a "disguised" poem, in which the pain of loss of one loved object is shifted to a fictitious one.[21]

At one time or other nearly every poet writing in the confessional genre has taken the pains to disavow the literal truth of his poems. Tennyson said of *In Memoriam*, "The 'I' is not always the author speaking of himself, but the voice of the human race speaking through him." More recently Roethke wrote (twice) on the difficulty of creating a reality, a verisimilitude, an "As if" world in his longer poems which traced the spiritual history of a protagonist. He insisted, in two different essays, on the fictitiousness of that protagonist ("Not 'I' personally, but all haunted and harried men").[22] John Berryman also insisted on the mythological or fictitious nature of the protagonist of his *Dream Songs*: "The poem then, whatever its wide cast of characters, is essentially about an imaginary character (not the poet, not me) named Henry." [23] Lowell's disclaimer begins, "This is not my diary, my Confession, not a puritan's too literary pornographic honesty, glad to share private embarrassment, and triumph." [24] James Merrill has cautioned the reader, "Confessional poetry . . . is a literary convention like any other, the problem being to make it *sound* as if it were true." [25] And Sylvia Plath, in her poem "The Burnt-out Spa," exclaims, "It is not I, it is not I." And so it goes.

Methinks the poets protest too much, though Anne Sexton has a very valid point when she states that *any* poem can be therapy, and that confessional poetry itself is not (for her) necessarily therapeutic: "You don't solve problems in writing. They're still there. I've heard psychiatrists say, 'See, you've forgiven your father. There it is in your poem.' But I haven't forgiven my father. I just wrote that I did." [26]

While sharing common subjects, a common vision, frequently a common tone, and obviously a common disclaimer to veracity, the confessional poets are not in agreement on matters of form. Nor should they be, since they are artists expressing themselves individually, finding themselves individually. For instance, whenever writing on the subject of madness, Robert Lowell seems to feel freer writing in free verse. Anne Sexton, on the other hand, would rather deal with that subject in strict forms. One could generalize and say that open statements usually give rise to open forms, and that the strict measures, symbol clusters, and dense phrases of Empson and early Lowell and early Kunitz give way to looser measures and simple diction, more like common speech. Some disciplined poets, when writing in the confessional mode, produce works which appear to have come out all in one rush—one breathless, reckless cloudburst, as in some of Mrs. Sexton's one-sentence poems and many of the *Dream Songs* of John Berryman. Stanley Kunitz's confessional poems are far and away his freest work, with only occasional lapses into the four-beat line, the measure he thinks most approximates the rhythm of human speech. Most poems by Mrs. Sexton, as well as Roethke and Lowell, are as tight and reveal as carefully a constructed rhyme scheme as one is likely to find. The Sylvia Plath of the last poems and Allen Ginsberg write the freest verse of all, with Ginsberg frequently swerving altogether out of control. Louise Bogan has theorized that the writing of such a poem is by its very nature bound to pull, or push, the poet out of the path of strict form:

> The classic confessors, from St. Augustine to Rousseau, were not poets; in reading them, it is possible for one to see that the kind of confession that is good for the soul requires not the condensation of poetry, but the discursiveness of prose. The Romantics were able to link up personal revelations with the sublime, and it could be argued that a negative attitude toward the sublime brings on a negative attitude toward form. . . . In our own day we find both Yeats and Rilke writing Auto-biographies in prose while continuing to write lyric poetry of striking formal beauty.[27]

Antistructural and antielegant in mode, the confessional poem is also antiestablishment in content. Alienation is a recurring theme. At a time when the nation's youth feel radically estranged from the country and leadership to which they are asked to pledge allegiance, it is not surprising to find that the older and more sensitive poets feel especially so. Indeed, they are confessional precisely because of this felt alienation. The English critic John Bayley is quite wrong, I think, when he dismisses this common theme of alienation as mere bandwagonship. Had Bayley lived in the United States during the same period, perhaps he would not have made the quip, "The camaraderie of alienation is not essentially different from the camaraderie of surfing or stock-car racing; it has the same cozy clubbable quality; it is the fashion in common." [28] Real frustration, not fashion, has made alienation a prime American experience.

Closely related to the current poems of personal dissociation are poems of personal failure: failure in marriage, in bed, in love, in career, even in coping. The confessional poet is very "democratic," too, often writing of the failures of his relatives as well as of his Self. But these family failures are usually of a more public kind: Lowell detailing his father's financial bust, Kunitz confessing his father's suicide, Mrs. Sexton and Roethke their fathers' drinking habits, Ginsberg his mother's madness. But the most successful confessional poetry is usually the immediately personal, rather than the familial or the historic. In the most personal of these, certain *leitmotifs* recur, to the point that several poets have poems with the same title as well as the same subject. Both Snodgrass and Mrs. Sexton, for instance, have works titled "The Operation," while Maxine Kumin, a close friend of Mrs. Sexton, has poems designated "Pre-op" and "Post-op." Sylvia Plath penned "The Surgeon at 2 A.M." and Stanley Kunitz an allegorical poem titled "My Surgeons." Operations claim the attention of poets whose work only otherwise skirts the confessional, for example, Helen Chasin and Joyce Carol Oates. Domestic poems also abound; both Lowell and Mrs. Sexton have pieces entitled "Man and Wife." Barbara Harr's first collection bears the disarming title, *The Mortgaged Wife*.

For the poet who does not dabble in confession, but is committed to it, such psychological self-probings and public exposures have their risks. Sylvia Plath, Randall Jarrell, and John Berryman took their lives. It also cannot be accidental that all, or nearly all, the great confessional poets of the 1950s and 1960s have at one time or other suffered mental breakdowns. "I saw the best minds of my generation destroyed by madness," Ginsberg states at the beginning of *Howl*. And, *"We poets in our youth begin in sadness; / thereof in the end come despondency and madness,"* Lowell attributes to Delmore Schwartz.[29] (Schwartz himself anticipated the lot of confessional poets with his verse play, *Shenandoah*, though his greatest confessional achievement is the unforgettable story, "In Dreams Begin Responsibilities," originally published in 1937, and imitated in poetic form by Kunitz in 1971.)

So predominant is this theme of mental illness in their work that at least one critic has called the confessional poets, collectively, The Madhouse Muses. Ever probing into the Self, they eschew the Romantics' equations of the cosmos for their own realities of the soul. The result frequently is poetry which screams of the suicidal. As Berryman put it, "We are using our skins for wallpaper and we cannot win." Yet why should we not, living in a suicidal culture where the waters are dead and the air is death, produce a suicidal poetry? A pastoral or affirmative verse would be a lie: the miracle is that we produce poetry at all. Elizabeth Bishop perceives this. In her jacket note to Lowell's *Life Studies* she writes, "Somehow or other, by fair means or foul, and in the middle of our worst century so far, we have produced a magnificent poet."

I would go so far as to say we have produced a group of magnificent poets. Better than any practicing novelist, they have penetrated to the heart of darkness which is the center of modern American life. Their intention is rarely to shock, as some have alleged, even for didactic purposes. Rather, their intention is merely to reflect. As Anne Sexton says, "I write very personal poems but I hope that they will become the central theme to someone else's private life . . . Any public poem I have ever written, that wasn't personal, was usually a failure." [30] When the confessional poet deals with his own feelings and fears, his intention is the same as that expressed somewhere by Victor Hugo: "When I speak to you about myself, I am speaking to you about yourself. How is it you don't see that?" Of the group, only Lowell has produced a significant body of overtly public and political poems, notably those in his *Notebook 1967–68* (later revised, expanded, and reissued under the title *Notebook*), together with a number from *For the Union Dead*. Generally these fall short of his best.

The universal implication toward which Mrs. Sexton claims to work is at the core of the best confessional poetry, though perhaps unintentionally so. In the hands of lesser poets like John Wieners, whose work is pure self-indulgence ("I blew him like a symphony"!), writers who create out of a determination to shock rather than to illumine, the effect is destructive rather than purifying. Even Lowell himself, when not in complete artistic control of his material, resorts to sensation rather than intensification of presentation and courageousness of subject matter. (I am thinking here of *Near the Ocean*, that very slender—if not thin—volume in which balance and detachment are lacking and which consequently seems artificial and coldly theatrical, and of Berryman's *Love & Fame*). Confession can wear thin. The human voice can become a whine. Put another way, Robert Bly has accused Lowell of offering his readers *nervous* excitement rather than *poetic* excitement. All of which are reasons why confessional poetry, when it is bad, seems very, very bad.

A final word on the question of universality. In the best confessional writing, transcendence of the personal arises from the human particulars recounted by the poet, rather than from design. Whereas the poets of the 1930s and 1940s consciously strove for universality through the invocation of mythological and psychological archetypes, the confessional poets of the 1960s and 1970s achieve the same end through "personalization"—the Self and family history.

Before examining the work of individual poets, let us summarize all, or most all, we have discussed as characteristic of the post-modern confessional poetry currently written in America:

It is highly subjective.
It is an expression of personality, not an escape from it.
It is therapeutic and/or purgative.
Its emotional content is personal rather than impersonal.
It is most often narrative.
It portrays unbalanced, afflicted, or alienated protagonists.
It employs irony and understatement for detachment.

It uses the self as a poetic symbol around which is woven a personal mythology.

There are no barriers of subject matter.

There are no barriers between the reader and the poet.

The poetry is written in the open language of ordinary speech.

It is written in open forms.

It displays moral courage.

It is antiestablishment in content, with alienation a common theme.

Personal failure is also a favorite theme, as is mental illness.

The poet strives for personalization rather than for universalization. (If totally successful, the personal is expressed so intimately we can all identify and empathize.)

M. L. Rosenthal has said that the best confessional poetry is that which rises above subject matter to achieve some sort of victory over pain and defeat, poems which are glosses on the triumph of life. Let me add to that one last word: As with all good poetry, the best confessional poems are more than conceptions. They are revelations.

2

Robert Lowell: Free-Lancing Along the Razor's Edge

After publication of *The Mills of the Kavanaughs* (1951), a book many regard as a failure, Robert Lowell stated it was difficult for him to find a subject and a language of his own. But by 1959 it was obvious he had found his subject—himself. And the more personal material gave rise to a more personal style, a style modeled upon Lowell's own voice, freed from the early echoes of Hart Crane, Eliot, and Tate, freed from all packed and baroque mannerisms and iambics. If Lowell's earlier work can be summarized as an attempt to reconstitute American history and the Christian experience, these later poems are an attempt to reconstitute his family history and personal experience. And his style changed as radically as his subjects. It is almost as if the abandonment of rigid Catholic dogma tripped a loosening in his own work. Lowell has told us this new form was the result of a suggestion of his wife's, the critic Elizabeth Hardwick.

> "I started one of these poems in Marvell's four-foot couplet and showed it to my wife. And she said, 'Why not say what really happened?' . . . the meter just seemed to prevent any honesty on the subject, it got into the cadence of the four-foot couplet. The style came out of a whole lot of things, and I don't know myself what was the dominating influence." [1]

As we have seen in the preceding chapter, the new style also might have derived from Lowell's reading of manuscript poems by both W. D. Snodgrass and Anne Sexton.

A third, partial, explanation for the new freedom of form is given by Lowell in his *Paris Review* interview, in which he admits the poems of *Life Studies* are the result of his attempting a prose autobiography:

> "I found it got awfully tedious working out transitions and putting in things that didn't seem very important but were necessary to the prose continuity. Also, I found it hard to revise. Cutting it down into small bits, I could work on it much more carefully and make fast transitions." [2]

Life Studies, then, began as prose. Its intention was to communicate personal history. With their free metrics, there is about the poems a great deal of the accessibility of a prose autobiography. Surely they are the most readable of all Lowell has written.

Readability, however, is not to be confused with ease of composition or ease of comprehension. Indeed, when the wife in one poem speaks of her husband's "free-lancing out along the razor's edge," we are given an adequate summation of the risks Lowell took in this book in general and its part four in particular. Lowell's *bildungsroman*, the book unflinchingly faces up to and addresses the poet's contempt for his inadequate father and the compensatory affection he lavished on his grandfather; the deaths of his father, grandfather, domineering mother, and young Uncle Devereux; the failures of his Aunt Sarah; his own imprisonment as a conscientious objector during World War II; his uneven marriage; his treatment in and return from an expensive "house for the 'mentally ill' "; and a final statement of acceptance and some little triumph even in a world in which the poet acknowledges, "I myself am hell."

This is a poetry of self-discovery and fact far removed from the fiction and melodrama of *The Mills of the Kavanaughs* and the religious allegory and ideology of *Lord Weary's Castle* (1946). One should by no means assume that every statement in *Life Studies* is factually autobiographical. But Lowell's inclusion of the long prose piece, "91 Revere Street"— labeled "An Autobiographical Fragment," and presumably what remains of the autobiography he attempted in prose—confirms that the poems are indeed autobiographical in intent. As never before in Lowell's work, the *persona* gives way to the person, fiction to fact. In the book Lowell gives up the Christ for himself, the crucifixion for his own trials on earth, and the Virgin for his unsaintly mother. In *Life Studies* Lowell himself becomes the man on the cross. He himself seems conscious of the role; in "Skunk Hour," the ultimate poem of the book, he describes himself as climbing "the hill's skull"—an allusion to Golgotha, the "Hill of the Skull," also called Calvary.

A great deal has been written about the book's structure, some more fanciful than illuminating. M. L. Rosenthal, for instance, has called *Life Studies* the most remarkable poetic sequence to appear since Hart Crane's *The Bridge* and William Carlos Williams's *Paterson*,[3] a comparison which confers upon Lowell's book a unity which may or may not exist. Charles Altieri is more cautious about structure, but sees in its progress "the anxieties characteristic of sequence poems like *Song of Myself,* the *Cantos,* "Comedian as the Letter C," *Paterson,* and *Homage to Mistress Bradstreet.*" [4]

One can disagree with the validity of these comparisons, but the book remains nevertheless the most carefully constructed of all Lowell's volumes. It is divided into four sections. Part one consists of four "public" (as opposed to purely private) poems which serve to place the remaining three sections in historical and emotional perspective: four visions of the breakdown of the world which predicate the breakdown of the poet. When Lowell leaves Rome for Paris in the first poem ("Beyond the Alps"), he is symbolically leaving the Holy City for a spectacularly secular one.[5] It is the only poem which seems to belong to his earlier manner, exploring as it does the meaning of history and religion, and religion within history. Perhaps the abandonment, after the first poem, of this earlier theme is but one of the many voyages in the book, of which the trip to Paris from Rome is but the first and most metaphorical. There follow many others: journeys from Boston to Cambridge, Cambridge to Maine, Rapallo to New York, Boston to Beverly Farms,

Manhattan subway rides, New England Sunday spins, and visits to family burial grounds. These are in addition to Lowell's numberless other journeys forward and backward in time and memory.

The three poems in the first section which follow "Beyond the Alps" discuss topics of economics, politics, and militarism, all concerns of the modern secular man who has left the City of God. The four are also all comments on private and public madnesses: the life of Marie de Medici, America's election of Grant and Eisenhower as president, and the ruminations of a confined mad Negro. By far the strongest of the four is the last, which establishes the tone of hysteria and the theme of alienation which inform the rest of the volume. The mad black confined at Munich, we come to feel, is a *doppelgänger* for Lowell confined in his CO cell, or committed to McLean's, or home but trapped within the cell of self. Each heart is "pulsing to its ant-egg dole." Despite the advantages of birth and position accorded a Lowell, that soldier's problems have come to be in many ways those of the "privileged" poet.

The second section of *Life Studies* is the autobiographical prose fragment already discussed. It gives us the background from which the poet's present condition has grown, and is the portrait of an only child born of an unhappy marriage. This prose version of the only child joins with the poem on Lowell's bachelorhood, "To Delmore Schwartz," to present a figure of the alienated self—one of the many "figures of isolation and human want in the land of plenty. The contrast of the potential and the denial, the tension of the fertility and the want, is the principle that governs movement throughout Lowell's work." [6]

Though the fragment discussed above fills many gaps in Lowell's life story, such as his early preoccupation with a distant and possibly Jewish relative, Major Mordecai Myers, it gives in prose what Lowell later renders better in poetry. (It is interesting to note the upper-class Protestant Lowell's fascination with the possibility of Jewish ancestry, a theme later explored on equally personal terms by the defiant, middle-class Protestant Sylvia Plath.) For this reader's taste, the prose section places rather too much stress on Lowell's father's ineffectualness, a spectacle the poet presents more movingly in part four. Perhaps Lowell himself came to feel this as well, since he omitted the passage from the English edition. The prose section does, however, serve to preview the autobiographical themes of the great later poems, and, in some important ways, counterpoints and illumines them. The section functions much as do the autobiographical short stories and sketches which Delmore Schwartz interleaved between the poems of his first and best book, *In Dreams Begin Responsibilities*.

Part three is yet another section of four poems, again concerned with the madness and the breakdown not alone of individuals, but of the whole of society. Each poem is about or is addressed to a writer for whom Lowell felt an especial affinity: Ford Madox Ford, George Santayana, Delmore Schwartz, and Hart Crane—all men with faith in nothing but art. (Lowell tells us satirically that Santayna had "found the Church too good to be believed," and has the writer declare, "There is no God and Mary is His Mother" [7]—a cryptic phrase in the spirit of the adolescent graffiti frequently observed around the Manhattan of the early 1970s, for example, "The Virgin Mary is nothing but a purity symbol!") What all four writers have in common with each other and with Lowell is an inability to survive as artists in the killing atmosphere of America. Santayana exiled himself, Ford died in want, Crane committed suicide, and Schwartz suffered mental breakdowns similar to Lowell's. "These writers become for Lowell the 'American' equivalents of the numerous Russian writers who were purged, exiled, or hounded to death; they honor and deepen *Life Studies* with their presence." [8] Like that of the mad Negro soldier of part one, these writers' defeats and isolation underscore Lowell's own plight. And just as the climax to part one comes with the depiction of the mad black, that of part three comes with the figure of Hart Crane stalking sailors and proclaiming, "Who asks for me, the Shelley of my age, must lay his heart out for my bed and board." The recognition of both sick figures foreshadows Lowell's own mental illness, which occurs in the book's last quarter, in which he becomes a night-stalker too.

Despite the undeniable power of the three preceding sections, it is part four for which *Life Studies* is revered and in which are found the poems of Lowell's mental breakdown and confessional breakthrough. Here he literally lays his own heart out for his bed and board. These are the poems which have been imitated so widely. Their centrality to the book can be inferred by Lowell's calling the section itself "Life Studies"—the title also given the collection as a whole. Here the poems become intensely personal; all but one speak in the first-person singular.

The section is subdivided into two parts. The first deals with the past—the writer's childhood impressions of relatives, especially grandparents, and with the writer's "nervous breakdown," which may or may not have been "caused" by that past. The childhood poems may be subdivided into three dealing primarily with Lowell's relationship with his grandparents and six dealing with Lowell and his parents. The nine accounts are at once sad and precocious, blooming with bittersweet details like those in the extraordinary novels of alienated childhood of Elizabeth Bowen, most especially in her *The Death of the Heart* and *The House in Paris*. The "breakdown" poems are but two in number—"Waking in the Blue" and "Home After Three Months Away," which catalogue the events of Lowell's manic phase.

The second part contains four poems dealing with the more immediate. Two speak of marriage, one of Lowell's opposition to the Second World War, and one of his current mental state. These last four poems serve as parallels to the volume's initial four. But now the secularism, politics, militarism, and mental illness are not those of historical figures, but of Robert Lowell. Lowell himself has become his own most important subject and symbol. Together the fifteen poems of part four are a testament to Lowell's past and present. The journey from Rome to Paris becomes ultimately the journey toward self-realization in the non-religious world.

At the book's conclusion Lowell discovers himself alone and acting strange, admitting to himself in a way no American poet had before, "My mind's not right." This final poem, "Skunk Hour," is one of the most famous poems of the confessional movement, and justifiably so. Posing as it does the question of personal survival in the modern world, it is one of the best single poems in the volume as well as a meet and right conclusion to all which has preceded it. (In the later paperback edition, Lowell added in the final place the poem later titled "For the Union Dead." Whereas this poem now rightfully concludes the subsequent whole volume of that title, as a finale to *Life Studies* it seems the afterthought it indeed was, reversion to the historical concerns of *Lord Weary's Castle*.)

"My Last Afternoon with Uncle Devereux Winslow" begins the "Life Studies" sequence. The year is 1922; the setting, the stone porch of Lowell's grandfather's summer house; the mood, one of a boy's suspended animation in the manly and comfortable world of Grandfather Winslow. The poem is divided into four sections and was originally cast in prose as part of the "91 Revere Street" fragment (according to Lowell in an interview with A. Alvarez).

The central contrast in the poem's first part, that which contributes most to the poem's premise, is that between opposite images—the cool black earth and the warm white lime on each of which the young Bobby Lowell rests a hand. But earth and finally lime combine to form a metaphor for mortality: Uncle Devereux, we learn with a shock, will be dead at twenty-nine, his bones and body fallen from ashes to ashes, dust to dust.

> *My hands were warm, then cool, on the piles*
> *of earth and lime,*
> *a black pile and a white pile. . . .*
> *Come winter,*
> *Uncle Devereux would blend to the one color.*

The inexplicable and inexorable toll of time is the poem's subject. The clock may be cuckoo but it cannot be halted. If the poem begins with frivolous details, these serve only to heighten the horror as we experience with the five-year-old boy in his frivolous milieu, the sight of the young uncle already a walking corpse whose "face was putty."

In addition to the black and white of earth and lime, and of the screen through which the boy looks (connoting that he has, until the time of the poem, been "screened" from reality?), the poem constellates other opposites as well: the warm and the cool, the quick and the dead, the healthy and the unwell, the young and the old, the active and the inactive, the appearance and the reality, the past and the present. (Lowell also effectively employs contrasts of black and white in "Sailing Home from Rappollo.") These contrasts contribute more to the poem's life / death theme than do the four elements, whose informing presence has led at least three critics (Jay Martin, Hugh B. Staples, and Jerome Mazzaro) to proclaim them to be the poem's patterning metaphors. To be sure, a predominating element is found in each of the four sections: earth in the first, as we have discussed; water in the second; air in the third; and smoke if not fire in the fourth. But of the four, only earth seems to me critical to the poem's meaning; the others are merely architecture raised on its indispensable foundation. But it is cool black earth which the poet treads, not warm, fecund earth. This is the earth of death, not life—burial places are suggested by the clay of the tiles the boy sees, "sweaty with a secret dank, crummy with ant-stale." It is the heart of dankness that the boy must confront. Even his dog is given a name of the earth, "Cinder."

The poem's first section thus novelistically gives us the setting for the boy's epiphany. The second, brief and bemused, gives us the boy. The third is a portrait from life and hearsay of the boy's Great Aunt Sarah, the first of Lowell's gallery of great family failures, which is inserted to contrast with Uncle Devereux's own brief life. (Here, too, air is less important than the empty concert hall's mournful Greek statues, "draped with purple / like the saints in Holy Week.") Whereas, even knowing he is dying, Uncle Devereux characteristically rushes out to embrace life, while Great Aunt Sarah withdraws from that same embrace. Jilting her lover to escape marriage, failing to appear on her recital day, she avoids reality by reading in bed and playing a soundless piano. Yet, Lowell infers, such people are allowed by God to continue their useless existences, whereas vital Uncle Devereux's life was taken.

It is the boy Lowell's first head-on encounter with death. No one, the poet reminds us, had died at his grandfather's house within his own lifetime. The effect was near-traumatic.

> *I cowered in terror.*
> *I wasn't a child at all—*
> *unseen and all-seeing, I was Agrippina*
> *in the Golden House of Nero.*

The line, "I wasn't a child at all," seems to say that with this summer's knowledge Lowell came of age, though by the calendar he was "only" five. This precipitate awareness of mortality is the first crisis Lowell portrays in the "Life Studies" section. The structure of the four-part poem suggests that of the four-part book as a whole, with its many journeys, animal images, and epiphanies. It is important to note that the poems and the poet do progress within the sequence. Like Anne Sexton's *Live or Die* and Roethke's sequence poems, Lowell's *Life Studies* moves toward and concludes with a note of affirmation and revitalization: the unseen boy acknowledging death's presence becomes the unseen man of "Skunk Hour"— the final poem—the man who, as that poem's skunks, "will not scare" from life, but rather will search for its meaning and survive as best he can.

As a confessional poet, what is Lowell here "confessing"? Within the tale of a terrified boy is an implicit fracture of faith in his parents, disapproval of his relatives' lives, an unusually strong regard for and dependence on his grandfather, and the early loss of a second potential father-figure with Uncle Devereux's death. This is a great burden for any poem to bear, and one could argue that the poem is successful only in parts. The first twelve lines, for instance, might have been cut, allowing the poem to begin with "One afternoon in 1922"—as indeed it essentially does. And not all the images succeed: I refuse to believe that yellow sun-flowers can at all resemble "Pumpkins floating shoulder-high." But as the first of the "family" poems, it announces many important conflicts later individually developed. As Lowell once observed, a confessional poem is possible only when one has something to confess.[9] At this stage in his career, Robert Lowell has much he wishes to disclose in the hope of receiving psychic absolution.

If the mood of the previous poem was one of fear and insecurity, "Dunbarton" reveals the boy to have found some measure of stability in the company of his Grandfather Winslow. That the elder Winslow found the boy's company preferable to that of others is fortunate. At this time Uncle Devereux is dead and the only-child's father is on sea duty in the Pacific. Lowell here spells out his specific relation to his grandfather: "He was my Father. I was his son." The importance Lowell placed upon the paternal figure perhaps is unintentionally signified by his capitalizing "Father" but not "son."

Grandfather Winslow is the Charon figure who guides the boy forward on his life's journey. In the poem the pair pay one of their annual visits to the family graveyard in Dunbarton, New Hampshire, for the purpose of ordering it. (There is, so far as I can see, no evidence to support Maz-zaro's assertion that the poem "records the funeral of Devereux in the family plot."[10] The poem is, to echo Mercutio's pun, a grave one. But if Uncle Devereux's living journey toward death frightened the boy, his later visit to the grave site seems melancholy but not terrible. For rather than dwelling upon the coldness of his uncle's grave, the boy now concentrates upon the warmth of his grandfather's love. Together they defy the dank weather, as they now defy all trials together. (Note Lowell's use of "dank" in both poems, with the sensation of disagreeable moisture per-vading both. Its presence is less oppressive in the second, however, the difference lying in the narrator's state of mind.)

Just as the boy feels the difference between his own inexperience and his grandfather's achievement (symbolized by the old man's cane carved with the names of all the mountains he has climbed), so he notices the difference between young and mature newts. The older newts are spotless, yellow and inactive, like Lowell's older relatives; he identifies with the younger variety, "neurasthenic, scarlet and wild in the wild coffee-colored water." Unlike his father and his great-aunt, the boy plunges himself into the element, into life, of which the millpond is surely a potent symbol — that dark ("coffee-colored") and festering body. Lowell here employs water as symbol for the source from which all life comes, the universal font of potentialities open to himself as a boy.

This symbology can be seen as more sophisticated as well, for Lowell's newt in the water is an interesting archetypal intuition and transformation; that is, in ages past the newt, or aquean salamander, has been a mythological fire-spirit, a kind of lizard said to inhabit the element of fire rather than water. In Marya Zaturenska's "The World of the Salamanders," for example, "They arise, and sing of fire, of fire-lit phantasies; / They summon marvels, legends, mysteries." [11] And fire, in the Egyptian hieroglyphics, is associated with the concepts of life and health (deriving perhaps from the idea of body heat). According to Enel's *La Langue Sacrée* (1932), fire is, as well, associated with control and superiority, being a physical manifestation of spiritual energy.

From this complex of associations, Lowell's boy-as-newt can be seen as submerging himself into the depths of life, and through such a "leap of faith" potentially achieving a better state of bodily and mental health and control. Within a specifically Christian framework, the act is equally beneficial, since it is a baptism, an act of initiation and purification. The boy of Dunbarton is more prepared to cope with life (and death) than in the earlier poem. Yet we must not forget Lowell's telling adjective "neurasthenic." The boy's emotional conflicts or insecurities are engendering a psychopathological condition, a condition in some probability caused by and/or exacerbated by guilt over his defection from his father. For this is the poem in which belong those twelve opening lines I wished to delete from "My Last Afternoon with Uncle Devereux Winslow." To begin "Dunbarton" with, "I won't go with you. I want to stay with Grandpa!" is to underscore the basic conflict, the disloyalty to his father and undue attachment to his grandfather. That he acknowledges he is out of place in his grandfather's life becomes explicit in the guilt-ridden lines, "I cuddled like a paramour / in my Grandfather's bed."

The strain of this guilt becomes even stronger in the third and last grandfather poem, called simply "Grandparents." The piece discovers the poet as owner of the grandfather's farm, with the old man dead ("altogether otherworldly"). In addition to the guilt of defecting from his father, the poet now bears the burden of remorse over somehow failing his grandfather as well, as Mazzaro rightfully concludes.[12] The poem moves from a nostalgic recreation of the grandparents and their world in the first stanza to the poet's remorseful act of doodling a handlebar moustache ("disloyal still") on a picture of the late Czar. We abuse our past, and when we finally realize what we have done it is too late. As in the Uncle Devereux poem, Time is the villain. The poem's climax is reached when the poet realizes the extent of his aloneness and helplessness and cries out in the empty house, "Grandpa! Have me, hold me, cherish me!" The old man who even shot pool for the boy is gone, leaving the poet emotionally behind the eight ball.

With the fourth poem in the fourth section the focus of the book shifts to Lowell's father. Actually, "Commander Lowell" contains harsh portraits of both Lowell's parents. His mother he portrays as a "daddy's girl"; his father as an ineffectual bumbler who even "took four shots with his putter to sink his putt." Moreover, Commander Lowell, in the boy's eyes, was as out of place on the sea as he was on the green. For this reason it is at once pitiable and ironic to find Lowell portraying his father singing "Anchors aweigh" in his bathtub. Perhaps only there was he a true "Commander." Leaving the navy for Lever Brothers, "He was soon fired." The point of the poem is disappointment —that and shame for his father's undistinguished career. Lowell, who as a boy had memorized "two hundred French generals by name," could not accept a father who could not even sail a small yacht properly. The poem concludes with a revelation of Commander Lowell's early and unfulfilled promise. The unseaworthy man had, as "the youngest ensign in his class," been " 'the old man' of a gunboat on the Yangtze." The effect on the boy of his father's public and private failure can be weighed by his description of himself as "bristling and manic." The "neurasthenic" boy of "Dunbarton" has become confessedly mad.

"Terminal Days at Beverly Farms" completes the boy's story of his father, who at this later stage has had two coronaries. That there will be a third and fatal one is implicit in the poem; Lowell carefully employs death-images in the second stanza: the railroad tracks shine "like a double-barrelled shotgun"; the sumac multiplies "like cancer." (The double-barrelled shotgun is an important symbol in Lowell's private mythology, used also in part 4 of "My Last Afternoon.") Yet the revelation of his father's impending death, like that of Uncle Devereux, is withheld by Lowell until late in the poem. The poet presents first a portrait of the man, bronzed and with a figure "vitally trim." Only then does he communicate that the diet is a precautionary measure, the vitality a false one, and the new house chosen for proximity to the medicos.

Even in this diminished state, his father is seen by Lowell as a contemptible figure. The unsuccessful commander who sang nautical songs in the tub has become the unsuccessful businessman in early retirement, loafing in the Salem Maritime Museum, wasting his days puttering with ship statistics and trading bad jokes with the curator. His father is shown as especially dependent upon his material possessions: his six-pointed star-lantern, his cream gabardine dinner-jacket, his indigo cummerbund, his black Chevie, his books, his ivory slide rule. Lowell seems to be saying that all the possessions add up to less than a man, and all the materialistic goods in the world could not save him. This is a theme he develops more fully in relation to his mother, in "Sailing Home From Rapallo." In this materialistic world, the young Robert Lowell is like the "uncomfortable boulder" in his father's garden, an irregular object foreign in its environment. When Lowell relates his father's last words— "I feel awful"—the flatness of tone, the withholding of emotion, is appropriate to the lack of sympathy the younger Lowell obviously felt for his father.

In an attempt to comprehend his dead father's life, the poet visits the dead man's empty bedroom. "Father's Bedroom" is an inventory of the objects found there. The most important (for the poet) is a volume of Lafacdio Hearn's *Glimpses of Unfamiliar Japan,* important because it illuminates the waste of his father's life. As a boy, the commander had been stirred toward a naval career through reading Hearn. This particular book had accompanied him on that youthful Yangtze journey. It was, perhaps, the first and last successful act of his life.

Besides the book, the contents of the room are described as sparse and manly and mainly blue: blue bedspread, blue dotted curtains, blue kimono, blue sandal straps. The color of course reminds one of the elder Lowell's undistinguished naval career. It also is the color of the spatial—the blue sky above, the blue sea below. In visiting the room, the younger Lowell is attempting to comprehend the meaning of a life spent within our universe.

"Father's Bedroom" is but a brief coda to the larger father poem, "Commander Lowell," as is the one which follows in sequence, "For Sale." As in the bedroom poem, this piece attempts to comprehend the man through place. Taking the Beverely Farms cottage is seen as but another prodigal act by his father, and its inappropriate town-house furniture was as out of place within its walls as the father was within real Boston society. The poem is notable largely for its shift in focus from the cottage to a view of the widowed Mrs. Lowell in the last five lines: "Mother mooned in a window, / as if she had stayed on a train / one stop past her destination." This is a powerful image for the bereft emotions of a marriage partner left behind.

Lowell's attention remains with his mother in the next two poems. (There is a certain inevitability about the book's progress, as the poet relentlessly moves on to exhaust, one by one, the lives of his great-aunt, his grandfather, his father, his mother—and finally his wife, his daughter, and himself.) Unlike the death of his father, his mother's passing, four years later, brings genuine tears. The finality of her death is cruelly contrasted with the continuity of the natural world, which all about the poet "was breaking into fiery flower." The lush Mediterranean is compared with the stark winter landscape upon the family graves at Dunbarton.

But even a poem upon his mother's death is an occasion for Lowell to flog his father's memory. (An illuminating comparison can be made between Lowell's attempts to "recapture" his father and those of Stanley Kunitz in *The Testing-Tree*.) Here Lowell sees his father as relatively unworthy to be buried beside his mother's family of Winslows and Starks. His is an "unhistoric" soul, and even in death his materialism, already noted in "Terminal Days," seems to prevail, he being buried beneath a new and unweathered "pink-veined slice of marble" on which "Even the Latin of his Lowell motto . . . seemed too businesslike and pushing here."

Yet Lowell's irreverence is not reserved alone for his father. Just as he was capable of recording those inelegant last words of his father ("I feel awful"), so also the poet is somehow compelled to describe his mother's corpse as "wrapped like *panetone* in Italian tinfoil." Such openness and moral courage, of course, are characteristic of confessional poetry as I have defined it. But many sensibilities would choose to repress such a grotesque comparison, together with the fact of the indignity of his mother's name being actually misspelled on the coffin. But of course indignity is what the poem is all about. That is why these two painful details are so essential. His mother may, even in death, travel first-class. His father may lie beneath pink marble. But both were mortal. Money and breeding could not save either from the ultimate indignity, mortality—

while meanwhile the natural objects of the world somehow perpetuate themselves, creating a kind of immortality. The Mediterranean flowers multipy. The New England evergreens remain ever green. But man is no more nor less a commodity to be consumed than is Italian bread wrapped in foil.

Robert Lowell's mother is portrayed for the last time in "During Fever," a poem occasioned by his own daughter's illness. The weight of his parental responsibility experienced in the first stanza gives way to memories of his own parents when he was a child. Implicit but unspoken is the contrast between Lowell's daughter's normal childhood ailment and his own "abnormal" childhood condition.

The poem re-creates the comfort and the stability which his mother attempted to maintain in his life—the milk and biscuits awaiting him, no matter how late the undergraduate returned home—and reveals how the two of them were pitted against the witless father, rehashing together his character in his absence. That the mother had little in common with her nautical husband is symbolically depicted by the positioning of her bedroom, which "looked away from the ocean." That Lowell viewed the union as a cold and mechanical one is epitomized by his description of the nuptial bed, "big as a bathroom." There are many size-comparisons which could be made; none are quite so sterile and functional as this. The poem is also consistent with Lowell's portrayal, in "Commander Lowell," of his mother as "her Father's daughter." She was happiest, he infers, in those "settled years" of World War I. The adjective is deliberately ironic: while the world was in turmoil, his young mother's affairs were marked by tranquillity. She was better off with her "Freudian papá" than in her marriage with its forced intimacies and quarrels.

With "Walking in the Blue," the book leaves off one movement and begins a new. The spotlight shifts from Lowell's forebears to Lowell himself. But this is not Lowell the father or Lowell the professor. It is Lowell the mental patient, discovered with dramatic abruptness in "the house for the 'mentally ill.'" The euphemism is employed wryly;

Lowell's comprehension of his predicament is complete. (Allen Ginsberg, on the other hand, refers in *Kaddish* to the place of his own confinement as the "bughouse"—a semantic difference which says much about the disparity between the two poets' sensibilities.) The blue in which Lowell awakes is more than day perceived through a window. It is a melancholy blue, indicative of his varying states of equilibrium. (We should remember that blue is the one color between white and black.) In the poem Lowell is less sick than most of the inmates he sees about him, but less well than outpatients on the street. In the poem he is shown also as a born patrician, but one who eschews patrician manners and mores.

Everyone in the poem has a problem. The night keeper's is to find "meaning"; Stanley's is to retain his youthful physique; Bobbie's is to return to the past; and Lowell's is loneliness for family and adjustment to current reality. Daylight for him is an "agonized blue." As M. L. Rosenthal states, the poem is not without traces of Lowell's ancestry-awareness. He feels condescended to by the youthful Roman Catholic attendants: "There are no Mayflower / screwballs in the Catholic Church." Surrounded by "these thorough-bred mental cases," Lowell at once identifies with them and rejects them. The moment of the poem is a difficult one: caught between two worlds, belonging to neither, the poet can only feel anguish and *déjà vu*: "We are all old-timers, / each of us holds a locked razor." The locked razor joins the double-barrelled shotgun as symbols of potential violence, a violence not physically manifest until the poem, "To Speak of Woe That Is in Marriage." Lowell describes the other patients in animal imagery, inasmuch as they lead lives largely instinctual rather than intellectual, thereby further differentiating themselves from the poet.

For these several reasons "Walking in the Blue" is, I think, a terrifying poem, though many have not read it as such. With its vision of the naked and insane French King and all the other "victorious figures of bravado ossified young," we come to be aware of what Charles Altieri has called "the terrifying inversion of normal life that madness is":

The common elements usually so taken for granted become potential instruments of violence or suicide. The choice of mirror as the specific focus for the shift intensifies the horror because the mirror, like art, is a way of defining the Self, of assuring some coincidence between inner and outer self. To see oneself in a metal mirror is to reverse this normal assurance, to receive in the attempt to grasp the self a reminder of the potential tenuousness of that existence.[13]

One is reminded of Sylvia Plath's memorable poem, "Mirror," as well of Lewis Carroll's Alice, for whom a mirror revealed the unreality of the real, and whose horrors of the adult world were magnified and dramatized by her total immersion into the image. Lowell's worst horrors are also reflected in his mirror. As Altieri concludes, "He too might become 'ossified' like the others into a too 'familiar' future, a future whose horror is suggested by the last inversion of normal life, the locked razor."

Doubtless it was a difficult poem to write. In an age when all institutions and physical states are labeled by euphemisms, Lowell penned a madhouse poem as forthright as the anonymous Elizabethan "Tom o'Bedlam's Song" (which both Edith Sitwell and Robert Graves attribute to Shakespeare), and whose narrator confesses,

> *With an host of furious fancies,*
> *Whereof I am commander,*
> *With a burning speare, and a horse of aire,*
> *To the wildernesse I wander . . .*

Lowell's is the contemporary madhouse poem which made hosts of imitations posible, poems like Sylvia Plath's "The Stones."

The companion piece to "Waking in the Blue" is "Home After Three Months Away," which gives the reader Lowell upon his return from the mental institution (McLean's). It is not a triumphant return. For the family, nothing has changed; for the poet, many things: the baby's nurse is gone, Lowell himself is no longer forty but forty-one, the flowers he planted are deteriorating, his physical state is one of enervation: "Recuperating, I neither spin nor toil." This comparison with the Biblical lilies of the field leads directly to a more personal one. The poet sees and empathizes with the seven tulips below. Like him, the tulips came into this world pedigreed. And like him, their ancestry has done nothing whatsoever to equip them to survive in an alien world. As Lowell is defeated by the weight of oppressive forces, the tulips too are "Bushed by the late spring snow." The link is completed by the image of their bed, a mere "coffin's length of soil." Mortality nags the poet even when supposedly well. ("Cured, I am frizzled, stale and small." The adjective "frizzled" suggests the physical aftermath of electric shock treatment, which may or may not have been part of Lowell's therapy.)

About these tulips one must ask a final question: Why seven? Could Lowell, writing in the mid-fifties, have remembered the exact number of tulips he saw three stories below? In all probability not. The number may have been consciously chosen by the poet for its traditional symbolism of perfect order (being the number forming the basic series of musical notes, of colors, of the planetary spheres and the gods corresponding to them, as well as of the capital sins and their opposing virtues). If this be so, the vertical tulips, now "horizontal," represent disorder—that state in which the poet finds himself—and possibly a death wish as well. (See Sylvia Plath's poem, "I Am Vertical," which begins, "But I would rather be horizontal. . . .") I might add that a more esoteric meaning for the number seven held by some scholars is that it is a symbol of pain. Such meaning is exceptionally appropriate here, though one cannot assume the poet's foreknowledge of it.[14] However, that these tulips are drawn more from the imagination than from life might be supported by the fact that in "New York 1962: Fragment," a poem from his next book, the seven tulips have been transmogrified into seven daffodils.

Whatever their precise connotation, the poet feels the press of Time. In an apostrophe addressed to his daughter he muses, "Dearest, I cannot loiter here / in lather like a polar bear." If Stanley of McLean's was as a seal, and

Bobbie a sperm whale, Lowell sees himself reduced to a bear. The poet now feels it is time to subdue the instinctual and return to intellectual things. The poem leaves the poet dangling, like the returned soldier of Snodgrass's "Ten Days Leave," a stranger in his own house. There is one note of hope, however: The sky-blue of his daughter's corduroy apparently gives the outpatient pleasure, whereas the azure blue at his hospital window gave pain. The color is the same; only the state of mind has changed.

Lowell begins a new section with "Memories of West Street and Lepke," which commences with reflections on the time when his daughter was only nine months old and he was teaching. Then the time-period changes, and in his mind the poet compares this earlier domestic scene with his even earlier "seedtime"—those months Lowell spent in prison for his "manic statement" of conscientious objection to war.

If Lowell's identification was with the struggling tulips in the preceding poem, his empathy here is for a fellow prisoner, Murder Incorporated's Czar Lepke. There is great irony here, of course, in Lowell's size-comparison of a jail-house walking-roof, seeing it as no bigger than his school's soccer court. The patrician soccer-player, for all his pedigree, is imprisoned with the drug-addicted Negro and the sentenced gangster. Yet just as his condition was spiritually comparable to that of the "Mad Negro Soldier Confined at Munich," so it is with Lepke. Lowell's fear, at the time of the poem's composition, seems to be that he shall become, like Lepke, "Flabby, bald, lobotomized"—a description not far removed from his own of himself as "frizzled, stale and small." The prison is not unlike the madhouse, and his own sentence to electric shock therapy not unlike Lepke's to the electric chair. Lowell's and Lepke's sheepish lethargy are, moreover, similar to Commander Lowell's. Having despised his father, Lowell later becomes him. Which is perhaps Lowell's greatest source of despair. In all his work, there is nowhere the sense of personal achievement one encounters in, say, the poetry of John Berryman —which goes too far in the opposite direction, and becomes

self-aggrandizement and egotism, but nonetheless indicates
a healthy ego. In the Lepke poem, one feels Lowell's failure
of intent. Wanting desperately not to conform with draftees,
he finds himself instead conforming to a world of the daily
walk and the "hospital tuck." He is surrounded by con-
formists of a different kind; even the garbage scavenger
"has two children, a beach wagon, a helpmate, / and is a
'young Republican.' " In the "Tranquillized Fifties," all in-
dividuality is suppressed. Lowell sees himself burnt out at
an early age. But, as in "Home After Three Months Away,"
he recognizes renewal and continuity through the person of
his daughter. If his fiery spirit is gone, every morning "Like
the sun she rises in her flame-flamingo infants' wear."

Two poems on marriage follow. The first, "Man and
Wife," appears to be a scene from Lowell's second marriage.
It reveals the poet twelve years prior, holding his wife's
hand in dependence all night long, and contrasts that scene
with a current evening during which the wife turns her back
upon him. What is wrong with the marriage is capsulized
in the first line: "Tamed by *Miltown*, we lie on Mother's
bed." The couple has to resort to medication to achieve re-
laxation; they make love on his mother's bed—that reminder
of Lowell's hagridden past. What is right about the marriage
also is clear: the poet obviously deeply loves his wife, that
"clearest of all God's creatures." Even her shrill invective,
which first caught his fancy, has not turned him off in the
dozen years since. Rather, it "breaks like the Atlantic Ocean
on my head." The Atlantic, according to Lowell's best
critic, Jerome Mazzaro, has always been a releasing force
in the poet's work; here it "indicates the direction his life
should be taking—away from tradition; yet the magnolia
and the house, and the security and direction they offer,
prey upon the poet's own sense of insecurity and indirection
and reassure him of his 'sane' grasp of reality." [15]

Just as the boy Lowell is "baptised" in the Dunbarton
millpond, the husband Lowell is purified by the Atlantic of
his wife's tirade. Yet he walks perilously close to the razor-
edge of insanity. The description of the magnolia tree
especially dramatizes what is essentially the poet's malevo-

lent world view: its blossoms "ignite / the morning with their murderous five days' white." One is reminded of the funerals of the Greeks and Romans, who always strewed flowers over the corpse, not as an offering or tribute, but as an analogy for the brevity of life and the ephemeral nature of pleasure. (The Egyptians brought a skeleton to their banquets, a jolly practice of *carpe diem*.) Even in the act of looking at flowers, these magnolias, or the earlier tulips, Robert Lowell cannot forget the pull toward death.

The second marriage poem is " 'To Speak of Woe That Is in Marriage.' " Borrowing his title from Chaucer and an epigraph from Schopenhauer, Lowell completes the indirection by casting the poem in the third person. It is the only poem of the "Life Studies" sequence which is not first person singular. Why he chose to do so is not clear. Perhaps he felt a portrait of the poet as seen by another would add, at this point, another dimension to his family gallery. While we cannot blindly accept the poem's couple as Robert and Elizabeth Lowell, details would indicate that much of the portrayal is based on fact. The murderous magnolia from the previous poem is still blossoming; the husband is still "mentally ill." Hopped-up and deranged, this husband is continually "free-lancing out along the razor's edge." The poem's most important image again is borrowed from the animal kingdom: a sacrifice to his lust, the wife is "Gored by the climacteric of his want, / he stalls above me like an elephant"—an image at once suggestive of the weight of the lovemaker upon the beloved, as well, perhaps, of the trunklike appearance (to the female) of the male sexual organ.

What the poem contributes to the sequence is a sense of the real danger of mental illness. If "Man and Wife" explored it within a muted domestic milieu, however uncozy, the manifestations apparent in " 'To Speak of Woe' " are precipitately homicidal. Only the comparative calm of "Skunk Hour," the final poem, allays the reader's anxieties. As in " 'To Speak of Woe,' " the husband is again out hitting the streets. But rather than cruising for prostitutes, he is engaged in the more passive activity of voyeurism. Instead of "whiskey-blind," he is unbearably sober. And instead of being a goring elephant, he is a calm spectator for a parade of skunks. The animal has become human again. The narrator of "Skunk Hour" is not well; but he is well enough to know he is not. The husband of " 'To Speak of Woe,' " on the other hand, is totally irrational and out of control. This represents a progression for the narrator / poet.

It should be apparent at this point that the poems in this last section are all attempts to regain life, the humanity achieved finally in "Skunk Hour," as opposed to Lowell's earlier work which was largely an attempt to regain his own Christian experience in historical perspective. The first four poems of *Life Studies* ("Beyond the Alps," "The Banker's Daughter," "Inauguration Day," and "A Mad Negro Soldier . . .") are close to Lowell's earlier subjects and style. The last four ("Memories of West Street and Lepke," "Man and Wife," " 'To Speak of Woe That Is in Marriage,' " and "Skunk Hour") closely parallel these first four in content. Only the secularism, economics, politics, militarism, and insanity are no longer Marie de Medici's, Eisenhower's, or the mad Negro's. They are Robert Lowell's. He has, as Jay Martin concludes, become his own central symbol. In "Skunk Hour" he achieves his most accomplished realization of the self-symbol.

So much has been written about "Skunk Hour" that my comments may be brief. As one of the best poems in *Life Studies*, and the one containing the essence of Lowell's then-new subject matter and style, it has received more explication perhaps than any other confessional poem of the fifties and sixties. There is, for example, twenty-six pages of commentary on the two-page poem in Anthony Ostroff's symposium, *The Contemporary Poet As Artist and Critic;* [16] a whole section is devoted to it in Richard J. Fein's *Robert Lowell.* [17]

"Skunk Hour" is a deceptively simple poem, one largely stripped of overt symbols and rhetoric. Richard Wilbur, among others, has remarked of it that "one must participate in the lines, discovering their implicit emotional value and generalizing from their relatively dead-pan specificities." [18] This statement, together with Hugh B. Staples's comment on Lowell's talent for "making an inventory a vehicle for psychological projection and sociological comment" [19] should be borne in mind.

What is essential to the poem, it seems to me, are the contrasts Lowell establishes between the worlds of yesterday and today, the natural and the unnatural, the rich and the poor, the sick and the well. The heiress of Nautilus Island thirsts for the "hierarchic privacy / of Queen Victoria's century"; she buys up all property facing hers and lets the "eyesores" fall. But even the purchase of such expensive privacy cannot restore the past to the heiress, the island, or the world. The summer millionaire, with all his false rustifi-cations, will no longer return; his yawl will no longer be used for pleasure but for lobstering. This unnatural state is further symbolized by the goods sold by the island's "fairy decorator," whose fishnets are filled with corks painted orange instead of natural ones. Though ironically he dreams of marriage as an escape from his unprofitable business, this would be but yet another unnatural state (for him) about to be perpetuated.

Discontent fills the poem. The heiress is unhappy with her surroundings, the decorator with his work and pay, the millionaire with his vacations, and, finally in stanza five, we find the narrator to be the most discontented of all. The other three characters were merely background for his greater malaise. This poet drives about on a dark night (the dark night of the soul, as many have suggested), hoping for a glimpse of lovers in their parked cars. As he admits, "My mind's not right." He summarizes his condition in the phrase, "I myself am hell"—echoing Milton's Lucifer in book 4 of *Paradise Lost* ("my self am Hell"). This narrator makes his way toward no Paradise, however; the poem is, instead, infused with death images: falling eyesores, dead millionaires, the fox-stain of autumn, the hill's skull, the graveyard, a hand at the throat, a chalk-dry spire, and more. The narrator summarizes his condition in this land of the living dead with the phrase, "I myself am hell; / nobody's here—" the opposite of Sartre's thesis (in *No Exit*) that hell is "other people."

The wandering, ill, and malcontent figure of the poet

exploring the wreckage of his life is one with that of the mother skunk who explores the town in search of something to nourish and sustain her. John Berryman reads her function as thus: "The skunk is an outcast; this is the basis of the metaphor, and how a mental patient feels." [20] William J. Martz, on the other hand, sees the skunk not as a figure for the poet, but for the poet's world: "The skunk suggests inescapable odor, the loathesomeness of the speaker's world, its refusal to be driven away (from the mind) no matter what effort the speaker makes to exorcise it—'Horror and doubt distract / His troubled thought.'" Martz goes on to suggest that, "the skunk is also a healthy creature of nature going about the business of caring for her young, who in column likely suggest to the speaker an enviable order, and though she is always a threat, she will not release her air-polluting odor unless frightened or attacked." [21] In this sense the order of the column of skunks repeats the order of the seven tulips.

In a world of garbage, the skunk and her kittens somehow survive. In an alien world they "will not scare." So too the poet somehow gets on, through tenacity, and hope, and courage. And so despite the poet's outright confession of mental derangement, the poem is less bleak than many which precede it. There is in the last two stanzas a glimmer of a better time for the narrator; he will not only endure, but prevail.

"Manic," "neurasthenic," "sick," "mental cases," "screwballs," "homicidal," "lobotomized," "hopped-up," "tranquilized," "*Miltown*"—all are key words from the fifteen poems of the "Life Studies" sequence. They are forthright and clinical words, then new to mid-century American poetry. They have since influenced the content and texture of poems by other important poets. In subject matter with Snodgrass, whom we shall discuss next, he changed the direction of mid-century American poetry.

It is a vision and a vocabulary which have served Lowell well. After the completion of *Life Studies* he stated, at the 1960 Boston Arts Festival, "When I finished *Life Studies*, I was left hanging on a question mark. I am still hanging

there. I don't know whether it is a death-rope or a lifeline."
It has proved undoubtedly to be a lifeline. His next book,
For the Union Dead (1964), extended his confessional autobiography with poems on his first as well as his second marriage, examinations of middle-aged love, and what is, hopefully, his final exorcism of his parents' ghosts. Early in that
book Lowell confesses, "At every corner, / I meet my Father,
/ my age, still alive," and concludes that the man left "death-
steps on the crust, / which I must walk," an ironic echoing
of Longfellow's poem on the lives of *great* men, who are
said to leave "Footprints in the sands of time." "Fall 1961"
continues Lowell's lament that his father left him un-
prepared for the world. Indeed, the book continues Lowell's
plaint for all those gone, "those aunts and aunts, a grandfather, / a grandmother, my mother—". Just as Lowell admitted in *Life Studies* that his grandfather meant more to
him than his father, in *For the Union Dead* he confesses
that Harriet Winslow "was more to me than my mother."

This separation, by death, from all his loved ones perhaps
accounts for the number of symbolic severed heads throughout the book. The Gorgon, "her severed head swung / like a
lantern in the victor's hand"; Sir Walter Raleigh, his head
"still dangling in its scarlet, tangled twine"; Sisera's "idol-
atrous, nailed head"; even the poet's own head, which he
describes in one poem as being like "a turtle shell / stuck
on a pole." (In *Notebook* [1970] Lowell continues the preoccupation and comes to write the inevitable poem of
Judith and Holofernes, only interpreting the decapitation
now in Freudian terms: "Smack! her sword divorced the
codshead from the codspiece." Sylvia Plath independently
seized upon this psychic symbol as well; in "Leaving Early,"
from *Crossing the Water*, she perceives cut chrysanthemums
the "size of Holofernes' head.")

In simplest terms, the head separated from the body is
symbolic of Lowell's lack of feeling for his parents. But
Plato, in *Timaeus*, posited the thesis that "the human head
is the image of the world." The graphic separation could
thus be that of Lowell from the world about him. Whether
Lowell's several severed heads are symbols of the body's

alienation from the intellect—which is highly probable—or the son's from the parents, or the poet's from the world, they continue as an important portion of his private mythology. One is reminded of that other poet of alienation, Lewis Carroll, in whose *Alice* books one finds the Queen of Hearts who wants to cut off everyone's head; a serious discussion of decapitation by the Cheshire Cat; and the decapitated Jabberwock.

In Lowell the poet's psychic wounds are given physical manifestations of another sort as well. In *For the Union Dead*, for instance, one poem deals with a cut cornea and a separated tooth; another has the poet-as-child wishing to be sawed in half; a third focuses on unfocused myopia; yet another on night sweats. Everywhere insomnia is omnipresent.

While that book is exceedingly pessimistic, with man's fate summarized in the terrifying lines, "We are like a lot of wild / spiders crying together, / but without tears," there are indications this later Lowell is more at peace with himself than the night wanderer of *Life Studies*. He has learned to ask his father to "forgive me / my injuries, / as I forgive / those I / have injured!" While working out his personal salvation in these poems, Lowell in no way exhausted the confessional mode. Unlike Snodgrass, whose second book reveals the strain of confessional overreach, Lowell's mammoth *Notebook*—which in its third printing contained over three hundred and ten poems—yields many confessional triumphs. It promises to be a book like Whitman's *Leaves of Grass*, amended and enlarged on each printing. Lowell continues to define the moral and intellectual passions which distinguish man as a social being, and his poems perform a civilizing function in an increasingly barbaric world. Looking inward, Robert Lowell continues to find images valid for the outward world, and powerful enough to illumine it.

3

W. D. Snodgrass and the Sad Hospital of the World

Lowell's confessional poems seem the result of an attempt to work out a separate peace between himself and his father's memory. W. D. Snodgrass's most famous work is clearly the result of forced separation from his daughter. While the jacket of his book informs us he is "the father of three children," the poems of the "Heart's Needle" sequence which gives the volume its title are clearly about the poet's relationship with his first child, a daughter. And in an epigraph taken from an old Irish story, Snodgrass reminds us that "an only daughter is the needle of the heart." It was this needle, pricking the poet's vitals, which hurt Snodgrass into writing the most admired sequence of confessional poems in our time short of Lowell's "Life Studies" cycle. The ten poems of the Snodgrass sequence are in their way as frank and as harrowing as the fifteen which compose Lowell's. (Both books were published in 1959.)

Then years later, under the pseudonym "S. S. Gardons"— Snodgrass more or less spelled backwards—he published an even more startling cycle of confessions under the title *Remains*. It is a lesser known work than *Heart's Needle*, owing to the disguise of the author, the limited number of copies printed (200) and the list price of forty dollars. No review copies were distributed. One can only speculate the reason for such anonymity. While the "Heart's Needle" sequence is about wife and daughter, for whom the poet has responsibility and presumably control, the "Remains" poems are about his father, mother, and the memory of a sister,

45

dead at twenty-five. The sequence is apparently so frankly based on actual familial love-hate relationships that the poet probably chose not to hurt his parents further by exposing them directly. As William Heyen observed, "it is difficult to send one's mother a book in which she is depicted as 'consoled by evil,' or in which one's dead sister is depicted as wearing 'Eyeshadow like a whore.' "[1] The important thing for American poetry is that Snodgrass did not repress his desire to write such a book or suppress the poems once written. However limited their readership at present, the *Remains* poems remain.

It was in 1959 that Snodgrass published what amounts to his poetic manifesto. He explained why the use of *personae* and third-person narratives and adopted poses and postures were, for him, a dead end. It was one of the earliest statements in print supporting a post-modern "confessional" school:

> I am left, then, with a very old-fashioned measure of a poem's worth—the depth of its sincerity. And it seems to me that the poets of our generation—those of us who have gone so far in criticism and analysis that we cannot ever turn back and be innocent again, who have such extensive resources for disguising ourselves from ourselves —that our only hope as artists is to continually ask ourselves, "Am I writing what I *really* think? Not what I think is acceptable; nor what my favorite intellectual would think in this situation; nor what I wish I felt. Only what I cannot help thinking." For I believe that the only reality which a man can ever surely know is that self he cannot help being, though he will only know that self through its interactions with the world around it. If he pretties it up, if he changes its meaning, if he gives it the voice of any borrowed authority, if in short he rejects this reality, his mind will be less than alive. So will his words.[2]

It is this dedication to "sincerity," to the "self he cannot help being," which individualizes the best of Snodgrass's work. In another of his infrequent essays he exclaims, "How could one be a first-rate artist without offending, deeply, those he most loves?" [3] Snodgrass has always written what he must. He is our poet of the anti-*personae*. Indeed one of his best poems is literally about just that, concluding, "You must call up every strength you own / And you can rip off the whole facial mask." [4]

This "sincerity," for want of a better word, when expressed in poems about the poet's own life, is what makes Snodgrass's confessions more sympathetic than Lowell's. Snodgrass is, somehow, his own best metaphor, a "seemingly miraculous embodiment as an individual of the age's stereotype." Living in suburbia, driving a Volkswagen, puttering in the garden, marrying a minor-league beauty queen, his life touches the reader's more deeply than does the aristocratic Lowell's, because in fact it more closely resembles the reader's own. Jerome Mazzaro says it neatly: "Lowell has to stand outside himself to become part of the age; Snodgrass does not. There is, as a result, less irrelevant poetry by Snodgrass and less strain in writing, for his own urgency touches the urgency of his readers." [5]

What Mazzaro does not go on to say, and what needs saying, is that for Lowell reality is deeply rooted in *things*. It was Wallace Stevens, that elegant poet who lived an elegant life, who said, "I am what surrounds me." But it could have been Robert Lowell. The very context and texture of *Life Studies* is, say, venerable stone porches, Edwardian clocks, pedigreed puppies, Rogers Peet pants, chauffeured autos, home billiard tables, and wall-to-wall leather-bound books. At times the sheer weight of possessions burdens Lowell's volume. Snodgrass, on the other hand, happily wears his relative poverty on his shirt-sleeve. Experience has taught him "That all the ordinary / Surrounds of social life are futile and vain." Or, put another way, "There is a value underneath / The gold and silver in my teeth." Snodgrass sees the typical American's materialism as spiritually stultifying. In "Flash Flood" he dramatizes the futility of such materialism by narrating how one act of God or man can splinter "the goods they had used their / lives collecting." He implies that such a severance is far from tragic. Indeed, after the stock market crash of the thirties, people in his opinion "then began to live." In this sense his second book, *After Experience*, is an American poetic counterpart of E. M. Forster's English novel, *Howards End*; both books relate, in symbolic acts, the poverty of the inner life of the middle and upper classes when possessions take precedent over persons. One poem is concerned with the "company men" who "will spend their lives / In glossy houses kept by glossy wives," a condemnation which echoes that of *Heart's Needle*, in which he assails "the young who sell / their minds to retire at forty." Another poem compares such men to moths who, trapped, are impelled by a "blind fanatical drive." But Snodgrass's consummate statement on materialism is found in "The Platform Man," a poem which sets forth his personal philosophy (platform) of minimal possessions and minimal expectations. Here he employs the figure of a double-amputee on a platform as symbol for man beggared by man. The poet concludes,

> *I'd travel light: taking nothing*
> *Free and give no quarter.*
> *The curse is far from done*
> *When they've taken your daughter;*
> *They can take your son.*

The taken daughter, as we shall see, is the event which gave rise to Snodgrass's most poignant poems.

The materialism of the company man leads to blind conformity, the subject of many other poems. "Lobsters in the Window" is a portrait of men as creatures, "heaped in their common trench." Snodgrass, obsessed with the individual's loss of identity in America, gives us poems on the anonymity of lovers checked into motels under assumed names; servicemen setting out for the East in camouflaged uniforms; businessmen who "dress just far enough behind the fashions / And think right thoughts"; black-robed academicians for whom a committee gives the proper "opinions on fine books" and chooses "clothing fit / For the integrated area where he'll live."

Like Lowell, Snodgrass obviously has experienced alienation in the no-man's-land of mid-century America. But if
Lowell is the poet of voyages, always traveling somewhere
in search of meaning—Rome to Paris, Boston to Dunbarton,
home to lovers' lane—Snodgrass is the poet of withdrawals
and returns—the soldier home on leave, the soldier revisiting
San Francisco, Ulysses brought home alone to no-man's-
land, the postoperative patient returned to consciousness,
the wandering lover restored to his beloved, the native returning home after fifteen years, the poet to his favorite
writing place, the professor to the classroom, the endless
return of the seasons, and especially the bittersweet return
of a separated father to his daughter.

Heart's Needle is a book composed of nineteen short
poems plus the ten poems of the title cycle. The pieces
are characterized by the essential egocentricity of the confessional poet. Indeed in one Snodgrass exclaims,

> *While civilizations come down with the curse,*
> *Snodgrass is walking through the universe.*[6]

Like the "Life Studies" sequence, *Heart's Needle* is arranged
roughly in chronological order to conform with the progression of the poet's life. But instead of childhood traumas
and father hatred, Snodgrass's emotional life seems to have
begun with the war, and his return from it. This leads into
a period of rumination, a teaching career, marriage, father-
hood, divorce, remarriage. Unlike the poems of Lowell and
those of a much lesser poet, Donald Justice, Snodgrass's
reveal no compulsion to return to the child's garden with
verses.

The first poem, "Ten Days Leave," strikes the chord of
alienation which reverberates throughout the book. The
serviceman on leave, feeling vastly changed by war and experience, finds that nothing at all has changed: "His folks /
Pursue their lives like toy trains on a track." This image of
the oval train track could stand for Snodgrass's determin-
istic world view: all things are cyclical; even the "seasons
bring us back once more / like merry-go-round horses."
Though we return to our point of departure, in our end is

not our beginning—either we or the departure point itself may have drastically changed during our absence. The returned serviceman, for instance, feels in his own home like "A tourist whispering through the priceless rooms / Who must not touch things."

"Returned to Frisco, 1946" continues the alienation theme. Stripped of identity by uniform and service number, the soldier shoulders along a rail with the others, "like pigs." Earlier they had scrambled up hostile beaches "like rabbits." Reduced to an animalistic state, the poet returns to the saintly city only to find the Golden Gate Bridge, that rainbow of promise, "fading away astern." On the other hand Alcatraz has been prettified with flowers. The war has canceled free will. Hope is dimmed, and over all looms the shadow of prison house.

"MHTIS . . . OU TIS" is centered on the famous pun from book 9 of the *Odyssey* (in which, at a banquet, Odysseus relates his adventures since leaving Troy, in particular his encounters with the Lotus-Eaters and the Cyclops). In this further exploration of alienation and lack of identity, Snodgrass adopts a rare *persona* in the figure of Odysseus, who disguised himself as No Man and was able thus to save himself. Perhaps, the poet is saying, by abandoning all past identity, one can create a new self. Like Odysseus, the returning warrior might begin again.

The poem, however, is not one of Snodgrass's best. Its lofty allusions, its untranslated title from the Greek, its dedication to a psychotherapist who is never identified as such (though knowledge of whose profession is essential to comprehension of the second stanza addressed to him), are all barriers to communication.

"At the Park Dance," with its dancing couples who are even in physical closeness "loving strangers," is a minor development of the alienation theme. "Orpheus" is something else again. Snodgrass here, more successfully than in the Odysseus poem, dons the mask of the legendary husband and poet who has lost his beloved. It may not be too much to assume that the poem is his expression of grief over the loss through divorce of his first wife. Though Snodgrass is at his best when speaking in his own voice, Orpheus's is singularly appropriate here. Returned from an expedition, married and then separated from his young bride, Orpheus like Snodgrass paid a heavy penalty for "looking back." We can even compare the verse Snodgrass makes with the Orphic poetry of early Greek writers; in true Orphism one finds the sense of guilt and the need for atonement, the suffering and the ultimate belief in immortality, which characterize his own poetry.

Dedicated to the poet's second wife, "Papageno" is about the poet's search for love after the fracture of his first union. Just as Orpheus had his lyre, Papageno has his flute —both symbols for the poetry Snodgrass employs to call the world to love. Snodgrass here seems to confuse Mozart's Papageno with the opera's hero, Tamino, who possesses the "stealthy flute." Papageno, on the other hand, carries a pipe of Pan and—later—a set of chimes (*Silberglöckchen*). In Mozart's opera, *The Magic Flute*, Papageno's instrument was bestowed by the Powers of Darkness and had the power to inspire love. So Snodgrass, in the dark time after divorce, "went to whistle up a wife," seeking love and purification.

That his search was a long and dark one is evident in the symbolic landscape—or psychescape—of the next poem, "The Marsh." The dead limbs, rotting logs, and snarled sun are emblems for the poet's state of mind. The low level of the swamp is an equation for the spiritual, negative, and destructive state he has entered. At the time, the water's surface is a mirror which presents an image for self-contemplation, consciousness, and revelation. In "heavy waters," Snodgrass recognizes the need to deliver himself out of this state: "Stick in the mud, old heart, what are you doing here?" (An interesting comparison can be made between his swamp poem, Lowell's "Dunbarton," Roethke's "The Premonition" and "First Meditation," Plath's "Full Fathom Five" and "Sheep in Fog," and Kunitz's "Father and Son." All five poets seek purification from the darkest waters.)

In Snodgrass's "September in the Park" the poet has emerged from darkness. But the world in which he finds himself is still hazy, a landscape of marginal things—a dim sun, some dying leaves, and squirrels gathering food for winter. The poet has traveled further inland, away from the bog of despair, but he is still wandering, has still attained nothing to replace that which he has lost. All he has is a memory of his hand upon his wife's breast. True tenderness is felt in these several poems. Whereas Lowell has never written a love poem, only poems of marriage, Snodgrass is capable of transmitting much more feeling in matters of the heart. He achieves this partially through great directness and simplicity, partially through a tone which one critic has described as "dreamy precision," giving us human encounters something like "snowdrops in water, that are so full of implications." [7] Compared to his tender apostrophes, Lowell's wifely poems are harsh indeed.

With "The Operation" the book shifts focus and the poet's quest is partially fulfilled. The dark of the swamp, the hanging smoke of the park, lift. The reader discovers the poet undergoing purification in a dazzling world of white. In the hospital the poet is symbolically reborn; the knife which shaves his body hair leaves him "White as a child." The knife also makes of him a sacrifice, the naked poet on display for strangers to flay. (The poem is related to "The Examination" from his second book, *After Experience*; in that poem it is the poet's brain and not his body which is operated upon.) Through totally delivering himself up, the poet regains the world. His last vision is of the world beyond, inverted and slow, but nevertheless quite "gay." He has awakened into a world of flowers and women. We can assume that one of the women by his bedside is the new partner he has spent so long seeking. Hers are the flowers which make the world gay.

"The Operation," then, is about human recovery and resilience. Using bodily recovery from an operation as metaphor, he explores the heart's recovery from lost love. Through sacrifice man can attain something greater than that which has been given up. The poem's two allusions are, as always with Snodgrass, highly relevant. It is not only his own long hospital gown which reminds the poet of Pierrot. "Little Peter" has traditionally been the artist-lover of soaring imagination who must grimly hide his real passion behind a comic mask. The second allusion, to "A schoolgirl first offering her sacrament," functions not only as a parallel to the hospital gown, but, as Donald T. Torchiana says, reinforces the theme of guilt purged through sacrifice.

For better or worse, "The Operation" is the poem which has occasioned scores of imitations by less skillful writers — works which constitute the "My-stomach-laced-up-like-a-football" school of poetry. (The quotation is from Anne Sexton, but Snodgrass's operation poem is the original.) With its clinical observations, its unflinching attention to such details as aluminum bowls and cold sponges, rubber gloves and pared pubic hair, the poem makes successful use of subject matter formerly thought unfit for poetry. The difference between this poem and many of its imitations is a vital one. Snodgrass contrasts the clinical with the emotional, the white-on-white hospital landscape with the world of flowers and love, the anesthetized patient with the recovered husband-lover. The poem is about deliverance from a bad time to a better, the salvation of the spirit. His imitators, by way of contrast, too often use the means and forget the end; they are clinical for the sake of being shocking. They shout, "Look, Ma! No cavity's too sacred to write about! The anus, the vagina, the Caesarian section!" This is a vision far different from and more limited than Snodgrass's sad hospital of the world, in which one dies to become resurrected, is cut to become whole.

It would be nice to leave the poet and his love together in that hospital room. Nice, but contrary to Snodgrass's book and life. So the autobiographical chronicle continues with "Riddle," a poem of separation from Jan, the second love, and "Winter Bouquet," a poem of reunion. In the latter, Snodgrass perhaps plays with his name when he inventories those "grasses gone to seed." The dry straw-flowers are a symbol for the poet without his love, a husk devoid of past vitality. Only a woman's love can revivify the poet's body / spirit, much as the love of women who gathered pods during the war years to fill life preservers saved shipwrecked men. Both acts save men from being lost. In the third and final stanza, when Jan returns, the poet blows the weed-seed to the March wind. This act of delight and fertility celebrates the reunion, as do the following two "Songs," erotic poems of man's dependence on woman, woman's dependence on man.

"Seeing You Have . . ." and "Home Town" reveal the poet, for all his new connubial bliss, to be haunted by other feelings. The first addresses itself to the fact that the poet is not quite happily monogamous. The second is a portrait of the artist as an older man, re-walking the streets of his youth and compulsively hunting what he has outgrown. It is a poem which invites comparison with Peter Taylor's short story, "Drug Store."

The poet's quest continues. He leaves the scene of his youth and the next poem, "A Cardinal," finds him in a gully within a wood. Yet even in this voluntary withdrawal, the poet cannot escape the world about him. Still he hears the uniformed college air cadets marching and counting cadence; trucks and trailers grinding on the turnpike; airplanes soaring in the air; factories turning out consumer goods. Even the woods itself is spoiled by the poet's contemporaries: toilet paper, lovers' litter, and beer cans spoil the habitat. One is reminded of the sweet, spoiled Thames of *The Waste Land*.

A writer of words no one wishes to read, a member of a military service but between wars, the poet finds hope in identifying with the bird of the poem's title. Snodgrass's search for meaning in life is encapsulized in the words of the "song" he attributes to that red bird:

> *I fight nobody's battles;*
> *don't pardon me for living.*
>
> *The world's not done to me;*
> *it is what I do;*
> *whom I speak shall be;*
> *I music out my name*
> *and what I tell is who*
> *in all the world I am.*

It is significant that, once more, as in "Winter Bouquet" and "These Trees Stand . . ." and "April Inventory," the quest for identity is linked to the ability to say his name. A name which, in one poem, he calls "absurd, miraculous as sperm, and as decisive"; and which, in many other poems, he changes entirely by reversing the letters and attributing authorship to "S. S. Gardons."

It is equally significant that the creature chosen for projection of the self is, first, a bird; and, secondly, a red one. Birds, of course, are very often used in literature to symbolize human souls. (Think, for instance, of the *Mirach*, in which Mohammed found the Tree of Life in the middle of heaven, about which perched those many brilliant birds, the souls of the faithful.) More specifically, Snodgrass's bird seems to be symbol of thought, imagination, or spiritual relationships. Certainly as a creature of the Element of Air it denotes loftiness and lightness of spirit, which can descend to the earth, then rise again and again in perpetual mediation between "heaven" and earth, as did Shelley's skylark.

The color of Snodgrass's bird determines its secondary symbolism. The color of blood, of the life force, as well as of fire and purification, the cardinal is a near-perfect figure for the poet surrounded by philistines. More brilliant than they, and dedicated to truth and beauty and art, he strikes a strong contrast to those who earn their living praising only "what it pays to praise" (for instance, Snodgrass suggests, soap and garbage cans). Like the cardinal in the wood, the poet is a bright spot in the thickets of commerce. Like "Papageno," the poet / cardinal whistles in the dark to drive the devils off. But whistle though he may, the poet is still, at poem's end, somewhere in the weeds. He has not yet emerged a whole self. He does, though, seem to know better than before who and where he is.

Condemnation of the American middle and upper classes continues in "The Campus on the Hill." The poet has at last progressed from the swamp to the weeds, and from the weeds to a house on a hill. The serviceman is now college instructor. But the America which surrounds him is the same. Even within the groves of academe, the values deemed important are not those of the mind. The poem rails at the children of the *nouveaux riches* for their unthinking conformity.

And was there ever a more poignantly modern couplet than this:

> *The pear tree lets its petals drop*
> *Like dandruff on a tabletop.*

From "April Inventory," these lines from the last poem to precede the "Heart's Needle" sequence convey the poet's frame of mind after all that has gone before. The man who chased girls must now nudge himself to look at his female pupils, so great is their age differential; the poet who has lost hair and teeth has gained a wife and an analyst. Yet through it all, the poet / protagonist has managed to adhere to his youthful ideals. He has not sold out. His "inventory" is not one of capital gains or material possessions. It is one of humble and modest achievements on the spiritual plane. While the "solid scholars" were pushing ahead for better situations and salaries, Snodgrass was teaching a girl a song of Mahler's; showing a child the colors of the luna moth ("and how to love"); and easing in turn a wife and an old man who was dying.[8]

While not learning a "blessed thing they pay you for," it is obvious the poet has learned how to be William DeWitt Snodgrass. In this poem he can finally name his full name. He is resigned to growing older without getting richer, to the loss of youth and physical beauty, because these resignations are firmly rooted within a great commitment to that which is of more value than youth, beauty, or money. A truly individual comprehension of one song of Mahler's, or of one butterfly's wing, is worth all the books on books. Above all, Snodgrass preaches the gospel of gentleness in a violent world, a gentleness which "will outspeak and has its reasons." It is this general gentleness which preserves the poet in a world of specialists.

Just as the writing of the poem "The Operation" marked a turning in Snodgrass's life, the entrance of a feminine muse to inspire and perhaps save him, so too is a similar milestone marked by the "Heart's Needle" cycle. Only it is the subtraction of a loved one rather than her addition which prompts the poetry. Inspired by the enforced separation from his young daughter, Cynthia, the sequence of ten poems—one each for each season over a two-and-one-half year period—shows the experienced father-poet groping for meaning and survival when the world he has created and grown into falls about him.

Appropriately the cycle begins in winter (of 1952), the terminal season, with a poem directed to the lost child. The daughter, born in another winter and during the martial Korean War and, by implication, during the marital war the poet waged with his wife, is seen as a victim of strife. Just as the snows of Asia are fouled by the war's fallen soldiers, so Snodgrass's daughter's mind ("A landscape of new snow") shall be disturbed by marital strife. As in "The Operation," white connotes purity. But the hospital white signaled a new beginning; here the same color portends a terminus, the end of family life as the poet has come to know it. Comparing himself to a chilled tenant-farmer, the poet surveys his daughter's purity and his own chances for restraining "the torments of demented summer." We later come to realize that this "demented summer" is a figure for the separation from his wife, which he was unable to forestall.

The next poem, of spring 1953, finds the daughter three years old. Father and daughter are portrayed planting seeds. He cautions her to "sprinkle them in the hour / When shadow falls across their bed." In other words, she should look toward the living in the presence of death or separation. He recognizes now that the daughter, his own seed, shall come to sprout in his absence. Someone else shall have to "weed" her. Yet the poet seems to be saying that she shall grow almost *because of* his absence. There is a recognition of the shadow which has fallen across that other garden bed, the nuptial; and when the poet declares, "Child, we've done our best," he speaks not just for himself and her in regard to the damaged garden, but for himself and his wife in regard to the ruined marriage.

Extremely subtle, these lyrics of "Heart's Needle" para-doxically cut deeper than Lowell's more overt outcries. Poem 3 of the sequence is a skillful symbolic portrait of the father / daughter / mother relationship during the summer after the spring planting. Employing the symbolic action of the child's swinging and tugging between them, Snod-grass communicates at once the tug-of-war between a mother with "custody" and a father with "visiting privileges" and the heavy tug of love on the human heartstrings. The Ko-rean War again forms a counterpoint and counterpart to the domestic clash; both parents are compared first to Cold War soldiers who never give ground but never gain any— stubborn and stoic parents between whose stations the child swings back and forth—and secondly, to prisoners of war. As with the opposing sides of a battle, "nobody seems very pleased." And with the poem's allusion to Solomon's wis-dom, the poet implies that, in order to save his daughter, he must first give her up. As in the biblical story, the true parent is the one who, rather than have the baby sawn in two, sacrifices all claim to possession.

Fall 1953. Poet and daughter walk in a public garden (in poem 4). Just as no one can hold back the autumn, the sep-aration is inevitable. That which was lovely and gay is now a ghost of itself; in the poem the dandelion heads have turned gray. Snodgrass renders a symbolic landscape of dwindling and termination:

> . . . the asters, too, are gray,
> ghost-gray. Last night's cold
> is sending on their way
> petunias and dwarf marigold,
> hunched sick and old.

The poet next translates this landscape into the language of sickness and analysis: the morning glory vines become "nerves caught in a graph." But this image immediately melts into one of the broken lines of the poems the poet cannot write. Separation, analysis, and writer's block are all part of one interior landscape.

Still, perhaps all is not futile. In the penultimate stanza

the pair find a flower among some late bloomers, a bud which may yet blossom in the daughter's room. Her life may yet flower after his departure. This possibility, however, is negated in the ultimate stanza. The poet tells, in a little parable, of a "Friend's child" who cried upon the death of a cricket who used to sing outside her window. The cricket of course is another figure for the poet. As William Heyen reads these lines, they are a portent of grief for the daughter and death for the father. But, as Heyen says, "unspoken here is also the realization that he must continue his writing." [9] Herein lies a paradox: only the destruction of his marriage provides sufficient impetus for the renewal of his creative abilities.

The fifth poem concludes the first year, beginning with winter again, and introduces a greater depth of feeling. The daughter's loss finally is hideously real, not future possibility but present reality. Through skillful use of halting enjambment ("Although you are still three, / You are already growing / Strange to me"), the poet conveys emotionally not only the girl's physical development but also her increasing mental alienation from her father. This loss and alienation provoke the strongest image in the first half of the cycle: the poet feels himself a fox caught in a trap, a fox whose only salvation is to gnaw off his paw. That paw, remaining behind, is the flesh of his flesh, the daughter surrendered to the machinery of divorce. As the Bible says (Matt. 5:29), "If thy right eye offend thee, pluck it out, and cast it from thee." It is better to enter the Kingdom of Heaven blind, lame, or maimed, than not at all.

The poem of the second spring is a memory piece occasioned by a walk on the riverbank with his daughter, who has brought an Easter egg. To interpret this egg as a traditional symbol of hope, potentiality, and immortality seems too painfully ironic. The Easter egg is here more precisely a symbol for the mystery of life, the poem's major theme. The second stanza is literally a rendering of the miracle of birth. The third relates an incident of flooded killdeer nests, the eggs lost to water. The fourth depicts a precarious nest, the fifth, dead starlings and a trapped pigeon. All these imitations of mortality are but preparations for the portrait of the father at his daughter's sickbed, when those miraculous lungs (of stanza two) become caught and will not take air.

These recognitions of the brevity and destructive nature of life are by way of apology to the daughter for the revelation, saved for the eighth stanza, that the poet has remarried. He has another child, another wife. It is Snodgrass's attempt to make the most of this bad situation, our life, in which we have few choices and those we have may prove destructive to those we love.

The image of the net which snares the pigeon is not unlike the trap which snares the fox of the preceding poem. Both, like marriage and divorce, are traps. In letting the pigeon go to its keeper, the poet is reenacting his letting his daughter go to the custody of his wife. In each case he fears he has brought about destruction. Yet, as Heyen has said, destruction is perhaps "the inevitable outcome of any attempt to live the individual life." [10] We can only try to choose what is best.

Blue July and the poet is swinging his daughter again. Once more the back-and-forth movement of a swing conveys the pendulum-like push-pull relationship. He voices his hope that though she climbs higher and farther from him, she may fall back to him the stronger for it.

Animals, war, and institutions are the three prevailing motifs of "Heart's Needle." In poem 8 the poet lives "next door to the jail"; the zoo's caged monkeys "consume each other's salt." (The image of caged animals recurs later as well.) When the poet's daughter visits, this autumn, he is Halloween, masquerading as a fox. (We remember the fox's foot left behind in poem 5; the fox indeed is the daughter, the life-red creature whose existence is so dear to the poet.) It is an irony that when the daughter strips off her mask, her father's new neighbors still do not know who she is. As the face she wears in public is not her own, so in the poet's new life she has no essential identity. The false face and the grinning jack-o'-lantern are a pair of masks, the appearances the poet tries to maintain. Yet the jack-o'-lantern's face fronts a hollow core. Behind the grin as behind the daughter's visits, there is an emptiness. The girl has no real participation in his life, only visits which should become less frequent for her own independence. That such independence is imminent is conveyed through her symbolic act of eating snow off his car. Years before she had, unrealistically, asked her father to catch a star, "pull off its skin / and cook it for our dinner." Her dining fare and her vision are already more down-to-earth. The poet knows he should relinquish his hold on the girl. Yet to do so would be to create an awful void, summarized in the line, "Indeed our sweet / foods leave us cavities."

Animals, institutions, and war are again the motifs for the penultimate poem of the cycle, a piece which must count as the strongest. Set within a museum in Iowa City, the poem's stuffed animals are arrested in motion "like Napoleon's troops." This institution is clearly Snodgrass's microcosm of the larger world where creatures are pitted against creatures in constant rage. The bison shoving at his calf is not unlike the poet fighting with his wife. The lioness standing over her cub is no less envious than the daughter's mother. The poet and his wife are the poem's two Olympian elk who stand bound and fixed in their everlasting enmity.

These animal images are succeeded by a catalogue of the museum's horrors: a two-headed foal, an hydrocephalic goat, a limbless calf, Siamese-twin dogs, and more. These are clearly outward manifestations of the poet's inner state, like the dwarf marigold of poem 4, those flowers so "hunched sick and old." Yet these visions are not of flowers, but of flesh. And the catalogue includes unborn and born, "putty-colored children curled / in jars of alcohol" as well. Man himself has fought no less than members of the animal kingdom. Only those here arrested in alcohol can avoid being born into the world and spilling blood. The poet cannot accept man's nature; he does not understand it, has no answers. He only knows that he lives less than one mile from his daughter, and has not seen her for more than three months.

It is a dark, almost suicidal poem, culminating in the terrible vision of a world which "moves like a diseased heart / packed with ice and snow." Unlike that other poem of a poet-scavenger moving among the garbage dump of a civilization — Lowell's "Skunk Hour" — there is here no glimmer of hope.

That hope, nevertheless, is to be found in the tenth and final poem. Winter gives way to spring. Separation yields to reunion. Images of life and re-creation crowd the short poem. Nothing has really changed, of course; the seasons merely "bring us back once more / like merry-go-round horses"; the train travels its oval track. But the poet is reconciled! He will not accept the advice of friends who state that he would leave his daughter alone if he truly loved her. (Job's advisors?) His life is inexorably bound to hers, however little of it he is handed. He is like the coons and bears of the park, "punished and cared for," those creatures who stretch forth fingers for whatever scraps are given. After ten seasons of separation, she is still his daughter. A book of both separations and reunions ends with the latter.

As poet-critic Heyen summarizes deftly, *"Heart's Needle* remains a poetry without answers, but it is a poetry of total awareness. Inherent in its criticism of the way things are is the ability of the intelligence that informs its lyrics to accept this reality and to struggle against it at the same time. *Heart's Needle,* without caterwauling, free from what Ezra Pound calls 'emotional slither,' takes on dimensions of the tragic." [11]

With the tenth poem the "Heart's Needle" sequence ends. Which is not to say that Snodgrass's poetic exploration of his relationship with his daughter ends. The second book, *After Experience* (1968), opens with four poems which seem to have been written at the time of *Heart's Needle,* and which continue the cycle though collected outside it. (A fifth additional poem to his daughter closes the *Remains* volume.) "Partial Eclipse" uses that meteorological phenomenon as metaphor both for the father's refusal to be blacked-out of the girl's life and for the very nature of the strained relationship. Like the full moon during eclipse, at least "one glint was left." Yet it is only a glint. That which was once full and bright is now "dim as a ghost." "September" is a brief chronicle of loss. The heron they saw together is gone, the newts in the creek are gone, and of course the daughter herself is gone. The dry landscape reinforces the impressions.

The ephemeral nature of human relationships is the subject of "Reconstructions." In each of three opening stanzas, Snodgrass slowly builds his evidence: a plant left behind, the Indian-gift of a doll, a pathetic owner / pet drama. Yet it is not relationships in general which agonize the poet, but that between himself and his daughter. And he realizes that in saying she did not mind leaving the plant behind, in snatching the doll away, and in leaving the sitting dog trembling for her command to relax, the daughter is reenacting roles she herself has been forced to observe or play during her parents' separation. She has turned grief into play. And nothing can be done to change this state of affairs. At the poem's conclusion the daughter is left at her mother's; the dog is given away. Always outward, away from the poet himself, the loved ones go.

"The First Leaf" seems to bid farewell to the subject which has sustained Snodgrass for fourteen poems. The daughter is now more than six years old and going away for a full year. The season is autumn and the first leaf which falls from its branch and spins across the windshield is like the daughter herself, torn free from her origins to spin out into the world. (Snodgrass together with Roethke seems intuitively to know, moreover, that the leaf is one of the eight "common emblems" of Chinese symbolism, being the allegory of happiness. With the fall of the leaf, happiness drops to dust.) The reader is told the daughter will travel by train, and when the poet posits the image of cattle transported in a trailer before his car, like men shipped to battle, we know he is associating by image the impersonal and mechanical process by which such a separation is decreed. The poet admits to a sense of guilt at having a life of his own at the expense of hers. He has been able to remarry only by shedding her mother; able to write poems again only through finding the subject of his daughter's loss. The result of all this suffering, then, is that "Now I can earn a living / By turning out elegant strophes." Another Snodgrassian irony. From out of the wreckage of his family life the poet has found a new life and new creativity. As someone once observed, some eggs must be broken to make an omelet. But what a terrible price to pay for a handful of poems! We feel the weight of his loss in the last four lines, carefully controlled and understated, yet unmistakably bereft:

> *You move off when I send you;*
> *The train pulls down its track.*
> *We go about our business;*
> *I have turned my back.*

That he did not, could not, turn his back is evident in the later poem, "To a Child," with its themes of fertility and futility. Published in *Remains* in 1969, it gives evidence that Snodgrass has not yet abandoned the relationship as his primary subject. Yet for all its obsessive quality, the subject has been handled in all fifteen poems with great emotional control. So obviously hurt into writing, the poet is, nevertheless, never mawkish or self-pitying. These are dry, brittle poems. Even in extremely personal revelation, Snodgrass somehow preserves a proper aesthetic distance between his psyche and his Smith-Corona. The "Heart's Needle" cycle and the five subsequent poems which might have belonged to it is an artistic victory over the defeats and pains of quotidian existence.

One of Snodgrass's most successful techniques for achieving this distance is a borrowed one, T. S. Eliot's "objective correlative." (We stated in the first chapter that Snodgrass was unique among the confessional poets in this respect.) In the poem in which the poet-father first acknowledges that his daughter has become a stranger to him, for instance, he shifts from the personal to the ostensibly impersonal. Snodgrass leaps from the situation at hand to the image of the fox who "backtracks and sees the paw, / gnawed off, he cannot feel; conceded to the jaw / of toothed, blue steel." The paw, as we have said, must be equated with the lost daughter, the trap with the divorce. But by translating the details of his life into metaphoric terms, Snodgrass avoids sentimentality without losing sentiment, and forcefully communicates the full measure of his personal loss. Indeed, "Snodgrass is walking through the universe" in his poems: Snodgrass the man is seen by Snodgrass the poet as a character in a drama viewed from afar.

Another check on direct emotional overflow is the use of his symbolic landscapes, really poetic psychescapes, as in the fourth poem of the cycle. Those dwarf marigolds, old and sick, are an objective projection of the father's subjective state when he realizes he must part with his little girl. The device is most effective in the ninth poem in which the poet contemplates the unnatural condition of their separation as well as the nature of man; the poet wanders through that museumscape of cysts, fistulas, and cancers. The poet is no Shelley, falling and bleeding upon the thorns of life. Rather, he records in apparently cool fashion the outer signs of his inner state. This technique is developed to near-perfection in Snodgrass's second book, in the poem "What We Said," whose twenty-eight lines detail scenery which mirrors every human grief. But the poems in *After Experience* also reveal the danger of this device when overworked. The symbols and symbolic acts show signs of strain. The moon obligingly disappears on cue, a kind of *dea ex machina,* in sympathetic synchronization with the daughter's departure; furtive lovers drop aspirin in a vase of motel flowers, unconsciously performing an act of sympathetic magic as they express their desire for a life with continuity if not permanence.

Sometimes of course these symbolic landscapes and acts coalesce for Snodgrass to form a magnificently reverberant poem, as in "Powwow," a trenchant comment on the destruction of the culture of the American Indian by the American "Americans." In performing their ceremonials now, the Indians "all dance with their eyes turned / Inward —like a woman nursing / A sick child she already knows /

Will die." At the poem's conclusion the tourist drives away from the performance "squinting, / Through red and yellow splatterings on the windshield." The bright guts of insects that go with him resemble the bright war paint of the Indians, who also flung themselves against the oncoming force and shall not live again. Here image and intention are one. (Many confessional poets have written of the shadow-images that slide across their bedroom walls, notably Delmore Schwartz in "In the Naked Bed in Plato's Cave" and John Berryman in "Beethoven Triumphant"; Snodgrass alone seems to find inspiration in the objects which cross his windshield.)

Such achievement is unfortunately rare in *After Experience*. Too often the landscape, the carefully planted symbol, the internal pun, seem too deliberate, too academic. The Snodgrass of *Heart's Needle* was a taker of risks; too many of the purely personal poems in *After Experience* smack of the ingrown nail—everything growing inward, with too much consciousness of Self and Craft. The four new poet-daughter poems seem blurry, heavy carbons of the sharp originals. They were, perhaps, written at the time of the cycle and deliberately withheld from the book for that reason. And as if aware his situation is no longer so unique, his revelations no longer so revealing, in the second book Snodgrass coarsens his language as if that alone might still shock. Elegance has fled from the poetry, the fine elegance of, say, "Winter Bouquet." When the poet passes a drive-in now, it must be described as one of the "hot pits where our teens / Finger fuck."

Not that Snodgrass need resort to gutter language to shock. The title poem, "After Experience," describing an act of self-defense so acutely painful no one can read it without a wince of the eye, a flop of the stomach, is ample evidence of his rhetorical powers. Aside from the purely personal and confessional poems with the manner, if not the power, of *Heart's Needle*, the poems in the second volume must be categorized in three other distinct groups. First come the more objective poems, including the supremely successful "A Flat One," which amplifies the hospital imagery of "The Operation" but makes the act of saving a life seem a selfish gesture and comments on modern life in a more devastating way than any other poem in recent American literature; "Lobsters in the Window," which imagistically re-creates the primordial life as it comments on mass conformity; and "The Platform Man," a poem in which guilt and mutilation fuse in a most beautifully placed and seemingly inevitable pun; as well as an uneven group of five poems attempting to reexperience particular paintings by Matisse, Vuillard, Manet, Monet, and Van Gogh. The last, a very fluid poem utilizing many quotations from the artist's letters, is the most successful of the group.

A third category is a generous selection of translations, fourteen in number, from Rilke, Bonnefoy, Rimbaud, and others. Though unqualified to comment on the linguistic veracity of these translations, we can say they are among the book's most moving poems. Snodgrass has managed to find in other languages poems which reflect his own plight —such as von Eichendorff's "On My Child's Death," that poet's loss by death paralleling Snodgrass's through divorce. In rendering these poems into the American idiom, Snodgrass has found a voice which at times seems more authentic than his own. As statements on grief, the translations are crucial to an understanding of Snodgrass and where the poet presently has arrived. (In the same year he published *After Experience* Snodgrass also published a quite different series of translations, the *Gallows Songs* of Christian Morgenstern, on which he collaborated with Lore Segal. This poet of fancy and lyricism, for whom "time and space are not realities," seems less suited to Snodgrass's personal vision than, say, Rilke and Rimbaud. To compare his translation of Morgenstern's "The Moonsheep" with that of E. M. Valk proves the point.) [12]

The fourth category is not a group at all, but a single poem, "The Examination," the only satire in the Snodgrassian canon. It is a dark allegory on the examining of Ph.D. candidates by university faculty members, perhaps the result of his own examination in literary history for the

Ph.D. in English at Iowa. During the course of the poem's examination the victim is physically and spiritually dismembered. The penultimate stanza concludes, "Well, that's a beginning. The next time, they can split / His tongue and teach him to talk correctly, and give / Him opinions on fine books and choose clothing fit / For the integrated area where he'll live." The poem is an elaboration of the theme of Berryman's "Dream Song #8," in which officials of an institution tell the patient, "if you watch Us instead, / yet you may saved be. Yes," this after "They blew out his loves, his interests." Snodgrass's poem also stands comparison with Swinburne's "In Sepulcretis," in which a man is dismembered by those who "Spy, smirk, sniff, snap, snort, snivel, snarl and sneer." Swinburne's conclusion is, "This is fame." Snodgrass would probably disagree, and say, "This is life." Snodgrass's poem seems to have started a spate of such poetic allegories in our time, of which a late example is Erica Jong's "The Book," from her *Fruits & Vegetables* (1971), in which another examining committee decides "to repossess my typewriter, my legs / my Phi Beta Kappa key, one breast, / any children I may have, / & my expresso machine."

After Experience, like Anthony Hecht's second collection, *The Hard Hours*, bears testimony to the effort of a truly excellent poet to push a unique vision and practice beyond viability. Snodgrass's major achievements remain *Heart's Needle* and sections of the tougher *Remains*. But when in the second volume he does connect, as he does at least nine times in the hefty book, it is with poems which probably shall endure. "What We Said," "The Platform Man," "Leaving the Motel," "A Flat One," "Powwow"—and, for sheer singularity, "The Examination"—are all poetic events for which we should be grateful.

If *After Experience* seemed too varied a collection, the "Remains" poems of "S. S. Gardons" is a highly unified sequence. Just as a daughter lost through divorce was Snodgrass's subject for the ten poems of the "Heart's Needle" sequence, the loss of a sister by death provides the occasion for this new eight-poem cycle. The sequence begins with a poem on the poet's mother and ends with one addressed to his daughter. In between the quality of his experience is rendered with infinite detail. In all eight the pivotal experience is the sister's death, which occurs ironically enough on Independence Day. Only through death does the mousy sister achieve a kind of independence from sickness, a dull life, and a domineering mother.

The title, *Remains*, reverberates with meaning. On one level it refers to the bodily remains from which the spirit of the girl has departed, and on which the undertaker has undertaken an elaborate cosmetic job (in "Viewing the Body"). But "to remain" is also to be left behind, which is the case with the survivors of the dead girl. To remain is also not to be included or comprised, which is the situation of the poet himself, an alien in a small town which thrives on conformity and misfortune. Finally the title may be intended for the manuscript of the poems itself, which is blurbed by the publisher as the literary remains of "S. S. Gardons":

> This sequence of poems was collected by his friends after his disappearance on a hunting trip in the mountains. From the condition of his abandoned motorcycle, it was impossible to determine whether he suffered foul play, was attacked by animals, merely became confused and lost, or perhaps fell victim to amnesia. At present, the case is listed as unsolved.[13]

For the time being, at least, Snodgrass has chosen to phase out his *nom de plume*.

Remains opens with portraits of Snodgrass's mother and father. The first is portrayed as one who "moves by habit, hungering and blind"; the second, one who exacts "no faith, no affection" and whose entire life has been a "programmed air of soft suspension" which he survives in, "cradled and sustained." To such a couple were born the poet and his sister, "The Mouse" of the poem by that title. Like the small mouse they once found outdoors, the sister—small and dull, yet ever so much more precious than the found creature—dies. Yet unlike the mouse, she is unmourned by the brother. As children they were taught to "be well-bred," not to cry over dead animals; so that when the genuine, human tragedy presents itself, the poet "wouldn't spare one tear." His upbringing bars the display of true emotion, an observation which holds true in relation to the writing of these poems themselves. William Heyen observes, "the potential for bathos is certainly here, but the metrical control and hard rhymes, because the employment of conscious technique always implies the poet is attempting to control highly emotional matter by mind, stop the voice from breaking, stave off the purely melodramatic." [14] The brother / sister relationship here is reminiscent of that of Tom and Laura in Tennessee William's moving *The Glass Menagerie*, with the mousy sister especially resembling Laura.

The mouse analogy is carried into the next poem, "Viewing the Body," in which the girl's grey life is contrasted with the gaudiness of her death,

> *Flowers like a gangster's funeral;*
> *Eyeshadow like a whore.*
> *They all say isn't she beautiful.*
> *She, who never wore*

> *Lipstick or such a dress.*

Rather, "Gray as a mouse," she had crept about the dark halls of her mother's house. The shadow sister of the youthful hero of Housman's "To an Athlete Dying Young," this girl paradoxically achieves her only glory through dying. Yet it is a false victory, as all deaths must be, and the worldly trappings are grotesquely unsuitable as props for this girl's earthly departure. The red satin folds of the coffin are "obscene." The deadly circumstance and pomp seem a hideous parody of her life style.

Exactly one year after her death the poet and his wife are back in the parents' house, aware of the family's awareness of the anniversary. The girl's unworn party dress is still closeted, her stuffed animals still shelved. The poet senses that his young wife is unforgiven by the family for being alive—why her, and not the sister instead, the sister, whose deathday is ironically the wife's birthday? More meta-physical than most others of Snodgrass, this poem shifts into speculation on the kingdom of the dead, a wondering at where, "Into what ingrown nation has she gone / Among a people silent and withdrawn." Entering the still-mournful house after some Independence Day fireworks display, the poet realizes the full extent of his personal alienation: "No one would hear me, even if I spoke."

"Disposal," the next piece, is in many ways redundant. Though it carries forward the action of the cycle—the dead girl's personal effects are finally disposed of—it contributes little new to the appraisal of the girl. Her one party dress unworn, she lived in dresses sewn of canceled patterns and markdowns. The poet's preoccupation with the gaudy casket is again manifest; he compares her daily dress with the way she was laid out in death:

> . . . *Spared of all need, all passion,*
> *Saved from loss, she lies boxed in satins*
>
> *Like a pair of party shoes*
> *That seemed to never find a taker.*

The last two poems shift focus from the dead to the surviving. Out of morbid curiosity the poet makes his journey (another Snodgrassian journey!) home on the first "anniversary" of the girl's death, as we have seen, to find nothing changed. He has survived, the parents have survived, but his mother and father seem more like the living dead. That they do not even acknowledge the world about them is communicated symbolically by the two stone lions which guard their house entrance: ". . . someone has patched / Cement across their eyes." The poem carries other symbolic freight as well, including some cherries from a tree the parents still try to protect from neighborhood boys. Is it too much to suggest that these cherries are symbolic of the virginity they also tried, too successfully, to protect from neighboring males? The cherries which now rot in their lawn are one with the now-rotting virgin in her grave.

The final poem, "To a Child"—already mentioned in conjunction with the "Heart's Needle" cycle—is an inventory of past events, the cyclical nature of life, and its ironies. The child addressed is obviously the daughter of the earlier book, to which this poem might rightly be appended in some future edition. This is a bittersweet catalogue, like the earlier "April Inventory"; the poet concludes there is much for the living to learn from another's death, be it that of a sister or merely that of "the glow of rotten / Wood, the glimmering being that consumes / The flesh of a dead trout." The verse moves forward into a region of parasitic existences which suggest the lives of his parents. He urges his daughter, who has observed both his sister's death and her mother's pregnancy, to attain the possibility and the meaning of love. Without love we die. Yet—the final irony—"With love we kill each other." Love is for the poet the mistress without whom he cannot live, yet with whom he cannot live.

This last is a horrifying group of poems, less sentimental and more sensational than "Heart's Needle," which it echoes in part; compare the conclusion of the latter, "We have to try," with the line from the earlier, "We try to choose our life"; compare, "And you have been dead one year" with "And you are still my daughter." The tone, the rhythm, and the effect are the same. Which is why Snodgrass can never truly disguise these poems, no matter what name he appends to them. In each book he speaks in a voice of suffering and guilt of marginal characters and separations.

4

Anne Sexton: The Blooming Mouth and the Bleeding Rose

Great poetry, it seems, has often been born of misfortune. Sir Philip Sidney would never have written "Astrophel and Stella" had he not lost, at age twenty-six, the girl Penelope whom he expected to marry. Henry Vaughan's "Silex Scintillans" poems were occasioned by the death from war wounds of his younger brother William. Sir Walter Raleigh's fall from the grace of Queen Elizabeth, John Donne's imprisonment and poverty, the death of Christopher Smart's father, Milton's blindness, Housman's academic failures — all were major calamities in the lives of the poets who went on to create masterpieces.

Of the moderns, Robert Lowell seems anguished most by his august ancestry and impotent father; Snodgrass by his enforced separation from his daughter and the death of his sister; Plath by her hatred for her father and perhaps of all men; and Kunitz and Berryman by love / hate relationships with their dead suicidal fathers. But with Anne Sexton the poetry of misfortune reaches some sort of apogee. So many are her afflictions, we recognize in the poet a female Job. One is able to reconstruct a hellishly unhappy life from her nakedly autobiographical poems: Birth into the well-to-do Harvey family in Newton, Massachusetts, in 1928; her mother's materialism and father's alcoholism; apparently an accident at the age of six, in which the young girl nearly lost an arm in a clothes wringer; the arrival to live with the Harveys of a great-aunt, who later suffered deafness and lapsed into madness; summers on Cape Cod; marriage to an unimaginative man; the deaths of two poet friends, John Holmes and Sylvia Plath; the birth of two daughters, Linda and Joy; the death of both parents within three months of one another, in 1959; her confinements in mental institutions; the temporary loss of a daughter; her search for release through religion, drugs, lovers, art. Her books, as she herself says, "read like a fever chart for a bad case of melancholy." [1]

These events, whether wholly autobiographical or only partly, all occur and recur in her work—they are the straws with which she weaves her therapeutic baskets, the terrible threads of her private mythology. Totally frank about each event, Mrs. Sexton renders it as if in a diary. One does not sit down with a volume of her poems to be entertained (though her work is laced with a wicked wit, especially the volume in which she goes most outside herself, *Transformations*). Indeed, her poetry has repelled a good many. Reviewing her early poems, James Dickey conceded their "sickeningly frightening appropriateness to our time," but felt it all had "so obviously come out of deep, painful sections of the author's life that one's literary opinions scarcely seem to matter; one feels tempted to drop them furtively into the nearest ash can, rather than be caught with them in the presence of so much naked suffering." [2] Another Dickey, this one William, found her fourth book equally repellent. That critic found himself out of sympathy with the world of her imagination: "For while Sexton's world is full of objects, they have no independent validity; they exist as projections of her own indulgent emotional states." [3]

I would suggest both critics have suffered an overreaction to Anne Sexton, as have others too embarrassed to criticize the work because it seemed so much a piece of the life that a criticism of one was a criticism of the other. Despite the autobiographical events cited above, which appear to adhere to the truth, one must be very careful in reading Anne Sexton to separate the truth from the fiction. For instance, she has no brother. Yet two of her fine poems, "For Johnny Pole on the Forgotten Beach" (from *To Bedlam and Part Way Back*) and "The Papa and Mama Dance" (from *Love Poems*) are addressed to a brother in uniform. This has led astray a number of critics, including Ralph J. Mills, Jr., who calls the Johnny Pole poem "The elegy for her brother" and includes it in his list of her "family poems." [4] Others have taken the "Unknown Girl in the Maternity Ward," from her first book, to be Mrs. Sexton herself, thereby endowing her with an illegitimate child she later gave away. (A symbolic act, by her own admission, for the temporary loss of her daughter due to her own madness. See the *Paris Review* interview of 1971.) [5] Others have assumed the act in "The Abortion" to be factual as well. What is essential to recognize is that, while more acutely autobiographical than most, including Lowell, Mrs. Sexton's work is also populated by a gallery of "real" yet totally fictitious figures, such as the old man, the seamstress, and the young girl in "Doors, Doors, Doors" (from *All My Pretty Ones*); and the one-eyed man and the mother of two sons (in *Live or Die*). Indeed as she publishes more books, Mrs. Sexton seems to have exhausted the autobiographical and to be turning increasingly to the fictional. Her fifth book, *Transformations* (1971), is a transmogrification of seventeen of Grimm's fairy tales, with popular mythology displacing the personal. It should also not surprise us to find, in 1972, the poet publishing a work of fiction. (See the short story, "The Letting Down of the Hair," in the *Atlantic* [229, No. 3].)

All these imaginary characters reveal Anne Sexton is very deft at assuming *personae*. Yet her best and most characteristic work invariably is her most autobiographical. This is the form of poetic expression to which she is firmly committed. As she has said in an early interview, "It's very embarrassing for someone to expose their body to you. You don't learn anything from it. But if they expose their soul, you learn something. That's true of great writers: They expose their souls and then suddenly I am moved and I understand my life better." [6] Elsewhere she has said, "I think if I had written twenty years ago I'd have written this way, whether it were stylish, whether it were a good thing to do or a bad thing to do. I can just do my own thing and that's the way I do it. I have been quite aware of criticism about this, naturally, because I do it; but I can't seem to change. I don't think I'm aiming at anything from an intellectual standpoint. I didn't make up my mind to write personal poems . . . You might call it an accident." [7] Despite the naturalness with which she produces "confessional" poetry, until recently Mrs. Sexton nevertheless resisted identification with the movement or the mode: "For years I railed against being put in this category . . . then about a year ago, I decided I was the *only* confessional poet. Well . . . Allen Ginsberg too. He holds back nothing and I hold back nothing." [8]

I hold back nothing: That could be the motto for all of Anne Sexton's work. Beginning with her first collection, *To Bedlam and Part Way Back* (1960), her work has stunned readers with its realism, its shocking details. That she intends to shock is made manifest by the epigraph which she appends to her second book, *All My Pretty Ones* (and part of which I already quote in the first chapter):

> The books we need are the kind that act upon us like a misfortune, that make us suffer like the death of someone we love more than ourselves, that make us feel as though we were on the verge of suicide, or lost in a forest remote from all human habitation—a book should serve as the ax for the frozen sea within us.

Written after her mother's death, but before her father's, the individual poems of this volume collectively chart the poet's drift toward madness and back to partial recovery, as the title graphically communicates. Mrs. Sexton is even more forthright about her mental illness and frequent institutionalizations than was Lowell, the first to make the subject permissible in such works as "Waking in the Blue," "Home After Three Months Away," and "Skunk Hour." (Berryman's madhouse sequence in part 3 of *Love & Fame* was not published until 1970.)

The first poem in Sexton's first book places the reader directly in bedlam without explanation, history, or apology. The first lines, "You, Doctor Martin, walk / from breakfast to madness" make use of apostrophe and halting enjambment for startling effect. The realities of the madhouse inform all the imagery in this collection, even that of nature: "It was the strangled cold of November; / even the stars were strapped in the sky / and that moon too bright / forking through the bars." It is doubtful that any poet never institutionalized would employ straitjacket imagery in relation to the stars.

Therapy and elegy are the book's two concerns. Those mourned are the poet's mother, grandfather, great-aunt, and, most important, the poet's lost self which she hopes to regain. In the poem about the great-aunt, "Some Foreign Letters," the young poet is surprised to discover, through reading the dead woman's correspondence, that she had once been young, had once led a life of her own. The poet can remember only the deaf and dying crone. From this particularization the poet generalizes about the nature of life, and concludes that the promise of youth is a false one. Wars come, lovers die, flesh weakens, and ultimately "life is a trick, life is a kitten in a sack." A most unsettling metaphor, that.

More poems of disillusionment follow. "The Farmer's Wife" is a *persona* through whose eyes one sees a marriage in which love has become routine, an unfulfilling pantomime. The protagonist wants the ordinariness of her life transformed, wishes her husband somehow transformed into someone more romantic—a cripple, a poet, perhaps even a dead lover. Another poem of contrasts, "Funnel," compares the largesse and love of life possessed by her grandfather with her current niggardly existence. The title predicts the shape of the poem's subject, the shape of more flowing into less, of dwindling. In "For Johnny Pole on the Forgotten Beach," the fantasy and innocence of children playing with toy boats is contrasted with the horror of war and a soldier's death on a beach front before a junkyard of landing craft.

These explorations of disillusionment are followed by poems in which the human need for rite, the attempt to right one's life, is expressed—such as "The Lost Ingredient." "Ringing the Bells" is about a more literal ritual, the games used in therapy, written as a nursery rhyme to enforce the realization of the regressive or restorative infantilism to which the self has been forced. (The childish language is buttressed by images of patients in diapers.) This is one of Mrs. Sexton's greatest gifts—her ability not only visually to present the precise mental state she intends, but to render the lines in the correspondingly correct musical mood as well.

Two of the book's most important poems are "For John, Who Begs Me Not to Enquire Further" and "The Double Image." The first is Mrs. Sexton's defense of her poetry, addressed to her former teacher John Holmes. Her probing of her mind's recesses, she explains, was done "Not that it was beautiful, / but that, in the end, there was / a certain sense of order there." The poem is related to "The Lost Ingredient" in its theme of the search for order. Introspection, however painful, is advantageous, for out of examination comes order and out of order, release. "The Double Image" repeats and embellishes upon the topic of the poet's guilt for neglecting her mother in her sickness, which was the theme of the shorter "The Waiting Head." Guilt, alienation, the necessity for loving oneself before one can love others, and the gulf between generations are the poem's concerns. Its central image is the pair of portraits of her mother and herself which capture the outward resemblance of the two, but which are symbolically hung on opposite walls. The subject of guilt is explored to include not only her own toward her mother, but also the effects of Sexton's own suicide attempts on her daughter. The double image becomes triple, the guilt multiplied in a hall of mirrors.

All My Pretty Ones (1962) followed the first book by just two years. It is a continuation of the themes of death and ruin, guilt and mortality. It could be called the second volume of Mrs. Sexton's autobiography in verse. In the first book she re-created the experience of madness; the second book explores its causes. At the time of its writing, her father also had died, an event which left the poet tired of being brave. The volume reveals she had reached a reconciliation of sorts with her father just before his death. Many poems (like "Young") contrast the innocence of her girlhood with her present world-weariness.

The imagery in this second collection derives less from institutionalization than from domesticity, a transition perhaps paralleling the poet's own removal from clinic to home. The images are in no way less sharp, however. In "The Starry Night" we see "one black-haired tree slips / up like a drowned woman into the hot sky"; in "Lament," a "Canada goose rides up, / spread out like a gray suede shirt"; in "Ghosts," women have "breasts as limp as killed fish"; and in "Woman with Girdle," the subject is seen as having "thighs, thick as young pigs." But when Mrs. Sexton does get clinical, she does so with a vengeance: "The Operation" is a poem full of psychologically and clinically precise observations, and revolves about the irony that she must have removed from her body the same type of malignancy which killed her mother. The poem concludes with the figure of Humpty-Dumpty, symbol of all which is precarious in life, the difficult balance we all must maintain.

There is a glimmering of optimism in this book, "A Curse Against Elegies," which posits the thesis that one must live for the living and not the dead. But what is really new in this second collection, besides the additional grief for and details of her father's dying, are the poetic evidences of Mrs. Sexton's search for faith. "From the Garden" expresses the need for the spiritual in the midst of the secular. In all probability the two deaths, and the attendant guilt which ensued, caused the poet to ruminate on the nature of life and of death and the existence of the soul as never before. In other poems, such as "With Mercy for the Greedy," "For God While Sleeping," and "In the Deep Museum," we experience with her a pull toward death which seems at times stronger than the will for redemption. The final poem of her first book, "The Division of Parts," had pointed the way, inviting comparison as it did between the sorting of her mother's earthly effects on Good Friday and the division of the crucified Christ's possessions. As Ralph J. Mills, Jr., observed,

> Since she is a poet without mystical inclinations, but rather is earthbound, committed to a vision that shocks

by its unvarnished realism, it is hardly surprising that she should approach religious belief through the person of Christ, who is, for her, the man claiming to be God and subjecting Himself to the extremes of bodily and spiritual torture as proof of His appointed task. He is the one who reminds her again of the destiny to which all flesh is ordered—death.[9]

A number of years after Mills's statement, Mrs. Sexton confirmed its contention in print, agreeing with a statement that the suffering in her confessional poetry should be associated with the kind of sufferers she examines in her religious poetry, and concluding: "That ragged Christ, that sufferer, performed the great act of confession, and I mean with his body. And I try to do that with words." [10]

While these "religious" poems are terrible in their detail, with Christ "hung up like a pig on exhibit," elsewhere the volume manages to reveal another neglected aspect of Mrs. Sexton's talent, a rare whimsy which rescues certain poems from bathos. At the conclusion of "Letter Written on a Ferry While Crossing Long Island Sound," a poem about the aftermath of a breakup with a lover, the poet is amazed to see the world going on as before. In need of some sign of the extraordinary, she playfully imagines the four shipboard nuns in a state of miraculous levitation, an imaginative act which predated the television series "The Flying Nun."

The volume concludes with an inconclusive "Letter Written During a January Northeaster," a six-part refusal to mourn "Those dear loudmouths, gone for over a year." Mrs. Sexton sees the dead as lost baggage—gone, beyond recovery, yet stuffed with aspects of the self. As in "In the Deep Museum," the poem expresses "both nostalgia for and denial of absolute love." [11]

Live or Die (1966), which won the Pulitzer Prize, continues the poet's search for reconciliations, her obsession with the limits of the body and its failures to be equal to the demands of the spirit. It marks a turning point in her work, a passage from pessimism to optimism. Chronologically arranged, the poems chart her inner and outer lives between January 1962 and February 1966. The book commences with the first direct account of her father's death, though its event had been accounted for earlier. The need for renewal and therapy is set forth in the second poem, "The Sun," symbol of all that is restorative in life. That poem prefigures a third, "Flee on Your Donkey," in which she proclaims, "Dreams came into the ring / like third string fighters, / each one a bad bet / who might win / because there was no other." Mrs. Sexton would agree with Nathanael West, who wrote in *The Day of the Locust*, "Any dream was better than no dream, and beggars couldn't be choosers."

During the time covered by the diarylike book, death ("that old butcher") hacks away at her dear ones again, this time taking her teacher John Holmes and her friend Sylvia Plath. During this stage of her life even nature seems malevolent: the rain "drops down like worms." Weary of the flesh again, she thirsts for the water of the spirit. Yet formal religion continues to fail her, and in its collapse she grows scornful ("Those are the people that sing / when they aren't quite / sure") and she turns from the church to the comforts of drug addiction and attempted suicide.

The book is riddled with guilt. There are more poems on guilt feelings toward her mother ("I did not know that my life, in the end, / would run over my mother's like a truck") and toward her daughter, who as a baby she may or may not have abandoned in a ditch during one of her illnesses. I suspect this is yet another of Mrs. Sexton's "disguised poems," with the fictional act of ditching the baby supplanting the actual act of leaving her to go to the mental hospital.

"Self in 1958" is a strong portrayal of deadened sensibilities. Mrs. Sexton here employs the figure of a plastic doll as symbol of the self (as did Plath in "The Applicant" from *Ariel*). Yet despite the stoicism which develops into negativism, *Live or Die* ends on the strongest note of affirmation found in all three books Mrs. Sexton had published up to that time. After the apparent exploration of pills and suicide, the poet can find in life values worth living for. Between the two alternatives posited in the title, she chooses life. The final poem, "Live," shows life opening up for her. Against seemingly overwhelming odds, Anne Sexton, like Faulkner's Dilsey, will not only endure, she will prevail. Unlike Sylvia Plath, who wrote her ultimate confessional poem in the act of killing herself, Mrs. Sexton prefers life.

Just where all this affirmation took Mrs. Sexton, if we are to trust the tales told in her fourth collection, *Love Poems* (1969), is to an unhappy extramarital affair. Anticlimax, oh yes. And not much more therapeutic than drug addiction or attempted suicide, one might say. Except that the poems are considerably less bitter than her early work. In seeking a lover at least one is serving the self. The old brooding over the death of parents has been, if not forgotten, at least put on the back burner and turned down to Low. As the new collection indicates, she has achieved more than the realization of some additional confessional poems. She has grown. She has abandoned her previous preoccupations with ancestry, madness, and partial recovery. Most of these latest pieces are ironic love poems, speaking more of alienation than of conciliation, more of loneliness than togetherness. Yet her rather loveless, unlovely love poems are apropos of our time. Based upon the physical rather than the metaphysical, their depiction of unsatisfactory relationships between lovers reflects the failure to communicate in the modern world. And they do reflect a new attitude, "an awareness of the possibly good as well as the possibly rotten," she herself has commented; "inherent in the process is a rebirth of a sense of self, each time stripping away a dead self." [12]

Mrs. Sexton's fourth book documents the pain as well as the absence of love. There is as much redness from blood as from roses and as many real broken bones as metaphorically broken hearts. Further, it employs the most homely or blatantly commercial images to communicate transcendental truths. Mrs. Sexton has become by this time a master at finding the telling image in domestic detail: as when "the other woman" perceives her lover's wife to be "real as a cast-iron pot"; and as when another comments to her lover, "We are a pair of scissors / Who come together to cut," a metaphysical conceit embodying the shape and the psychological effect of the physical contact. It is a figure worthy of comparison with Donne's celebrated compass conceit in "A Valediction Forbidding Mourning." The difference between Donne's stiff-twinned compasses, symbolizing tender married love, and Sexton's mutilating scissors-figure for her adulterer reveals how basically images of juncture have come to be conceived as destructive rather than constructive in the anxious modern mind with pathological tendencies.

Individual pieces in *Love Poems* examine love in its many guises: sensual, filial, adulterous, self-—and the impossibility of reciprocal love (there are numerous poems on the struggle against loneliness). Others, some of the best in the collection, fall altogether outside the range of love. These include two powerful war (more correctly, antiwar) poems, "December 9th" and "The Papa and Mama Dance." Another group recounts the various states of womanhood: "In Celebration of My Uterus"; "The Nude Swim"; "Song for a Red Night Gown"; "Loving the Killer"; and "December 18th." Significantly, Mrs. Sexton's poems on loneliness are among her most fully realized. Especially fine is the volume's initial poem, "The Touch," in which a severed hand serves as synecdoche for the isloated self. It is followed by "The Kiss," in which a boat is metaphor for the self / female body, "quite wooden / and with no business, no salt water under it / And in need of some paint." The boat / body / self is related to the severed hand; both embody unfeeling and neglect. "The Ballad of the Lonely Masturbator" relates one woman's solitary solution to such intense frustration and loneliness. Its rather startling subject matter (startling even in the post-Portnoy era, and only alluded to guardedly by Roethke in his sequence poems, more openly by Allen Ginsberg and Frederick Seidel) is hammered into the Procrustean bed of the ancient ballad form with the recurring refrain, "At night, alone, I marry the bed."

This is a pathetic vision. So is that conveyed in "December 12th," one of the volume's most difficult poems. Here the lonely poet seeks solace in volunteer hospital work. The unnatural states of body and mind which she sees there parallel the unnatural state in which she finds herself—that of sharing her lover with his wife. The poet-narrator is like the abnormal children in the ward to whom permanent possessions are forbidden. The only thing she is allowed to bring for the children's amusement is—herself; just as the only thing she can share with her lover is her body. The poet's need for love is shown ultimately to be as intense as the need of the hospitalized children whom she visits.

Not all the "loneliness" poems are pathetic, however. "The Nude Swim," yet another of spiritual isolation, culminates in the narrator's triumphant floating on the water, mistress of her element. Another affirmative poem, "It Is a Spring Afternoon," concludes that, as death is the way of the natural world, so time and nature are restorative: "Everything is altogether possible / And the blind men can also see." The collection's second recurring theme, adulterous love, is treated in "You All Know the Story of the Other Woman," a fine firm poem which elaborates upon the irregularity of any affair with a married man: "When it is over he places her, / like a phone, back on the hook." The same subject is treated in "For My Lover, Returning to His Wife," with the permanence of the wife's position (the already-quoted "as real as a cast-iron pot" image) contrasted with the impermanence of the other woman's ("As for me, I am water-color. / I wash off"). A third poem in this category, "December 16th," also deserves attention for its diction, which emphasizes the story-book quality of the lovers' lives.

Among Mrs. Sexton's celebrations of sensual love—the third classification—are the poems "Us," "Now," "Barefoot," and "Song for a Lady." "Us" concludes with an almost Biblical sexual metaphor: "And we rose up like wheat, / acre after acre of gold, / And we harvested, we harvested." A *carpe diem* poem, "Now" carries such sexually symbolic freight as bullets and blood, a hammer and balloons. "Barefoot" is an ambitious poem in which the predatory nature of lovers is compared to the predatory nature of wildlife. The poem displays another of Mrs. Sexton's borrowings from nursery literature: "All spirited and wild, this

little / piggy went to market and this little piggy / stayed."
The tenderest of the love lyrics, and the poem containing
the most striking sexual metaphor, is "Song for a Lady,"
one of Mrs. Sexton's few poems "sung" from a male point
of view. This male voice is sentimental, in contrast to the
strident female voice of "Mr. Mine." The poem climaxes in
a miraculous image for male virility: "Oh my Swan, my
drudge, my dear wooly rose, / even a notary would notarize
our bed / As you knead me and I rise like bread."

A fourth group defines the impossibility of fully reciprocal
love. Mrs. Sexton registers this conviction in "The Interrogation of the Man of Many Hearts," declaiming: "Every
bed has been condemned, not by morality, or law, but by
time." As in "The Breast" (which employs the nipple as
eye and *I*, with a woman's physical inadequacy mirroring
her emotional instability), she sees the narrator/beloved
not only as a surrogate wife, but as a daughter- and mother-
figure as well. "Mr. Mine" asserts that one reason lasting
love is impossible is the egotisim implicit in every sexual
act. The lover's selfish conquest of the beloved's body recalls the building of a city, the woman's flesh yet another
material thing to be possessed. And the female is shown to
be as much the predator as the male in "December 18th,"
where the vagina is called "my tiny mail." (See also "Loving
the Killer" for a variation on this theme.) That both parties
are responsible for the failure of love is affirmed in "December 10th," the poem yielding the scissors image cited earlier.
To effect a cut, blades must oppose one another.

The physical and emotional aftermaths of an affair are
conveyed in "The Break" where the literal fracture of bones
parallels the metaphorical fracture of the heart. The break
of the title refers, on a third level, to the severed relationship. The literal fall down the stairs, a reversal of the
conventional Freudian metaphor for the sexual act, is rendered with the homely description of her fractures: "I was
like a box of dog bones." But the poet immediately gives
us a mythic account as well: "What a feat sailing queerly
like Icarus / until the tempest undid me and I broke." (One
could quibble that it was *hubris* and the sun that undid

Icarus, not a tempest, but one won't. Mrs. Sexton has earned her poetic license.) Once again she repeats the rose / blood duality found throughout the volume: "My one dozen roses are dead. / They have ceased to menstruate. They hang / there like little dried-up blood clots." (Mrs. Sexton's imagery may have been influenced by Theodore Roethke's, who wrote in "The Lost Son" of "The big roses, the bloody clinkers." Much later, in "Poppies in July," Sylvia Plath described her flowers as resembling "A mouth just bloodied.")

"Pro Femina" poems could be seen as constituting a fifth group. The title of "In Celebration of My Uterus" tells all: the poet sings of the universality of womanhood and sexuality. "Song for a Red Night Gown" details the wildness inherent in all women, the sanguine color of the gown symbolizing their blood allegiance to barbarity. The poem's world in which a rose bleeds and a mouth blooms relates directly to and repeats that of "The Kiss" and "The Break." One of the most ambitious poems in the volume, "Loving the Killer," explores domestic love in the midst of wilderness and danger. A corollary theme of the eighty-four-line poem, the persistence of the past, relates it also in this respect to the concerns of her first three books. Yet the poem's two themes are organically entwined: though the lovers have escaped their native New England for Africa, the past accompanies them. The big game hunt becomes the larger hunt for selfhood; and the bones and skins of beasts that accompany them back to the States are symbols of what Whitehead has called "the withness of the flesh" (a concept which receives consummate poetic treatment in Delmore Schwartz's "The Heavy Bear"). The final stanza reveals the woman as the ultimate predatory beast, whereas her lover, the hunter, is mere skin and bones like the wildlife he has stalked.

The disparity between appearance and reality is felt or seen in the volume's many uniforms, costumes, and masks. "You All Know the Story of the Other Woman" vividly contrasts the comforting illusions of night with the harsher realities of day. "Again and Again and Again" features once more the image of the blood clot, only this time analogous to the manner in which the poet wears her *persona*: "It is a mask I try on. / I migrate toward it and its frog / sits on my lips and defecates." The poet's mask is akin to the death mask worn by the animals in "It Is a Spring Afternoon." And in "December 14th" we find a circus used as an extended metaphor for the reality behind the illusions of the love affair.

Though only two in number, war poems constitute a final grouping. "December 9th" is a strong, ironic statement on the Vietnam War. The irony is implicit in the poem's central action, the unloading of bodies from a Starlifter jet. In death the men are accorded a dignity and consideration denied them in life. Unfortunately, the poem echoes two other well-known ones. "This is the stand / that the world took" sounds uncomfortably like the closing lines of Eliot's "The Hollow Men." Similarly, the hero's being addressed as "carrying / your heart like a football / to the goal" recalls Mrs. Sexton's own, "The Operation" from *All My Pretty Ones*, with its notorious line, "My stomach laced up like a football for the game" (which prompted one critic to ask if footballs were laced up just prior to game time). Nevertheless, "December 9th" is an important new poem and a strong one, as is "The Papa and Mama Dance," in which a brother in uniform prompt his sister to recall their childhood masquerades, when they played "dress-up" in their father's academic robes as black-clad bride and groom. The color now is seen as prefiguring their ultimate doom. The poem is a companion piece to that other, and even more impressive, Sexton poem about the reminiscences of a woman with a brother in uniform, "For Johnny Pole on the Forgotten Beach."

In "The Papa and Mama Dance," the apostrophe to the brother, Mr. Gunman, is but one of many—far too many!— that flood the book's pages and threaten to inundate even the best poems: my Nazi, my louse, my swan, my drudge, my absentee, my dear wooly rose, Mr. Mine, Mr. Bind. A device can be overworked. The same is true of Mrs. Sexton's favorite images, the clot and the roses and the balloons resting on the ceiling. (See "For My Lover Returning to His Wife," "Now," and "December 12th" for more balloonabilia, as well as Sylvia Plath's poem in *Ariel*, "Balloons.") Mrs. Sexton's persistent use of a very small private mythology reminds one of Edith Sitwell's penchant for honey and gold, lions and apes, all ubiquitous in her *Collected Poems*. (The word *gold* appears 280 times, the word *golden* 94!)

Love Poems concludes with a sequence of a dozen and a half short poems under the collective title, "Eighteen Days Without You." I have treated the component pieces as separate poems, because that is how they are best perceived. All of the above mentioned concerns are included in the group, but—except for those designated "December 9th," "December 12th," and "December 16th"—the sections are not as strong as the individual poems in the volume. As a whole they add up to considerably less than Snodgrass's "Heart's Needle" sequence, to which the group inevitably invites comparison, since both are confessional cycles on the enforced absence of a loved one. What is unquestionably Sexton's is the superimposition of surreal dream imagery upon the no less horrifying realities of modern life. She writes, for example, of falling in love the day John F. Kennedy was shot, and accuses her lover of having dragged her off by a Nazi hook. The times themselves are justification for such savage imagery, if justification is necessary. The conventional love poem seems anachronistic.

There is less regression in *Love Poems* than in the previous three collections. The book's general effect is one of stoicism and self-reliance rather than of self-pity and dependence. There are of course deliberate regressions in language for special effect, much as Roethke uses them throughout his sequence poems. Mrs. Sexton has used this device effectively in the past, notably in "Ringing the Bells" from *To Bedlam and Part Way Back*: "And this is the way they ring / the bells in Bedlam / and this is the bell-lady." She repeats the technique several times in *Love Poems*, however, to the point that it seems now a gimmick rather than a technique, a trick rather than an organic part of the poem. In "That Day," a poem written in schoolgirl nursery rhyme rhetoric ("This is the desk I sit at / And this is the desk where I love you too much"), we become conscious not only of the Mother Goosery of "This Is the House That Jack Built," but also of the other Sexton poems in which she has cribbed from the nursery. Lowell has done much the same. In "Waking in the Blue" he parrots, "This is the way day breaks in Bowditch Hall at McLean's." One of Sylvia Plath's asylum poems is also written in nursery rhyme: "This is the city where men are mended," etc. And one of Donald Justice's poems, "Counting the Mad," begins, "This one was put in a jacket, / This one was sent home." To be sure, there is something undeniably infantile about institutionalization. Yet Sexton and Lowell and Plath and Justice must be aware that it was Elizabeth Bishop who first made this particular voice her own, many years before (1950), in "Visits to St. Elizabeth's": "This is a wristwatch / telling the time / of the talkative man / that lies in the House of Bedlam," etc.

Despite these faults, the achievement of *Love Poems* is considerable. If one counts the parts of "Eighteen Days Without You" as separate poems, as they were originally conceived, the volume contains forty-two new poems written between 1966 and 1969, making Anne Sexton one of our most productive artists. Of that number, more than a quarter deserve to be listed with the indispensable Sexton. And this time she has forsaken the indignities of the body for the more uniquely human dignities of the heart.

Earlier I observed that Mrs. Sexton's body of work evinces a definite progress in personalization. This progress made a giant leap when, in 1971, appeared *Transformations*, a rich collection of seventeen long poems. Each begins with a contemporary observation or application of the "moral" of some fairy tale, then segues into a contemporary recasting of the fairy tale itself. These "transformations" of Grimm's tales into grim parables for our time are deftly done, and in them Mrs. Sexton continues her practice of transforming the dross of commonplace experience into pure poetic gold — and vice versa, for shocking effect. The ancient is remythologized into the modern: Snow White's cheeks are as "fragile as cigarette paper"; the wicked queen's bodice is laced "tight as an Ace bandage"; the dwarf Rumpelstiltskin's body "wasn't Sanforized." And so it goes.

Mrs. Sexton retells the mythological stories, those master keys to the human psyche, in images and metaphors of Hitler and Eichler, Linus and Orphan Annie, Isadora Duncan and Joe DiMaggio, speed and electroshock, Thorazine and Thalidomide. By transforming the stories into the language and symbols of our own time, she has managed to offer us understandable images for the world around us. The tales focus on the psychological crises of living, from childhood dependence through adolescent trauma, adult frustrations through the deathbed. The two most successful are her versions of "Cinderella" and "Sleeping Beauty." The former she takes to be a prototype of the old rags-to-riches theme ("From diapers to Dior. / That story.") Cinderella is said to have slept on the sooty hearth each night and "walked around looking like Al Jolson"—a comparison indicative of the level of invention and humor in the book. At the end, when Cinderella marries the handsome prince to live happily ever after, Mrs. Sexton pulls a double whammy and reveals that that ending, in itself, is another fairy tale within a fairy tale, totally unreal and unlikely. How could anyone live

> *like two dolls in a museum case*
> *never bothered by diapers or dust,*
> *never arguing over the timing of an egg,*
> *never telling the same story twice,*
> *never getting a middle-aged spread,*
> *their darling smiles pasted on for eternity.*
> *Regular Bobbsey Twins.*
> *That story.*[13]

The "Briar Rose (Sleeping Beauty)" tale is not so rich in imagery, but is fraught with frightening implications evoked by examining, as no poet has done before, what happens to a girl's psyche after she has been disturbed from the sleep of death, her renewed life becoming a life after death and bringing with it fear-induced insomnia. (This sleeping beauty also has an Electra complex, but in the words of Mrs. Sexton, that's another story. The reader is referred to my chapter on Sylvia Plath.)

While technically not "confessional" poetry, these verses of *Transformations* do at times strip the poet bare, as when she uses the wolf's deceptions in "Red Riding Hood" as occasion to reveal that she, too, practices such masquerades:

> *Quite collected at cocktail parties,*
> *meanwhile in my head*
> *I'm undergoing open-heart surgery.*

In her fifth book then, as in her first, Anne Sexton is domesticating our terrors. With outstanding artistic proficiency, she renders the particular pain of her life into universal truths.[14]

5

John Berryman's Literary Offenses

"These Songs are not meant to be understood, you under-stand. / They are only meant to terrify & comfort," John Berryman wrote in his 366th Dream Song. And understood many have not been. Packed with private jokes, topical and literary allusions (Berryman's reading and personal library are legendary), they boggle many minds. When the first 77 *Dream Songs* (1964) were published, Robert Lowell admitted, "At first the brain aches and freezes at so much darkness, disorder and oddness. After a while, the repeated situations and their racy jabber become more and more enjoyable, although even now I wouldn't trust myself to paraphrase accurately at least half the sections."[1] The situation was considerably beclouded when, four years later, Berryman dumped on the world a truckful of 308 additional Dream Songs, under the title *His Toy, His Dream, His Rest*.

This latter title could apply to all the Dream Songs. At once Berryman's plaything, hope for immortality, and major achievement, after which he could repose, the cycle consists of 385 impossible dialogues by Berryman with his possible selves. Daydreaming and nightmaring on the printed page, Berryman broke from his earlier, academic, Audenesque verse into confessions of over-drinking, over-smoking, over-sexing, pill-popping, whathaveyou. That these poems are confessions is undeniable—though Berryman claimed they are about a character named Henry. Let us simply say that Henry has a daughter, as did Berryman; when Henry goes to Ireland, Berryman was on the ship as well.

Of the two volumes, the second and fatter is the superior. For this reader, 77 *Dream Songs*, with its twisted syntax, Negro minstrel-show dialogue from the mouth of the narrator's unnamed friend (who addresses the narrator as "Mr. Bones"), and the sheer sloppiness of its several sequences, has not worn well. As one critic noted, "The dreams are not real dreams but a waking hallucination in which anything that might have happened to the author can be used at random. Anything he has seen, overheard, or imagined can go in." [2] While continuing in the same vein, *His Toy, His Dream, His Rest* is more coherent, and the minstrel friend is kept in the wings for most of the performance. Moreover, many of the second set of Dream Songs give off a great shimmer of beauty.

The difference is the difference in the poet at the time of composition. 77 *Dream Songs* seems the work of some randy contender, youthful despite his years. *His Toy, His Dream, His Rest* is mellow, sad, and at times maudlin. Death in the first book is discussed in detail only in several poems centering on Robert Frost—whom Berryman acknowledges was no friend and, by his count, slandered him at least twice—and in one brief stanza on his father's suicide. The second collection, on the other hand, is filled with accounts of friends' deaths and suicides, events which took their toll on Berryman's psyche: Randall Jarrell, Sylvia Plath, R. P. Blackmur, Yvor Winters, William Carlos Williams, and above all, Delmore Schwartz, to whose memory Berryman dedicated the book and penned Dream Songs 146–157 and also number 344. These personal losses were experienced during a time of great public loss as well: John Kennedy, Robert Kennedy, Martin Luther King, Ernest Hemingway, William Faulkner. Yet none of these personal or public deaths figure so importantly in the volume as the suicide of Berryman's father which is, in one sense, the sole subject of the latter collection.

What these losses did to Berryman the man can be deduced from the great number of poems on death or contemplated suicide. A. Alvarez was wrong when he wrote, in *Beyond All This Fiddle*, that Henry's unnamed friend is "Mr. Bones," and not the poet. Nevertheless, that critic's

suggestion that the nickname stands for Death is an intriguing and plausible one, raising the possibility that from
Dream Song 1 to the very end, Death stalks the poet. Indeed the first fourteen Dream Songs of the second volume
are designated as "op. post.," as if written after the fact of
the poet's death. Only one Dream Song in all, number 259,
seems directly counteractive and assertive of joy in life:
"My desire for death was strong / but never strong enough.
I thought: This is my chance, / I can bear it." [3] That the
desire for the grave became stronger and overcame the desire
to accept the chance and bear up to life, was tragically
made public on January 7, 1972, when spectators saw Berryman jump from a bridge onto the ice of the Mississippi
River.

Berryman was, in this final act, following the example of
his suicidal father, whom he claimed alternately to hate and
to love, and whom he could never forget. The elder Berryman's ghost popped up on the next-to-last page of 77 *Dream
Songs* ("in a modesty of death I join my father / who dared
so long agone leave me"),[4] and it hovers as this unholy
ghost above all of *His Toy, His Dream, His Rest,* filling the
pages with dread. It is in this sense that, though both collections are confessional, the second is far more personal,
bearing greater witness to Berryman's attempt to confront
his past. These are poems not unlike Stanley Kunitz's
father-son poems of *The Testing-Tree.*

In Dream Song 143, "the like of which may bring your
heart to break," Berryman first relates how, when the poet
was a little boy, his father began taking a pistol everywhere.
The man also threatened to swim out too far into the gulf
and take the young boy or his brother with him. Instead
of death by water and with a son, the father settled for
lead and solitude (Dream Song 145):

> he only, very early in the morning,
> rose with his gun and went outdoors by my window
> and did what was needed.

The event was, from that moment, the center of the poet's
life. Ever after he spent his days attempting to read his

dead father's wretched mind, "so strong & so undone." Yet more than a quest for an understanding of his father's motives, the poet's search in the ensuing decades was for the strength to forgive his father for leaving him to live on alone. In one late poem Berryman confesses, "Father being the loneliest word in the one language / and a word only, a fraction of sun & guns . . ." (Dream Song 241). Much later, hearing of Hemingway's suicide in the sixties, Berryman wrote (Dream Song 235):

> *Mercy! my father; do not pull the trigger*
> *or all my life I'll suffer from your anger*
> *killing what you began.*

Near the end of the sequence, the reader encounters Berryman making another of the repeated pilgrimages to his father's grave in Oklahoma. The occasion gives rise to one of Berryman's bitterest songs (Dream Song 384):

> *I spit upon this dreadful banker's grave*
> *who shot his heart out in a Florida dawn*
> *O ho alas alas*
> *When will indifference come, I moan & rave*
> *I'd like to scrabble till I got right down*
> *away down under the grass*
>
> *and ax the casket open ha to see*
> *just how he's taking it, which he sought so hard*
> *we'll tear apart*
> *the mouldering grave clothes ha & then Henry*
> *will heft the ax once more, his final card,*
> *and fell it on the start.*

The "indifference" to his father's death which he sought so long to attain was obviously never achieved; these lines are more terrible, in their way, than Sylvia Plath's poetic act of driving a stake through the heart of her father's corpse. As Helen Vendler notes,[5] by murdering his suicide-father, Berryman fulfills the guilt expressed in that most memorable of the *77 Dream Songs,* "There sat down once, a thing on Henry's heart . . ." (Dream Song 29). By violating the father's grave, the poet symbolically enacts the desire of his subconscious. (It is fascinating to note that in Berryman's one book of literary criticism, a psychoanalytic study of Stephen Crane, his analysis traces what he calls "oedipal elements" in Crane's "rivalry against the father, the wish to *be* the father," perhaps an instance of criticism's telling us more about the critic than the subject.) [6]

Berryman was a long time coming to a method which would allow him to expiate his guilt, to confront his demons if not exorcize them. His earliest verse was, as I said, elegant, his mentors Auden, Housman, Hopkins, and Yeats. Only when he wrote *Homage to Mistress Bradstreet* (1956), a long, intricate and anguished poem, did he break with literary tradition and find his own quirky style. Berryman's voice spoke for and through the mask of Anne Bradstreet; her impulses were not unlike Henry's of *The Dream Songs*. Just as Anne Bradstreet was temperamentally more an Indian than a colonist, Henry House in his blackface is more a Negro than a white—the alienated individual in America. But using Mistress Bradstreet as self-spokesman was only partially satisfactory or satisfying, and it was through Berryman's later development of the *personae* of Berryman / Henry / Mr. Bones that the poet was able to let go.

And let go he did, for 385 Dream Songs' worth. It was Robert Lowell who pointed the finger: "Henry is Berryman seen as himself, as *poète maudit*, child and puppet. He is tossed about with a mixture of tenderness and absurdity, pathos and hilarity that would have been impossible if the author had spoken in the first person." [7] It is this third-person singular device which struck a necessary note of distance in the Dream Songs. Whereas Anne Sexton's best work is her most personal, as we have seen, the reverse is true of Berryman. So long as Berryman does not wallow in the first-person singular, he is capable of striking, if not important, poetry; after the completion of the Dream Songs, unfortunately, he chose to do so. In Dream Song 324 he confesses admiration for William Carlos Williams and for "the mysterious late excellence which is the crown / of our trials & our last bride." Sadly, Berryman himself did not follow the admired pattern, did not marry that particular muse. His last works are his least. In them, something seems to have happened to the poet or the poet's method; the two books which came after *The Dream Songs*—*Love & Fame* and *Delusions, Etc.*—were derived from the same imagination and the same life; but the result was altogether different.

"He was interested in love and money; and if he had found a combination of them in something else, he would have dedicated himself to it instead of poetry," Berryman pronounced of Theodore Roethke in 1970.[8] Yet in the same year, he himself published the most blatantly self-aggrandizing sequence of autobiographical poems, *Love & Fame*. It is a book which sadly reveals Berryman's accusation of Roethke to be a classic case of projection. For Berryman clearly came to equate fame with money. The book also demonstrates that for him love had become equated with lust. It is this self-aggrandizement and lack of compassion which make Berryman's late confessions a series of false notes. Instead of confessing for therapeutic or purgative purposes, he appears to have done so to gratify his formidable ego. (William Wasserstrom posits the theory that the Dream Songs' Henry was the embodiment of Berryman's ego, Mr. Bones the id.) [9] Rather than displaying moral courage, these poems display instead immoral callowness. In place of love and fame, we have lust and notoriety.

These tendencies were present in *The Dream Songs*, of course, but were held in check by Berryman's use of the Henry *persona*. When in *Love & Fame* he abandons altogether the third-person singular fiction, he gifts us only with unprecedented breast-beating. The Dream Songs are motivated by the ego; *Love & Fame* is sheer vanity. Berryman tries to make himself egoistic, but in fact becomes egotistic—which is why his confessions seem false.

At this point let me announce my intention to discuss the 385 Dream Songs no further. The format prescribed for this volume, one of a series, is limited. Besides, the Dream

Songs already have had a disproportionate number of admirers. One critic went so far as to compare them with
those other "good elegies," *Lycidas* and *In Memoriam!* [10]
No, the two books of Dream Songs have admirers enough
without me. As Sainte-Beuve said with true French gal-
lantry (and no small amount of malice) to Louise Colet,
that bad "poetess" who solicited from him an essay on her
work, "Madame, allow me to worship you in silence." It
would be more instructive, I maintain, to examine Berryman's last two books, especially *Love & Fame*, that poetic
sequence published on the heels of *The Dream Songs* and
which critics have dismissed as a trifle. They *are* trifling,
but the poems reveal much of what is wrong with bad
confessional poetry, and can educate us to what makes a
confessional poem go wrong. (For what makes a confessional poem go "right," I refer the reader to the body of
Sexton, Snodgrass, and Lowell's *Life Studies*.) We shall
see that, when Berryman dropped the third-person, that
which had been latently bad in his work became out-
rageously so.

As I have noted, the very title *Love & Fame* sets the key.
(Berryman may have taken his title from the last line of
Keats's sonnet, "When I have fears, that I may cease to
be.") Lowell is concerned in his book with *Life Studies*—
studies of lives. Mrs. Sexton weighs those heavy alternatives,
Live or Die. But Mr. Berryman, well, Mr. Berryman, alas,
was toting up his relative successes in the game of love and
the game of fame. And about love Mr. Berryman seemed to
know sadly little, though of lust he wrote a lot. The poems
literally attest to his status as a "sexual athlete" (his words,
not mine). There are poems on his researches into the size
of women's breasts, on cunnilingus ("I sucked your hairs"),
about his twenty-year-old fantasy to "satisfy at once all
Barnard & Smith / & have enough left over for Miss Gibbs's
girls." The poet-protagonist (and once again the poems
closely parallel Berryman's autobiography) brags in one
poem that he has been "fiddling later with every wife / on
the Eastern seaboard." In another, that he has made out a
list of his sexual conquests: "it came to 79." [11] So much for

love. We would suggest that this catalog of sexual perform-
ances, without passion or personal commitment to other
values than satisfying the itch, is indicative of the poet's
total lack of commitment to other higher values as well.

About fame Mr. Berryman is equally boastful, and the
matter-of-fact attitude toward celebrity found in Dream
Song 133 ("It doesn't matter, truly") has vanished. The
point of one poem seems to be that Elizabeth Bishop, a
writer he thought our best lyricist since Emily Dickinson,
once sent him a fan letter. Another informs the reader that
Alumnus Berryman does not send Columbia University any
money: "They use my name / Now and Then. That's
plenty." A third poem contains an eight-line put-down of a
minor American poet (Robert Creeley) in the form of a
letter written by Berryman from his seat on Parnassus. The
letter would best have remained unpublished.

Being famous, of course, provides opportunities for the
poet to meet others famous. Berryman, I fear, is guilty of
dropping names as readily as he says he drops his trousers,
and always on a first-name basis so that the reader can see
how very well he knows them. He mentions Saul (Bellow),
Mark (Van Doren), Delmore (Schwartz), Allen (Ginsberg), others. This may seem an unfair charge: after all, if
these men were his friends, why shouldn't he mention them?
Nevertheless, such charity does not explain the mentality
which is not only thrilled by, but moved to write a poem
about, the fact that "Anthony Eden passed within ten feet
of me." The truth seems to be, Berryman is guilty of the sin
of *hubris*, a sin which has been the downfall of greater men
than he. Here he brags as much about his friendships as he
does his money. Berryman's *hubris* is not a trait as in the
Aristotelian hero's fall. The reader will neither thrill with
horror nor melt with pity at what takes place. He might be
a little disgusted, though. Berryman might well have
heeded Wallace Stevens's dictum, "Life is not people and
scenes, but thought and feeling." [12]

The *lucre* which dirties the pages of *Love & Fame* reminds us of Robert Graves's aphorism, "If there is no
money in poetry, neither is there poetry in money." Because

Berryman has been fortunate enough to disprove the first half of that statement, he takes the second half to be equally untrue. So he writes about receiving "elephant checques" for his readings and books, and once, in discussing children and high art, feels compelled to add, "Money in the bank is also something."

If the amount of money a poet makes seems a supremely trivial topic for poetry, it is absolutely Olympian when compared to some of Berryman's others. He writes of losing the vice-presidency of his class in school "by five bare bitter votes." One poem is on getting a C in a course at Columbia, which occasion put him "squarely in the middle of Hell." These could be topics for poems, of course: ironic or spritely light verse by John Betjeman or deliberately deprecating and played-down lines by Philip Larkin. But in Berryman's heavy hands they are mawkish at best: Is receiving a C in a course, however much is riding on it, really sufficient impetus to place a soul "squarely in the middle of Hell"? Is the poet guilty of overwriting or, worse, of failing to see through the personal experience to the poetic experience? This can be seen as a major fault of bad confessional poetry, and time and again Berryman seems unwilling to sacrifice the personal meaning to the poetic.

Berryman's questionable topics are at times elevated by superior poetics, as they indeed are in certain of the Dream Songs. But in fact his rhetoric and glib abbreviations and slang here help not at all. We single out two bad puns as examples of Berryman's poetic offenses. The first is perpetuated when the poet engages in intercourse with (we can't say "makes love to") a woman who is menstruating. He chortles, "So there on my floor she did her bloody best." Indeed. The second, within another poem about intercourse, has the poet lament, "O this has been a long long night of wrest." The spirit of Ogden Nash lives!

Moreover, there seem to be no memorable images or metaphors in *Love & Fame*, nothing to compare with, say, Mrs. Sexton's "life is a kitten in a sack." Weighing the six hundred pages of his last four books, Berryman might have done well to heed Ezra Pound's dictum: "It is better to present one image in a lifetime than to produce voluminous works." [13]

All that has gone wrong can be examined in the book's first poem, "Her & It." The "it" ultimately is fame, and how it gets in the way of the poet's recovering his past. But initially "it" is also the vagina of a girl the poet once knew; or, as Berryman indelicately puts it, "a gash." The poet in times past seems to have been in love with a disembodied female organ, if one trusts the poem. In stanza one he conjectures that this "gash" must now have "seven lousy children," though why the children should be lousy is not indicated. This immediately leads to the parenthetical confession "(I've three myself, one being off the record.)" In the fourth line of the book, Berryman already sandbags the reader with an unnecessary confidence, a confession which does nothing to advance the poem and is merely an irrelevant posture of supermasculinity. To confess is not synonymous with to make art. It is selecting from among all that one *might* confess which leads to poetry.

The second stanza is offensive for a different reason: the poet wishes the girl would now write to him: "After all, I get letters from anybody," he boasts. (Later in the book he brags of one from the White House.) The famous poet boasts about his correspondence—the old woman displays her medals. Stanza three continues the *hubris*. The poet is flying East "to sing a poem." Although it is decades since he has seen his "gash," he will look for her when "Admirers . . . surge up afterward."

The fourth stanza contains the offensive description of Berryman's "elephant checques," plus the observation that his Dream Songs are selling well in Tokyo and Paris, and that his publishers are very friendly both in New York and London. Selah.

In the fifth stanza the poet compares his reputation to that of Saul (Bellow, of course, but with Poundian pride unidentified). Berryman further lets the reader know he himself was in *Time* magazine the year before: "Photographs all over!"

The poem concludes with the promising line, "She muttered something in my ear I've forgotten as we danced." Promising, because for the first time in a poem titled "Her & It" we finally have a portrayal of the "her" in a human (as opposed to dehumanized, disembodied, anatomical) way. The poem's missed potentialities are for a moving contrast between human relations when one is an unknown lover and when one is a famous poet. But all the bravura and insecurity of the narrator have stood between him and the unrealized poem.

Further, one cannot examine that final line too long without realizing even the convoluted rhetoric which has become Berryman's signature actually bars direct communication. Clearly the girl muttered something in his ear as they danced, which he has since forgotten. But as the line stands, the girl muttered something in his ear, and he has now forgotten it as he danced. Further, did she really mutter something while *in* his ear, or did she mutter something *into* his ear?

In light of such syntax one should recall Yeats's definition of the poet as one who "is never the bundle of accident and incoherence that sits down to breakfast," but one who "has been reborn as an idea, something intended, complete." [14] Berryman in his last poems seems to have eschewed this process of synthesis completely, coming to the table all disheveled. The publishers' blurb on the dust jacket of *Love & Fame* proclaims, "One of the most astonishing things about this astonishing book is that it follows so closely in time the enormous achievement of the author's *Dream Songs*." But Berryman devoted some eleven years to the writing of those songs, and only one to *Love & Fame*. It shows.

Which is not to say the entire collection is ragged. Part four, subtitled "Eleven Addresses to the Lord," reveals (briefly) a Berryman capable of contemplation, reminding us of the religious poet of Dream Songs 194 and 234. It was a mode he was to continue in the first section of *Delusions, Etc.* as well. In these eleven short lyrics *hubris* is displaced by what would appear to be a genuine humility, and we trust the poet when he thanks his Lord "for such as it is my gift." The self-aggrandizement gives way to a search for salvation. The poet here admits he does not know all the answers, but is willing to commend his spirit into the hands of the Lord, and "Whatever your end may be, accept my amazement." Berryman's choice of the word "amazement" is fresh and vital within this context, and the entire sequence possesses imagery and insight superior to the callow autobiography which precedes it: here the world becomes one of "candelabra buds sticky in Spring," a world in which "Jonquils respond with wit to the teasing breeze." The Berryman of the school and university poems was too busy noticing Berryman to notice God in the world's flowers.

Recently Jerome Mazzaro has argued persuasively that Berryman's model for the entire book was Augustine's *Confessions*, that history of self-disaffections which culminates also in a final affirmation of the Lord. Mazzaro sees the opening two sections of *Love & Fame* as a parallel to Augustine's preoccupations with love and school in the earliest books of the *Confessions*, "and, in part three, Berryman substitutes a kind of agnostical Freudianism for the period of Augustine's Manichaenism." [15] It is precisely here that Mazzaro's argument, for this reader, begins to degenerate into the wildest sort of speculation. But there certainly are valid parallels to be made between the early religious training and influence by his mother, St. Monica, which Augustine received, and Berryman's own Catholic boyhood and motherly attachment. Augustine's schooling at Carthage could be a parallel to Berryman's at Columbia and Cambridge. And one further parallel which Mazzaro might have drawn is that—as in Berryman's book—Augustine's *Confessions* recount his wild youth, during which time he also fathered an illegitimate child. If Berryman had all these parallels in mind, which is unlikely, then his seemingly gratuitous confession of having a bastard son is not so gratuitous after all. [16]

But Berryman was no Augustine. Despite the bathetic beauty of these late confessions, I am not convinced of the poet's repentance. The formidable ego which wrote the poems of the first three sections has never been sufficiently doubtful or suffered the mental disquietude which would trigger such a full-scale embracing of Christianity. The face of Berryman's Christian mystic, like the figure of Henry House, was yet another false one behind which to hide.

Nevertheless, after Berryman's suicide it was debated whether the embarrassing and downright unlikeable poems of *Love & Fame* were profanity and the product of a lapse in taste (as Robert Lowell said) [17] or deliberate caricatures of the bumptiousness of his youth, caricatures which did not quite come off (as Walter Clemons claimed).[18] I hold to the former view. But, happily, it can be stated that Berryman redeemed himself in print. His last collection, *Delusions, Etc.*, which, unlike the posthumous books of Sylvia Plath, was given order by the poet himself and seen in proof before he died, shows the extroverted poet to have assumed a new tone of humility in his final years. If *Love & Fame* was Berryman's loudest work, *Delusions, Etc.* is surely his quietest. The pathetic boasting and glory-seeking somehow segued into movements of melancholy and finally of cold despair.

The difference is noted immediately in a line such as, "At fifty-five half-famous & effective, I still feel rotten about / myself." [19] The fame so touted in the former book is now seen, perhaps more realistically, as only "half-fame." The lust which has supplanted love is now replaced by tenderness for a wife and worship of God. Berryman was surely moving in these directions with the "Eleven Addresses to the Lord" which conclude *Love & Fame*. Beginning where that book left off, *Delusions, Etc.* opens with a group of eight meditations. But a return to Catholicism is not to save the poet, any more than a return to the origins of his boyhood and youth had done in the previous volume. All are, as the title testifies, delusions, etc. He is still sick in life and more than ever haunted by death. One of the best and longest poems is "about" Beethoven and that composer's death. Another is on the death of his friend, Dylan Thomas. Robert Frost is once again invoked, this time with charity.

No mention is made of the old man's slights, only awe for his work: "Frankly, sir, you fill me with joy." And that old, unlaid-to-rest ghost of his father pays Berryman one final visit. Even then Berryman seems more forgiving than before, now calling his father merely a man who was "not . . . very able." It is as though, in his own new-found humility, Berryman was finally able to forgive others. Even his suicidal father.

This humility is best expressed in the opening section, "Opus Dei," a sequence of eight poems based on the offices of the day from Lauds to Compline, though Berryman's language throughout the book reflects his sympathetic reading of meditative literature from the Book of Psalms ("Let us rejoice on our cots") to the Book of Common Prayer ("There's no health in here"). The second section consists (much as did the part 3 of Lowell's *Life Studies*) of poems about historical figures and personal friends who, in one way or another, touched the poet's life. Berryman's quintet are George Washington, Beethoven, Emily Dickinson, Georg Trabel, and Dylan Thomas.

The third section is a mixed bag of thirteen poems on various personal, theological, and historical topics. A fourth, arranged as a scherzo, briefly) reintroduces the figure of Henry (from *The Dream Songs*). Henry's randyness has turned to pure despair. "Henry By Night" depicts Berryman's insomnia, night sweats, and shakes, concluding, "Something's gotta give." "Henry's Understanding," a companion piece, presents the poet's certainty that some day he will take his own life; in this case he imagines walking "into the terrible water . . . under it out toward the island."

The fifth and final section, meditations and reflections, culminates in "The Facts & Issues," the true climax to the book and to Berryman's life ("*Let this be it.* I've *had* it. I can't wait"), though a short poem ("King David Dances") follows as a sort of coda. In David's dance before the Ark, as in Beethoven's death, Berryman perceives a joyful triumph after trial and adversity. In the Beethoven poem we find identification by the poet with the composer; let us hope that in his vision of the survival of art after the death of the maker ("You're all over my wall! / You march and chant around here! I hear your thighs") Berryman saw and believed in a probable parallel in his own life and work. *Delusions, Etc.* is not Berryman's best book. But it redeems his reputation, tarnished so badly by the offenses of *Love &* *Fame*.

6

The Inward Journeys of Theodore Roethke

It has been remarked of Jane Austen that she lived during some of the most stirring events of world history—the French Revolution, the Terror, Napoleon's rise and fall—and yet made no mention of them in her work. Theodore Roethke flourished during the years of the Great Depression, World War II, the atom bomb, the Korean War, and more—and yet made no mention of them. Of all poets discussed in this book, Roethke is the least "public," his poems almost entirely untouched by history or current events. Whereas Robert Lowell appends to his *Notebook* a checklist of fifteen important dates which figure "directly or obliquely" in his text (the Vietnam War, 1967, 1968, 1969, 1970; the Black Riots in Newark, 1967; Robert Kennedy's murder, 1968, etc.), and Denise Levertov prefaces her *To Stay Alive* with a statement expressing her hopes that the book will be "seen as having some value not as mere 'confessional' auto-biography, but as a document of some historical value, a record of one person's inner / outer experience in America during the '60s and the beginnings of the '70s," Roethke's work seems to have been produced in a vacuum. When his poems do not involve a journey to the interior of self, they extend no further outward than toward what he calls "the minimal"—nature's smallest things: slugs and roots and stones.

Roethke's personal mythology, then, does not include the cataclysmic events of our century. He sees himself instead in relation to the herons and the bats, the flowers and the weeds. And though the first poem in his first book proclaims,

> *My truths are all foreknown,*
> *This anguished self-revealed.*
> *I'm naked to the bone,*
> *With nakedness my shield . . .*[1]

one could argue that Roethke was not, at least blatantly, a "confessional" poet at all. Surely he fits more comfortably into the Romantic tradition of Wordsworth and Coleridge, with his attitude toward the quotidian: "O to be delivered from the rational into the realm of pure song," he exclaims in "What Can I Tell My Bones?"

Yet a confessional poet Roethke often is. Ralph J. Mills, Jr., in the introduction to his edition of *Selected Letters of Theodore Roethke,* for instance, declares Roethke's poetic voice to be "the voice of the total self, nothing withheld, moving through and articulating the whole range of the poet's experience, from his origins to the threshold of death, and touching, often terrifyingly, the areas of madness and of mystical perception."[2] Elsewhere, Mr. Mills, Jr. has written of Roethke's "preoccupation with the poet's own self as the primary source of artistic exploration and knowledge"[3] as well—surely a description of the confessional poet as I have defined one.

The reader may ask, How can a poet be both romantic and confessional? We remember how Roethke hated the ambivalence of his "Kitty-Cat Bird," who sat on a fence in the poem of the same name. Like the work of Lewis Carroll and Edward Lear, the poems Roethke categorized as "Nonsense Poems" often make exceeding good sense. The "Kitty-Cat Bird" is no exception. Roethke is telling the reader to "Be sure that whatever you are is you." And romantic or confessional, whatever Roethke's poems are, they are him. His body of work can be read as one long search for psychic identity and spiritual enlightenment, however obscure and private that search may become. About his poems he once wrote:

1. To go forward (as spiritual man) it is necessary first to go back.
2. In this kind of poem, to be most true to himself and to that which is universal in him, the poet should not rely on allusion.
3. In this kind of poem, the poet should not "comment" or use many judgment-words; instead he should render the experience, however condensed or elliptical that experience may be.[4]

Taken as a sort of poetic manifesto, Roethke's three points illumine his work and its confessional nature. The second of these, the abolition of allusions, has been shown to be fairly characteristic of all confessional poets (except for John Berryman, whose private allusions often mar his work). The first and third are more unique to Roethke, and help explain his uniqueness among confessional poets.

"*To go forward (as spiritual man) it is necessary first to go back . . .*": Roethke did not discover this principle or truth until after publication of *Open House* (1941), that creditable but nonetheless derivative first volume which bore marks of then-current poetic fashion. Only in a handful of poems — "To My Sister," "The Premonition," "Mid-Country Blow," "The Heron," "The Bat" — does Roethke truly return to his roots and in so doing produce poetry in the voice and manner for which he later was to be acclaimed. Too much else in the book is either Audenesquely witty — "Academic," "Poetaster," "For an Amorous Lady" — or too embarrassingly sentimental — "Ballad of the Clairvoyant Widow," "Night Journey." Indeed only the title poem seems mature Roethke as we come later to read him.

Seven years passed between that book and the next. The change in Roethke's work is phenomenal. The second collection, *The Lost Son and Other Poems* (1948), is one of the truly original and worthy volumes of twentieth-century American poetry. Of Roethke's six books, it is indisputably the great one, as Stanley Kunitz and others have agreed. One reason for its great success is that Roethke did indeed "go back," as the title would indicate. For his subject he journeyed backward in time to his youth, to discover at the small end of the funnel the person he had been—in order to find the person he was. For his style he obeyed his own third dictum, and rendered his experience direct ("however condensed or elliptical that experience may be"). The mannerisms and exercises of *Open House* were abandoned.

The subject of *The Lost Son* is the progress of the spirit from conception toward death, though many of the shorter lyrics with which the volume opens have often been interpreted solely as acutely lapidary exercises in imagism, descriptions of the greenhouse world in which the young Ted Roethke was reared. Yet there is deep personal history embedded in even these thirteen short vegetal lyrics. They are radically different from anything in *Open House*. Rather than making poetic observations of plants in nature, Roethke here employs Keatsian "negative capability" to convey the essential identity of hothouse flowers, and, by extension, to discover the essential identity of the boy who also grew there. It was a risk Roethke was willing to take—to focus all his powers upon capturing the spirit and laws of the flowers, and hoping thereby to capture his own growth as well. These poems differ from the earlier as well in their fierce intensity and infinite concern with detail. It is as if nothing the poet was later to observe appeared to him with quite the same clarity as it did to the child who lowered himself to the level of flowers. Like Thomas Traherne, Roethke knew "I must become that child again." There are several reasons for Roethke's "flower fixation." The most obvious of course is purely autobiographical. The young Roethke grew up in and worked around his father's greenhouses, which were said to be among the largest in the state of Michigan. To project his spiritual history he must revisit the floral world, the garden which figured as his Edenic Paradise in childhood. But an aesthetic reason also must be considered: His poetic journey into the underworld of the mind demanded an appropriate symbology, and the shoots and roots and weeds and mosses of these poems symbolize the submerged self. Further, the annual cycle is another aspect of the world of Roethke's imagination—repeating as it does the mysteries of death and resurrection. When, in the first poem, "Cuttings," the one nub of growth asserts itself, it can and must be likened to the human spirit which miraculously survives even when severed from the parent plant. The image is a uniquely personal one for the strivings of a son separated from his beginnings. (So unique that it perhaps went unnoticed until Kenneth Burke, that astute critic of language and literature, noted in essay form the personal history embedded in these thirteen short vegetal lyrics.[5] Perhaps this is giving Burke too much credit, since he was a personal friend of Roethke's, and more than any other critic was in a position to discuss with the poet the makings and the content of his work.)

"Cuttings (*later*)," the second poem, makes clear with the addition of a human comparative that the poet intends the imagistic figuring as one for man's condition:

> *This urge, wrestle, resurrection of dry sticks,*
> *Cut stems struggling to put down feet,*
> *What saint strained so much,*
> *Rose on such lopped limbs to a new life?*

Roethke moves from the saintly situation of the cuttings, in the first stanza, to his personal situation in the second: "I can hear, underground, that sucking and sobbing, / In my veins, in my bones I feel it—" The poet himself struggles toward some sort of resurrection. Like the cuttings, he has returned to a prenatal state. Like an embryo floating in amniotic fluid, "Slippery as fish, / I quail, lean to beginnings, sheath-wet."

"Root cellar," the third, is a symbol for the poet's psyche, that dark and deep-down place in which "Nothing would sleep." He is tormented by the past: "Nothing would give up life." Roethke's preoccupations here can be interpreted both as a yearning toward ancestry—those ripe roots—and toward sexuality ("shoots dangled and drooped, / Lolling obscenely from mildewed crates"). Like the bulbs in the root cellar, the poet finds himself in the dark. He must hunt for light. The poem is an assertion of stubborn existence and the will to survive, as was "Cuttings." His is a frantic search for the growth symbolized by the "Forcing House," an un-natural situation, manmade, to induce "Fifty summers in motion at once"—which feat could only be duplicated by human memory. Yet just as the steam pipes which make possible such hermetic growth are in danger of break-down (in "Big Wind"), so too is the poet. Roethke's obsession with roots fascinates. Clearly a symbol of physical growth in reverse, and return to beginnings, the roots are an emblem of inversion and involution.

The already-hinted-at sexual imagery is supra-abundant in "Weed Puller," with its "black hairy roots" and "lewd monkey-tails." But to comment on those symbols is to achieve not much other than to note that the poet has observed the correspondence between nature and human sexual anatomy. A more important correspondence is to be found in the image with which Roethke concludes the poem:

> *Me down in that fetor of weeds,*
> *Crawling on all fours,*
> *Alive, in a slippery grave.*

On the physical level this might be seen as an image of the poet's desire to have sexual congress with a woman. But "Alive, in a slippery grave" is more likely an overt image for the prenatal self in the maternal womb, thoroughly consistent with the birth and rebirth imagery traced so far ("Slippery as a fish . . . sheath-wet"). Like the seeds and the bulbs, weed-puller Roethke is spiritually himself in a hole, awaiting rebirth. Readers skeptical that Roethke could have had such overt symbolism in mind must realize that the poet was well versed in both Freud and Jung, and that in at least one essay he calls the greenhouse "My symbol for the whole of life, a womb, a heaven-on-earth." Certainly Roethke used language to mean just what he meant; at the same time he was quite aware of the purposeful ambiguities inherent in his lines. The many holes and graves in his poems thus signify more than the sexual and the biological. The scholar J. E. Cirlot would tell us that as a symbol of heaven "the hole also stands specifically for the passage from

spatial to non-spatial, from temporal to non-temporal existence, and corresponds to the Zenith." [6] Whether in intercourse, within the womb, or inside the grave, the poet in
his suspended state seems on a threshold between one world
and another. The weed puller, the young worker attempting
to make whole fields of flowers inviolate, is a superb figure
for the poet as artist.

The analogy between the human and natural conditions
is pushed even further in "Orchids," an impressive series of
images set forth in the spare and economical language of
an H. D. (Hilda Doolittle) or T. E. Hulme. In their mossy
cradles the orchids seem to the poet "so many devouring
infants" with "soft luminescent fingers." In their living
they are no less demanding than babies. Roethke may or
may not have had in mind various other meanings of these
orchids: their lavender color, for instance, in T. S. Eliot and
elsewhere traditionally the color of spirituality and sublima-
tion; their shape, essentially phallic. The poem as it stands
is, without further commitment or comment, merely another strong link between the vegetal and the human conditions. Perhaps the orchids are best interpreted as symbolic
of the poet himself and his spiritual suspension, with "Lips
neither dead nor alive, / Loose ghostly mouths / Breathing."
(Roethke was, in fact, possessed of a fleshy mouth and wrote
in several poems about "fat lips.")

From this almost totally imagistic statement the volume
moves toward the overt confession of guilt of "Moss-
Gathering." As the florist's son, Roethke often gathered
mosses to line cemetery baskets. He never returned with the
moss from the wood or marshes without feeling as if he
had "Disturbed some rhythm, old and of vast importance."
Even as a boy he obviously enjoyed learning from nature
without violating her. But now he can no longer afford to
examine the natural world of his youth without also disturbing the psyche. For the poet, pulling moss off the
planet's face is like pulling off his own fleshly mask: both
acts are painful, both engage the conscience. (Karl Malkoff
has suggested the guilt occasioned by these woodland visits
stems from the poet's having masturbated there. He cites

as evidence the phrase "pulling off flesh." [7] I would maintain that such an interpretation can only be read *into* the
poem, rather than *out of* it. Malkoff is more convincing
on the theme of masturbation in Roethke's work in his discussions of the long sequence poems.)

The greenhouse becomes a ship sailing through a savage
storm in "Big Wind," one of the most memorable poems in
The Lost Son. The boy helping his father save the roses
from the ravages of water is, again, a symbolic figure. First,
the greenhouse as a ship is a metaphor for Roethke's life, a
sailing toward death, carrying with it always the memory
of his father and flowers. Surely the poem can also be seen
as an expression of Roethke's desire to transcend existence,
his romantic yearnings. The symbolic act of saving roses
from the elements can be read as Roethke's desire to preserve his Edenic childhood or Dantean paradise from destruction. The roses as symbols of perfection are threatened
by waters which may not necessarily be outside forces – the
dull roar of the outside world – but more likely the oceanic
unconscious of the poet. Seeing the greenhouse as an ark,
his father as Noah and Roethke as Noah's son, the flowers
instead of beasts as cargo, we can entertain the notion that
the young Roethke was afraid to learn to sail the sea of
passions in order to reach the mountain of salvation. (The
greenhouse becomes a symbolic ship, the ship a symbol for
the physical and spiritual body, the ship of life or death.)

Otto Roethke, that prime mover and the poet's father,
finally is given a solo performance in the ninth poem. Unlike Sylvia Plath's, John Berryman's, or Robert Lowell's
portraits of their fathers, Roethke's depiction of his is of an
essentially kindly and revered figure. This poem does not
convey the boyish terror later evident in "My Papa's Waltz,"
and elsewhere. Most important here are the godlike quali-
ties with which the poet endows the father: he can elim-
inate rot, resurrect the dying flowers, and "drown a bug in
one spit of tobacco juice."

Like "Orchids," "Transplanting" is chiefly imagistic. It
is another instance of Roethke's adherence to his third poetic principle – i.e., to render direct a condensed experience

without judgmental asides. It is distinguished by a remarkable second stanza, which renders—as if by time-lapse pho-
tography—the growth of a bud into blossom. (One is reminded of "Tulips," a later poem by Denise Levertov, in
which the reverse process is made tangible, showing the
reader image by image, step by step, the gradual disintegra-
tion of flowers from bloom to wilt.)

A more resonant poem of Roethke's is "Child on Top
of a Greenhouse." One is struck first by the pathetic fallacy
—"The half-grown chrysanthemums staring up like accus-
ers"—so human, this vegetal world! Again the poet-as-child
sees the greenhouse as a vessel. Implicit in the gesture of
child riding the top of the roof in the wind is the desire to
transcend existence, to travel through space to other worlds.
And implicit is the inevitable drift toward death: with its
verticality and height, supports forming a mast in the center
of the vessel as well as a cross or cosmic tree, the greenhouse is at once a Ship of Life and a symbol of the inexhaustible life-processes of growth and development. It is
significant that the "Flower Dump" lies outside the greenhouse. Yet even the poem named after that repository for
all flower-flesh remains is not unduly negative: on top of
the dead heap one tulip still swaggers its head. One might
say the poet identifies with that tenacious tulip, surviving
still an alien environment. The tulip atop the dump heap is
a figure for the romantic poet in America in this century.
That tulip and the flowers of "Carnations" are both positive
visions, portents of eternity and the perpetuity of art and
life, in sharp contrast with the dying cannas and the ghostly
orchids found elsewhere in Roethke's work.

The final poem of the cycle, "Frau Bauman, Frau
Schmidt, and Frau Schwartze," turns from the vegetable
to the human. Roethke here summons from so long ago the
memory of three female greenhouse employees, those ancient ladies who kept creation at ease, summons them now
to blow "lightly over me in my first sleep." The important
word is "first." Is this the poet's first sleep because he has
just been (re)born? Is the poet to be no longer "alone and
cold" in his bed? The poem contains no solutions, merely

questions. There is about this and all the greenhouse poems a sense of wonderment at life and creation. It seems singularly appropriate that the section should conclude with "Frau Bauman, Frau Schmidt, and Frau Schwartze" (the first editions of the book did not contain the poem; Roethke appended it later). Because, for this reader at least, the three ancient crones strongly suggest the three Moirae (called Parcae by the Romans), Clotho, Lachesis, and Atropos—the three Fates who serve as allegorical divinities of the duration of life. Cutting and pruning, Roethke's three German ladies recall the spindle and cutting instruments with which the Moirae are classically represented. Just as they kept life going in the greenhouse, so now the ancient ladies nurture Roethke in his own life.

In these first poems Roethke merely raises the questions of his existence, and revisits the scene where answers can and must be found. And the pieces which conclude the volume reveal that the greenhouse did indeed hold answers. As Kenneth Burke has perceived, in the world of flowers Roethke "was trained to a symbolic vocabulary of subtle human relations and odd strivings, before he could have encountered the equivalent patterns of experience in exclusively human terms." [8]

The seven poems which comprise section 2 of *The Lost Son* are portraits of the poet in various stages of his life. The first, "My Papa's Waltz," shows him as a young boy, not playing or working in the greenhouse but, for once, in that other house, the Roethke home. For the first time his mother is mentioned; his quest for identity seems previously to have revolved almost solely about the figure of his father and their relationship. Though the mother plays a role in "My Papa's Waltz," it is by definition a very minor one. The poem is primarily an impressionistic view of the small boy romping about the kitchen with his drunken, or at least drinking, father. At first impression the poem is a happy one. But this happiness is only momentary, for as the poet tells us, "Such waltzing was not easy." The boy is dizzy and afraid. His ear keeps scraping his father's belt buckle. His head becomes a drum, beat time upon by the man. Then, still clinging to the elder's shirt, he is danced off to bed while his mother (emblematically in the background) frowns disapproval. The poem in truth recounts neither the boy's waltz, nor the boy's waltz with the father, but "My Papa's Waltz," an adult indulgence which discomforts the son. Yet there can be no doubt of his love for the father. This waltz, a dance performed by the two bodies linked, symbolizes his cosmic and psychic alliance with the father. In his adult life they are united still, in memory. In this sense the whirling figures of the dance embody the passage of time as well as the corporeal image of becoming. As Yeats pondered of the same figure, "O body swayed to music, O brightening glance, / How can we know the dancer from the dance?"

The remaining six short pieces in section 2 show the young Roethke in evolution. In "Pickle Belt" he is a youthful worker in a factory, having broken away from the greenhouse but still working with products of the vegetable kingdom. Here the ripe fruit passing on the conveyor belt suggests the ripeness of the boy's adolescence, "the fruit and flesh smells mixed." Just as the young boy was one with flowers, these pickles are one with the boy. His sixteen-year-old lust is ready for picking. The phallic implication of his predicament, the pickle he is in, need not be mentioned.

"Dolor" presents a sharp contrast. Instead of the itching adolescent we have the world-weary adult, possessed of an intelligence which has been dulled by the conformity and sterility of institutions. There is nothing of the spontaneity of nature here, only the "inexorable sadness of pencils," the "dolor of pad and paperweight," the "Desolation in immaculate public places." The poem sustains a tone of misery throughout, and contains two arresting images—one the duplicating machine which in fact effects an "Endless duplication of lives and objects"; the other the dust from institutional walls which drops its film on "the duplicate grey standard faces." Too much institutionalization, the poet is saying, kills something in us all. By extension, we know Roethke believes it is in the freedom of nature we find ourselves, from the "study of lives on a leaf" (as in "The Minimal").

"Double Feature" is yet another view of the young poet, a restless seeker whose search for meaning takes him to the movies. Reluctant to leave, he is yet unsatisfied: "there was something else I was hoping for." The poem concludes with the poet lingering, neither wholly in the real world, nor totally committed to that of make-believe. "The Return"—a poem of entrance—and "Lost Words"—a poem of exit—present an older version of the poet in two stages of despair. "Judge Not" is an ironic statement of the poet's world view. The first stanza positions him as one praying for the blessings of life to descend on all the unfortunate living. The second reverses that view. Having heard the howl of drunkards, seen the wretchedness of women, he prays instead for the blessing of death to descend on all. While there are no shifts of time evident here, we can read the first stanza as Roethke's Song of Innocence, the second as his Song of Experience.

Section 3, five lyrics not more than seventy-five lines long, can be seen as a calm before the Sturm und Drang of concentrated self-exploration which was to follow in the concluding section 4, those long sequence poems "The Lost Son," "The Long Alley," "A Field of Light," and "The Shape of the Fire." These five "little preludes," as it were, clarify Roethke's world view and introduce a new dimension of *déjà vu* ("And I knew I had been there before") and pantheism ("I wasn't alone / In a grove of apples"). The final lines are redolent with a Dylan Thomasean joy: "all the waters / Of all the streams / Sang in my veins / that summer day." Again we have a genuine progression from darkness (the crow) to light (the summer waters), a movement repeated in the sequence poems. And what I have called *déjà vu* has been seen by at least one critic as an instance of Jung's reactivated archetypes.[9]

All the pains and anxieties treated individually in the shorter poems—the isolation of the artist in America, the separation of the son from his parents, the uncertainties of sex and death and God—are found in the sequences which follow. Of these sequence poems Roethke has written, "each in a sense is a stage in a kind of struggle out of the slime; part of a slow spiritual progress, an effort to be born, and later, to become something more." [10]

In "The Lost Son" the struggle specifically is one from a lower state to a higher, a dark time to one of illumination, depression to joy, alienation from the father to reconciliation, atheism to religion. Unlike the poems which follow it, "The Lost Son" maintains a linear narrative line. "The Flight," section 1, begins with a reference to death (Woodlawn), which recalls his father and his own past; and the poet's intimations of mortality ("the softening chalk of my bones"). In his dark time, the poet wishes to return home, emotionally if not physically, "home" being the only home the poet ever felt at-home in, the world of his father, the greenhouse and childhood. Ironically he sees such a return as a progression forward for his mental state, progression in regression. It is noteworthy that the two sentences which constitute stanzas two and three each lack a subject, the first-person pronoun "I" being deliberately omitted. The poet clearly is projecting his identity crisis, or, more specifically, his crisis of lack of identity, by omitting the pronoun. He is defenseless in a stagnant world and, finding no other help, asks the smallest creatures (the minimal) to give him a sign, some subhuman clue to the meaning of human existence. Yet there is no creature comfort to be found in the animal or vegetable kingdom; the poet must leave them behind and come to terms with human relations and human relatives.

The last four stanzas of the section employ the rhythms and vocabulary of the nursery, signifying the poet's homecoming. The protagonist, the reader realizes, has been reborn to a childlike and perhaps even subhuman state. (Remember: "Except a man be born again, he cannot see the kingdom of God" [John 3:3]). In Roethke's search for salvation he undergoes flights of irrationality, alternating between the animal and human states: "It's sleek as an otter / With wide webby toes / Just under the water / It usually goes."

This agonizing quest brings the poet to "The Pit," the site of section 2 and geographically (but not emotionally) the low point of the poem. Initially described in images of roots, mosses, leaves, and thereby serving as a symbol of origins, the poet is seeking his beginnings, the true author of his nativity: "Who stunned the dirt into noise?" a mole / phallus image for the act of paternal impregnation of the mother. The question asked is, then, Who is my father? In this section Roethke repeats the womb-imagery seen earlier, with the protagonist now depicted as inside a pit, a slimy wet nest.

"The Gibber," a third section, concerns the poet's sexual failures: "Dogs of the groin / Barked and howled, / The sun was against me, / The moon would not have me." This failure, in tandem with all others, instills a death wish within the poet. For this reason he reaches a lower state than even in "The Pit," despite that section's designated title. He sees salvation in parental reconciliation, or at least in reconciliation with the memory of his parents if not with their flesh. For the first time he admits his "father problem":

> Fear was my Father, Father Fear.
> His look drained the stones.

It is a severe look (and father) which can metaphorically drain stones. Much of this section's imagery derives from the Book of Job: like Job, Roethke too is being tested and is estranged from the father. The difficult next movement in the section is described by Roethke himself as a "rising agitation . . . rendered in terms of balked sexual experience." [11] The poet works himself into a state of hallucinatory frenzy and blackout: "Kiss me, ashes, I'm falling through a dark swirl." This is, of course a dark night of the soul, the ashes falling upon him are the remnants of his expended energies on both the animal and spiritual levels.

"The Return" is a memory of a time past. It finds the poet literally inside the greenhouse, his body and soul calmed once more, his emergence out of depression into serenity, madness to sanity, symbolized by the coming of dawn over the glass house, a state made possible by the coming once more of his father into his life: "Ordnung! ordnung! Papa is coming!" Coming to terms with the father figure creates order in the poet's disheveled life. The ashes of the last movement give way to the roses of "The Return," roses which symbolize regeneration, new growth from old, as opposed to the sterility of ashes. With the approach of the florist father, heaven and earth become one for the poet. As he now accepts his earthly father, so too can he acknowledge a Heavenly one as well.

The final section, labeled "It was beginning winter" but which more correctly would be titled "The Illumination," removes us to an in-between time. For the poet sees things now neither as completely black—as at the poem's beginning—nor clear as dawn—as in "The Return." The bones of weeds survive in the wind, but they are bones nonetheless. Can these bones live? The near-grown poet feels they can. Yet his illumination is far from complete; he must await further spiritual insight. He is still uncertain of the nature of his especial spiritual insight. Is it external or internal? He only knows it came once, and shall come again. Salvation is attainable by him who seeks it. Like the coming of dawn and the coming of the father, another advent is promised.

This long confessional sequence eventually was to be followed by seven more of similar construction, each following the progression and retrogression of the poet / protagonist's mental states. Besides "The Lost Son," three more sequence poems were included in this important second volume. Three others appeared in *Praise to the End!* and the last in *The Waking*. A generalization can be made. The earliest of these appear to be confessions of the fears and pangs of growing up—resentment of, then reconciliation with, the father; guilt over onanism; alienation from the commercial world. The latter sequences, on the other hand, deal with troubled sexuality and alienation as well, but "the childhood themes are displaced by more mature reflections on love, death, and questions of being." [12]

The alienation from the world of childhood evoked in

"The Lost Son" gives way to adult alienation from the world-at-large in "The Long Alley." The first line of the poem, the evocation of Eden, is immediately displaced by images of destruction and pollution, the dead fish floating belly upward in the river. This is later reinforced by the water's being described as sulfureous, the banks made of cinder. It is obvious that the poet has fallen from whatever state of grace he had achieved at the conclusion of "The Lost Son." The polluted air and water and earth are at once sources of his mental disturbance and symbols for his disturbed mental landscape, or *psychescape*. In this regard Roethke must be seen as a symbolist poet, with his various states of being represented as certain definite kinds of landscape in which additional symbols of level, light, color, and shape all play a role. The dirty serpentine river with which this piece opens is a good example: it connotes the fallen Paradise, innocence to experience, purity to pollution. Serpents can as well connote the primordial, the most primitive state of life (to which the poet now finds himself reduced?), as well as the evil, since snakes are vicious, and it was the serpent which tempted Eve. Jung tells us that, psychologically, "The snake is a symptom of anguish expressive of abnormal stirrings in the unconscious, that is, of a reactivation of its destructive potentiality." [13] All these and more are possible readings of the mood-landscape painted here, particularly when Roethke himself identifies with a serpent in the third section, as we shall see.

Compared with the conclusion of "The Lost Son," here, in "The Long Alley," the poet's mental health seems to have worsened. But at least his preoccupations are of time present rather than time past. (Or are they? In a still later poem, "Where Knock Is Open Wide," Roethke declares, "My father is a fish." Is the dead fish which opens "The Long Alley" a symbol for the lost father? Or for the failure of religion—the fish as Christ symbol—to be of aid? The reader must decide.) The second stanza shifts from the poet's environmental alienation to one of frustrated eroticism: "There's no joy in soft bones." The inability to touch flesh is paralleled with the failure to invoke the infusion of the holy spirit.

Then comes the identification with the snake: "This wind gives me scales," a line immediately followed by, "Have mercy, gristle: / It's my last waltz with an old itch." The sexual implications are undeniable, and the serpent identification for Roethke must in this instance be read as phallic. Yet failed sexuality permeates the poem, which appropriately lapses into unmanly nursery rhyming and culminates in the emasculation symbol of a head of a decapitated match. The old itch conceivably is a penchant for masturbation which, when practiced by the poet, results in guilt feelings because he has not found true sexual satisfaction.

Yet there is another aspect of the serpent symbology which must be considered. Because it sheds its skin, the snake is also an emblem of new life. And in section 4 the poet seems resurrected from his bad time. The earlier stagnation gives way to revivification: "This air could flesh a dead stick." The dead stick suggests at once a greenhouse cutting, the poet, the impotent phallus, and the serpent. The poet reverts to childhood once more, summoning the solace of flowers, and for the first time "The Long Alley" of the title is seen not merely as an image of darkness, confinement, and restriction—one more avenue in the terrestrial maze through which the poet must find his way back to the center, or soul —but also a greenhouse memory of rows ordered by string. And the flowers are said to have "fish-ways," presumably not only to float in their element as fish do in theirs, but also to suggest the poet's father, who "is a fish." (It is tempting to conjecture whether Roethke remembered reading Faulkner's *As I Lay Dying*, in which a son laments of his lost mother, "My mother was a fish." More likely the traditional connotations of the symbol are intended. Specifically, Roethke's search for his father is like that for the Holy Grail. Like Roethke's quest, the path of the Grail was marked by a number of miracles. When Parsifal meets the King of the Grail he is a fisherman. "My father is a fish" also can mean, "My father is Christ." The fish like the father is mystic and psychic, living in another element and thereby symbolizing renovation and regeneration.)

This stanza, as permeated by light as the first three are by dark, concludes with the realization that

The leaves, the leaves become me!
The tendrils have me!

The leaves "become" the poet, not only in the sense that they complement his existence; they literally become one with his existence, much as Daphne was metamorphosed into a laurel tree. (The reader is referred to the *Collected Poems* of Horace Gregory for many poetic manifestations of this leafy transmogrification.) For Roethke, to become one with the leaves is to attain mental peace, an ancient concept: of the eight common emblems of Chinese symbolism, it is the leaf which represents happiness, a fact Roethke most likely never knew but intuited. Certainly for Roethke any return to the flowering leaf was a happy one. The last stanza, in which the poet rejects the material world for the natural one, reinforces this interpretation. More important, the "low" psychic and bestial physical level in which the poet had been living, represented by his identification with both the snake and the dog, is finally shed ("my paws are gone"), to allow him to assume his place as a man in the world. When he declares he will "take the fire," he means he will turn his back on death and mental illness to embrace life and health. A purifying symbol of regeneration and transformation, this vital heat is also an expression of the spiritual energy the poet hopes to achieve. (The spiritual connotations of fire are submerged in favor of sexual ones in the later "The Shape of the Fire.") In this sense the poet has reached a condition similar to that at the conclusion of "The Lost Son." Or at least he tells us he has. From out of a dark time he confesses to have attained a state of receptivity to spiritual strength and illumination, "light within light."

It is then chronologically and emotionally appropriate that the next poem be titled "A Field of Light." The shortest of the sequence poems, it also repeats what for Roethke has by now become a formula: a beginning in the lower order—the slime, the stagnant, to symbolize a probing of the unconscious or a dark night of the soul—and then a working toward a higher state of grace and light. What is new here, however, is a reciprocity with natural things. The poet can kiss a stone. He can see the separateness in all things. Instead of depending on nature for his identity, he has earned a disparate unity of soul which allows him to see himself in nature, but not of it. The poem ends with the poet walking "through the light air."

Another poem, another setback. Paralleling Roethke's own continuing shifts in mental balance, the last poem, "The Shape of the Fire," throws the protagonist back into the pit of darkness and confusion, into a place of black rocks and crying spiders (the latter very singular image perhaps later borrowed by Robert Lowell in his "Fall 1961"), a place where the vegetal kingdom is not happiness or unity but actually vicious: "These flowers are all fangs," a point of view recalling Tennyson's "Nature, red in tooth and claw."

The initial search here is not for spiritual unity, but carnal knowledge: in the face of the fire, the lost son can offer only a "lewd whisper." The obliquely rendered eroticism of the earlier poems seems more explicit in "The Shape of the Fire." And in this last search for psychic identification, Roethke goes back to earliest beginnings, to a prenatal state, into the womb, that "cave of sorrow" from which he prays someone will "Mother me out of here." He is one with the wasp who waits; the eye coming out of the wave is his on entry into the world.

Roethke's regression at this point is reminiscent of the ancient Hindu path of *pitri-yana,* or "The Way of the Ancestors," as set forth in the *Bhagavad-Gita.* That is, freeing himself from the material world, he follows the path of detachment which is the very inverse of that route he took upon entering it. Instead of ever moving forward, he retreats in his journey of the soul. To quote from the *Bhagavad-Gita*:

At this juncture, those who tend towards union, without having actually achieved it, leave manifest existence behind them, some to return to it later, others never to return . . . Fire, light, day, the crescent moon, the half-

year of the sun's ascendence . . . —these are the lumi-
nous signs which lead to Brahma those who acknowledge
Brahma. Smoke, night, the waning moon, the half-year
when the sun descends toward the south—such are the
signs that lead to lunar light and immediately to the
return to states of manifestation.[14]

The images of fire and illumination are pure Roethke. Out
of this regression the poet is again reconceived, reborn, re-
greenhoused, reloved, and therefore reconciled. Once again
he tells us he enters a plane of light which fills and falls
("often without our knowing, / As an opaque vase fills to
the brim from a quick pouring"). The ways of grace are
mysterious, the poet says, the state can be achieved almost
unconsciously. In the midst of the most torturous mental
anguish, the weight can suddenly be lifted.

Four long and agonized explorations (exploitations?) of
the mind; four long journeys out of the darkness into light,
turbulence into peace: Does Theodore Roethke finally
achieve something resembling peace of mind from these
traumatic confessions? Sadly not, as a reading of those
poems which fill the subsequent books reveal. Indeed, the
implied action and use of language as psychic shorthand
in these early poems, making them more truly "dream
songs" than anything John Berryman wrote under that
designation, together with their concealed hordes of half-
confessions (masked masturbation images, for instance)
ultimately give way to such open and frank confessions of
mental illness as "Heard in a Violent Ward," "Meditation
in Hydrotherapy," and "Lines Upon Leaving a Sanitarium"
—late poems more in the manner of Anne Sexton than
Theodore Roethke. Stylistically they are lucid exceptions.
For the better part of his writing career Roethke was not
content merely to swim on the surface of the unconscious.
His was a compulsion to dive down deeper and stay down
longer than any other of the confessional poets. And he
alone of the group attempts a poetry of mysticism.

Yet after getting it all down, the 274 pages of his Collected Poems, Theodore Roethke was ever "the lost son."

We find "The Shape of the Fire" concluding with a cut flower, the very image with which the volume *The Lost Son* began. To the end Roethke *was* that severed bloom, the offspring inexorably separated from the parent stock, the intellect (blossom) isolated from the brute body (ancestry, roots, sexual forces). The severed flower functions for Roethke much as does the severed head for Robert Lowell. But Lowell, a more political man, continually proves to find sustenance from the world about him. Roethke had only the self upon which to feed. The limitations of his work, aside from the chameleon-like ability of his verse to absorb the colors and voices of the poets he currently was reading—particularly Yeats, Eliot, and Thomas —is the insincerity of its sincerity. It is true enough that the spirit of man can gain strength or a renewal of grace in a period of conflict and of trial. And in wanting so desperately to achieve just such an epiphany or illumination, Roethke concludes poem after poem with a description of a mystic or spiritual event. It is a bit like a whore claiming to have an orgasm with each new customer. The fact that the poet rarely if ever achieved these visions makes it impossible for the reader to experience them from the printed page. It is ecstasy unearned, and the unattained vision cannot be shared.

7

The Dark Funnel
A Reading of Sylvia Plath

"Such a dark funnel, my father," Sylvia Plath cries out in her "Little Fugue." And Otto Plath is a funnel indeed, leading her psyche from the openness of youth down toward the small dark point of death. Jan B. Gordon has touched upon this mythos of the father in his important essay, "Who is Sylvia? The Art of Sylvia Plath." [1] But to date no one has traced the trajectory of her father's memory in the body of Plath's work. We suggest that a pattern of guilt over imagined incest informs all of Plath's prose and poetry. When Otto Plath died of natural causes in a hospital on November 2, 1940, he might just as well have been a lover jilting his beloved. Indeed, in all her poems Plath makes of this separation a deliberate desertion. In poem after poem the father drowns himself.

This is the central myth of Plath's imagination. Critics have called hers a poetry of annihilation, poetry in which her own suicidal impulses are set against the larger framework of a world which deliberately destroys—the Nazi genocide of the Jews, the Kamikazes, Hiroshima. Even a train is said to eat its track. A favorite Plath image is that of the hook: from the bend in a road, to the corner of her son's smile—both traps for the unsuspecting. Plath's is a terrible, unforgiving nature; in feeling victimized by her father's early death, and later by an unsatisfactory compensatory marriage, she makes no distinction between her tragedy and those of Auschwitz or Nagasaki.

Indeed, in the poem "Daddy," Plath claims to become

a Jew, an identification which reaffirms an earlier *persona* assumed in the autobiographical novel, *The Bell Jar*, in which she chooses the name "Esther Greenwood" for the protagonist. That the heroine was, in experiential terms, "green wood," can be seen from such passages as, "How could I write about life when I'd never had a love affair, or a baby or seen anybody die?" [2] But it is the forename which is telling. Esther of the Old Testament was the Jewish queen who kept her nationality secret until the evil Haman conceived a plot to destroy all the Jews in the kingdom. It was Esther who saved the Jews by pleading with the king. Such an identification would also appear to confirm the Oedipal nature of Plath's work. Queen Esther (and the further identification with queen bees must be explored later) was more than a deliverer of the Jews. She was also the beautiful young virgin with whom King Ahasuerus united after his wife, Queen Vashti, treated him with contempt. Plath reveals in *The Bell Jar* that Mrs. Plath treated her husband's memory in similar fashion: "My mother had taught shorthand and typing to support us ever since my father died, and secretly she hated it and hated him for dying and leaving no money because he didn't trust life insurance salesmen." [3]

The mother's contempt for the father is paralleled in the novel by Sylvia Plath's own violent distaste for men, a reaction triggered by her "abandonment" by the father. The novel's most heartless character, Buddy Willard, is—like her father—a scientist. (Dr. Plath was known for work in ornithology, entomology, ichthyology, and biology, and was author of a book on bumblebees.) [4] Only instead of frogs and bees, Buddy dissects human cadavers. By extension he dissects the sensitive human fibers of Sylvia Plath's being. For her, Buddy clearly represents the male species, which she found cruel and deceptive. Her attitude toward men is nowhere more clear than as echoed in the words of the second voice in her radio play, *Three Women*: "They are jealous gods / that would have the whole world flat because they are." This "flatness" is the same as insensitivity, which for the female—and especially for the female artist—is intolerable. (Dr. Plath was said to possess a coldly scientific mind. He also taught scientific German.) When Buddy makes Esther view a birth, and tells her the woman is on a drug which afterward will make her forget she has had any pain at all, Plath concludes, "it sounded just like the sort of drug a man would invent. Here was a woman in terrible pain, obviously feeling every bit of it or she wouldn't groan like that, and she would go straight home and start another baby, because the drug would make her forget how bad the pain had been." [5]

The Bell Jar is full of contempt for the hypocrisy of men and their double standard. Even Esther's friend and saviour, Doctor Nolan—another scientist!—like her father, betrays her. But the real turning point of the novel comes, appropriately, when she goes looking for her father (her father's grave) and cannot at first find him. When she finally approaches his grave, the marker's insignificant appearance, coupled with memories of her mother's remarks on how much "better off" he was in death than in life, cause the girl to collapse. In this love triangle it was obviously the daughter who loved Otto Plath more than the mother.

That Sylvia Plath felt consciously rejected by the father in his lifetime is not apparent (though he as much as did so when it was revealed to him his newborn was not a boy. On October 27, 1932, the day she was born, he declared: "All I want from life from now on is a son born two and a half years to the day." With remarkable efficiency, Mrs. Plath gave him the wanted son on April 27, 1935. Professor Plath's teaching colleagues toasted him as "the man who gets what he wants when he wants it").[6] But while he lived Sylvia never felt second-best. In her own words, she was never happier than when she "was about nine and running along the hot white beaches with my father the summer before he died." [7] That she felt rejected by him in his act of dying is documented in poem after poem. Had he lived, she elaborates in the novel, she was certain he would have taught her German and Latin and Greek, as well as everything there was to know about insects. She would even have become a Lutheran for him. In short, her life would have been totally different.[8]

That she tried to keep her dead father alive within her can be seen from her interests over the years. She began the study of German, though openly admitting a hatred for the language. According to her high school yearbook she continuously played on the piano the "Bumble Boogie" — that frantic bit of pop music approximating the sound of bees. As a pet expression she used "God save the Queen," unconsciously incorporating bees into her conversations. And, after her marriage to Ted Hughes, she began bee-keeping. The author of *Bumblebees and Their Ways* was with her yet. It does not surprise that, when she entered the casualty ward for removal of a splinter from one eye, she confesses to have been "babbling frantically about Oedipus." [9]

We suggest that Plath was a modern Electra. Her unnatural love for her father, who "abandoned" her in death, caused her subsequent hatred of all men, a hatred we shall document by examining the four collections of poems and the novel. (Electra, as no one needs reminding, took vengeance on her mother, Clytemnestra, for murdering Agamemnon, thereby robbing the girl of her beloved father.) Agamemnon was killed in his bath; in Plath's mythology her father died in water. This charge would appear to be substantiated in the overt and uncollected poem, "Electra on the Azalea Path," which reads in part, "Oh pardon the one who knocks for pardon at / Your gate, father — Your hound-bitch, daughter, friend. It was my love that did us both to death." [10] In another uncollected poem the father is like Thompson's hound of heaven, pursuing the daughter to her end: "There is a panther stalks me down: / One day I'll have my death of him: / His greed has set the woods aflame; / He prowls more lordly than the sun." [11]

Such is the case of a daughter having great difficulty freeing herself emotionally from her infantile milieu. In psychological terms, Plath's untoward attachment for her father precipitated a conflict and ultimately a psychotic disturbance. Her libido, already sexually developed, poured into the Oedipal (Electral) mold and "set," in her poems and radio play and novel, in feelings and fantasies which until the time of composition had been totally unconscious and more or less inchoate.[12]

Jung differentiates between two types of conscious behavior as a consequence of the formation of intense resistances against such "immoral" impulses resulting from the activated complex. The first is direct, in which the daughter displays violent resistences against the mother and a particularly affectionate and dependent attitude toward the father. The second is indirect—or "compensated"—in which the daughter displays, instead of resistance to the mother, a marked submissiveness combined with "an irritated, antagonistic attitude" toward the father. Jung also acknowledges that these direct and compensated consequences can sometimes alternate, as they seem to have done in Plath. The heroine of *The Bell Jar* seems a perfectly-realized embodiment of Jung's first type of behavior; the protagonist of "Daddy" a violent example of his second. What we have is perhaps not so much an alternation of behavior as a development from one state into another. Certainly the poet of "Daddy" had grown into a depth of self-knowledge far beyond that possessed by the protagonist of the novel.

Naturally, if the sexual libido were to function unchecked in this manner, daughters would go about killing their mothers and sleeping with their fathers, or vice versa. Fortunately, in life the libido is forced to seek new love objects, as Plath did in marriage. These new subjects for affection, according to Jung, serve as a check against parricide and incest: "The continuous development of libido toward objects outside the family is perfectly normal and natural, and it is an abnormal and pathological phenomenon if the libido remains, as it were, glued to the family. Nevertheless, it is a phenomenon that can sometimes be observed in normal people." [13] Sylvia Plath's libido never became totally unglued. Only instead of ending in parricide ("Daddy") her identification with her father grew so intense she committed suicide. It is with a great sense of irony, then, that we turn to the penultimate page of Plath's first book, "A Note on the Type," and read there the publisher's innocent note: *The text of this book is set in Electra.*[14]

Jung has also said that experience shows the unknown approach of death often casts an *adumbratio*—an anticipatory shadow—over the life and the dreams of the victim. Plath's poems in this sense were her dreams, and a preparation for death expressed through art—words not unlike tales told at primitive initiations or Zen *koans*. The *Ariel* poems, her greatest achievement, rather than conforming to Christian orthodoxy, are formulated more on primitive thought drawn from outside historical tradition and taken from the psychic sources which have nourished religious and philosophical speculation about life and death since prehistoric times. A case can be built stating that such an *adumbratio* informs Plath's imagery from the first, as if her future suicide were casting its shadow *back* by arousing in her certain archetypes which, usually dormant, were tripped by death's approach. And while the specific shape of the archetypes in Plath is very personal, albeit confessional, the general pattern of the archetypes is collective. Her use of the yew tree, the rose, the moon, and the bee—while deriving from autobiography—have universal implications. One encounters parallels in Dante and Leopardi as well as in Coleridge and Eliot.

The first collection, *The Colossus* (1960), is the poems of a young woman whose mental disturbance can be detected in subject and image. Poet-critic Richard Howard even reads the poems' forms as unhealthy—the rhymes all slant, the end-stop avoided like a reproach—and calls the book a "breviary of estrangement." [15] More important, there are no people in this first book, only the poet's conflict between her need to reduce the demands of life to the unquestioning acceptance of a stone (what Howard calls "the lithic impulse") and the impulse to live on. Always in these first poems one observes Plath's identification with the lower forms of existence—mushrooms and moles, snakes and insects, stones and bones. Ultimately her search through the lower forms reaches an ultimate depth in whiteness and in death, not unlike Ahab's obsession with the whiteness of the whale. Every landscape in *The Colossus* is a nightmare-scape—or, as Jan B. Gordon would have it, a *psychescape*—of dead sea creatures and boat wrecks. (In her transitional poems, those written between that collection and the maturity of *Ariel*, Plath's vision lifts from the earth's depths and surfaces to the moon's and the clouds beyond. But there is no psychic relief, and her mental sickness becomes personified in many physical images of surgery and bandages as well.)

The first line of the first book contains an image for death: "The fountains are dry and the roses over. / Incense of death. Your day approaches." [16] In Plath's beginning is her end. Reversing the usual cause / effect progression, in the second poem we are given the cause of the previously posited effect: a medical student in a dissection room ("Buddy Willard"?) cruelly hands her "the cut-out heart like a cracked heirloom." His act seems the kind of male role which causes the spiritual death imaged in the opening poem. The dissection room is a microcosm of the world, and Buddy's is the ruling cold male intellect in a universe in which flesh, not spirit, prevails. Plath of course would beg that the male see both function and beauty, both flesh and spirit. The poem parallels the later "Pheasant," from *Crossing the Water*, in which the male also is callous and a destroyer.

The male principle of power and thrust is symbolized in the silver factory's undershirted workers and machinery of "Night Shift." The obvious analogies with the physiological function of sex are continued in a later poem, "Blackberrying," in which Plath also speaks of silversmiths "Beating and beating at an intractable metal"—a more violent sexual metaphor. (In "Years" she exclaims, "The piston in motion— / My soul dies before it.") Even the poem "Sow," which appears to render a fecund earth-mother type, is really "about" the state of the female when reduced to pure reproductive functions, the sow a symbol of the transmutation of the higher order into the lower. That Sylvia Plath saw herself so reduced is evident in the title poem, "The Colossus," in which she becomes a broken idol and issues from her lips "mule-bray, pig-grunt, and bawdy cackles." (This translation of the typically male colossus figure, e.g., the Colossus of Rhodes, into the female is typical of Plath's inversions, as we shall see. In her rebellion against typical sexist attitudes she reverses conventional male-female roles.)

The lowered estate of the female is seen in "Strumpet Song," in which Plath positions the Self as whore, made so perhaps because of her incestuous wishes, and in "Fever 103°," in which she calls all her selves "old whore petticoats." These denigrations of self finally give rise to a poetry of utter escape, and in both "The Eye-Mote" and "Ariel" Plath uses a horse as symbol of freedom. Then she confesses a desire for a return to the purity she possessed before the fact of men: "What I want back is what I was / Before the bed, before the knife." Such an unspoiled world is shown in "Hardcastle Crags." Man is seen as the spoiler, and in "Faun" he is projected as a Pan-figure—Pan traditionally being a figure dreaded by maidens, and rightfully so, with his overt sensuality, horns, pug-nose, and goat-feet. (Goats held none of the charm for Plath that they have for Picasso; in "Departure" she depicts them as "rank-haired" and "morose.")

It is Plath's hatred of men and the unhealthiness of her mental condition, then, which is figured in the title poem, "The Colossus," in which the poetess identifies with a broken idol out of the stream of civilization, one whose "hours are married to shadow." No longer does she "listen for the scrape of a keel / on the blank stones of the landing." Man, personified by a ship, has no place in her scheme. The marriage to shadow is Plath's marriage to the memory of her father, and therefore to death itself. The pull toward that condition is the subject of "Lorelei" as well as the central symbol of "A Winter Ship." That Plath perceived the nature of her own condition is clear not only in the identification with the broken idol of "The Colossus," but the broken vase of "The Stones" as well.

Plath makes a metaphor for her reversed misogyny in "The Bull of Bendylaw," in which she transmogrifies that traditionally feminine body, the sea—*la mere*—into a brute bull, a potent symbol for the active, masculine principle. The bull here is a symbol of both destruction and power (as the figure of the bull clearly expresses in all palaeo-oriental cultures). Yet our own reading must not stop there. As with many of Plath's symbols, there is a complexity, a muchness. According to Leo Frobenius, for example, a black bull is linked in the unconscious with the lower heaven, that is, with death.[17] This could be substantiated, one supposes, by the historical fact that in India the bodies of princes were burned specifically in bull-shaped coffins. Yet Jung would disagree, claiming in his *Symbols of Transformation* that the bull, like the he-goat, is a symbol for the father. And while it is possible to read "The Bull of Bendylaw" with all these suggestions in mind, the bull which overpowers the existing order by devouring the royal rose must, primarily, be seen as the male principle, personified by her dead father—a presence so real to Plath it ultimately caused her destruction. In the world of her private mythology, the sea and her father and herself become one. If the single rose is taken as a symbol of completion and wholeness and perfection, Plath says in this poem that her father destroyed all that—her sanity—with the line, "the royal rose in the bull's belly." This was a charge she was to repeat in "Daddy" and other poems.

In "All the Dead Dears" Plath acknowledges outwardly and not metaphorically the influence of relatives upon her own psyche:

> *From the mercury-backed glass*
> *Mother, grandmother, great-grandmother*
> *Reach hag hands to haul me in.*

But the pull of the past cannot be explored without further contemplation of the "daft father" who drowned himself, "With orange duck-feet winnowing his hair," an imaginative event explored at greater length in "Suicide Off Egg Rock," in which the father resolutely turns his back on the imperfect landscape.

The crime of renouncing his daughter is ultimately

equated by Plath with the Nazi destruction of the Jews. The first manifestation of this occurs in "The Thin People," who are at once the Jews and the ghosts of the past which haunt her. Then in "Frog Autumn" the "fold" who "thin / lamentably" are both frogs and all withering races with which she identifies. "Mary's Song" (from *Winter Trees*) continues the exploration of persecution, as does "Getting There" (from *Ariel*). The subject receives its fullest and most sensational treatment in the poem "Daddy" in which, as I have said, Plath literally becomes a Jew, her father a Nazi.

"Mushrooms," a very Roethkesque poem of Keatsian negative capability, seems to mean not what it appears to say, that the meek shall inherit the earth, but rather that the parasites shall prevail. Her father, in her view, was one of the latter living off her blood, which is the reason why at the conclusion she must drive a stake through his heart —as she literally does at the end of "Daddy," killing the vampire memory.

"The Ghost's Leavetaking," in which to awaken in the morning is to experience the Fall, mourns Plath's lost innocence and childhood. "Full Fathom Five" lays that lost innocence once again at the feet of her father. Alluding as it does by title to Ariel's speech from *The Tempest*,

> *Full fathom five thy father lies,*
> *Of his bones are coral made,*
> *Those are pearls that were his eyes . . .*

the poem begins with a god-figure, perhaps that of Neptune, perhaps that of a god of that other dark deep place, the unconscious; then progresses to the death of her own father in his "Shelled bed" (never the hospital bed!). She concludes that she herself is like a fish, finding the air she breathes killing, and would breathe water with her father instead. Her search for such a father / god figure can only end in death.

In "Man in Black" the figure of the father clad in "dead / Black" balanced on the spit of stone in the sea is the figure of Death who stands on the shred of Plath's sanity, the balance of which can be tipped by evoking the father figure. Indeed men in black pervade all of that later book, *Ariel*, as well, culminating in "Years" in which God is seen clad in "vacuous black." The search for the father and the search for The Father, as in Roethke and Kunitz, ultimately become one. And just as the impulse to enter water was seen in "Full Fathom Five" and "The Lorelei," Plath would become a mussel in "Mussel Hunter at Rock Harbor," a poem in which she pursues the Wholly Other. The body of the fiddler-crab, one who "saved / Face, to face the bald-faced sun," seems also a symbol for the father.

Only once in *The Colossus*, in "The Disquieting Muses," is the mother really portrayed. Then it is as one who is comforting but ineffectual in protecting the daughter from Mother Nature. ("Point Shirley," on the other hand, de-·picts Plath's genuine love for her grandmother.) Plath's attitude toward her mother is tempered, as I have said, by an unconscious feeling of rivalry and resentment. It also may derive from her feelings toward the institution of marriage generally, and particularly in her own case. Her fullest treatment of this in the first book is the veiled little poem, "Spinster," which is a literary curiosity. The overall tone and diction of the poem are clearly derived from John Crowe Ransom ("By this tumult afflicted . . ."; "a burgeoning / Unruly enough to pitch her five queenly wits / Into vulgar motley—"; and other Ransomed kidnappings). Yet Plath's story of the maiden who retreated from love is a neat parable of the necessity for a woman-poet to resist the temptation of "romance." Read in such a manner, the poem gives up undeniable echoes of Elinor Wylie ("Puritan Sonnet") in stanza three; and Edna St. Vincent Millay ("Spring," with its celebrated image of the season as a babbling idiot strewing flowers) in stanza four. In writing of the feminine artist's necessity for independence from the male, Plath invokes—purposefully, I would submit—the work of two very independent woman poets.

Perhaps the most overt of all incestuous poems is "The Beekeeper's Daughter," in which the father, "Hieratical" in his frock coat, is a father / priest who initiates the daughter into holy mysteries. The beehive is seen as the boudoir, a place rich in sexual suggestion and appealing so immensely to Plath's imagination because it ironically inverts the double standard, making the queen bee the goddess of the harem, the males all drones. Incestuous suggestions are found in the lines,

> *Here is a queenship no mother can contest—*
> *A fruit that's death to taste; dark flesh, dark parings.*

I suggest the latter word is a pun, conscious or unconscious, on dark "pairings"—pairings which can end only in insanity or death. That Plath sees the poem's sacred marriage as an incestuous one cannot be doubted:

> *Father, bridegroom, in this Easter egg . . .*
> *The queen bee marries the winter of your year.*

This is a poem of a defiant spirit, albeit an unhealthy one. Here too is the explanation for the situation of the volume's final poem, "The Stones," perhaps the only poem in the entire first volume which truly points the way to Plath's more mature style and approach. With its first sentence, "This is the city where men are mended," we are pitched into a mental institution where the poet finds herself after falling from grace into the "stomach of indifference." In the tenth stanza she re-creates the experience of electric shock treatment. As in "The Colossus," Plath gives us an image for the broken self—this time a vase which must be mended. Like that earlier poem which eschewed the possibility or even the desirability of love, we are here told that "Love is the bone and sinew of my curse." The devoured rose of "The Bull of Bendylaw," here clearly a symbol of Plath's spirit, is momentarily resurrected: "The vase, reconstructed, houses / the elusive rose." And in the last line she tells us, "I shall be good as new."

But of course she will not be, and knows that she will not be. A vase once broken is never totally new again. The seams always show, no matter how cleverly held together. The permanent damage to Plath's psyche is manifest in the other three volumes which follow.

The poems of *Crossing the Water*, written during 1960 and 1961, a transitional period between *The Colossus* and the late work of *Ariel* and *Winter Trees*, continue Plath's preoccupations with death, drowning, and terminations. The feminine protest against the masculine ego, will, and violence, seen in the earlier collections, is first manifest here in "Pheasant," in which Plath urges the aggressive male to "Let be. Let be." [18] (In *Three Women* Plath's one contented wife is compared to and empathizes with a pheasant.) In Plath, man's rage for order is as despicable as his violence. If woman gives in to man, she becomes the robotlike modern female of "An Appearance": "From her lips ampersands and percent signs / Exit like kisses." Elsewhere, in "A Birthday Present" (from *Ariel*), Plath rails against the rigidity of "adhering to rules, to rules, to rules."

"I Am Vertical" announces, on the obvious level, the poet's death-wish. But buried in the language is protest against the image of woman as seen by the male chauvinist pig:

Nor am I the beauty of a garden bed
Attracting my share of Ahs and spectacularly painted,
Unknowing I must soon unpetal.

The real components of this statement are evident. The symbolic components only less so: "the beauty" who is "spectacularly painted" and who receives her share of "Ahs" from admirers is no flower, but modern woman who must dutifully "unpetal" for the male in that not-so Edenic (garden) bed, the nuptial.

A new preoccupation merges in this second collection, that of lost youth. "The Baby Sitters" is pure nostalgia, and indeed "Face Lift" is the fantasy of a woman who wishes to appear with her face rendered "Pink and smooth as a baby," perhaps a metaphor for Plath's desire to become again her daddy's little girl. "Parliament Hill Fields," the next poem, displays a sensibility numb to adult responsibilities and emotions; the death of the narrator's own infant is described as barely entering her consciousness—perhaps prompted by the narrator's own desire never to cease being a child herself, which the condition of motherhood would make impossible. The wish to return to childlike innocence is seen in "Child" (from *Winter Trees*) as well. This theme of aging reaches its apogee in "Mirror":

In me she has drowned a young girl, and in me an old woman
Rises toward her day after day, like a terrible fish.

The earlier preoccupation with split personality, in "The Colossus" and "The Stones," is bettered by "In Plaster," which explores the dualities of sane / insane, saint / sinner, wife / daughter. It also repeats the symbol of the rose as soul. Surprisingly, the volume contains several poems in praise of heterosexual relations, such as "Love Letter" and "Widow"—a portrait of a woman's loss of identity without the company of a man. "Heavy Women," by way of contrast, portrays each mother as a Virgin Mary. But more often Plath is one with her own "Candles": that is, "Nun-souled, they burn heavenward and never marry." (In "Small Hours" she describes herself as "nun-hearted.") When a baby is born to her, "a black gap discloses itself" and she feels "dismembered." She would like to conform to the world's expectations of her as a thoroughly modern mother, stated satirically as a "Mother of a white Nike and several bald-eyed Apollos," to become part and parcel of the mechanized male-oriented world, and even to contribute to it. But she cannot. "The Tour" satirizes and ridicules the "normal" domestic scene, with its bald wife and exploding furnace, a machine gone wrong, a machine which, predictably true to Plath's mythology, disfigures the female.

The depersonalized male appears in "The Surgeon at 2 A.M." (a poem which should be compared in vision and intention with the earlier "Two Views of a Cadavar Room"). In the later poem a doctor sees human flesh as nothing more than "a pathological salami," something less efficient and desirable than "a clean, pink plastic limb." In his white coat he walks apparently godlike among the wards; in reality he is not human, let alone godly. He is as impersonal as the Danish jeweller in "On Deck," a man who "is carving / A perfectly faceted wife to wait / On him hand and foot, quiet as a diamond"—a vision the Women's Lib gang will find right-on. As doubtless they would applaud Plath's nightmare visions of the "Zoo-Keeper's Wife," that sensitive soul lost in a world of hairy, obscene beasts who copulate out of pure boredom. The animals and the male are here inseparable. As heartless as the earlier medical student, and later the surgeon, this Mellors figure of a zoo-keeper "checked the diet charts and took me to play / With the boa constrictor in the Fellow's Garden." The snake here is the powerful crushing phallic principle. The destructive element pervades the poem, nowhere more harrowingly than in the image of the "bear-furred, bird-eating spider / Clambering round its glass box like an eight-fingered hand." Plath is the bird devoured.

This then is Sylvia Plath's psychological view of life, and all the preoccupations of the first two books are summarized in the final lines of "A Life":

Age and terror, like nurses, attend her,
And a drowned man, complaining of the great cold,
Crawls up out of the sea.

The ghost of her father is with her yet.

After these beginnings Plath played only theme variations in her two remaining books (Ariel, which was published soon after Plath's death; and Winter Trees, which was not, although its poems were written at the same time as those of Ariel, during the last nine months of her life).[19] The title poem, "Winter Trees," for instance, displays Plath's identification with trees (the name Sylvia, after all, is the feminine form of Sylvanus, "living in the wood") and her envy of them for their freedom from woman's fate of copulation, abortion, and bitchery. Tree weddings are seen as merely the quiet accretion of new growth-rings; their seedings are totally effortless, unlike the sweat and heave of human procreation. Like Leda, they are full of wings and otherworldliness. (When Zeus coupled with Leda, he did so in the form of a swan.) Yet we should not forget that in Plath's radio play, Three Women, one of the three equates winter trees with death, perhaps the natural conclusion of such inhuman congress. Another of the women cries that there "is a snake in swans." Sex in any form seems to repel.

The poem is followed by a series of bitter portraits of men. Unlike the zoo-keeper of the previous volume, the "Gigolo" in the poem of that title is repellent not for his sweat and animalism, but for his clean efficiency and glitter. He is possibly an *animus* figure for Plath, who elsewhere was concerned with female prostitutes. Yet he is no less repellent than the zoo-keeper, with his "way of turning / Bitches to ripples of silver." Here is yet another man who, in seeing women as mere instruments, becomes himself such an instrument. The gigolo is also the male as Narcissus, a new exhibit in Plath's chamber of horrors. He is soon joined by "Purdah," Sultan, who is "Lord of the mirrors." The poem's violent climax is the assassination of the male ego by one who has been too long a mere member of the harem.

"The Rabbit Catcher" performs the role of the male who snares his prey, in a world which is "a place of force." (We recall the passage from *The Bell Jar* about the male treachery of anesthesia in childbirth.) Like rabbits, women are caught to attend the brute violence; like hunters, men have minds "like a ring / Sliding shut on some quick thing." The rabbit, we assume, was chosen not only for its fecundity but also for its connotations of the world of subhuman instinct. Plath concludes with the confession that such constriction kills her as well. After which, as in "Stopped Dead," there is always "a goddamn baby screaming." (In "Lesbos" there is always "a stink of fat and baby crap.") The car stopped just short of the cliff's edge is a figure for Plath's life, especially her marriage, an event which left her suspended just above the abyss. We can only wonder that she did marry, and not have just one child but two. But then she herself gives us her own interpretation for her action in "Daddy," which I discuss shortly.

Such discord between the sexes is communicated not only by the male narcissism of "Gigolo" and "Purdah" but also through the absenteeism of the father in "For a Fatherless Son" and "By Candlelight." [20] The latter is a satirical poem, spoken somewhat in the chiding voice of "The Tour." The almighty male, reduced to a "little brassy Atlas" statue, is at best a poor heirloom. As a figure for the absent father and husband, he has no child or wife, nothing save his masculine bluster—bawdily synthesized in the image of his five brass balls, which he can use "To juggle with, my love, when the sky falls."

Another satirical male portrait is that of the friend's husband in "Lesbos," whose "Jew-Mama guards his sweet sex like a pearl" and whose wife used to play-act quick orgasms to thrill her lovers. In such a world the image of woman—traditionally identified with the moon—now is nothing more than a "bloody bag." The logical conclusion is that "Every woman's a whore." (The statement has been made implicitly earlier in "Strumpet Song.")

The roles women must play, then, is the theme of *Winter Trees*: daughter, beloved, wife, mother, girl friend, sister, friend of girls—they are all explored in the "Poem for Three Voices," *Three Women*, which concludes the volume. Plath chooses three different attitudes to be embodied by her characters. The first is a woman who is gladly a mother. The second, one who loses her child through miscarriage. And the third is one who gives her child, unwanted, away.

The mother who retains her child accepts her lot as naturally as a seed breaks. It is the second and the third who seem to speak for Plath, however, the second finding men flat as cardboard, a flatness which she herself caught like some fatal disease:

> *That flat, flat, flatness from which ideas, destructions,*
> *Bulldozers, guillotines, white chambers of shrieks*
> *　proceed . . .*

And the third envisioning women as victims of men's torturing:

> *They hug their flatness like a kind of health.*
> *And what if they found themselves surprised, as I did?*
> *They would go mad with it.*

Indeed, this unlikely shared vision of male "flatness" by both women can be seen as a shortcoming of the play. Plath stacks her deck too high. Clearly all three women are, in many ways, aspects of Plath's personality. Even the docile mother-wife confesses that she too is too open: "it is as if my heart / Put on a face and walked into the world." In a prayer echoing "Born Yesterday," a poem of Philip Larkin's, she begs that her child be unexceptional, for "It is the exception that interests the devil. / It is the exception that climbs the sorrowful hill."

Sylvia Plath, an exceptional individual, climbed that hill to the summit. The full revelation of her agony comes in *Ariel*, her most famous book, and the one which contains her most striking poems. What one must realize, however, is that the poems of all four books were written between 1959 and her death in February 1963. As the shapes of the poems grow sparer and sparer, the tones darker and darker, she follows her father into the small end of the funnel. The poems are all part of one great confession. The publication, seven years after *Ariel*, of the poems in *Crossing the Water* and *Winter Trees*, shows us how wholly obsessed with her themes Plath really was. *Ariel* was no one-shot love affair with death. She courted it all her life, and won.

Ariel is filled with poems of marriage, estrangement, and suicide—a pattern which follows that of Plath's life. In the marriage poems the modern wife is "A living doll" who performs mechanical functions ("It can sew, it can cook, / It can talk, talk, talk"). Here the mechanistic images of "A Vision" (in *Crossing the Water*) become more pointed and satirical. In "Tulips" the wife sees the smiles of her husband and child as "hooks," that is, as lures to snare and catch her. She would rather return to her nunlike state, being afraid of human emotions and feelings.

Ironically, emotion is strong in Plath's poems of estrangement. Her estrangement from her own children is the subject of "Morning Song"; and that from her husband the subject of "The Couriers." In the latter the wedding band is tested and found to be nothing but fool's gold:

> A *ring of gold with the sun in it?*
> *Lies. Lies and a grief.*

Here as in "A Winter Ship," Plath employs the sun as the symbol of unattainable happiness. Finally, the theme of estrangement from the father is pursued, with parables of the lost lamb looking for the promised land and the Good Shepherd serving as vehicles for her own search for the earthly father. She fears, in "Sheep in Fog," that her own search will lead instead to a "starless and fatherless" heaven, into dark waters. Such dark waters are the subject of "Lady Lazarus," a much-quoted poem in which Plath compares herself to that biblical figure once resurrected by Christ, and also to a cat with its nine lives, because she has been "resurrected" from attempted suicide three times. The poem is also an act of revenge on the male ego.

> *Out of the ash*
> *I rise with my red hair*
> *And I eat men like air.*

Emasculation of the female occurs in "Cut," in which the lacerated thumb is a "little pilgrim" whose scalp has been axed by an Indian. Plath is the pilgrim, her husband (or all men) the savage, an Indian as well as a Kamikaze man or Ku Klux Klanner—any man violent and unmindful of humane values and depriving the female. In "Elm" we find another outward symbol for Plath's inner injuries, with that poem's concluding two stanzas presenting an implicit image of the Medusa, whose "snaky acids kiss." The Medusa is introduced here also for its connotations of guilt. In mythology she was a once-beautiful maiden whose hair was changed into snakes by Athena in consequence for her having had carnal knowledge of Poseidon in one of Athena's temples. The act resulted in the birth of both Chrysaor and Pegasus. Plath develops this theme of guilt more completely in the poem titled "Medusa," in which she communicates with her unconscious, becoming the poetess with a divining rod who summons the image of the Father-God who is "always there, / Tremulous breath at the end of my line." If Plath is at the end of her rope, it is, she feels, the father's fault. The lust in the temple is incest in the sacred home, an obscenity instead of something sacred. This attitude toward sex permeates "Berck-Plage" as well.

The male predator becomes Death the predator in "Death & Co." Because she feels continually victimized, Plath can identify with the Jews in "Getting There." Ideally she would unite this male element with the female, the bestial with the poetic, as she does symbolically in "Ariel." In that poem she is a woman poet riding Pegasus (offspring of Medusa!). But as a woman riding the godly horse, Plath becomes a female centaur, another inversion of the usual male order, with the creature half-man, half-horse becoming half-woman, half-horse. This inversion is related to the image of the order of the beehive, another sexually inverted symbol. A. Alvarez is correct in noting of "Ariel" that "the detail is all inward. It is as though the horse itself were an emotional state." [21] But Alvarez is too simplistic in saying the poem is "about tapping the roots of her own inner violence." Rather, mounted on Ariel, hers is at once the drive toward death, toward God, the moth toward the flame and the red eye of morning.

The drive toward God is explored in "The Moon and the Yew Tree," in which Plath identifies with the moon and longs for religious belief. The moon identification is simple to comprehend, with its connotations of the imagination and the maternal, its mysterious connection between the lunar cycle and the menstrual cycle. Like woman, the moon is the celestial body which suffers painful changes in shape (as did Plath in pregnancy). There is also a parallel between Plath's being subject to changes as is the moon, with both hiding their dark sides. The moon is a female symbol because it is the passive sphere, only reflecting the glory of the male sun, a state of being similar to Plath's view of the conventional roles assigned wife and husband.

The poem's other central symbol, the yew tree, is also a conventional one, traditionally implying inexhaustible life and immortality. The ancient tree also seems to me to function here as a representative of the growth and development of Plath's psychic life as distinct from the instinctual life symbolized by animals such as the rabbit and the horse Ariel. That it is an important symbol to her is implicit in the fact that the yew appears in other poems, "Little Fugue" and "The Munich Mannequins" as well. In "The Moon and the Yew Tree" the tree's "Gothic shape" reinforces the implication that Plath aspired toward Christian belief and the Church, a quest which was to end only in coldness and blackness. There is no comfort to be found in institutional Christianity. Yet she repeats her desire to see, and therefore to enter the temple of God, in "A Birthday Present," the poem which follows. But ultimately religion fails her, and only through hallucination does she achieve Paradise, as in "Fever 103°," of which Plath herself wrote, "This poem is about two kinds of fire—the fires of hell, which merely agonize, and the fires of heaven, which purify. During the poem, the first sort of fire suffers itself into the second." [22]

The only way Plath was to achieve relief, to become an independent Self, was to kill her father's memory, which in "Daddy" she does by a metaphorical murder of the father figure. Making her father a Nazi and herself a Jew, she dramatizes the war in her soul. It is a terrible poem, full of blackness, one of the most nakedly confessional poems ever written. From its opening image onward, that of the father as a "black shoe" in which the daughter has lived for thirty years—an explicitly phallic image, according to Freud—the sexual pull and tug is manifest, as is the degree of Plath's mental suffering, supported by references to Dachau, Auschwitz, and Belsen. (Elsewhere in Plath the references to hanged men also are emblems of suffering while swinging. In Jungian psychology the swinging motion would be symbolic of her ambivalent state and her unfulfilled longing as well.) Plath then confesses that, after failing to escape her predicament through suicide, she married a surrogate father, "A man in black with a Meinkampf look" who obligingly was just as much a vampire of her spirit—one who "drank my blood for a year, / Seven years, if you want to know." (Sylvia Plath was married to the poet Ted Hughes for seven years.) When Plath drives the stake through her father's heart, she not only is exorcising the demon of her father's memory, but metaphorically is killing her husband and all men as well.

It is a poem of total rejection. And when she writes that "The black telephone's off at the root," she is turning her back on the modern world as well. Such rejection of family and society leads to that final rejection, that of the Self. Plath's suicide is predicted everywhere in the book, in poems of symbolic annihilation such as "Totem" and statements of human fascination with death, such as "Edge"—in which to be dead is to be perfected. Plath's earlier terror at death becomes a romance with it, and her poems themselves are what M. L. Rosenthal called "yearnings toward that condition." [23] Freud believed the aim of all life is death, and for Plath life was poetry. By extension, then, poetry for Plath became death, both conditions inseparable. She herself as much as said so: "The blood jet is poetry, / There is no stopping it." In the act of committing her confession to paper, she was committing her life to death. The source of her creative energy was her self-destructiveness. She did not have Mrs. Sexton's or Roethke's humor to save her. (Instead of committing suicide, Roethke continually became a child again.)

And what burden of her life led Plath to cancel it? Many, surely. But none so overpowering as the psychological necessity to link herself with her father, spiritually and physically. Suicide then became a sexual act, the deathbed the marriage bed. This obsession is nowhere more apparent than in the four bee poems which, as an informal group, are the glory of the concluding pages of *Ariel*. Plath's fascination with bees, of course, is yet another attempt to reconstruct her father's life. Not only that Otto Plath was the author of a book on bumblebees, I have noted; but also bees themselves, with their monarchic organization, are a potent symbol for order and obedience. To be a bee is to report to an authority figure.

"The Bee Meeting" opens with a vivid imaging of Plath's vulnerability before the hive. In the poem all the villagers but her are protected from the bees, and she equates this partial nudity with her condition of being unloved. In the symbolic marriage ceremony which follows, a rector, a mid-wife, and Plath herself—a bride clad in black—appear. Plath seems always to remember that even the arrows which Eros used to shoot into the ground to create new life were poisoned darts. And just as her search for a Divine Father was tempered by her fear there was none, so too her search for consolation from her earthly father created an intensity of consciousness in which she no longer had any guarantee of security. Eros was for her ever accompanied by the imminence of death. We are reminded here of the frequent word play, in Italian literature, between *amore*, love, and *morte*, death.[24] Certainly every mythology relates the sex act to the act of dying, most clearly perhaps in the tale of Tristan and Iseult. And in nature the connection is even more explicit. Sylvia Plath's personal mythology of the hive anticipates this: the male bee always dies after inseminating the queen. When the central figure of authority, the queen, is her father, the daughter / worker must die after the incestuous act, as she does at the conclusion of "The Bee Meeting." The long white box in the grove is in fact her own coffin; only in this light can she answer her own questions, "what have they accomplished, why am I cold?"

In the second bee poem, "The Arrival of the Bee Box," the coffin analogy is made again, and Plath confesses she "can't keep away from it." The unintelligible syllables of the bees are the mystery of the unknown, the cipher of her life and her father's. In "Stings" she herself becomes the queen, the Self that needs recovering captured in a wax house, a mausoleum. The queen is the father and the daughter united, for by assuming his body she effectively kills him (just as Freud assured us the joining of the bodies in sexual congress results in a kind of death, speaking of the "likeness of the condition of that following complete sexual satisfaction to dying, and for the fact that death coincides with the act of copulation in lower aniamsls. These creatures die in the act of reproduction because, after Eros has been eliminated through the process of satisfaction, the death instinct has a free hand for accomplishing its purpose").[25] Such a symbolic death of her father provided for Plath enormous psychic and physical release, and the occasion for one final invective against men ("Winter-ing"):

> *The bees are all women,*
> *Maids and the long royal lady.*
> *They have got rid of the men,*
>
> *The blunt, clumsy stumblers, the boors.*[26]

Sylvia Plath ended her life in the early morning of February 11, 1963. At the time she was living separately from her husband.

Notes

Introduction

1. "The Art of Poetry," an interview with Allen Ginsberg by Tom Clark, *Paris Review*, 37 (Spring 1966), 13–55.

1 — The Confessional Mode in Modern American Poetry

1. *The New Poets* (New York: Oxford University Press, 1967), p. 23.

2. "A Meaning of Robert Lowell," *Hudson Review*, 20, No. 3 (Autumn 1967). Reprinted in *Robert Lowell: A Portrait of the Artist in His Time*, ed. Michael London and Robert Boyers (New York: David Lewis, 1970), p. 222.

3. Dan Wakefield, "Novel Bites Man," *Atlantic*, 206, No. 2 (August 1970).

4. See "Poetry Therapy," *Time*, 13 March 1972, p. 33.

5. "The Art of Poetry XV," *Paris Review*, 52 (Summer 1971), 158.

6. *Sappho: A New Translation*, trans. Mary Barnard (Berkeley and Los Angeles: University of California Press, 1958), p. 6.

7. *The Poems of Catullus*, trans. and with an introduction by Horace Gregory (New York: Grove Press, 1956), p. 151.

8. *Leaves of Grass and Selected Prose*, ed. and with an introduction by Sculley Bradley (New York: Rinehart & Co., 1949), p. 107.

9. T. S. Eliot, "Tradition and the Individual Talent," *The Sacred Wood* (London: Methuen & Co., 1928). Reprinted in *Modern Poets on Modern Poetry*, ed. James Scully (London: Fontana, 1966), pp. 58–68.

10. Interview with Robert Lowell by Frederick Seidel, in *Writers at Work: The "Paris Review" Interviews*, Ser. 2, ed. Malcolm Cowley (New York: Viking Press, 1963), p. 347.

11. Anne Sexton, "The Barfly Ought to Sing," *Tri-Quarterly*, 10 (Fall 1966), 89.

12. "Craft Interview with Anne Sexton," *New York Quarterly*, 1, No. 3 (Summer 1970), 8–12.

13. "The Art of Poetry XV," p. 158.

14. Robert Lowell, "Foreword," in *Ariel*, by Sylvia Plath (New York: Harper & Row, 1966), p. ix.

15. "The Art of Poetry XV," p. 160.

16. "The Barfly Ought to Sing," p. 89.

17. Ibid.

18. T. S. Eliot, "Hamlet and His Problems," *Selected Essays* (New York: Harcourt, Brace & Co., 1932).

19. Barnard translation, p. 6.

20. For discussions of the *anima* and *animus,* two of the archetypes in Jungian analysis, see chapter 1 ("Concerning the Archetypes, with Special Reference to the Anima Concept") of *The Archetypes and the Collective Unconscious,* in *Collected Works of C. G. Jung,* Vol. 9, Part 1, ed. G. Adler et al., trans. R. F. C. Hull, 2nd ed. (Princeton: Princeton University Press, 1969); chapter 3 ("The Syzygy: Anima and Animus") of *Aion: Contributions to the Symbolism of the Self,* in *Collected Works of C. G. Jung,* Vol. 9, Part 2, ed. G. Adler et al., trans. R. F. C. Hull, 2nd ed. (Princeton: Princeton University Press, 1968); chapter 3 ("The Relations Between the Ego and the Unconscious") in *The Basic Writings of C. G. Jung,* ed. Violet De Laszlo (New York: Modern Library, 1959).

21. "The Art of Poetry XV," p. 160.

22. The wording was identical in both Roethke's "An American Poet Introduces Himself and His Poems," BBC Broadcast (30 July 1953), Disc #SLO 34254; and also in "Theodore Roethke," in *Twentieth Century Authors,* 1st suppl., ed. Stanley J. Kunitz and H. Haycraft (New York: H. W. Wilson, 1955), pp. 837–38.

23. "Note," in *His Toy, His Dream, His Rest* (New York: Farrar, Straus & Giroux, 1968), p. ix.

24. "Afterthought," in *Notebook* (New York: Farrar, Straus & Giroux, 1969), p. 159.

25. "An Interview with James Merrill," *Contemporary Literature,* 9 (Winter 1968), 1–2.

26. "Craft Interview with Anne Sexton," p. 11.

27. *A Poet's Alphabet* (New York: McGraw-Hill, 1970), p. 370.

28. "Robert Lowell: The Poetry of Cancellation," *London*

Magazine, 6, No. 3 (June 1966). Reprinted in *Robert Lowell. A Portrait of the Artist in His Time*, pp. 187–98.

29. Robert Lowell, "To Delmore Schwartz," in *Life Studies* (New York: Farrar, Straus and Cudahy, 1959), p. 54. If Schwartz indeed spoke these lines, he was misquoting, for his own purposes, a line from stanza 7 of Wordsworth's "Resolution and Independence."

Schwartz was known as one of the most brilliant conversationalists of his time. Related to the above quote is one from James Scully's *Avenue of the Americas* (Amherst: University of Massachusetts Press, 1972), in which he has Delmore Schwartz saying, "Even paranoids have enemies."

30. Interview with Anne Sexton, *Talks with Authors*, ed. Charles F. Madden (Carbondale, Ill.: Southern Illinois University Press, 1968), p. 160.

2—Robert Lowell

1. A. Alvarez, "Robert Lowell in Conversation," *London Observer*, 21 July 1963. Reprinted in *Profile of Robert Lowell*, ed. Jerome Mazzaro (Columbus, Ohio: C. E. Merrill Co., 1971), pp. 32–40.

2. Interview with Robert Lowell by Frederick Seidel, in *Writers at Work: The "Paris Review" Interviews*, Ser. 2, ed. Malcolm Cowley (New York: Viking Press, 1963), p. 346.

3. *The New Poets* (New York: Oxford University Press, 1967), p. 76.

4. "Poetry in a Prose World: Robert Lowell's 'Life Studies,' " *Modern Poetry Studies*, 1 No. 4 (1970), 182.

5. This interpretation is not uniquely mine. The fact is, the few poems of *Life Studies* have been so thoroughly mined for meaning that almost anything one can say about them has been touched upon in one way or other by someone else. I am pleased to note my indebtedness especially to the books by Hugh B. Staples, Jerome Mazzaro, and Richard J. Fein.

6. Philip Cooper, *The Autobiographical Myth of Robert Lowell* (Chapel Hill: University of North Carolina Press, 1970), p. 63.

7. *Life Studies* (New York: Farrar, Straus and Cudahy, 1959), p. 51. All quotations are from the original American hardbound edition, to which Lowell added a poem for the American paperback and deleted the prose passage for the British edition.

8. Richard J. Fein, *Robert Lowell* (New York: Twayne Publishers, Inc., 1970), p. 52.

9. "Robert Lowell in Conversation," in *Profile of Robert Lowell*, p. 33.

10. Jerome Mazzaro, *The Poetic Themes of Robert Lowell* (Ann Arbor: University of Michigan Press, 1965), p. 111.

11. From *Collected Poems of Marya Zaturenska* (New York: Viking Press, 1965), p. 209.

12. *The Poetic Themes of Robert Lowell*, p. 112.

13. "Poetry in a Prose World," p. 182.

14. Here and elsewhere in this study my interpretations of symbols depend heavily upon symbological studies by C. G. Jung and J. E. Cirlot.

15. *The Poetic Themes of Robert Lowell*, p. 116.

16. *The Contemporary Poet as Artist and Critic* ed. Anthony Ostroff (Boston: Little, Brown and Co., 1964), pp. 84–110.

17. *Robert Lowell* (New York: Twayne Publishers, Inc., 1970), pp. 63–68.

18. "On Robert Lowell's 'Skunk Hour,'" *The Contemporary Poet as Artist and Critic*, p. 87.

19. *Robert Lowell: The First Twenty Years* (London: Faber and Faber, Ltd., 1962), p. 81.

20. "Despondency and Madness," *The Contemporary Poet as Artist and Critic*, p. 99.

21. *The Achievement of Robert Lowell* (Glenview: Scott, Foresman, 1966), p. 12.

3 — W. D. Snodgrass and the Sad Hospital of the World

1. "A Note on S. S. Gardons," *Western Humanities Review*, 25, No. 3 (Summer 1971), 253.

2. "Finding a Poem," *Partisan Review* (Spring 1959).

3. "Master's In the Verse Patch Again," *The Contemporary Poet as Artist and Critic*, ed. Anthony Ostroff (Boston: Little, Brown and Co., 1964), p. 114.

4. "After Experience Taught Me . . . ," in *After Experience* (New York: Harper & Row, 1968), p. 39. All references to poems in this book are to the original hardbound edition.

5. "Public Intimacy," *Nation*, 16 Sept. 1968, p. 252.

6. All quotes from *Heart's Needle* are from the original edition (New York: Alfred A. Knopf, 1959). No paperback has been published.

7. Donald T. Torchiana, "Heart's Needle: Snodgrass Strides Through the Universe," in *Poets in Progress: Critical Prefaces to Thirteen Contemporary Americans*, ed. Edward B. Hungerford (Evanston: Northwestern University Press, 1967), p. 114.

8. Torchiana, who seems to know Snodgrass personally, identifies the Mahler song as the *Lob des Hohen Verstands* and the girl as Rachel Chester, a promising young painter; the girl of the moth lore lessons, as one of Jan Snodgrass's daughters by a previous marriage; and the dying man as Fritz Jarck, whom Snodgrass had attended in a hospital. This must surely be the same Old Fritz of the later poem, "A Flat One" (in *After Experience*).

9. "Fishing the Swamp: The Poetry of W. D. Snodgrass," *Modern American Poetry: Essays in Criticism*, ed. Jerome Mazzaro (New York: David McKay Co., 1970), p. 358.

10. Ibid., p. 359.

11. Ibid., p. 361.

12. The Valk translation is readily available in *Modern European Poetry*, ed. Willis Barnstone (New York Bantam Books, Inc., 1966).

13. "A Prefatory Note on the Author," unsigned preface to *Remains: Poems by S. S. Gardons*. Limited edition. (Mt. Horeb, Wis.: Perishable Press, Ltd., 1969). All references are to this edition.

14. *Western Humanities Review*, 25, No. 3 (Summer 1971), 253.

4—Anne Sexton

1. "Author's Note," *Live or Die* (Boston: Houghton Mifflin Co., 1966), p. xi. All six of Mrs. Sexton's books were published by this firm. Quotations are from the original editions.

2. *Babel to Byzantium* (New York: Farrar, Straus & Giroux, 1968), p. 133.

3. "A Place in the Country," *Hudson Review*, 22, No. 2 (Summer 1969), 34.

4. *Contemporary American Poetry* (New York: Random House, 1966), p. 221.

5. "The Art of Poetry XV," *Paris Review*, 52 (Summer 1971), 182.

6. "Oh, I Was Very Sick," *New York Times*, 9 Nov. 1969, pp. D1, D7.

7. *Talks with Authors,* ed. Charles F. Madden (Carbondale, Ill.: Southern Illinois University Press, 1968), p. 162.

8. "Oh, I Was Very Sick," p. D7.

9. *Contemporary American Poetry,* p. 232.

10. "The Art of Poetry XV," p. 187.

11. Beverly Fields, "The Poetry of Anne Sexton," in *Poets in Progress: Critical Prefaces to Thirteen Contemporary Americans,* ed. Edward B. Hungerford (Evanston: Northwestern University Press, 1967), p. 284.

12. "The Art of Poetry XV," p. 163.

13. Anne Sexton, *Transformations,* with a preface by Kurt Vonnegut, Jr. (Boston: Houghton Mifflin Co., 1971), pp. 56–57.

14. A sixth collection, *The Book of Folly,* was published after completion of this study.

5—John Berryman's Literary Offenses

1. "The Poetry of John Berryman," *New York Review of Books,* 28 May 1964, p. 3.

2. Ibid.

3. *His Toy, His Dream, His Rest* (New York: Farrar, Straus & Giroux, 1968), p. 188. All quotations are from the original, separate editions. A single-volume edition of all *The Dream Songs* was issued for a book club at a later date. Pagination naturally differs.

4. *77 Dream Songs* (New York: Farrar, Straus & Giroux, 1964), pp. 9, 83. Original, separate edition.

5. "Savage, Rueful, Irrepressible Henry," *New York Times Book Review,* 3 Nov. 1968, p. 1.

6. *Stephen Crane* (New York: William Sloane Assoc., 1950).

7. "The Poetry of John Berryman," p. 3.

8. Richard Kostelanetz, "Conversation with Berryman," *Massachusetts Review,* 11, No. 2 (Spring 1970), 343.

9. "Cagey John: Berryman as Medicine Man," *Centennial Review,* 12, No. 3 (Summer 1968), 334.

10. Christopher Ricks, "Recent American Poetry," *Massachusetts Review,* 11, No. 2 (Spring 1970), 313.

11. *Love & Fame* (New York: Farrar, Straus & Giroux, 1970), p. 48. [Berryman dropped poems from the 2nd printing.]

12. "Adagia," in *Opus Posthumous,* ed. Samuel French Morse (New York: Alfred A. Knopf, 1957). Reprinted as "Selec-

tions from 'Adagia,' " in *Modern Poets on Modern Poetry*, ed. James Scully (London: Fontana, 1966), p. 157.

13. "A Retrospect," in *Pavannes and Divisions* (1918). Reprinted in *Modern Poets on Modern Poetry*, pp. 28–43.

14. "A General Introduction for My Work," *Essays and Introductions* (New York: Macmillan Co., 1961). Reprinted in *Modern Poets on Modern Poetry*, pp. 13–27.

15. "False Confessions," *Shenandoah*, 22, No. 2 (Winter 1971), 86–88.

16. My earlier reservations about Mazzaro's Augustinian parallels must be qualified after reading Berryman's *Paris Review* interview, in which he admits Augustine was a hero of his (Vol. 53, Winter 1972).

17. "For John Berryman," *New York Review of Books*, 6 April 1972, pp. 3–4.

18. "Man on a Tight Rope," *Newsweek*, 1 May 1972, pp. 54–55.

19. Quotations from *Delusions, Etc.* (New York: Farrar, Straus & Giroux, 1972), p. 59.

6 — The Inner Journeys of Theodore Roethke

1. From *Open House*. Reprinted in Roethke's *Collected Poems* (Garden City, N.Y.: Doubleday & Co., 1966), p. 3.

2. *Selected Letters of Theodore Roethke* (Seattle: University of Washington Press, 1968), p. xi.

3. *Theodore Roethke* (Minneapolis: University of Minnesota Press, 1963), p. 8.

4. *Selected Letters of Theodore Roethke*, p. 142.

5. See "The Vegetal Radicalism of Theodore Roethke," *Sewanee Review*, 58 (Jan. 1950), 68–108. Reprinted in Kenneth Burke's *Language as Symbolic Action* (Berkeley and Los Angeles: University of California Press, 1966), pp. 254–81.

6. *Diccionario de Simbolos Tradicionales* (Barcelona, 1962).

7. *Theodore Roethke: An Introduction to the Poetry* (New York: Columbia University Press, 1966), p. 43.

8. "The Vegetal Radicalism of Theodore Roethke," p. 254.

9. *Theodore Roethke. An Introduction to the Poetry*, p. 59.

10. "Open Letter," in *On the Poet and His Craft: Selected Prose of Theodore Roethke*, ed. with an introduction by Ralph J. Mills, Jr. (Seattle: University of Washington Press, 1965), p. 50.

11. Ibid., p. 38.

12. Ralph J. Mills, Jr., "Theodore Roethke: The Lyric of the Self," in *Poets in Progress: Critical Prefaces to Thirteen Contemporary Americans,* ed. Edward B. Hungerford (Evanston: Northwestern University Press, 1967), p. 16.

13. See *Symbols of Transformation,* in *Collected Works of C. G. Jung,* Vol. 5, ed. G. Adler et al., trans. R. F. C. Hull (Princeton: Princeton University Press, 1956).

14. As quoted by René Girenon, in *Man and His Becoming according to the Vedanta* (London, 1945).

7 – The Dark Funnel

1. *Modern Poetry Studies,* 1, No. 1 (Fall 1970) 6–34.

2. References are to the Faber edition of *The Bell Jar* (London, 1963), p. 128.

3. Ibid., p. 40.

4. Biographical facts are taken from Lois Ames, "Notes Toward a Biography," in *The Art of Sylvia Plath,* ed. Charles Newman (Bloomington: Indiana University Press, 1970), p. 156.

5. *The Bell Jar,* p. 68.

6. *The Art of Sylvia Plath,* p. 156.

7. *The Bell Jar,* p. 77.

8. Ibid., p. 175.

9. Ibid.

10. *Hudson Review,* 13, No. 3 (Fall 1960), 414–15.

11. *Atlantic,* 199, No. 1 (January 1957), 65.

12. See Jung's "The Oedipus Complex," in *Freud and Psychoanalysis,* in *Collected Works of C. G. Jung,* Vol. 4, ed. G. Adler et al., trans. R. F. C. Hull (Princeton: Princeton University Press, 1961).

13. Ibid., p. 155.

14. For this and other observations I am indebted to Judith Bloomingdale.

15. *Alone with America: Essays on the Art of Poetry in the United States since 1950* (New York: Atheneum, 1969), p. 413.

16. *The Colossus* (New York: Alfred A. Knopf, 1962), p. 3. All quotations are from the first American edition.

17. *Histoire de la Civilisation africaine* (Paris, 1952).

18. *Crossing the Water* (London: Faber and Faber, Ltd., (1971), p. 13. All quotations are from the first British edition.

19. *Winter Trees* (London: Faber and Faber, Ltd., 1971).

20. After I had worked out this segment of this essay I was fortunate to read in manuscript Raymond Smith's excellent review of *Winter Trees*, written for volume 2 of *Modern Poetry Studies*. Dr. Smith confirms and elaborates upon these images of absence and narcissism.

21. *Beyond All This Fiddle. Essays 1955–1967* (New York: Random House, 1969), p. 49.

22. Quoted in *The Art of Sylvia Plath*.

23. *The New Poets* (New York: Oxford University Press, 1967), p. 88.

24. Rollo May, *Love and Will* (New York: W. W. Norton & Co., 1969). May's discussion of the relationship between love and death is directly reflected in several of my conclusions.

25. Sigmund Freud, "The Two Classes of Instincts," in *The Ego and the Id*, Standard Edition (London: Hogarth Press, 1961), p. 47.

26. All quotations from *Ariel* are from the Faber edition (London, 1965).

Selected Bibliography

Note: Listed here are primary sources only. Secondary sources are given in the footnotes to individual chapters.

BERRYMAN, JOHN

Poems. Norfolk, Conn.: New Directions, 1942.

The Dispossessed. New York: William Sloane Associates, 1948.

Homage to Mistress Bradstreet. New York: Farrar, Straus & Cudahy, 1956.

His Thought Made Pockets & the Plane Buckt. Pawlet, Vt.: C. Fredericks, 1959.

77 Dream Songs. New York: Farrar, Straus & Company, 1964.

Berryman's Sonnets. New York: Farrar, Straus & Giroux, 1967.

Short Poems. New York: Farrar, Straus & Giroux, 1967.

His Toy, His Dream, His Rest. New York: Farrar, Straus & Giroux, 1968.

The Dream Songs (collected edition). New York: Farrar, Straus & Giroux, 1969.

Love & Fame. New York: Farrar, Straus & Giroux, 1970.

Delusions, Etc. New York: Farrar, Straus & Giroux, 1972.

Recovery (novel). New York: Farrar, Straus & Giroux, 1973.

GINSBERG, ALLEN

Howl and Other Poems. San Francisco: City Lights Books, 1956.

Kaddish and Other Poems. San Francisco: City Lights Books, 1960.

Empty Mirror: Early Poems. New York: Totem Press/Corinth, 1961.

Reality Sandwiches: 1953–1960. San Francisco: City Lights Books, 1963.

TV Baby Poems. New York: Grossman, 1967.
Planet News. San Francisco: City Lights Books, 1968.
Airplane Dreams. Canada: Anansi, 1968.
The Fall of America. San Francisco: City Lights Books, 1973.

HARR, BARBARA

The Mortgaged Wife. Chicago: Swallow Press, 1970.

HEYEN, WILLIAM

Depth of Field. Baton Rouge: Louisiana State University Press, 1970.

JONG, ERICA

Fruits & Vegetables. New York: Holt, Rinehart & Winston, 1971.
Half-Lives. New York: Holt, Rinehart & Winston, 1973.
Fear of Flying (novel). New York: Holt, Rinehart & Winston, 1973.

KNIGHT, ETHERIDGE

Poems from Prison. New York: Broadside Press, 1968.

KUMIN, MAXINE

The Nightmare Factory. New York: Harper & Row, 1971.

KUNITZ, STANLEY

Intellectual Things. Garden City, N.Y.: Doubleday, Doran, 1930.
Passport to the War. New York: Henry Holt, 1944.
Selected Poems, 1928–1958. Boston: Little, Brown, 1958.
The Testing-Tree. Boston: Little, Brown, 1971.

LOWELL, ROBERT

Land of Unlikeness. Cummington, Mass.: The Cummington Press, 1944.

Lord Weary's Castle. New York: Harcourt, Brace, 1946; 2nd ed. rev., 1947.

Poems, 1938–1949. London: Faber and Faber, 1950.

The Mills of the Kavanaughs. New York: Harcourt, Brace, 1951.

Life Studies. New York: Farrar, Straus & Cudahy, 1959.

Imitations. New York: Farrar, Straus & Cudahy, 1961.

Phaedra (translation). New York: Farrar, Straus & Cudahy, 1961.

For the Union Dead. New York: Farrar, Straus & Giroux, 1964.

The Old Glory (drama). New York: Farrar, Straus & Giroux, 1964; rev. 1965; 2nd rev., 1969.

Near the Ocean. New York: Farrar, Straus & Giroux, 1967.

Prometheus Bound (drama). New York: Farrar, Straus & Giroux, 1962.

The Voyage and Other Versions of Poems by Baudelaire. New York: Farrar, Straus & Giroux, 1968.

Notebook 1967–68. New York: Farrar, Straus & Giroux, 1969. 3rd ed. rev. and expanded, issued under the title *Notebook*, 1970.

History. New York: Farrar, Straus & Giroux, 1973.

For Harriet and Lizzie. New York: Farrar, Straus & Giroux, 1973.

The Dolphin. New York: Farrar, Straus & Giroux, 1973.

MAZZARO, JEROME

Juvenal's Satires. Ann Arbor: University of Michigan Press, 1965.

Changing the Windows. Athens: Ohio University Press, 1966.

PLATH, SYLVIA

The Colossus. New York: Alfred A. Knopf, 1960.

Three Women: A Monologue for Three Voices. London: Turret Press, 1963.

The Bell Jar (novel). London: Faber and Faber, 1963.

Ariel. New York: Harper & Row, 1966.

Uncollected Poems. London: Turret Press, 1965.

Crossing the Water. London: Faber and Faber, 1971.

Winter Trees. London: Faber and Faber, 1971.

Crystal Gazer. London: Rainbow Press, 1971.

Lyonnesse. London: Rainbow Press, 1971.

ROETHKE, THEODORE

Open House. New York: Alfred A. Knopf, 1941.
The Lost Son and Other Poems. Garden City, N.Y.: Doubleday, 1948.
Praise to the End! Garden City, N.Y.: Doubleday, 1951.
The Waking: Poems 1933–1953. Garden City, N.Y.: Doubleday, 1953.
Words for the Wind. Garden City, N.Y.: Doubleday, 1958.
I am! Says the Lamb. Garden City, N.Y.: Doubleday, 1961.
The Far Field. Garden City, N.Y.: Doubleday, 1964.
Collected Poems. Garden City, N.Y.: Doubleday, 1966.
On the Poet and His Craft. Seattle: University of Washington Press, 1965.
Selected Letters. Seattle: University of Washington Press, 1968.
Straw for the Fire. Garden City, N.Y.: Doubleday, 1972.

SEXTON, ANNE

To Bedlam and Part Way Back. Boston: Houghton Mifflin, 1960.
All My Pretty Ones. Boston: Houghton Mifflin, 1962.
Selected Poems. London: Faber and Faber, 1964.
Live or Die. Boston: Houghton Mifflin, 1966.
Poems (with Kinsella and Livingston). London: Faber and Faber, 1968.
Love Poems. Boston: Houghton Mifflin, 1969.
Mercy Street (produced but unpublished play). 1969.
Transformations. Boston: Houghton Mifflin, 1971.
The Book of Folly. Boston: Houghton Mifflin, 1972.

SEIDEL, FREDERICK

Final Solutions. New York: Random House, 1963.

SNODGRASS, W. D.

Heart's Needle. New York: Alfred A. Knopf, 1967.
Gallows Songs (trans. with Lore Segal). Ann Arbor: University of Michigan Press, 1967.
After Experience. New York: Harper & Row, 1968.
Remains, (under the name S. S. Gardons). Mt. Horeb, Wis.: The Perishable Press, Ltd., 1970.

Index

165

Wendell had an urge to crush his lips on hers, but . . .

"I'll scrunch down like this," said Tanya, "and if you stand on tippy-toe . . ."

Wendell tossed his crystal champagne glass in the fireplace, flipped up the collar of his Italian silk smoking jacket, and, standing on tippytoe, pulled Tanya close, crushing his lips on hers.

With a musical sigh Tanya swooned onto the antique Victorian sofa, the back of her hand pressed to her forehead.

Wendell placed another log in the fireplace and lighted his pipe with the embers. Slipping his hand into the inside pocket of his smoking jacket, he withdrew a diamond-studded necklace and draped it around Tanya's neck.

Tanya reswooned.

Wendell blew a smoke ring.

"Oh, Wendell, Wendell," she muttered, "you really know how to make a young woman feel . . ."

"QUACK, QUACK, QUACK . . . DADDY SAID you'd never amount to anything. All you want to do is sit at that computer. Don't be surprised if you come home some night and find it in the garbage. If you spent your time thinking about how to improve yourself, you could get a better job, we'd be able to take vacations like other people . . . quack, quack, and quack. . . ."

Wendell shut down his computer, put on his jammies, and went to bed hoping to dream dreams of Tanya.

In the morning Wendell dressed quickly, ate a bowl of bran flakes and half a grapefruit. He fired up the Rambler station wagon and headed for work. Wendell's car was not flashy like the cars young people drove, but it got him from point A to point B and it was paid for. Of course, it had a small oil leak and the exhaust produced a lot of smoke and Wendell was planning to pin a blanket to the upholstery to hold in the stuffing, but other than that, she was as good as new, except for the paint.

Wendell stopped at a red traffic light.

Honk, honk, honk!

Hold your horses, okay? So Wendell made a mistake, okay? So the light was green and not red when Wendell stopped, okay? And honking your horn won't do any good because now the light is red, okay? And he and Wendell were going to sit there until it turned green again, okay?

When the light did turn green again, Wendell goosed the engine of the Rambler, leaving the impatient driver behind him in a cloud of smoke.

Wendell maneuvered into the left lane to make his usual left turn onto Taylor Street, his left turn signal lights flashing.

Honk, honk!

Hold your . . .

Honk, honk, blaaaaat!

. . . horses, okay? Wendell could have made that left turn safely, okay? But the oncoming Cadillac appeared to be moving faster than it really was, okay? And he could just cool his heels for a while, okay?

Honk, honk, beep, beep, blaaaaat!

The young woman standing on the corner, the one with the blonde hair, miniskirt, and large, you know, was on that corner every morning. Maybe she was . . .

WENDELL INSTRUCTED HIS CHAUFFEUR TO complete the left turn and ease the limousine to the curb. The young woman with the blonde hair, miniskirt, and large, you know, was smiling now and blowing kisses. Wendell told his chauffeur to hop out and open the door for her.

She slid in gracefully. Wendell could feel the warmth of her thigh pressing against his. Her breath was minty fresh.

"Hi," she breathed, "I'm Tanya."

Wendell excused himself, his cellular phone was ringing. It must be Hong Kong returning his call. If she would look in the little pocket on the back of the front seat, she would find a diamond-studded necklace, just a little something he had picked up for her at Tiffany's.

With a musical sigh Tanya swooned on the Moroccan leather seat, the back of her hand pressed to her forehead.

Wendell showed her his jar of Grey Poupon.

"Oh, Wendell, Wendell," she muttered, "you really know how to make a young woman feel . . ."

HONK, HONK! BEEP, BEEP! BLAAAAAAAAAAAT!

Wendell completed his left turn onto Taylor Street when he was good and ready, and a few minutes later he was at the office for another day of the same-old-same-old, unless of course Tanya was one of the young women at the office.

There were only two young women in the office, the boss's new secretary and the new salesperson. If Wendell had to guess which one was Tanya, he would choose the salesperson. She had a cute way of snapping her chewing gum, and Wendell could tell she liked him by the way she refused to look at him.

But Wendell had work to do. He had accounts to balance, statements to reconcile, checks to write and more accounts to balance and more statements to reconcile and more of the same-old-same-old.

"May I have your attention," said the loudspeaker. "Mr. Leroy wants all employees in the lunchroom at eight fifteen for a brief meeting. Doughnut holes will be served compliments of Mr. Leroy."

Wendell knew there was no such thing as a "brief" business meeting. He wished he could be left alone to do his work. He never did understand the rhetoric of business meetings. The language of business, it seemed to Wendell, consisted of random words filling the air with no meaning or logical sequence. The words sounded meaningful, but when Wendell asked himself what was said, he didn't have a clue.

Mr. Leroy was stout but impeccably creased and starched with perpetual beads of perspiration on his upper lip. "As members of the Central Division," he said, "we should be proud of last month's performance. Let's give ourselves a hand."

Clap, clap, clap.

So far so good. Wendell had no problem understanding that. They made money last month.

"I want to thank you personally," continued Mr. Leroy, "for proactively reducing variable and fixed costs and . . ."

Proactively? What the hell did that mean? Wendell had looked it up in his dictionary after the last meeting. It wasn't there.

". . . implement new strategic initiatives . . . revitalize our sales force . . . centralized processes . . . oink, oink, oink. . . ."

Sales force? Did he say sales force?

". . . Capitalize on new business trends and opportunities . . . oink, oink, and oink . . ."

There she was, the new salesperson, leaning seductively against the refrigerator, chewing.

". . . identifying leadership team . . . reorganization . . . oink, oink, oink. . . ."

THE NEW SALESPERSON WAS STARING at Wendell, a playful smile forming and reforming on her lips. She sashayed through the maze of lunchroom tables and chairs, her eyes never leaving Wendell's, her long blonde hair bouncing with each step. She stopped inches in front of Wendell. Her breath was minty fresh.

"Hi," she breathed, "I'm Tanya."

Wendell took Tanya's hand gently but firmly in his and led her to the parking lot. He opened the passenger door of his red Ferrari convertible, and she slid in gracefully, giving his hand a playful squeeze. Wendell liked it when his girlfriends squeezed his hand like that.

Wendell slipped his hand into the pocket of his English tweed jacket, the one with the elbow patches, and produced a large roll of one hundred dollar bills. He peeled two of them off the roll and handed them to Tanya.

"Are we . . ." she stammered ". . . are you really going to take me to . . ."

Wendell smiled and lowered the back of Tanya's seat to near horizontal, anticipating that she might swoon.

". . . to . . . to . . . Six Flags?"

Wendell nodded, and the Ferrari's engine roared to life.

With a musical sigh Tanya swooned in the seat that Wendell had so thoughtfully lowered, the back of her hand pressed to her forehead.

Wendell adjusted his Italian silk scarf, leaving one end five times longer than the other, anticipating that it would flow behind him as they sped down the highway.

"Oh, Wendell, Wendell," she muttered, "you really know how to make a young woman feel . . ."

". . . OINK, OINK . . . EXTENDED LEADERSHIP GROUP . . . performance objectives . . . implementation of technological enhancements . . . oink, oink, and furthermore, oink."

Wendell's day was slow in passing. He took his morning break, his lunch break, and his afternoon break. In between he totaled columns, produced reports, and wrote checks, the same-old-same-old.

Wendell left the office at five sharp and drove home, stopping only twice to add water to the radiator of the Rambler. When he got home, he took a small brown paper bag from his briefcase, as usual, smoothed it out, as usual, and laid it in the drawer in the kitchen, as usual, for reuse the next day.

Normally Wendell would have spent half an hour after work tending the roses in the tiny back yard of their mobile home. But this evening he sat at the computer and signed on to the Internet as soon as he got home.

"You expecting something special?" asked his wife.

Wendell's usual routine was to sign on at seven P.M., after the evening news. He had aroused her suspicions.

"You expecting another e-mail from Tanya?" she asked.

How did she know about Tanya? There was no way she could have seen that letter. Wendell's access code was known only to him. Besides, she knew nothing about computers, and he had trashed the message so nobody else would see it.

"That's right, you worm. You trashed it so I wouldn't know about your little affair."

Tanya must have called her.

"Nobody called me, you demented virus."

She must have bumped into Tanya at the grocery store.

"I didn't bump into her anywhere, you cockroach."

Then how did she know?

"I know because *I* am Tanya."

Wendell couldn't remember the last time he'd laughed so loud or so hard. He removed his horn-rimmed glasses and brushed the tears from his eyes and cheeks. She couldn't possibly be Tanya.

"Why not?" she demanded.

Well, for openers, Tanya was young and pretty and sensitive and loving and kind and gentle and full of life and exciting to be with and . . .

"You know all that from one little e-mail letter?"

Damn right! His wife couldn't be Tanya. She didn't even know how to turn on the computer.

"That's true," she said. "I don't know the first thing about computers, but I have a friend who does. She's on the Internet, too, and she wrote the letter for me. I told her what to say, and she sent the letter to you from her computer. I wanted to see if you'd tell me about it, if you'd be faithful."

That couldn't be. There had to be a Tanya. His wife was screwing with his mind. Without Tanya he was a ghost, with her he was alive and young.

Wendell's wife recited Tanya's letter from memory, including the punctuation, stopping on occasion to ask if it sounded familiar. She folded her arms across her chest and smiled.

Wendell was not one to lose his temper. He rose from the computer and walked to the kitchen. He checked the knives for sharpness. He made stabbing and slashing movements with each knife and decided that the large carving knife had the best grip.

"You're going to kill me, aren't you?"

Wendell went to the toolshed. He picked up a small hatchet, checked it for sharpness. He swung it several times. The hatchet was comfortable in his hand. He placed it on the kitchen counter next to the carving knife.

"You won't get away with it," said his wife. "I'll scream."

Wendell rummaged in the bedroom closet. He found his .38 revolver. It was loaded. He released the safety and placed it on the kitchen counter between the knife and hatchet.

"You'll fry in hell."

It was difficult for Wendell to make decisions. He paced the kitchen floor, hands clasped behind his back, trying to decide which of the weapons would be best for the job. He decided against using any of the weapons—too cold, too impersonal. Wendell would have to kill her in a more intimate manner. He felt he owed her that after twenty-five years of marriage. The right way would be to throttle her. Wendell placed both hands around his wife's throat and squeezed.

"Qua . . . ack . . . qua . . ."

Wendell heard the doorbell ring. At least, he *thought* it rang. Wendell released the hold he had on his wife's throat.

". . . ack . . ."

The bell *had* rung. An exotic young woman with hoop earrings and dark lips was standing in the living room. She must have let herself in. Now she was slinking toward Wendell, a seductive smile forming and reforming on her lips. Her long black hair swished with each step. She stopped inches in front of Wendell. Her breath was minty fresh.

Maude Miller is an author who makes regular appearances in *Alfred Hitchcock's Mystery Magazine*, among others. She lives in Twin Falls, Idaho, but can write deftly about anywhere else. Her story "The Last Word" takes sibling rivalry to a new extreme.

The Last Word
MAUDE MILLER

Life had been rather uncomplicated before Leona moved in, Edith thought wistfully. Leona with her blue-grey hair and real gold earrings and remarkably unlined skin, seventy-three-year-old woman that she was. Theo said she'd had a facelift while living in America; Theo said they all had facelifts there once they passed fifty. Leona *had* certainly changed since living in California with her American husband for so many years, even Edith admitted to that. She had found a way of using up all the sisterly love and patience that had existed among them in the past; she always had to have the last word.

"Theo, your skin would be as nice as mine if you'd use my special formula facecream on that turkey gobbler neck of yours," Leona said in her reproving voice, used when she was pointing out some particularly galling inadequacy of her sisters'.

Seventy-five-year-old Theo, with her short, softly waving white hair and tallish, amply proportioned figure, did indeed have several folds of loose skin hanging off her neck, but so what?

Leona, she thought with irritation, didn't know everything. She rebelled against her sister by using no youth-restoring remedies at all. "I like my skin the way it is, Leona."

"I don't see how you could," Leona replied doubtfully. "No harm in trying to look your best."

Leona never concentrated long on Theo's appearance, however. Theo never took her excellent advice, and there were the more challenging short-

108

comings of younger sister Edith to attend to. Edith was a dowdy spinster with straight, iron-colored hair that fell just below her fading chin. A deeply lined face was interrupted by two small, pale grey, frightened looking eyes, a facial mole, and a prominent nose. Leona had tried on numerous occasions to make Edith over so that *someone* might want her, but it was no use. Edith insisted on looking like a wallflower; she'd had the same haircut for thirty years and dressed like one of those bag ladies who push a grocery cart around.

Each time Leona had visited in the past she'd had Edith's hair done, left her with makeup (and lengthy demonstrations on how to use it) and a new wardrobe of smart clothes. They were Leona's own castoffs, but Edith was naturally thin and could fit into most of them. On subsequent visits, however, Edith would always be back to her old self, the clothes mysteriously gone and the makeup relegated to the back of a cluttered drawer.

Leona blamed Theo for that.

She often wondered why she was so unappreciated by her sisters. Didn't they *want* her help? She thought they ought to; they were always in such a muddle. And she herself was a paragon of organization and efficiency. Give it time, she told herself reassuringly. She'd soon have them both straightened out and doing things her way. They'd soon realize she knew best.

But in the meantime she wanted a traveling companion. She didn't think seriously of taking Theo along on the trip she was planning to Morocco. Theo was too troublesome and scarcely listened to her advice. But Edith was still—pliable. And without Theo along, Edith would do what Leona told her to.

Leona had been all over the world (courtesy of two late husbands' generous life insurance policies), and she was itching to take off again. Travel brochures were piling up, but this time she was set on having a warm holiday. Rainy, bone-chilling England was not as she'd remembered it in her childhood. Morocco would remind her of sunny California and her years of tolerable marriages and blissful widowhood.

"Let's go to Morocco, Edith."

"Isn't Morocco a place to visit in the winter?" Theo asked snidely. "It'll be scorching there this time of year."

"Mind your own business, Theo," Leona answered. "Besides, it always feels like winter here. Don't you ever get any sunshine? If I'd known how cold it was going to be, I'd have stayed in California."

More's the pity, Theo thought ruefully. She continued in a brusque voice. "Edith doesn't want to go to Morocco." Theo thought she would rather have unanesthetized dental surgery than suffer a holiday with her know-it-all sister. And poor Edith couldn't speak up for herself.

Leona raised her arched, penciled-in eyebrows at Theo and turned back to Edith, who was seated uncomfortably on the green chintz settee in front of the fireplace. "Of course you want to go with me, don't you, Edith? You need to have some fun."

Edith shrugged her shoulders helplessly before a look of panic crossed her wrinkled face. She'd never had much *fun*, as Leona called it, but the thought of actually getting on an airplane and setting foot on foreign soil was terrifying.

What if the plane crashed or terrorists seized it? Any number of things could go wrong and often did. She'd read the papers, hadn't she? Edith shuddered. She'd never been any farther than Peterborough, and that with Theo. She only felt safe with Theo at her side. The thought of adventure made her heart flutter with fear.

"I don't think I could go, Leona. I like it better here," she protested weakly, sinking deeper into the soft cushions of the settee, rather wanting to disappear.

Leona ignored her. "Stuff and nonsense. I'll get the tickets at the travel agent's next week." Then she added in a breathy voice, "Oh, it'll be *such* fun!" She smiled gleefully as she clasped her slim hands together, her blue hair shining in the lamplight of the cosy sitting room. She was already formalizing plans to transform Edith's appearance once again, away from Theo's watchful eye. They had to be a handsome pair, after all. Not that Leona wanted a third husband, she was finished with marriage. But possibly a flirtation? She had to be prepared, just in case. Perhaps she'd have another tint put on her own hair, bluer this time. She thought her hair was her best feature, although she did have a girlish figure as well. Lots of self-restraint and careful attention to her diet, she told herself proudly; if Theo and Edith would follow her example, they'd be much better off, any fool could see that.

"JUST BECAUSE SHE HAS MONEY doesn't mean she can tell us what to do," Theo said acidly to Edith the next day as they were working on their embroidered tea towels for the annual summer fete at the vicarage.

"It was your idea to have her move in with us," Edith pointed out meekly. She reached for another jam tart.

"In case you hadn't noticed, little sister, we're rather hard up," Theo replied. "Before Leona came, I didn't see how we could afford to live in this house for another six months, what with all the repairs and taxes." She attacked the embroidery on the tea towel with renewed vigor. "I don't see that I had much choice."

"I expect not," Edith answered, eyeing Theo's tattered cardigan and well-worn housedress. Theo shouldered all the responsibilities for them both and had done so for over twenty years since their invalid mother had died and left Edith without a home or a purpose in life.

"Don't you think we'd better hide this tray of tarts before she gets back from the hairdresser's? She'll really be on us if she sees us eating again."

Theo rolled her bright blue eyes. "For pity's sake, I can eat what I want. If I want to be *fat*, I'll be *fat!*"

"No need to bite my head off," Edith answered in a hurt voice.

Since Leona had moved in several months before, the arguments between the sisters had escalated. Edith and Theo had never quarreled before *she* came. Leona was trouble. It was then that Theo decided something had to be done about their meddling sister.

THE FOLLOWING WEEK, LEONA STARTED in on doing the house over (it needed refurbishing, didn't it?). Edith listened agreeably, but Theo felt a rising irritation. It wasn't enough to do *them* over, the house had to be changed as well. Leona planned to revamp the garden, too.

"I think we should put a row of pansies along the walkway in back. And get rid of that awful gazebo."

At this Theo bristled. "Oh no, we won't. The gazebo was Cecil's favorite place to sit in the evenings." Cecil had passed on twenty years before, but Theo still felt strangely loyal about the house they'd lived in for the thirty-odd years of their contented marriage. They'd had a child, one child only, a boy who'd lived to be ten, then died of viral pneumonia during a relentlessly cold winter. Oddly enough, Cecil had taken it much harder than Theo had. He'd built the gazebo in memory of their son and was, during the remainder of his lifetime, fiercely dedicated to it. She'd told Leona that before, of course, but Leona never paid any attention to her.

"It's dreadful, Theo," Leona persisted. "We'll have it bulldozed and build a new one, a modern one."

"I don't want a new one," Theo said, thrusting her strong chin out for emphasis, the turkey gobbler skin hanging below it. "I want *this* one."

Leona flashed dark, angry eyes at her.

"The gazebo *stays*," Theo said, folding her arms tightly across her broad chest.

Leona could buy some new things for the house if she wanted, Theo thought angrily, but she wasn't to change anything, not without Theo's approval. In an effort to calm her nerves, she reminded herself that they needed Leona's money. After all, that was why she'd come to live with them (from Theo's standpoint, anyway). Theo had known about Leona's sizable pension of over a thousand pounds each month and the large sum in the bank, too. Leona had paid for the new roof, repaired Theo's old car, and hired the painters to repaint the outside of the peeling white Victorian. Having Leona live with them had seemed like an ideal arrangement at the time.

But Theo had forgotten how bossy Leona was. Maybe she'd wanted to forget.

The following week, Theo returned from a full day of shopping in Peterborough to a trio of workmen fitting out the lavatories. Theo had dearly loved her old fashioned baths with the big iron tubs. There was one on the ground floor and another upstairs. She had soaked in them often in the days before central heating.

"Nonsense," Leona said firmly when Theo expressed her dismay. "The tubs are positively ancient, Theo. I can *afford* to have them replaced, you know. It's no good pleading poverty when I can pay for it all."

Theo's head was aching, and her back hurt; a day at the shops as a prelude to this was simply too much.

"I can see it's too late to do anything about it now, Leona. The lavatories will have to be done, since they're already half demolished. But I'm warning you," she said hotly, a purplish color flooding her pale cheeks, "next time you are to consult with me first. It's my house, isn't it?"

The next day at teatime Leona was out. Gone off to London to see her solicitor or something, Edith said vaguely. Theo didn't ask for details; she wasn't speaking to Leona.

It was over scones, marmalade, and a cuppa that Theo first voiced her plans to Edith. They were seated at the scrubbed oak table in the kitchen, looking out the picture window into the garden. The flowers were blooming although the weather was only sporadically warm. Lilies of the valley were nestled in their shaded spot in the garden, the oblong leaves sheltering the white, bell-shaped flowers. Soon the fragrance of the garden would waft through the open leaded windows in the sitting room and hall, sweetening even the soured atmosphere Leona had brought with her. But Theo looked skeptically at the garden and the gazebo, bringing herself back to reality. Leona would change it all. There was no stopping her; in time she'd have the gazebo down and the garden destroyed. Leona always had to have the last word.

Theo couldn't allow it, not anymore.

"I'm afraid we're going to have to do something about Leona, Edith. I've been trying to think of some other way, but I don't see how it can be avoided." Theo spoke calmly, as matter-of-factly as if she were considering what to do with the family dog.

Edith looked up from her plate of scones, swallowing hard. She was trying to down as many as she could before Leona got home; a large chunk of orange marmalade was suspended from the corner of her mouth. "What can't be avoided?" she finally asked, picking up another scone.

Theo raised her napkin to Edith's mouth. "You've got marmalade on your face, dear." She put the napkin down. "We must get rid of Leona."

"But we need her money, don't we? How would we get on without those pension checks?" Edith bit into her third scone nervously. She was thinking of the impending trip to Morocco. The tickets had been secured and her passport sent for, but nothing had eased her fears. In fact, she was more frightened than ever about getting on that airplane with Leona. If Leona moved out, of course, she'd be spared the trial of actually going.

Theo daintily took a sip of tea and dabbed the corners of her mouth. "We're not going to give up the pension checks, Edith."

"What do you mean?"

"I mean," Theo said coolly, "we're going to do her in. We'll say she's traveling around the world—although no one's likely to ask—and that she'll be away for some time. We'll continue to get her pension checks and there's the bank account in London as well. They're not likely to know her by sight. And I've been practicing her signature."

"You can't be serious," Edith said in alarm. "You're not serious, are you, Theo?"

"Of course I'm serious. You don't think I'd joke about something like that, do you?"

Edith didn't know what to think. All she could think was that she had been momentarily relieved when she'd thought Theo was going to ask Leona to move out, for she'd have been spared the holiday in Morocco, since it wasn't until next month. But she certainly wasn't relieved about this. With shaking hands she poured herself another cup of tea, until it poured over the top of the cup and onto the lace tablecloth. She didn't notice until Theo placed a steady hand on her shaking one. "You're spilling, dear."

Theo cleaned up after her.

WHEN EDITH WOKE UP THE following morning, she trudged downstairs with a heavy heart. Theo had gone round the bend, she thought with panic. And there was nothing to be done about it. Edith had never taken care of anything herself. Theo did that. Maybe, however, it was just nerves. Many things could be attributed to nerves, it seemed. She comforted herself briefly with the notion that this was so; Theo had sometimes been afflicted with a nervous condition.

Theo and Leona were sitting at opposite ends of the kitchen table in a morose silence. Leona brightened when she saw Edith heading unsteadily towards them and started an energetic flow of chatter.

"We're all set, dear Edith. We're leaving on Wednesday next."

"But I-I thought," Edith faltered, "we-we weren't leaving until next month. My passport . . . I-I won't be ready next week."

Leona dismissed this triviality with a wave of her hand. "I hurried up your passport; it should be here in a couple of days. And really, why wait? The weather next month will be better here, and now it's miserably chill, so why not escape England now and have our little holiday in the sun sooner rather than later?''

Why not indeed? Edith asked herself unhappily. Well, mainly because she didn't want to go at all and she thought that maybe by next month Leona would be gone. She looked at Theo, but Theo gave her a smug smile as if to say, *I'm doing what's best for both of us, Edith.*

Edith took to her bed for the rest of the day with a headache.

Theo retired to her bedroom early that night, with a book on poisonous plants.

Leona made plans to have the kitchen redone. That big, fat Theo couldn't scare *her*. Leona would do as she liked.

A FEW DAYS LATER, ON Friday, Theo set to work early in the shadows of the kitchen, making a soup. It was chilly out, and the dark clouds hovered overhead with menace. The impending storm cast an ominous gloom over the shining white house, almost hidden by a rapidly leafing forest of decid-uous trees and an occasional spruce. They had no neighbors nearby; living off by themselves had always been deeply appealing to Theo. And now it was crucial that they be alone, away from the interference of well-meaning neighbors. There was their activity in the local church, of course—she and Edith had always taken part in the occasional women's group and had a casual acquaintance with the young vicar—but people seldom came to visit. Edith was dull as nails, and Theo hadn't the patience for many friendships. Friends got on her nerves. Leona, of course, thought she was better than most of the villagers. It would have been beneath her to become too friendly with any of them.

There *were* the workmen to contend with. But only vaguely interested in completing a job (it was infinitely more interesting to begin one), they had not shown up since Tuesday and had told a spewing Leona that they wouldn't be back for a fortnight, at the *earliest*, they'd added bravely.

Theo had carefully worked through all the details of what she was about to do; further delay could create problems. She felt invincible.

By lunchtime it had started raining, drizzling at first, then rapidly esca-lating into a downpour. Although it was midday, the inside of the house was dark and the atmosphere funereal. Only the light in the kitchen was switched on.

"I'm making a low-fat soup for you, Leona. Lots of vegetables and no meat at all." Theo stood stirring the soup on the cooker and glanced over her shoulder at Leona, who was scrubbing away at some invisible dirt on the table. "As a peace offering, dear," Theo added in a pleasantly soothing voice.

Leona stopped cleaning and stared at Theo's broad, strong back. She was struck dumb for a moment, an oddity for Leona. "Why, how . . ." she stumbled, "how lovely!" She returned to her work with a satisfied smile. Theo had come around, she told herself smugly. She had known all along that she would.

"I think you'll be quite surprised what a low-fat diet will do for your figure, Theo. And for your health. You could live forever on a healthy regimen like mine."

Theo looked down at the soup she was stirring and the extra smaller pot in back, made especially for Leona. The vase in the corner of the counter-top, previously filled with lilies of the valley, was now empty. Not bloody likely that *you'll* live forever, she thought maliciously. She said sweetly, "I should have listened to you long ago. Of course you're right, about the house, too. Those lavatories needed renovation."

Edith looked back and forth from Leona to Theo, confused by the sudden truce. What were they playing at? She watched Theo ladle out the soup as Leona stepped into the W.C. to wash up.

"Why do you have two pots of soup, Theo?" Edith asked suspiciously.

"Because I've poisoned one of them, dear," Theo answered.

"You didn't! Please say you didn't, Theo. I can't believe you could do such a thing."

"But I did. I poisoned it with the lilies of the valley from our very own garden. The garden Leona wants to destroy."

"Then why are you being so nice to her?"

"Because otherwise she won't eat the soup."

Edith backed away with a squeak, her frightened grey eyes terror-struck. "But she'll notice and won't eat it."

"Leona's not interested in cooking, you know that," Theo said. "Cooking to her is a piece of unbuttered toast and a tin of pears."

Leona walked in just then. "Smells lovely! Let's eat." She sat down at the table, waiting to be served.

Theo served Edith and Leona both. She couldn't risk Edith's shaking hands' dropping Leona's soup.

Leona talked feverishly while she ate. It was no surprise that she didn't notice the soup's odd taste. She was too busy handing out as much as advice as possible while Theo was still listening to her.

"I don't know what you were thinking when you bought that settee in the sitting room, Theo. It's such a ghastly shade of green. Now, my advice would be to get a new one, something carnation pink, perhaps?"

Oh yes, Theo thought disdainfully. Carnation pink would be just the thing to go with Leona's blue hair. "I'm sure you're right, Leona," was all she said.

Leona smiled happily. Edith opened her mouth, without thinking, to tell Leona not to eat her soup. What Theo was doing was all wrong. She had to stop it. Before she could speak, however, Leona said, "We'll be eating lots of strange food in Morocco, Edith. But it'll be quite an experience for you. Can you believe it? Less than a week before we're on that plane!" Edith couldn't say a word. She was almost ashamed for being such a coward.

Leona finished the bowl of soup. Almost immediately she started having hot flushes, and a headache set in. She complained of violent stomach pains while Edith led her upstairs to bed.

Theo dutifully followed and sat beside her the rest of the day, watching Leona's face cover itself with red patches just before she started vomiting.

"I need to go to the surgery, Theo. You're trying to kill me. I can see that," Leona panted. "You're not going to get my money, though. I've been to see my solicitor. It's all to go to charity."

"Don't upset yourself," Theo told her. "You'll be just fine by tomorrow."

"It was the soup, wasn't it?" Leona gasped before she collapsed.

Edith peered over Theo's shoulder at Leona, small and flushed, lying between the fluffy white pillows at the top of the brass bed.

Suddenly Theo regretted what she'd done. Leona deserved many awful things, she told herself, but she didn't really deserve to die. What she actually deserved was to be born again, to be fat, ugly, and poor. But it was too late for recriminations. Leona was dying, and there was no way they could get anyone to help her. The inevitable had to be accepted.

Theo and Edith shut the door behind them and spent a tense, silent evening downstairs in front of the fire, listening to the rain beat against the leaded windows and watching the lightning crackling around the gloomy house.

Theo finally rose, retrieved the shovel from the garage, and contemplated the grim task of burying Leona tomorrow.

BY MORNING THE STORM HAD abated. It was muddy out, but there was no time to waste. The task would have to be completed in privacy. Theo opened Leona's door timidly.

But the brass bed was empty.

Theo pulled back the duvet, certain that skinny Leona must be hiding somewhere. She looked in the cupboard, filled to overflowing with Leona's designer clothes. She lumbered anxiously into Edith's bedroom, but it was unoccupied as well. She heard voices downstairs. Gingerly, nervously, Theo started down the stairs. At the bottom she stopped in shock. Leona was chatting amiably with a pale Edith, as if last night was a forgotten nightmare.

Theo held onto the stair rail for support. "Are you feeling better then, Leona?"

"Right as rain," Leona answered blithely. "Edith told me I was ill yesterday, but you know, I can't remember a thing!" She laughed, shook her shoulders helplessly, and started in on the unsightly mole on Edith's cheek and how she'd be much more attractive without it and Leona knew just the doctor to take it off. But they'd have to wait until after Morocco. . . .

Edith blanched.

And so it went. The three sisters spent the remainder of the day in the house because a light rain had set in, keeping it wet outside. Theo was strangely relieved that Leona hadn't died, although she was still left with the dilemma of what to do about her, short of murdering her. They couldn't go on like this. Theo seemed to hear her from a great distance even though Leona was sitting right next to her on the green settee (soon to be shipped off to a jumble sale, no doubt).

"And, Theo, I think we should send you to a diet clinic, to take that weight off once and for all. I'll pay for it, of course." Theo felt her shoulders tighten and her blood pressure soar.

By late afternoon the sky had blackened prematurely as another thunderstorm gained momentum. Theo switched on the porcelain lamps in the sitting room and lit the fire. Edith did embroidery while Theo read a murder mystery. By eight o'clock Leona had retired, exhausted, it seemed, from all that advice giving. After an hour or so, they heard a thump from upstairs.

Theo was unconcerned, but Edith scurried up quickly, into the dark corridor illuminated only by intermittent bolts of lightning. Moments later Edith screamed, and Theo followed her up the mahogany staircase and through the open door of Leona's bedroom. Leona was lying on the wood floor beside her bed, bluish and most certainly dead. Theo checked her pulse; there wasn't one. She determined that Leona must have tried to get out of bed and collapsed. Heart failure perhaps? She wondered guiltily if it was a delayed effect of her insane attempt to poison Leona yesterday, but she promptly dismissed that notion: lilies of the valley were supposed to have an immediate effect.

"We murdered her," Edith said in a small voice, fighting back the tears.

"We didn't murder her," Theo replied sensibly. "She just died on her own. If we'd killed her, it would have happened yesterday. It's just coincidence."

"What are we going to do?"

"We're going to bury her."

"Shouldn't we call the doctor?"

Theo put her hands on her hips, Prussian soldier style. "And what if they find poison in her blood? Who do you think they'll blame for that?"

Edith looked at the floor.

"And what about the pension checks?" Theo continued. "This is perfect, Edith. We didn't actually kill Leona, but we get the benefits all the same. You heard her last night, didn't you? She was going to give all her money to charity. That's why she was visiting her bloody solicitor the other day. To make sure we didn't get any of her money if anything happened to her."

"But we tried to kill her," Edith said tearfully.

"We didn't succeed, dear. Though I must say I'm not sorry she's dead. We need those pension checks, little sister."

Theo buried Leona under the gazebo. She felt surprisingly calm about the whole affair.

SEVERAL WEEKS PASSED. THE TRIP to Morocco was canceled and the tickets cashed in to pay for the restoration of the lavatories (Leona had prepaid half). Two pension checks came, and Theo had no trouble cashing them. They had done nothing wrong in the end, Theo told herself reassuringly, and life was better than ever. She and Edith were alone again with no one to advise them about their many faults. Leona was safely tucked away underground beneath the gazebo. Cecil wouldn't have liked that, but at least Theo had saved his gazebo, hadn't she? She told Edith that Leona was still with them, of course, she was just in a more suitable place. Where she couldn't have the last word in every conversation.

Things went along swimmingly until one day when Theo and Edith motored to Peterborough for a day of shopping. It was a sunny day in June, and Theo felt blissfully happy. Edith was back to her old self, too. They'd bought a fair amount of goodies to munch on and a new housedress for each of them. When they pulled into the driveway, however, they saw a backhoe in the garden, digging up the gazebo. Leona must have ordered the work done weeks ago, and the workmen, being the procrastinators they traditionally were, had just now gotten around to it.

Theo jumped out of the car to stop them, but it was too late. She heard one workman call out to the other, "Take a look at this, Melvin. Why, it's . . . my god, it is. It's a dead body! We'd better call the police right away."

Leona had had the last word after all.

David Corn is the Washington editor of the *The Nation* magazine. He is also a prolific author, having written for magazines and newspapers including *Harper's, The New Republic, The Washington Post, The New York Times,* and others. "My Murder" is an intriguing story set around a brilliant concept. What if someone claimed to have committed a murder and wrote a best-selling book about it? His study of this idea was nominated for the 1996 Edgar Award.

My Murder
DAVID CORN

Ever have a notion that you couldn't get out of your head? No matter how hard you tried, it was still there. Always creeping around, whispering to you: here I am, here I am. Becoming part of you. The notion does not wither. You might forget it for a while. But turn a corner, and there it is, and the game you play with yourself of not thinking about it—for how can you think about not thinking about it?—is lost again. Sure, you recognize this feeling. Pulled into such a state, the answer many of us reach is this: yield. No choice is there. To be free, you must do it. And then figure out how to deal with the consequences. Start that affair with your office-mate. Tell your boss how bad he smells. Cook the books. Steal from the collection plate. Hurl a brick through your neighbor's window. Answer that adult services ad placed by that person who specializes in you-know-what. I, too, took the yielding path. I killed a person—just to kill, for no other reason—and I have gone unpunished.

"THERE IT IS, THE OPENING page of *My Murder*." I watched Hal Hemmings shut the book and stare into the camera. "This week, this book is on best-seller lists across the country. A fanciful exercise in imagination? Or, as the author claims, a true confession of a senseless murder he committed and got away with? Today we have with us the author of that book, Webb Seiden."

The red applause light ticked on. The studio audience began clapping.

119

"Stay with us. We'll be right back with the man who says he is a cold-blooded killer."

Gail Renda ran her fingers through my hair and complained about the makeup artist. I watched the monitor and worried about the strands her long fingers were collecting. Her broad, moon-shaped face was flush.

"There's not enough under your eyes. They probably want you to look evil. Remember what I told you: If I were them, I would load the audience with relatives of victims of unsolved homicides. They'll spring them on you in the second segment. We negotiated with them an exclusive—no other guests on the show—but we cannot control how they might fix the crowd. Be ready. Be natural. Talk to him, not the camera. And say the title whenever you can—especially when you come back from a break."

I listened to my agent, as she again straightened the tie we had purchased this morning. Ready, I was ready. The first time out is the hardest, everyone said. Get past this, it all will be easier. In my pocket I fingered the small stone I had picked up years ago at the grave site of Faulkner. Margaret had been with me then. We thought we soon would be married. Now she was gone. Now I was about to step before television cameras. With no complaints: this was what I had asked for. Now I was a published author.

"Say the title," Renda said, as I left the room.

A producer guided me to the chair. The audience stared. The host stood on the other side of the stage. He did not say hello. Someone shouted, "Fifteen seconds." The lights were hot. On cue, Hemmings did his lead-in. He then ran toward me, yelling his first question: "Mr. Seiden, did you actually kill someone just to kill them?"

"Yes."

"And then you capitalized on this heinous crime by writing this book?"

"Well, I did write . . ."

"So you're making money—I'm told the book is flying out of stores—off this act of murder?"

"I do have a book out. Its title is—"

"Mr. Seiden, you do understand why many people—myself included—are outraged that . . ."

He carried on. I waited. I knew I would be waiting for weeks to come. Just one moment after another, I told myself. I answered the questions when he allowed me the chance. Yes, I had tried to be a screenwriter. Yes, I had not succeeded. Yes, the only script I had been able to sell was the one for a B movie called *Lust Island*. Yes, I had committed a murder merely to see what it would be like. But, no, I didn't do it to write this book. In fact, several years passed between the event and the publication of *My Murder*.

"The event? What a sterile term. And who was she? The other person in this 'event.' You do say in the book your victim was a woman."

"Actually, Mr. Hemmings, I made it clear in the book that I would not disclose details that might assist any investigator. I explained that I would refer to the victim as 'she'—I never knew the person's name—but that did not mean that the victim had been a woman. It's all in the book."

"Excuse me, I haven't read it. Nor do I plan to. And I would urge anyone watching not to buy your . . . your deplorable book."

Before I could respond, he jumped into the audience and placed his microphone in front of the face of a white-haired mountain of a woman wearing thick glasses.

"Pretty sick, isn't it?" he said.

"Hal, he's a real sick fuck," she said. Later I would learn that someone in the control room had dubbed a tone over the last word of her sentence.

"We'll be right back," Hemmings said.

In three minutes, we were. We covered some details of the event. I had been driving, picked up a hitchhiker. Talked a bit. Stopped an hour or so down the road. Used a knife. Ditched the body in the woods. Went on my way.

"Why? I don't get it. Why?"

"Read the first page. That's the best explanation."

"Here's another page," he said.

The power. The surge. It can only sound like a cliché. But, then, this must be one of the oldest acts known to our species. I felt I had joined a club. Yet, strangely, not one that meant a great deal—or as great a deal as I had anticipated. I half-expected another club member to find me out, to come to my home one night, present his credentials, and tell me the secret. "You see, it's not as special as you thought. But welcome anyway." As with so much in life, it was the joining that was notable, not the ever-after state of having joined.

"Mr. Seiden, I respectfully submit you are full of you-know-what and should be locked up with all the other murderous creeps. Why should we believe you won't do this again, if your sorry little heart so desires?"

Time for another break—no answer.

Renda had been wrong. It was not until the third segment that Hemmings introduced audience members related to the victims of unsolved murders. "Maybe you killed my Janey," an older man shouted. "My Manuel," a woman said. "My Daddy," a girl shouted. "No details," I said, "none."

"Can't you even have the decency to look at these people and tell them that you are *not* responsible for the death of their loved one?"

"Was it on Route 38, near Yucaipa?" yelled a man in the front row.

In front of me were the images: the road, the sky, the face, the woods, the body, the leaves, the stillness.

No details, I repeated, no details.

"Some people think this is a hoax, that you didn't kill anyone, that you're in this only for the big bucks and some perverse ego thrill. I don't know which would be sicker."

"Mr. Hemmings, I stand behind my work."

"The book or the murder?"

"*My Murder*, my book."

58:10 into the hour. Done. An assistant escorted me off the set and to the green room. The makeup artist wiped my face clean. Hemmings came in. "Great show," he said and departed. Renda and I left the building through the rear entrance. We stepped into a waiting limousine. "Terrific," she breathed into my ear.

MORE SHOWS. MORE CONFRONTATIONS. NEWSPAPER columnists condemned me. Members of the clergy sermonized against me. Politicians promised legislation. The President pronounced me despicable. I was all that was wrong with society. A national newsmagazine put my face on its cover, above the line, "The Most Hated Man in America?" I was grateful for the question mark. A tabloid television show reported I was having an affair with an older actress. I had never met the woman. A supermarket gossip sheet claimed that Renda secretly had offered to provide to that magazine proof my book was false, if it would pay her $150,000. She released a statement denying the story. I bought a black convertible. There were symposia across the nation on the responsibilities of publishing houses. Doesn't promoting books such as this one, ponderous moderators asked, only encourage people? I declined invitations to all such affairs. A former professor of mine called Renda. I lost the message. My parents were snubbed at their tennis club. The obsessed pored over each page, searching for clues, some to crack the case, some to prove I was a fraud. Development execs at the studios rang. They promised I could write the screenplay. The book sold. My roommate moved out of the Melrose bungalow we shared. I retained a realtor to look for a place in the hills. I changed my phone number three times.

Renda kept pressing me on the next "project." She never called it a book.

"Move fast, capitalize on all this," she said one afternoon, while we ate salads at a sidewalk restaurant in Santa Monica. "No turning back, honey."

She suggested the next project chronicle this whole episode. Another bestseller, she said. The advance would be high six figures, initial shipping of two hundred thousand at least. She even had the title: *The Murder Wars*.

"A little too violent?" I asked.

She looked crossed at me when I informed her that I had begun a novel based on a series of hunting trips taken by my great-grandfather when he was a young man in Montana. She said nothing while the waiter poured sparkling water into our glasses.

"Webb, dear, people have stood by you. Taken flack, a great deal of it. Been talked about in none too pleasant fashion. Don't abandon them to follow a fancy."

"I am always with you," I told her. She leaned over and tussled my hair, again taking several strands with her.

"I am almost always here," I told the police detective who came to my front door later that day. It was my way of apologizing for having missed her earlier. Look over there, I directed her. I had placed by my phone the note—written on LAPD stationery—she had dropped in the mailbox. This was proof of my intention to phone the number she had left. I had been intrigued by the name on the note: Anna Rixt. How could one pass up the opportunity to meet an LAPD cop with this name? But I had been distracted by a host of e-mail messages I had received that day from members of a Gothic literary electronic conference I had joined under a false name.

Now Anna Rixt stood a foot or two into the living room. She began by noting that I did not have to let her in or speak with her. I waved aside her obligatory remarks.

"German?" I asked. "Flemish?"

"Dutch," she said, as I invited her to sit.

Her father had been a Dutch jazz drummer; her mother, a black American movie extra. At her prime, the light-skinned mother had a lovely, smooth and oval face. That was before the heroin. I learned all this later. Anna Rixt had kinky, sandy hair, wide lips, sharp lines at the side of her hazel eyes, broad shoulders, long, slender arms. Thirty-seven, I guessed silently. She wore no wedding ring.

"Lemonade?" I asked. "Fresh from my own tree."

"As long as there's not too much sugar."

I went to the kitchen and fetched the lemonade.

She informed me she had not come to question me directly about the murder in my book. But she wondered if she could discuss with me in general terms the subject of killing.

"It might help me in my work."

I did not believe her, but felt like helping her. My contact with the police had been on the cool side during these past weeks. A sergeant at the local station had called twice to notify me that the department had received a death threat concerning me. Each time he noted brusquely that a patrol car would swing by periodically. I, too, had received threats in letters and calls, despite having changed my number. But it would have been bad form to request assistance from the authorities. On a couple of evenings in a row, I noticed the same car slowing when it passed my house. Another victim's relative or a detective from Nevada assigned an unbreakable case, I guessed.

I waited for a confrontation, but the car never stopped. My book, my choice, my problems. No need to burden the police.

I felt sympathy for homicide detectives who believed my book mocked their arduous existences. So whatever I could do for Rixt—within reason—I would do. And I was curious. She told me she had wondered about the internal justifications that occur within the psyche of a murderer ever since her first case—a woman found with her mouth and nostrils glued shut by epoxy. That case, Rixt noted, was never solved.

But I suspected that another imperative had brought her to me. I pictured a scene: Detective Rixt at her desk. The phone rings. Some Higher Up had just been ripped a new anus by another Higher Up for not doing anything about that jerk on television who is making a million for having bumped off a party unknown with complete impunity. Down the chain of command, the order came: do something. And Rixt, at her cluttered desk in an office in dire need of a fresh coat of paint, was the order's final recipient. She had to visit the most hated man in America.

"There's a portion of the book that intrigued me." She sipped the lemonade and took a copy of my book out of her bag.

"I hope the office paid for it."

"No, I did." She did not get the joke. She began to read:

Guilt had been my greatest fear. I realized before I acted that I could not be sure what emotions, what compulsions would be borne of this event. Would they be as powerful—or more so—as the original impulse, the original sin? Would the commission of this murder create another force within me that was beyond control? I thought of the old cinematic depictions of the murderer so racked by remorse he confesses. I had no desire to be found out. Yet who could predict with rock-fast certainty that he—and he would have to be speaking for his entire conscious—would stick to this path? Who could be truly sure that some Sunday-school part of him would not rebel, without any declaration of intent, and purposefully drop a clue? There was now a killer inside me, and I could not be certain that I saw all of him in broad daylight.

I waited for him to cause trouble. For him to leverage the guilt. Nothing came. Yes, there were pangs. This had been a shitty thing to do. I realized that. But no heavy weight descended. And, as far as I could tell, there was no inchoate urge for penance. Someone might argue that the writing of this book is driven by guilt. It is not. If I were not fully convinced that I could write this book and escape legal punishment, these words would never have appeared. All of us have read a news report of a grisly action—a thug raping a nun, a colonel torturing a child, an army destroying an entire town of civilians, bayoneting babies, dropping napalm—and wondered, "How could they do it?" I would hazard a guess that many of us harbor the innate knowledge that no matter what horrible deeds we may do, eventually we will be all right. That the guilt, if present at the start, will fade. One of the few universal lessons of human existence is that everything fades. The guilt I never knew is gone. There might be others who are consumed by guilt, but I happen to be one of the lucky ones.

Anna Rixt put down my book. "No guilt at all?"
"As I said."
"When dealing with murderers, many of us count on, if not guilt, then the nervousness that we assume is the product of guilt."
"Nervousness might be of assistance," I said, as I placed my hands behind my head and gazed at the ceiling. "But I can only advise that you do not unduly associate it with guilt. A person in your custody would have reason to be nervous with or without guilt."
Good line, I thought.
We chatted for almost an hour. I did my best to answer her, until she checked her watch and said, "Thank you for your time, Mr. Seiden." She stood up and knocked over the pitcher of lemonade—it shattered on the floor.
"Don't move," I said and got the broom and dustpan. She stood by awkwardly in the puddle as I cleared the broken glass from around her. When I was done, she headed toward the front door. I asked if she intended to call on me again. She turned to look at me but did not reply. When I returned to the living room I saw that she had left her copy of my book. I opened it. She had underlined passages and written notes in the margins, in some spots rather extensively. I shut the book. It would be an intrusion upon her privacy, I thought, to read her jottings.

SEVERAL DAYS LATER, I SAT at the kitchen table, thinking about Anna Rixt, wondering if she would return. It was late afternoon, that portion of the day that cinematographers call "magic hour," when the long rays of a declining sun cast a glow. I was sifting through brittle letters my great-grandfather had written as a young man to an uncle in Philadelphia. One described when he was trapping near Flathead Lake in Montana and met an Indian man and a white woman who lived together in a cabin. The pair were startled to have a visitor, but with a storm front moving in, they invited him to supper and offered him a spot on the floor for the night. Neither the man nor the woman said much. They never mentioned their names nor asked his. In the morning, as he packed up to head out into the rain, the woman said, "We'd prefer you not say anything to other folks about us." My great-grandfather vowed not to and in his letter allowed himself but one observation on this episode: "Only far away from the rest of us could they find civility."

The phone rang. "Turn on the television."

"Who is—"

"Turn it on, you damn idiot," Renda said and hung up.

I went to the living room and picked up the remote. I only had to flip through several channels before I found where I was supposed to be. A woman surrounded by a group of reporters stood in front of LAPD headquarters: ". . . he's making all this money off of"—she was crying, stammering—"off of . . . of me." She paused while the cameramen jostled in front of her. The woman was thirtyish. She wore oversized sunglasses. A red scarf covered her hair. Not much of her face was exposed. An older woman in a business suit touched her hand, and she continued. "He tried to kill me. It was awful, I never wanted to ever see, to think about—but then I was watching television and there he was. He was right up there, talking about this as if it were nothing, as if I were not even a . . . a dog."

The older woman introduced herself as the speaker's attorney and declared that her client had been my victim, that I had not killed her as I had written, but that I had severely wounded her and left her for dead. Six years ago, the lawyer said, the woman in the red scarf was the hitchhiker I had picked up. After being stabbed repeatedly and then dumped in a ravine, this woman had managed to crawl a few hundred feet and had been discovered by two hunters. The attorney noted that her client barely survived the assault and emerged traumatized, with a murky recollection of her assailant and no memory of his car. She had been able to provide only sketchy information to the local police. The attorney read from the police report: "Victim identified assailant as male Caucasian in mid-thirties, of slim build, about six feet tall and 170 pounds, with dark or light brown hair." Close, I thought, but heftier than me.

"I never could remember the face," said the woman in the red scarf. "I never wanted to. Such a horrible, horrible. . . . But I saw his face on television. It was like I was there again. Everything came back. Even how, when he thought I was dead, he came over to me and said, 'Thanks for the company.' Then walked away. And I remember hearing the engine of the car turn over."

The attorney took charge. She explained that she had turned over relevant information to the LAPD and that the police in Yermo—where her client had been assaulted—had requested assistance from the Los Angeles department. "Would there be a lawsuit?" one reporter yelled. "Anything is possible," the lawyer replied. "A book deal for her, too?" "If anyone deserves money it's this poor woman."

"How do we know this is for real?" another journalist asked.

"Real? Real?" the woman shouted. "How's this for real?" She lifted her blouse. Her abdomen was covered with ugly scars. She pulled down her collar. A thick, crooked scar on the neck. She took off her glasses. Another one below her eye. "Real enough?"

I picked up the phone. "Is it—" Renda began to ask. "You know, I've never once asked you."

"I know. Are you asking, now, Gail?"

"No, not really. But are you prepared for all the shit that's about to rain down?"

"No."

"Well, I hate to say this, but this will sell more books. I'll be right over."

THE REPORTERS ARRIVED BEFORE RENDA. When a pack had gathered, I stood outside the front door and said that I could not corroborate the woman's account.

"She's not the one who you cold-bloodedly executed for the hell of it?" I could not see who had asked that.

"I've said before that I would not address any specifics."

"You deny her story 100 percent?"

"No denials, no confirmations."

"When you kill someone, they stay dead, don't they?"

I waited for the next question.

"What is your response to the statement from LAPD that it will examine these allegations?"

"It's what I would expect the LAPD to say."

"If the police ask you to supply an alibi, will you?"

"I will try to be helpful, in accordance with the guidelines I've already established."

"Do you think this is a publicity stunt to cash in?"

"By who?"

Renda's aquamarine BMW pulled up. She jumped out of the car, pushed through the crowd and grabbed me.

"Thank you all for your time," she said to the reporters and pulled me into the house.

Renda left several hours later—aggravated. No, I would not reappear on the Hemmings show with my accuser. No, I would not grant any magazine an exclusive interview. No, I would not hire a high-priced Beverly Hills defense attorney. No, I would not reconsider my refusal to write a follow-up book. Yes, the appearance of this woman would provide an entirely new dimension to such a book.

"You're going to have to fight back," Renda said as she walked toward the street.

Why?

"Because that's the way it works." She climbed into her BMW.

"By the way," she said as the window glided shut, "this fellow named Shea keeps calling me. Says he taught you at USC. He's a pain in the ass. Will you call him or something?"

THE WAITRESS BROUGHT ME MY second beer, as I waited for the ceviche and read an article in a science magazine about a type of DNA that passes only from mothers to their children. So, I thought, no men in these near-infinite chains of evolutionary evidence. And then Rixt appeared. She explained she had been directed to this tacky Mexican restaurant by a neighbor. I knew which one: the retired claims adjustor, who tracked all the details of my life that could be discerned from his windows. I suspected him of falsely informing a tabloid that I had received nocturnal visits from the leading actress of a popular situation comedy.

"I hope I am not disturbing you."

She sat at the table and with no further conversation asked me if I could account for my whereabouts on a specific date six years ago. I told her I would check my records, but I doubted they were organized enough to be of use. She said that she had DMVed me and discovered that I did not own a car at that time. "Living in L.A. without a car?" she asked. I told her that I had been sharing a car with a friend. "And that was?" I gave her Margaret's name and asked if she would like a drink. She ordered a rum with ice and lime.

"This is going to be a waste of time for you," I said.

"Her story is a persuasive one."

"Entirely convincing?"

"Well, her cousin is the assistant sheriff in Yermo and the one who signed the police report she's handed over to LAPD."

"Are you suggesting this might be a—"

"No. Just one more item to check."

"If the point was to murder someone, don't you think whoever did that would make sure the subject was murdered?"

"If people didn't screw up, I'd have no job."

My food came, and I pushed it aside. "What's her name?"

"Haven't you watched the news?"

"I did but I blanked on her name."

"Connie Dicomini."

"You think there is a case to be made here?" I asked.

"There is a point to be made."

"A point?"

"That you cannot smartass the law. Let more people think that and the world will be even nastier for cops and people like me."

"So better any resolution than the accurate one?"

"Everything depends. Every time is different." She finished her drink.

"What if the wrong person is used to make the point?"

"That would be a terrible thing. And it happens. Most people in jail deserved to be there long before they were caught. But I know a few who don't. They're living their own private hells. No system can process all the intake we get these days and not screw up. But I will say one thing. When the wrong person is blamed and punished, a small good is still committed."

She waited for me to ask, but I did not.

"And that is, all the rest of us are shown it's not getting any easier to rob, beat, shoot, slice, rape, kill and avoid the consequences."

"Yes, but in those cases the person who performed the deed falsely credited to another learns that this lesson is a lie."

"That's why I called it a 'small good.' "

She stood up to leave. I offered to walk her to her car. She declined and said she would stop by in the morning, after I had had a chance to check on the date in question. I listened to her boot heels click against the floor tiles.

"You left your copy of my book at my house," I called after her.

"That's okay," she said. "I don't think I need it right now."

Rixt did not come by the next day. I screened all my calls, refusing to talk to an assortment of journalists, a bevy of lawyers, and Renda. "We must develop a plan," an agitated Renda said to my machine. "And do something about that professor of yours. He keeps bothering me." I tried to work on the Montana novel, but every half an hour another television producer rang the doorbell. I sent them away.

Shortly after noon, the bell sounded again. At the door was a woman who looked familiar. I impatiently asked what she wanted. She stared for a moment. I asked again.

"You don't know, do you?"

The red scarf. Connie Dicomini. And behind her was a mob of reporters, photographers and camera operators.

"I wanted to see you," she said.

"Now that you see me, are you still so sure?"

"Yes, yes I am. It was buried in my mind. Now it's not. Answer me one question. I have to know: how could you?"

Lines of water ran from her face; her expression remained steely. The end of a scar peeked out from behind the sunglasses. The scene was being broadcast live.

"I can't say anything," I told her.

"Yes, you can. You choose not to say anything. So you can continue to torment me and collect millions. But I won't stand for it. Maybe they'll put you away, maybe they won't. But I want an answer. I don't care how long it takes. I'll be waiting. I'll be everywhere until you can tell me why what happened to me happened to me."

She spat in my face and walked away.

"Got it good," one cameraman said to his producer.

For the next week, she was constantly nearby. Wearing her sunglasses and red scarf, she sat in a car outside my house. She followed me when I walked to the corner each morning to get a coffee and a paper. Her car was in my rearview mirror whenever I checked. She never said another word to me. At night, I stayed up late, sitting at the window, with the lights out, and watched her alone in her car. For the first couple of days, the news people followed her as she followed me. I stayed away from the television to avoid the alleged-victim-keeps-lonely-vigil stories. Renda, who paid daily visits, never mentioned her.

I considered crafting a response for Connie Dicomini. But nothing came. I would not be able to satisfy her. I waited too for Rixt. There was no word from her. But early one morning, I heard from Margaret. She had not returned any of the calls I had placed to her when my book was about to be released. Now, she informed me, she was calling as a "courtesy to the past."

"I'll accept any courtesy I can get."

"This detective came by last night, she had an odd name. She asked me questions about you. But mostly she wanted to know where you were on a certain weekend six years ago."

An obliging Margaret had checked an old personal calendar for Rixt and discovered that she had been traveling that weekend. In the calendar, she had written "Webb—Joshua Tree," which she interpreted as a reference to one of my many solo overnight trips to the national park. Margaret had gone through phone records and found that no long-distance calls had been made from our phone on the relevant days.

"Webb, I couldn't say I knew where you were."

"I probably can't either."

"I did ask her, what if we assumed you had gone to Joshua Tree, would it still have been possible for you to, to . . ."

She was crying.

"And she said, 'Maybe.' " The old silence. "And I can't cover for you. I can't."

"If you want to know Margaret, I'll tell you. No one knows. But I'll tell you."

"I've got to go. Goodbye."

I STAYED IN MY HOUSE as much as I could. I kept up with the e-mail correspondence I maintained under various screen names. I listened to all the one-way conversations people held with my answering machine.

There were several calls from Maury Shea, a washed-out screenwriter whose course I had taken at Southern Cal. Decades earlier a script of his had been nominated for an Oscar. And every screenplay he wrote after that had gone unproduced. By the time I had come to sit in his classroom, he was dishing out stale recitals of his eight principles of successful screenplay writing and recounting for the millionth time the stories of his lunches, dinners and drinks with Welles, Huston, and Brando, during which they beseeched him for the opportunity to direct or appear in his next film— the one that never came. His eight principles were conventional but useful. I recalled being quite pleased that I had incorporated seven of them into the script for *Lust Island*.

I had no particular feelings toward Shea and ignored his calls as I did all others. Then when I was picking up the phone to order a linen jacket from a catalog, I found Shea on the line, trying to call me. He was mad that I had not returned his messages and told me that we had to talk right away.

"Let's talk," I said.

"No. No. Not like this. Come see me. I have to show you something."

"I'm pretty busy."

"If you don't, I'll, I'll go and . . . I already told . . . I can prove you a fraud."

"How so?"

"Just come, if you want to know. Believe me, you want to know."

He was right. I wrote down his address. We agreed I would drop by the next morning.

When I woke up I engaged in my new daily ritual. I went to the living room and, shielding myself behind a curtain, peered outside. She was still there. I realized I was waiting for two women to act. I wanted Connie Dicomini to vanish; I wanted Anna Rixt to reappear. For the first time since my book had come out, I wanted an end to all this.

Another ring of the doorbell. Two detectives from the homicide division of LAPD introduced themselves and asked if they could come in and talk to me.

"About what?"

"About certain allegations that have been made," one said.

I told them that I did not think I should talk to them without a lawyer present. The tall one—only he talked—informed me that they would appreciate it, then, if I came down to their office later in the day with my attorney. He handed me his card.

"If that is not convenient for you," he said, "we will be happy to call upon you again."

"What about Detective Rixt?"

"We're handling the case," the talking detective replied with a frown. "We'll be seeing you."

I found the note Rixt had left me and called the handwritten number on it.

"You have reached Anna Rixt, please—"

Voice mail. I phoned the station house and asked for her. Someone there suggested I contact headquarters. "Rixt, Rixt—sounds familiar," a downtown desk sergeant said. "Hold on." He checked and then asked if I wanted to speak to someone else in homicide. "Detective Rixt left the force two years ago."

I picked up the copy of my book that Rixt had left behind. I found a passage next to which she had scribbled a few words I could not decipher. I had not read the book since it had been in galleys and now could not recall having written these lines.

I was keenly aware that this was a dividing point. Whatever change occurred in me between the "before" side of the event and the "after," there would be no returning. So much in life can actually be undone. You can divorce a spouse you come to hate. You can quit a job. You can declare bankruptcy and start anew. You cannot undo a death. Once I had a conversation with a friend before he had a tattoo of a cup of coffee drawn above his right shoulder-blade. What if you change your mind someday? I asked him. What if you grow to dislike your tattoo? That's the whole point, he said. It is forever. How often do you do something that is forever?

Renda pounded on the door until I let her in. She held a fax. "See this. See this. They want a deal."

I told her I was not interested.

"Even with all the shit with that woman—or because of it—and they still want a deal. Some people have been scared off. You better take it now. They could easily turn around and offer it to her."

"Not interested."

Renda tried to convince me. I knew that she saw this as a step toward obtaining a studio job—her dream for many of her forty years. "What's the point," she shouted, "in representing someone who doesn't want to be represented?"

"Gail, what would happen if I declared that the whole book was a ruse?"

"That would be it for you. Nothing, no more. Not too good for me, either."

She sat down on the couch and was silent for a moment. "Would that be the truth?"

"I was only thinking aloud."

I made her a cup of tea, and she settled down. I didn't mention the detectives. I told her I was going to visit Shea.

"What for?" she asked.

"Old times, I suppose. Get him off your unduly burdened back."

Before she left, she tousled my hair. I thought about complaining this time. I was becoming possessive about the hair I had, and I never cared for this overdone display of tenderness. But there already was enough tension between us. Let the small stuff rest, I decided. "Honey," she said, "please think about the deal. But I can see I am going to have to start searching for other opportunities."

CONNIE DICOMINI FOLLOWED ME ONTO the freeway. I did not know what Shea wanted, but I figured it would be best if I arrived without my usual escort. I brought my black convertible up to 90. I assumed that Dicomini would be caught off guard; I had never tried to escape her watchful gaze. She dropped behind, but soon was back, matching my speed. I slowed to 40; she slowed. I returned to 90. She was there. I repeatedly switched lanes, and she stuck with me. I moved into the right lane and cruised along. She remained close. As I was coming upon an exit, I checked the mirror. The lane to the left was open, and there was little traffic behind us. I jerked the wheel to the left and slammed my foot on the brake pedal. Connie Dicomini went flying past. I then pulled the wheel to the right—in time to jump across the right lane and make the exit. Too many hours of television, I told myself and rode along surface streets in Universal City.

Shea lived in a seedy portion of Van Nuys. I drove past his house, parked down the block at a 7-Eleven, picked up a package of cigarettes—I had not smoked in years—and walked back to Shea's house. I rapped on the frame of the screen door, and he opened it for me. Shea was tall, gaunt, pale, covered with liver spots. Dull gray stubble ran across his face. Long strands of limp white hair hung from the back of his head. He wore a fraying bathrobe over pale blue pajamas. He led me in, relying on a cane and shaking as he walked slowly. "Aneurysm operation," he said by way of explanation. All the blinds were drawn inside the house. Old newspapers and magazines were piled in various corners. Movie posters from the 1960s were crooked on the walls. He shuffled to a couch and fell into it. As I made contact with the Barcalounger, a cloud of dust emerged, and I coughed.

"You sick too?" Shea asked.

"No."

"Never let them operate. Three years ago they said they had to fix this aneurysm. It didn't bother me any, but they said she could blow any moment. So I let them. Now I can hardly walk. Can't drive. Tired all the time.

All these damn headaches. And I haven't had a boner since. Insurance covered most of it, but it's cost me thousands. Rehabilitation, physical therapy. Can't afford the cable now. Look a lot different than when you last saw me?"

"A little."

"You don't look different to me, 'cause I can't remember what you looked like. My memory's almost as useless as my pecker."

From lunch with Brando to a San Fernando Valley hermit, I thought. On the mantel were framed photographs covered with dust.

"So if I had seen you on any of all those television shows or read about you in the paper—but I don't read the paper anymore—I wouldn't have remembered you at all. Nothing. Nada. Like thousands of people I once knew—a zero to me now. All gone."

He looked up from his hands. "Name them."

"What?"

"The fuckin' eight principles."

"Professor Shea, what did you want to tell me?"

"Okay, okay, screw the fuckin' eight principles. Maybe there were nine and I missed one."

He pulled on his hair. A woman came to see him several weeks ago. He can't remember her name. She said she's a reporter. She found out that I had been a student of his. She asked if he remembered anything about me. He explained to her all about the aneurysm operation, the bad memory, the bad pecker.

But, he told her, he has boxes. In the other room, boxes and boxes. Everything is in the boxes. Together they went through dozens of boxes—until they found the one from USC. Took awhile because it was labeled "insurance forms and warranties." And in the box are all the records from all his classes. Had this exercise he made all the little shitheads do, he explained to her. Sprung it on them like a trap. Came into the classroom, said, no lecture today. You have thirty minutes to write ten fuckin' fantastic film ideas—each no more than two sentences. Let's see what happens if you run into Mr. Studio Big-Dick this afternoon at a car wash. I graded them and gave them back, he told her.

But not before copying them. Not that he was going to swipe their ideas, most of which sucked. Not that. But they were good kicks to his own brainstorming. Sometimes he'd pull out the ten-idea sheets, rummage through them, get the juices flowing. And he still had every damn paper. Including mine.

I had forgotten all about Shea's ten-ideas exercise.

"Right here," he said and knocked a stack of *TV Guide*s off the table in front of him. He held it up for me. I reached out my hand.

"No, no, no. . . . Let me read it to you."

Number one: the Devil, disguised as a high-power lawyer, takes over a large New York corporate law firm. A young associate in the firm discovers this and attempts to thwart him.

"Not bad. I can see that," Shea said.

Number five: Instead of being blackmailed by a political opponent, the President of the United States, at the start of an election campaign, announces he is a transvestite. He then tries to convince the country—and his wife—that he deserves another term.

"Ahead of your time, Mr. Seiden."

Number ten: A washed-up minor-league pitcher, who is a former Special Forces veteran, stumbles upon a terrorist plot to blow up the Astrodome during the World Series. He and his teenage punk-rock nephew derail the scheme.

"Clearly, you were running out of steam. Oh, I skipped this interesting one."

Number four: Someone claims responsibility for a murder he did not commit and then proceeds to cash in on it.

"A little on the vague side, but we can easily fill in the details."
Shea wanted money. He said he would let me start the bidding. What did I think was fair? "Never done this before," he said.
"What about the reporter?" I asked.
She had wanted to take it. He had demanded she pay for it. She said that if she needed it she would come back—and then she never did.
"Drink?" He pointed to a bottle of bourbon and two crusty glasses on the table.
"No, thank you."
"Need some ice." He stood up and grabbed my list. "Think I'll keep this close." He hobbled off to the kitchen.
I tried to think quickly and thoroughly. The list was not solid proof my book was a ruse, but it was strong evidence for that proposition. He thought I would want it buried. In a perfect world, yes. But perhaps it now was more important for the paper to be disclosed. If so, how the paper became public would be crucial. If I refused to pay him and stormed out, would he find another reporter to sell it to? Or would he consider Connie Dicomini's accusations and come to realize that the paper, if revealed, might help me? Then would he sit on this list until I paid him? But if I

bought it from him, could I release it myself? Probably not. I would be accused of having faked it. Shea would not be a reliable source for confirming the origins of the paper. A reporter had seen it. She could attest to its validity. But her name was lost.

The door to the kitchen squeaked, and Shea entered the room. One hand held the paper. The other grasped a bowl of ice and the cane. A finger slipped, and the bowl fell.

"Shit," he said—and slipped on a piece of ice and fell backward. He landed hard and did not move. I rushed to Shea. My paper lay next to him. I kicked an ice cube away from it. He was still, but breathing. I heard a car drive past and saw that the front door was open. What if someone came in now? Shea on the ground, my paper beside him, me in the house. All easily twisted. Taking the paper would do me no good—unless I was certain I never wanted it to become public in a credible way. The postman could be next door and heading this way. But I had to proceed through all the calculations. When Shea came to, no doubt he would call me and we could start negotiations again. Let's say he didn't revive. Would it be better for my list to be there by his side or not? I could not figure that out. Should I stay with the path chosen, do what had to be done, round out rough spots, tidy everything up, be in control? Or leave him this way? I considered dragging Shea to the couch. Go, said a voice. Do it, said a voice. I realized I had not touched anything in the house, only the armrest of the Barcalounger. If—just if—he was not going to be fine, it probably would be best for my fingerprints not to be on the chair. The voices in my head were hard to separate. They created a fog. I stood over Shea. I felt lost in the fog. Then it lifted. I wiped the chair and walked out the door without looking back at him.

THE TRIAL LASTED LESS THAN three weeks. The jury needed seven hours to declare me guilty and another five to decide upon a sentence: death. It had been easy for the prosecutor to convince the jurors that I had been the person who had bashed a bourbon bottle into the front of Shea's head and had killed him. Connie Dicomini testified that I had lost her on the freeway, heading in the direction of Shea's home. Gloria Renda testified that I had informed her I was off to see Shea. After her testimony, on the courthouse steps, Renda announced that she would be representing Dicomini in negotiations with several publishing houses. A clerk at the 7-Eleven told the jury that she remembered recognizing me that day as "that awful man from the TV shows." A criminologist appeared with charts and showed that hairs found at the crime scene were consistent with my hair. The deputy county coroner noted that Shea had experienced blows to the back and front of his skull. He could not be positive which had been the lethal one, but he assumed it had been the one to the frontal lobe. Throughout the trial, there was no mention of any paper that had fallen next to Shea. It apparently had not been there when Shauna Fowbray—yes, of the U.S. Postal Service—had discovered the body.

I never took the stand. My lawyer advised me not to do so. During preliminary hearings he had fought successfully to prevent the prosecutors from referring explicitly to my book. The judge ruled that the prosecution could only mention my book if I testified. My lawyer also argued that due to my notoriety I could not receive a fair trial. The judge angrily replied that there was no way on God's green earth that he would allow the fact that I had bragged about committing one murder to prevent me from being tried for another. Throughout jury selection, he asked potential jurors if they had heard of my book. Most said yes. He asked those whether they could judge this case purely on its merits and the evidence presented in court. All said yes.

The district attorney's office only had one problem: my motive.

"We will admit we are puzzled by the 'why' of this murder," the lead prosecutor said during his summation. "We can only guess at what goes on in the mind of such a heartless, soulless person." The media reported that the prosecutors, having learned that I had been in Shea's class at the time of the assault on Connie Dicomini, believed that Shea had known something about my supposed attack upon her. The tabloids reported that Shea and I had been lovers.

My lawyer complained that he had no case. I had told him why I had gone to Shea's home and about the paper. "But it was not on the police list of recovered items," he said. Had I kept the original? he asked. I could not recall. I was being held without bond, so he rummaged through the filing cabinet in my garage and found nothing there. There was a possibility that my graduate school papers might have ended up in one of the boxes that Margaret had taken, but whenever my lawyer phoned, she hung up.

During a pre-arrest interrogation—to which I had submitted voluntarily, against my lawyer's advice—I had told the detectives on the case, the two men who had come to my home, about the paper and where I had last seen it. "There was no paper to save your pink-ass butt," said the talking member of the pair. "You did it. You know you did it. Read your million-ass-dollar book: *'No, it didn't feel like a dream. But time was odd, soft. Not until I pulled over for a coffee, did I reenter my own life again.'* The expert speaks. Tell yourself you know, and you'll remember. You say it all got foggy when you were standing there. People tell us that all the time. You wouldn't believe how many people. 'It went dark,' 'It went hazy,' 'It went fuckin' mauve.' "

During the preparation for the trial, I had told my lawyer about Rixt. He promised he would have an associate check on her. A week later he handed me a file. Rixt had been a cop, with a solid performance rating.

One night she shot her partner. The newspaper articles told how they had been caught in a shoot-out in an alley behind a warehouse. Her story was that they had been responding to a tip and were fired on by unknown assailants. She returned fire; her partner went down. The review board concluded that he had been killed by a bullet from her gun. Prior to his death, the newspaper clippings noted, her partner had come under internal investigation for trafficking drugs. Rixt was cleared of any wrongdoing in the shooting—and refused to talk about it publicly. She left the force and became a private detective. The file contained an old publicity still of her mother in her heyday and a few jazz magazine references to her father.

My lawyer went to see her. She had a small office above a copying store in Silver Lake. She had been hired by a client to look into my case, she explained. She would not say who the client had been. Nor would she say whether she had discovered anything of use to my defense. Rixt did disclose she had been visited by the detectives working my case. I told them the same thing I am telling you, she said. My lawyer concluded she could not be of any help to us. But I never stopped wondering who had retained Rixt.

Throughout my incarceration, I considered the alternative scenarios. Assume Connie Dicomini managed to follow me. After I left Shea's house, she knocks on the door. Not hearing anything, she enters and spots the old man on the ground. She picks up the paper, reads it, and realizes it might be proof that the man she is accusing might be innocent of the charge. Does she kill Shea to protect her version of the truth?

But she could not have trailed me. I had lost her on the highway.

Had Renda seen Shea's address at my house? Say she did. She then drives there and it's the same setup as with the first scenario. Renda does not want to be the partner of a proven fraud. There's no deal in that. Maybe Renda's association with Dicomini began before the trial, before my trip to Shea's house. Could she that day, on the way out of my home, have stopped by Dicomini's car and slipped her Shea's address?

How about this: both arrive and enter the house after my departure. Renda had this habit of tousling my thinning hair and grabbing a few strands. So she plants the hair in Shea's house and collects the paper. Who grabbed the bourbon bottle—and then walked away with the broken-off neck of the shattered bottle, the other piece of evidence that the police never found?

You have no proof, my lawyer reminded me repeatedly.

Renda never visited. I read in the paper that she had brokered a book deal for Dicomini. My lawyer, with no great enthusiasm, worked on an appeal. Months after the trial, I was able to start working again on the Montana novel.

I was in the prison library fruitlessly searching for information on the silverite movement in the West in the 1890s, when I realized that I had

overlooked something. The first chance I had I called Rixt collect. She
hung up on the operator. I wrote her. There was no reply. Over the next
six months, I called whenever possible and wrote her a letter every day.
Finally, one Sunday morning, I was informed a visitor was waiting for
me. I was brought from the wing reserved for those sentenced to death
to the high-security visiting room. Behind a thick pane of plastic, there
was Rixt.

"Hello," she said through the small holes in the plastic.

"You saw Shea, didn't you?"

Rixt shifted in her seat. "I came because I want you to stop writing and
calling."

"So, then tell me. Did you go to Shea's house?"

"It doesn't matter."

"You told him you were a reporter—like you told me you worked for
LAPD."

"I never actually told you that. You'll have to forgive me if I don't apol-
ogize for that. You should always ask to see a badge."

"And you were working for Renda, right? Trying to find out if the book
was true or not?"

"I can't tell you who I was working for."

"Did you ever look into Dicomini's cousin in Yermo, the one who signed
the police report on her case?"

"The client took me off the job before I got to that."

"But you saw that stupid test of Shea's. You read it. Did you tell Renda
about it?"

"I can't—"

"And the cops came to see you and you didn't say anything."

"I don't work for LAPD anymore."

"But you have to say."

"Listen, it wouldn't help you now. If I did say that the test existed, what
would that mean? It could mean that it was there and you killed the guy
so he wouldn't blackmail you with it, and then you destroyed it. Maybe
you did want it to come out because you were worried about Connie Dicomini. But how can you prove that? And if that's the case, maybe the old
jerk wouldn't part with the test, so you knocked him."

She was right. I shut up for a moment.

"If you had said something at the time," I said, "it might have made a
difference. You can't say it wouldn't have."

"You did too good a job in your book. I couldn't find any clear evidence
one way or the other—that you did it or that you made it up. But I was
willing to believe you. I've always found that when somebody declares
himself an asshole, you're better off taking him at his word. So I never had
much desire to help."

"None of the Shea business would have happened had it not been for you. He'd still be alive today. That doesn't bother you?"

"You should talk. I don't live in a make-it-up world. Where I come from, something goes wrong and some fool you don't care about is dead. I can't change that. You get used to it. It'd be great to keep an old man alive or maybe even help prove a fucker was framed, if he was. But you don't always get to write your own story. At least, I don't. And I can live with that—or I try to. So, yeah, you and me are in a way tied together by Shea. But it's not a bond that means anything. It's just there. And I've got plenty of it's-just-there in my life. I don't like what happened. But I don't like a lot of things."

"You came because you feel guilty."

"I suppose I'm not one of the lucky ones."

"Then will you tell me?"

"It won't help you any."

"Yes, it will. I want to be sure that I didn't kill him."

I often think about Rixt's reply. She shook her head and said, "You know, it's odd what you can convince yourself of."

Then she left. I never contacted her again.

Dicomini's book was published. An emotional highlight, one critic said, is the scene in which the victim meets my agent, and Renda breaks down. I found that the book was ambiguous as to when this encounter occurred.

During the publicity wave that accompanied Dicomini's book, a reporter wrote me and asked for an interview. I had spurned all such requests so far, but accepted this one. He came with a photographer. We were allowed to use a conference room for an hour. For his first question, he asked if I had any regrets. I'd be a damn fool not to, I replied.

"Did you really kill someone for your book?"

"I have nothing new to say about that. A death sentence doesn't change everything."

"No jailhouse confession, then?"

I had nothing to confess.

We talked about the appeal. I was not hopeful, I explained, but I did view it as a way to postpone my execution for a year or two. In that time, I could finish the Montana book. I am really pleased with it, I told him. I sent the first three hundred pages to a small press in Vermont, and the editor there expressed an interest in publishing it.

But please don't print that, I asked. I had submitted the manuscript under a pseudonym.

Edward D. Hoch is another Edgar Award–winning author who quietly produces some of the finest crime fiction around. A master of the short story, his work has appeared in every issue of *Ellery Queen's Mystery Magazine* since 1973. When he's not writing, he edits anthologies as well, having put together twenty volumes of *The Year's Best Mystery and Suspense Stories.* Luckily, he doesn't edit all the time, otherwise he wouldn't have time to turn out perfect little stories like "The Narrow House."

The Narrow House
ED HOCH

It was Andrew who taught Emily Rhodes the fundamentals of growing marijuana, but it was from the gang at the Shades of Purple Lounge that she first learned the advantages of growing it indoors. The narrow three-story brownstone that she leased in Greenwich Village provided a back yard only a bit larger than a postage stamp, and the one time she'd tried growing a few plants among the wild ferns there, they'd been dug up and stolen before she could harvest the leaves.

Andrew was gone by then, off to San Francisco with a gay lover who'd stolen him from innocent and trusting Emily. The gang at the Shades of Purple sympathized. "Make sure the next one is straight, honey," the bartender told her, pouring a drink on the house. When she came in a few weeks later to grumble about the stolen pot plants, he didn't pour her a free drink. Instead he sent her over to Lou and Toni Nelson.

The Nelsons were a Village couple who turned up at the Shades of Purple once or twice a week. Emily didn't know them well, but they seemed friendly enough. Lou was a bearded man in his late thirties who'd crashed in New York after a decade of dullness as a suburban breadwinner. Emily knew he was into drugs because once at a Village party he'd brought enough pot for everyone. Toni, who was probably his wife, had the drawn look of an addict. Emily liked her and felt vaguely sorry for her, though Toni never complained.

She told Lou about her latest misfortune with the stolen plants but she found him surprisingly unsympathetic. "You're still living back in the sixties, kid," he told her. "First of all, no one grows pot for the leaves any more. You smoke sinsemilla, the bud of the female plant. Whoever stole your plants just didn't know any better."

Emily reminded him of the party a few months back when he'd brought a plastic bag full of marijuana leaves. "What about that?"

"I like you, kid. You've got a good memory. I was going to throw them out when Toni said I should bring them along. She figured the crowd at that party wouldn't know the difference and she was right."

Toni nodded, exhaling a bluish cloud of tobacco smoke. She was rarely without a cigarette or a joint. "You got your own house, Emily. You should be growing indoors. Then you don't have to stay up half the night with a shotgun stuck out your back window."

"I wouldn't know the first thing about that." She laughed at the idea, shaking her head. "I'm not in the business. I was just growing a little for my own use."

"If you grow it, you're in the business," Lou Nelson assured her. "If you want, Toni and I could drop over and look at your place, see how much room you got."

"Do you grow indoors?" Emily asked.

"Sometimes," he answered vaguely.

So it came about that the Nelsons called on Emily at home two nights later. Her living and dining rooms were on the main floor, along with the kitchen. The bedrooms and bath occupied the second level with the top story being unused. "Storage!" Lou Nelson exclaimed upon seeing it. "You use this lovely third floor merely for storage?"

"It's a bit large for a single room and I'd have to get the owner's permission to make any substantial changes." She sighed, staring at the walls. "It's such a narrow house."

"Poe called a coffin a narrow house," Toni Nelson interjected. "And I suppose it is."

"You could grow a thousand plants up here," Lou decided while pacing off the room, "and no one would ever be the wiser."

"Wouldn't I need special equipment, lights, all sorts of things?"

He smiled benignly. "We could advise you on what you'd need. We could even supply some of the manpower—or womanpower—if you wish."

"I think a thousand plants would be a bit much. Wouldn't I be breaking the law?"

Toni coughed lightly and took out another cigarette. "A hundred plants means a mandatory five-to-forty. Years, that is. No parole."

Emily felt a shiver run through her. "My God, you can kill somebody and get less time than that."

"They have to catch you first," Lou Nelson assured her. "With me and Toni helping you, that's not a worry."

"What sort of equipment would I need to do it fast?"

"With six hundred-watt sodium lights you can harvest buds in sixty days. That fast enough for you?"

"Just right," she decided. Two months and she could turn a good profit and be out of business before the law caught on. "Where do I get the seeds?"

"I have a little stash. How many would you want?"

"Less than a hundred. Why tempt fate?"

"Any special variety?"

"I don't know. The ones that were stolen were a Northern Lights hybrid."

Lou nodded. "That's good pot."

But Toni interrupted. "Hell, Lou, you get a hundred of those in a room and they smell like sulphur. Sell her some Bubble Gum seeds."

He was quick to agree. "The Bubble Gum hybrid is best for indoors. It's got a nice sweet smell like candy or chewing gum. You still better keep the door closed, but at least the odor isn't offensive."

So it was decided. Lou and Toni would come over the following week with the necessary supplies, and because Toni was hopeless with her fingers he'd bring along Carol Knox to help with the installation. Emily had met Carol at a couple of Village parties. She was tall and slender like Emily, not particularly pretty, but with shoulder-length red hair that attracted attention. Like the Nelsons, she was into marijuana-growing in a big way.

Emily was employed by a temporary agency that sent her out to various office jobs in lower Manhattan. She barely earned rent money working as a temp, but she had a few hundred dollars saved up. It was enough to pay Lou for the plastic tubing, ceramic heater, carbon dioxide tank, four sodium lamps with timer, and other equipment she'd need.

"How many seeds?" she asked him when he handed her the packet.

"Ninety-five. You said to keep it under a hundred."

"Fine. How much space will they need?"

"These hybrids don't need much space; they get very tall before they start producing buds. We could grow them all on a large tabletop."

"What about that folding table in the dining room?" Carol suggested. She had an odd throaty voice that commanded attention.

"Good idea," Emily agreed. "I won't be throwing any dinner parties while that stuff's growing up here."

The table was six feet long when unfolded, and three feet wide. The seeds, each in its own peat pot, easily fit on top. "You'll have a sea of green in sixty days," Lou promised. Then, while Emily and Toni watched, he and Carol Knox went to work running the tubing that would supply water to the plants. The heater was for the roots and the sodium lamps provided the closest thing to sunlight twelve hours a day.

"Remember," Carol instructed Emily, "drapes closed, door closed at all times. You can check on them if you want, but don't leave the door open. This tank will supply carbon dioxide to sweeten the air, and they'll have heat, light and water. So long as the system's working you don't have to lift a finger until it's time to harvest the buds. Then I hope you'll remember your friends."

"You'll all get some," she promised. "But I'll be selling the rest. I need the money now that Andrew's gone."

The weeks after that passed uneventfully. Emily saw the Nelsons occasionally at the Shades of Purple, and once she saw Carol Knox there too. "How's it coming?" Carol asked.

Emily gave her a thumbs-up sign. "Perfect. Only a few more weeks."

When the time came they helped her with the harvest. There were multiple buds on most of the plants and when she smoked them she achieved a glowing high. Lou sold the rest at two hundred and eighty dollars an ounce.

It was time to dismantle the equipment and return the table to the dining room, but Emily decided it had been so easy she'd try it again.

WHEN THE SECOND PLANTING WAS halfway through its two-month cycle, Emily dropped in at the Shades of Purple Lounge for their monthly drag queen night. She was watching the entertainment with half an eye when Carol Knox came in and headed straight for her. "Bad news, Emily. Your old beau Andrew's back in town. He was here earlier and told the Nelsons he was heading over to your place."

"Damn!" Emily was on her feet. "Thanks for the warning, Carol."

"He doesn't have a key, does he?"

"I hope not." She went out the door fast.

She'd been too casual about keys while Andrew was living there, she realized now. Once she'd let him borrow hers to have a duplicate made, and he'd returned it when he moved out. But there was nothing to have stopped him from making a second duplicate. The room on her third floor wasn't even locked. If he got in and happened to wander up there . . .

She ran the last two blocks to the narrow house. There was no sign of entry and the place seemed empty as she turned her key in the lock. Then she heard it—the sound of her stereo playing up in the bedroom. Andrew was back.

Her heart was thudding as she climbed the stairs to face him. "Hello, Andrew. What are you doing back here?"

Seeing him now, his lanky body spread across her sofa while he flipped through her pile of CDs, she wondered how she could ever have loved him. "Don't you buy the new stuff anymore?" he asked, tossing the CDs aside.

She held out her hand. "I want my other key. Then I want you to get out."

"Hey, just a minute! I thought we had something going."

"What happened to your friend?"

"I'm sorry about that, Emily. I must have been drunk or crazy to go off with him."

"Give me the key, Andrew."

"Can't we—"

"No, we can't."

He stood up and reached into the pocket of his jeans. For an instant she feared he was going for a weapon, but when his hand came out it was only holding the key. "Sorry about that. I thought you'd be pleased to see me."

"I'm not. Goodbye, Andrew."

He went down the stairs and out of her life once more. For the final time, she hoped.

EMILY USUALLY CHECKED THE THIRD floor in the morning, and it wasn't until after breakfast that she went up and found the door to the plant room slightly ajar. She was certain she'd closed it tightly the previous morning. Didn't she always close it?

Andrew.

Had he been up there snooping around?

The room seemed undisturbed and nothing had been taken. The sodium lights still bathed the plants in a healthy sunny glow, and a small electric fan circulated the air. Water and fertilizer were delivered automatically by the plastic tubes. The tank of carbon dioxide helped freshen the air. Everything was as it should be.

Except that the door hadn't quite been closed.

Was Andrew planning to return in a month when the pot was ready for harvesting? She had two pounds of buds last time. At $280 an ounce that meant nearly nine thousand dollars.

He'd surrendered the key, but maybe he had another one. Maybe he had a whole box full of keys.

She decided it was time to get the lock changed. She phoned the landlord and told him she would pay for it herself. He offered no objection, but insisted a duplicate key must be sent to his office. Later, at the Shades of Purple, she told Carol and the Nelsons about it. They agreed she'd done the right thing.

"He might have found a new companion," Carol speculated. "I haven't seen him around the last few nights."

Emily went to jobs for the temp agency most mornings, and finally landed a month-long position at a travel agency. It was easy work, mainly simple computer things, and she liked the people. It did involve a certain amount of overtime with the vacation season approaching, and most week-nights she'd head straight home instead of stopping at the Shades of Purple. She hadn't seen the Nelsons in several days when Toni phoned her one evening just as she walked in the door. "There's a bit of a problem, Emily. I don't want to discuss it on the phone. Could I come over?"

"Come ahead. If you haven't eaten yet you can join me in some macaroni and cheese."

Toni Nelson arrived within thirty minutes, looking serious. She sat down in the living room and said, "We've got problems. Lou's been arrested."

"What for?"

"Dealing. He went down to Wall Street this morning with a plastic bag of freshly harvested buds. He'd never had any trouble before, but this time his customer turned out to be an undercover cop. Would you come with me to see him?"

"Of course. Let me get my coat."

Lou was being held at Centre Street overnight, awaiting arraignment the following morning. Toni was allowed to see him while Emily waited out-side in a cramped visitors' area. She'd been there about five minutes when a large black man wearing a photo ID pinned to his shirt came over to talk with her.

"I'm Sergeant Wendt," he said, settling down on the bench next to her. "You came to see Louis Nelson?"

She nodded. "But they'd only let his wife in. I'm just a friend."

"This is my case. I'm anxious to wrap it up."

"Then let Lou go. He didn't do anything."

Sergeant Wendt smiled at her, revealing a gold tooth. "He says he grew the pot himself and I tend to believe him, but that doesn't change the charge that he was selling it. Possession of a small amount of marijuana has been decriminalized in New York State, but it's still a crime to sell it. And grow-ing it can be a federal offense. Would you be knowin' anyone in your neighborhood growing pot?"

"Nope."

"Wouldn't be likely to tell me if you did know." His smile had faded. "What about Nelson and his wife?"

"I've never been to their place. I see them at the neighborhood bars."

"Let me give you some advice, Miss. Stay clear of Nelson and his wife. This investigation is just starting, and folks that get caught up in it are goin' to be facing big troubles."

"Thank you for the advice, Sergeant," she said primly.

TONI DIDN'T SPEAK UNTIL THEY were back in the car. Then, as she took a firm grip on the steering wheel she said grimly, "He thinks they're going to throw the book at him. He couldn't say much with them listening, but he wants me to post bail for him as soon as it's set. He doesn't think it'll be too high. It's not as if he was selling cocaine or heroin."

"Do you have the money?"

"I have it. But I'll need your help on something else tonight, Emily."

"Sure. Any way I can help—"

"I have to get rid of all the indoor gardening equipment tonight. That detective, Wendt, could have a search warrant by tomorrow morning." She thought some more and added, "I'm sorry now that I took you along, Emily. Maybe you need to get rid of your garden, too."

"I'm only ten days from harvest, Toni. I need the money. I can't quit now. You and Lou just brought in your crop. It's different with you."

Toni shrugged. "You're taking a chance. The heat's going to be on."

"They need probable cause to get a search warrant, don't they? They've got no reason to suspect me of anything."

Toni parked in her usual spot a block from the place they were renting. Emily had been mostly truthful when she told the detective she'd never been there. She'd never seen the basement room where the pot was grown, and seeing it now for the first time was almost more than she could grasp. There were twice, no, *three* times as many plants as she had—certainly way over the safe limit of one hundred—and most of them were just starting to bud. Tubes carried water and fertilizer back and forth across the basement floor.

"Everything goes," she said. "This basement has to be bare in an hour's time."

"But there's a small fortune here!" Emily objected.

"There's also life sentences for Lou and me if it's found like this. Are you helping me or not?"

"Of course I'm helping."

There was a Dumpster next door behind some stores, and they filled it with everything that would burn, including the plants. Then Toni threw in a lighted match and they watched the fire from a block away. Carol came by to watch with them, holding her nose at one point. "That's high-grade stuff for a bonfire."

"Lou's locked up," Toni explained. "They'll be here with a search warrant."

"God, Toni! What are you going to do?"

"If he gets bail we'll probably skip."

A fire engine came roaring out of the night, finally dousing the blaze with a high-pressure hose. The three of them moved on quickly.

LOU MADE BAIL THE FOLLOWING morning, and they celebrated at the Shades of Purple that night. As the word got around, all of their friends showed up. No one put it into words, but everyone seemed to know it was really a farewell party. By the weekend, when Emily dropped in the place again, Carol Knox told her they were gone.

"Doesn't that make him a fugitive?" she asked.

"I think they were heading west. There's lots of space out that way. Maybe they'll find a wheat field big enough for ten thousand plants. Hell, it's the biggest cash crop in America, now."

Emily went home that night and climbed the stairs to the third floor. The buds were almost ready. Just a few more days and they'd be money in the bank. Then she could dismantle the system and lay low for a while. Lou wasn't around to sell the stuff for her, but she wasn't worried—there were plenty of buyers at the Shades of Purple on any given night.

It was just at harvest time that the travel agency got especially busy. She was supposed to have dinner with Carol, but had to call up and cancel. As it turned out, she finished the computer work sooner than expected, and, by eight-thirty, was headed home.

As she fit the key into the shiny new lock on her brownstone's door, she noticed scratches she was certain hadn't been there before. She entered cautiously, hardly breathing, and stood in the downstairs hall. After a few moments she heard a sound from far above. Someone was in the plant room.

She tiptoed to the kitchen and took a hammer from one of the drawers. Andrew had come back, just as she'd feared, and picked the lock when his old key wouldn't open it.

Emily moved cautiously up the stairs, the sounds growing just a bit louder as she reached the second floor in the dark. The door to the plant room, at the top of the next flight, was slightly ajar as she'd found it that other time after Andrew's visit. She could see the beam of a tiny flashlight moving back and forth among the plants.

This last flight was the most dangerous because of the squeaky steps. She avoided the worst of them, keeping her eyes on Andrew's flashlight. Then she heard the snip of clippers and the rustle of a plastic bag. He was cutting them off, cutting the buds.

In a fury she burst into the room as the flashlight went off. "Damn you, Andrew! I'll kill you for this!"

His strong hands grabbed at her wrist, went for her throat. They tussled for a moment in the dark and then she swung the hammer in a high, deadly arc. There was a crunch of bone as it connected and her assailant went down without a sound, scattering some plants as he fell.

She snapped on the sodium lamps and gasped.

The figure on the floor of her plant room, in a widening circle of blood, wasn't Andrew. It was Carol.

She'd killed Carol Knox.

* * *

EMILY SLUMPED TO THE FLOOR, half-fainting, and sat for a long time staring at the body. She was finally forced to move by the thin trail of blood inching across the floor toward her. She stood up then and realized for the first time that she was no longer holding the hammer. It lay there among the plants, blood red at its tip. She went out in the hall and turned on the lights.

Trying to collect her thoughts, trying to realize what she had done, Emily looked back into the plant room and reached down to pick up the plastic bag full of clipped-off buds. Carol had indeed been stealing them, and chances were it had been she who'd sneaked up once before and left the door ajar. Andrew had nothing to do with it. Carol, her good friend Carol, had been trying to rip her off. She still felt bad about what had happened, but maybe Carol had deserved it.

Now the problem was what to do about it. All she'd done was kill a burglar, really, although the papers would immediately brand it a drug-related killing and that never sounded good. Perhaps she—

Her thoughts were interrupted by the ringing of her doorbell. God, who could that be? Lou and Toni were gone. Could it possibly be Andrew, after all?

At first she didn't answer it, but the ringing continued. It was only nine o'clock and whoever it was could see that the upstairs lights were on. Finally, she crept down and tried to see out through the curtains. There was a large shape silhouetted against the glare from the streetlight. She turned on the hall light, checked quickly to be certain there were no spots of blood on her, and opened the door.

It was the black detective, Sergeant Wendt.

"Oh! Hello."

"Sorry to bother you this late, Miss Rhodes, but I need to ask you a few questions about the Nelsons. May I come in?"

"Of course." She led him into the living room, turning on lights as she went. "How can I help you?"

"Lou Nelson has dropped out of sight. He missed a scheduled court appearance today and that probably means he's skipped bail. It would go a lot easier on him if he came back and surrendered."

"I have no idea where he is," she answered truthfully.

"When's the last time you saw him?" he asked, his eyes shifting from her face to study the room.

"Last week. I think it was the night he got out on bail. They had a little party at the Shades of Purple Lounge."

"Nothing was said about Lou and his wife leaving town?"

"Nothing. I was a friend. I'm sure they would have told me. Maybe he just forgot about the court date."

"The place they were renting is empty of all their personal stuff. They're not coming back."

She shrugged. "I couldn't tell you."

"I understand there was a fire in a Dumpster near their place the night he was arrested."

Fire!

Suddenly, all in a flash, she saw the way out. "I heard the fire engine and went down to see what was going on."

"Any idea who started it? Was Toni Nelson involved?"

"I doubt it. More likely it would be a girl named Carol Knox. She hangs around the Shades of Purple and she's been acting strange lately, especially about fires. She was here one night and set a couple of paper napkins ablaze, just to see them burn."

He made a note of that. "Carol Knox, you say?"

Emily nodded. "Tall, slender, long red hair. You can't miss her."

"Where does she live?"

"They could tell you at the bar. I try to stay away from her when I can. She's been acting spooky lately."

"A friend of the Nelsons?"

"She knew them. We all did."

That seemed to satisfy him and he closed his notebook. "Thanks for your help, Miss Rhodes. I'll call you if I need anything else."

As she closed the front door behind him, Emily felt her body relax for the first time since he'd entered.

SHE WORKED QUICKLY AFTER THAT. There was no way she could get Carol's body out of the house by herself, and she had no friends to ask for help. Now that Lou and Toni had left town she was alone. She could hardly walk into the Shades of Purple and tell them she'd just killed Carol Knox.

No, Carol would have to stay there along with the plants, and that meant Emily's only chance was to destroy everything. The detective's mention of the fire had given her the idea. The narrow house was going to burn to-night, and Carol's body along with it. She'd already noticed that they were about the same size, and now that she forced herself to carefully study the body of her victim she saw that even the bone structures of their faces were similar. The main difference in their appearance was the hair. Emily's was short and black, but Carol's long red hair would be destroyed by the fire. Her fingerprints would be gone too, if they were ever on file.

What else? Dental records, of course! The police were always checking dental records for identification. Emily had gotten this far in her young life without any cavities, although her wisdom teeth had been removed. She forced herself to pry open Carol's mouth and discovered that she was in luck. No wisdom teeth there either, and only one cavity that she could see, along the upper left side. In a bad fire, with falling debris, that could easily be knocked out and lost. She picked up the hammer and aimed one more blow.

When it was over she was breathing hard. Somehow she realized for the first time that she'd become a criminal. The blow that killed Carol had been something of an accident. This blow, knocking out the tooth, had been deliberate.

She had a quart bottle of kerosene for an old lamp in the living room that she'd never lit. Now she sprinkled the kerosene around, especially onto Carol's face and hands. She put crumpled newspapers in the plant room to feed the fire once it got started. It didn't really matter if some of the pot-growing equipment survived the blaze. The body would be identified as Emily's and the police would be searching for the missing Carol Knox.

Next, she rigged up a crude fuse made from a length of clothesline dipped in the remains of the kerosene. She gathered up a few clothes and some money, and even took twenty-four dollars in loose bills she found in Carol's pocket. There was no identification. Emily lit the fuse on her way out.

She watched from down the block until she saw the bright glow in the third-floor windows. Then she hurried away. She was disappearing into a subway entrance when she heard the first distant siren.

EMILY DYED HER HAIR BLOND and took an apartment on the upper west side of Manhattan, many miles from her previous home. The newspaper accounts of the fire mentioned suspected marijuana-growing and stated that the dead woman had been tentatively identified as Emily Rhodes. Police were investigating.

She'd determined that New York was a big enough city to hide in, especially if everyone thought she was dead. Staying clear of the Village was no problem and the upper west side had always appealed to her, anyway. What she needed was a new identity and a job. Lou Nelson had shown her once how to doctor social security cards. "Don't change the first three numbers," he said, "because those are the code for the state that issued the card. But do change the first letters of your last name. Computers do everything by the alphabet. If Rhodes becomes Jodes they'll never find you."

Emily knew the number would be quickly revealed as a fake if anyone checked it, but she also knew the employment agency wouldn't bother to check unless they had a reason. She chose a small agency near her new apartment, and they sent her out the first day. Her resume said she was from Ohio and listed a couple of stores she knew were out of business.

She worked in the office of a catering service for a few days and felt like she'd been there for months. The apartment was a good one for the price, with a partial view of the Hudson River. There was a tiny spare room and she even found herself pacing off the square footage and thinking of a new plant room.

But no, not yet.

Oddly, on the weekend she thought of her mother back in Ohio. How had she taken the news of Emily's death? It was better not to speculate about that.

On the following Monday morning she was back at work at the catering service. Shortly before eleven the manager summoned her to his office. She walked in and faced two big men standing there. One of them was Sergeant Wendt. He sighed and said, "That's her." Then, in a formal voice, he added, "Miss Emily Rhodes, I am placing you under arrest. You have the right to a lawyer. Anything you say may be used against you—"

"What's the charge?" she asked.

"You are suspected of murdering Carol Knox and setting fire to your residence in Greenwich Village. There may be additional charges involving drugs."

They had to handcuff her when they took her out. That was the rule. "How did you find me so soon?" she asked in the car.

Wendt was silent at first. Then he said, "I figured if you were still in New York you'd try for more temporary employment. We've been checking agencies for the last several days."

"I was supposed to be dead. How did you know Carol's body wasn't mine?"

"That was the easy part," he said. "Carol Knox was a man."

Alan Russell's first career was as a hotel general manager. When he switched to writing, he used the experience he had gained for novels such as *The Forest Prime Evil* and *The Fat Innkeeper*. His series character is Am Caulfield, who is, naturally, a hotel security director. He puts the hotel industry on hold for this story of a society matron who meets a multiple murderer and both hear—wedding bells?

Married to a Murderer
ALAN RUSSELL

". . . murderers get sheaves of offers of marriage."
—George Bernard Shaw

Danielle Deveron thought of herself as an *outmate*. She liked the expression, because in the word there was an element of outcast, as well as the notion of being mated. It was accurately descriptive, she thought, of those carrying on a relationship with a prisoner.

Not that Danielle thought she had much in common with other outmates. Most of *them* she considered pathetic, women with no self-esteem. As she saw it, their relationships with prison inmates offered them little more than a perverse nunnery. Danielle was sure her situation was different. Her wealth, reputed to be in the neighborhood of fifty million dollars, was only a part of what Danielle believed distinguished her from the other outmates. Perhaps she'd read too much Fitzgerald, who insisted that the very rich "are different from you and me." Or perhaps she was just being realistic.

Her money had brought Danielle to the prisoner. Helen Bernard had been the inadvertent matchmaker, guilty Helen who'd always been somewhat ashamed about her own vast wealth. Helen believed it was her duty to sit on philanthropic boards and work for the betterment of society, and was always dogging Danielle to become involved with one do-gooder organization or another. Usually Danielle escaped such duties by writing a check. In the end that's what they always wanted anyway. But on this occasion, Horseface Helen had piqued her interest. She had wanted Danielle to accompany her on an afternoon outing to San Carlos Prison.

Prison. Not some luncheon, or fashion show, or gathering of serious-looking people talking about addressing some pervasive wrong. Danielle had never been to a prison before. And what truly intrigued her was that Helen was scheduled to meet with a murderer. In her thirty years on the planet, Danielle had never met a murderer. She had dated the gamut of males, including poets, stockbrokers, race-car drivers, royalty, near royalty, surgeons, CEOs, and even a junior senator from the state of Colorado, but she had never spent any time with a murderer (or at least with anyone who boasted of having made a killing in anything other than the market).

What did they see in their first look? There was an immediate attraction for both of them that went beyond the physical. Clay Potter had been on death row for a dozen years. He was thin and pale, had sunken cheeks and a consumptive cough that caused a lock of his long dark hair to fall up and down on the bridge of his nose. There was a scar running along his right cheek. His arms, exposed to his elbows, were a canvas of tattoos, displays mostly of naked women, but his painted ladies, even in their exaggerated forms, disappeared in the presence of Danielle. Preternaturally pale, her milk complexion set off her dark lashes and blue eyes. Her pressed, shoulder-length golden hair glittered.

Gold, he thought. The hair, the woman. She personified his dreams and his fantasies of wealth. He had always had visions of what it must be like to be wealthy, and had pursued lucre, Jason after the fleece, Jason willing to fleece, or worse. Clay's problem was that he had never been able to distinguish fool's gold from the real thing.

The attraction wasn't one-sided. Clay didn't have the looks of the pretty boys Danielle usually associated with, but there was something about him that beguiled. She remembered attending a party replete with movers and shakers. There were familiar faces everywhere, household names from the entertainment industry, superstars from the sporting world, but the person that drew the most murmurs and looks was a mobster. "He's arranged murders," were the whispers.

Clay had done more than arrange murders. He had committed them, Danielle thought, though as might be expected, he still proclaimed his innocence. His pronouncement was made to the two women without any enthusiasm, words from a tired old script, words that had been uttered too many times to audiences that never listened or believed. Anyone who works in the criminal justice system knows that most inmates proclaim their innocence as a matter of course. Though lockup wasn't anything new to Clay, he tried to explain to Danielle and Helen that murder was.

"I've always been a B and E man," he said, explaining that meant "breaking and entering." It was just his bad luck to have broken into the wrong house. Everything had been quiet, he said, too still. It was one of those Hillsborough mansions, the kind where there should have been noises. He had been cruising the neighborhood, looking for some easy pickings, when he stopped at this one house. "Just a feeling," he said. He said his suspicions should have been aroused by the off-line burglar alarm, but he had encountered lots of homes where people had deactivated their systems just because they didn't want to be bothered with them.

"I'm an opportunist," Clay said. Was he warning Danielle? "I take advantage of circumstances."

He told them how he quietly went through the house, relieving it of rare coins, stamps, jewelry, and silverware. He took his pickings from the den, dining room, and family room. Clay said he was not a confrontational thief, wasn't the kind to hold a gun on the occupants. He liked his houses unoccupied, and he began to wonder whether anyone was home. He decided to sneak a peek into the master bedroom, and that's where he saw the blood and what looked like bodies.

"I panicked," he said. "I ran out of the house. I was so scared I even forgot my booty. I drove away fast. Unfortunately, my car didn't fit the neighborhood profile. That's why I got stopped by the police. If I'd had another car, I wouldn't be here."

Unsaid, but directed to Danielle with a telling look, he proclaimed the injustice. And somewhere in the look was also the hint that he should have been driving a new European sedan with the kind of shaded glass that hides its occupants from admiring eyes.

"The police didn't hold me," Clay said, "but after the murders were discovered, they picked up one of my prints on the gold coins I left behind. Taking off my gloves was felony stupid, but I never expected it would get me convicted of felony murder."

His initial statement was what hung him, Clay told them. He had tried to deny ever being in the house, and later, when he recanted, the prosecution made much of his changing stories and admitting to "fabricating." The jury, faced with four bodies (two of them children, aged eight and twelve), and having a hardened criminal at the scene of the murder, sentenced him to death. The Golden State had decided not to let Clay see his golden years. His death was scheduled in six months.

"My lawyer says you've helped others," Clay said, addressing Helen with his eyes and words. "I don't have many cards left to play, but the one survivor in the family was an older son that was away at college. He and his parents weren't getting along. Apparently he had a drug problem. That's what they call it when you have money. You're a junkie otherwise. The day before the murders, there was a big family fight. The parents said enough was enough, and that they wouldn't be supplying the kid with any more money."

Clay theorized that the night after the fight, the son had left his university apartment, driven home, turned off the burglar alarm, and then bludgeoned his family to death. Their son was the one who would have benefited from their deaths, Clay said. And who would benefit from his as well.

"That little preppy did whatever he could to help build the state's case against me. He hired some private dicks, and they dug up the dirt on me."

"Was there a lot of dirt?" Danielle asked.

Clay shrugged. "I was never any angel, but they made it sound like I was up to my ears in it. Their tactics didn't only work on the jury. They worked on me. I felt dirty, especially when preppy showed up every day in his thousand-dollar suits. He was always quick with his silk hankie too. Pulled it right out of his fancy suit like a magician, and started with the waterworks.

"Maybe if I'd had one of them suits, and a fifty-dollar haircut, and a Swiss timepiece, I wouldn't be in here."

Helen was too polite to disagree, but in her own mind she thought sheep's clothing would not have helped Clay Potter. He looked like a criminal. No. He looked like a murderer. When driving home later, Helen made a point of apologizing to Danielle.

"This wasn't what I expected at all," she said. "I often assist with prisoner's aid. But this is not the sort of case I would involve myself in. There are not the extenuating circumstances here which would warrant my involvement."

Danielle only half listened. She knew Helen liked to throw herself into frays that made her feel good about herself. Helen needed her noble causes, relished helping the disadvantaged and the downtrodden, especially if they were victims of persecution or prejudice. But assisting an unlucky criminal or—more to the point—an inventive murderer, was not something that would benefit society, and more importantly, Helen.

"I might help him," Danielle said.

"What?"

"Yes. I might."

DANIELLE DIDN'T PROMISE HIM ANYTHING at first, and he didn't ask. Visiting a prison, talking through a reinforced window, isn't the usual way men and women get to know one another. But there was an intensity to their talks that neither could have imagined. They only had minutes with each other, but those were the kind of minutes many couples never experience. There wasn't music, or food, or a movie between them. There wasn't physical contact, or shared passions. There was only death around the corner, death and the discoveries between them.

A week after they met, Danielle offered Clay her financial support. Her money, she said, would buy him the best lawyers, the best tacticians. If her wealth could buy him another day's life, it was there for him.

There for the taking. Clay was usually good at that, but he wasn't sure how to respond in this case. Now that everything was being offered, he felt off balance. He had heard about things like this happening, but only in fairy tales. He felt like the frog being kissed by the princess. Clay had always enjoyed stealing from the rich because he thought it brought him closer to them, almost made him one of them. And now everything was being offered on a golden platter. She was his last wish come true.

"I couldn't just take," he said.

"It's not taking," she said. "It's sharing."

"Like we were married?"

"Till death do us part."

"What would your friends say?"

"About what?"

"You know," he said, then struggled for the words, "if we were to get married."

"They'd say," she said, " 'Married to a murderer.' "

Neither of them spoke. The words hung between them. Each felt a thrill. He, that this one in a million (no, make that one in fifty million, he thought) woman could be at his side, and she, at the audaciousness of his notion.

Married to a murderer. Each of them thought about that. Marriage suited their desires, though each wanted different things. He wanted respectability, and she wanted notoriety. Both perceived the other as being powerful, as belonging to worlds they had only imagined.

"Will you marry me?" he asked.

"Yes," she said.

THEY DIDN'T WAIT. TIME WAS not on their side. Their nuptials set off a media frenzy. Why would one of the richest and most desirable women in the world marry a murderer? Danielle didn't offer answers, so the media tried to find their own. The life and times of Clay Potter were examined. If Danielle Deveron saw something good, and noble, and attractive in the man, then the reasoning was that there must be something there. Witnesses surfaced that remembered a different Clay Potter than was evidenced on his rap sheet. Even before his new team of lawyers went to work, the press began to call for a reexamination of his murder conviction.

"There is a God," said Clay Potter. And he knew there was an angel—his wife.

While desperate motions were filed, man and wife continued in their jailhouse courtship.

"People whisper behind my back," Danielle confessed. "Everyone is talking. And mostly what they say is, 'Married to a murderer.' "

"They're wrong," said Clay, his voice rising, red suddenly appearing in his ashen face. "They're wrong."

He coughed long and hard, the coldness of his years of imprisonment, and the harshness of the lies directed at his wife, making him burn with anger. Danielle consoled him. He didn't understand that she hadn't been complaining. Quite the opposite. Being married to Clay set her apart, made her something novel. Others might have five diamond rings, and Learjets, but she had something they didn't: she was married to a murderer.

They were quite the odd couple, but to all appearances, Danielle and Clay savored their moments together. Despite all the tumult going on around them, despite the clamor for a new trial, neither of them expected that Clay would be alive for very long. In some ways they found a freedom in his execution date. "Carpe diem," Danielle often said. Clay didn't know the Latin meaning, but he did like the excited look on her face.

The reprieve call never came from the governor. But Clay's lawyers found enough extentuating circumstances to allow for a retrial. Clay was ecstatic. He had been proclaiming his innocence from the day of his arrest, and now, at long last, people were beginning to believe him.

Clay's retrial was blessedly short. On further review of the so-called evidence, Clay was found innocent. In the arms of his beautiful wife, Clay left the courtroom. He told the media that he had never been happier, but he coughed all the while he made the pronouncement. It was clear to all that Clay was very sick, his body wasted from his long confinement. Many wondered whether his freedom had come too late.

His death was announced a week later, and the press treated it like a Greek tragedy. Center stage was the widow in black, poor little rich girl Danielle Deveron, but the public was not quick to rid itself of their early take on the story. Behind the widow's back, Danielle still heard the whispers: "Married to a murderer."

The words were all too familiar to Danielle. They had been Clay's last words to her. He had made his pronouncement minutes after his last dose of medication. Clay had been obedient and adoring almost to the end. It was only when he took that final swallow of medication that he finally awakened. His face had undergone a remarkable transformation, beginning with a cherishing gaze, to a questioning glance, to a piercing stare, and then, at the end, a horrified look. He was staring at death, and something else, something that must have appeared even uglier to him.

From the first, they had both seen what they wanted to see, both seen what wasn't there. For a time, each had thought the other perfect for their needs. Danielle had been married to a murderer, and her beloved was to die for his deeds. When it turned out Clay was innocent (just her luck, she thought), everything changed. This wasn't a man Danielle had wanted to spend a life with, but a death with. She had married a guilty man. She had married a murderer. She wanted that distinction, wanted the whispers. But even more, she had wanted his death.

"Married," Clay had gasped, trying to shout out his last words, trying to raise an alarm, "to a murderer!"

Then he died. Poisoned, but that was something only his widow would know.

Of their relationship, the public would always judge, "Married to a murderer."

They would never know, thought Danielle, how right they were.

Reginald Hill is another mystery writer who really needs no introduction. His novels, such as *Born Guilty* and *Matlock's System*, speak for themselves as fine examples of the craft. Whether he's plotting the perfect Sherlock Holmes pastiche or examining a man who's fantasies go a little too far such as in "The Perfect Murder Club," his stories are noted for their superb plot and pacing. Read on and see if you agree.

The Perfect Murder Club
REGINALD HILL

I switched on the news.

Starvation in Africa. Earthquake in Asia. War in Central Europe. Bombs in Belfast. And so many murders only the most gutting merited a soundbite.

Life was cheap.

One of the bodies lying by a roadside looked a bit like my bank manager. No way it could be. Nothing to do with him ever came cheap.

But it got me thinking. All these dead people and I didn't know any of them. What a waste!

I found a sheet of paper and started making a list of everyone I wouldn't mind seeing dead. I drew three columns; the first for the name, the second for the offense, the third . . . I wasn't yet sure what the third was for.

It turned out to be a surprisingly long list even though I limited myself to those I knew personally. Once start admitting people I didn't know, like those neanderthal yobs rampaging round the Arndale, or this horse-faced telly-hag now droning on about the Health Service, and the list could have gone on forever.

Finished, I read through it slowly, excising one name (gone to live in Provence, which surely must be regarded as some sort of sanctuary for the unspeakable) and adding two more.

On the box a weather forecaster was being brightly facetious. I studied her vacuous smile and was tempted. But no. Rules are rules.

So I turned to the problem of the third column. No problem! It was obvious what it was for. Mode of dying.

I had a lot of fun with this, making the death fit the life. Thus *he* whose halitosis had nauseated me these many years should choke on a pickled onion, while *she* whose voice had cut through my sensibility like a buzz saw should swallow her tongue.

But eventually the game palled. It was more interesting than TV but just as empty. What I needed was a strong shot of reality. I took another look at column three and soon saw where I'd gone wrong.

It wasn't for mode of dying, it was for method of killing.

Now fancies fled away. Now there was only one real consideration. How to do it and get away with it.

I had to devise the perfect murder.

An hour later I was still staring at a blank column. Perfection, I'd discovered, was surprisingly difficult. Or perhaps what was surprising was that I should have been surprised. After all, I'd never come close to achieving it, not even in the things I used to do every day. Perhaps if I had I might still be doing them. But it was no use brooding over what had gone forever. What I needed was expert assistance. But there was no government retraining scheme in this field, and it was pointless turning to the Yellow Pages. One obvious condition of the perfect murder is that you don't advertise.

I let my mind go blank in the hope of enticing inspiration, and suddenly I found it being invaded by that most ephemeral of messages, a Radio 4 *Thought for Today*. It had been uttered by one of those bouncy bishops who like to be known as Huggable Henry or something equally expectatory. After the usual mega-maunderings, he had cast the following already soggy crumb of philosophy upon the morning waters.

Sometimes what looks like an insurmountable barrier can turn out to be an open door.

On the whole you'd be better off pulling Christmas crackers. But this time, in this one respect, it struck me that Bishop Henry might unawares have come within hugging distance of a truth.

Think about it. If you've committed a perfect murder, the last thing you do is go around shouting about it. But what's the point in perfection without appreciation? It must be like running a mile in under three minutes, and no one knowing about it. Of course, some people would probably be content to hug such knowledge to themselves. But if even a small fraction of the probable total of perfect murderers were as eager to talk about it as I was to listen, then all we had here was the classic marketing problem of how to match supply and demand.

Now this was something I *was* quite good at. I'd already established that *they* couldn't advertise. But there was nothing to stop *me*.

The next morning I went down to my local newspaper office. The young man I spoke to first proved singularly stupid and I found myself wishing I knew him well enough to put him on my list. But finally the advertising manager appeared, and after I explained to him that I wanted to place the ad in connection with a TV programme I was researching, all went smoothly. You could persuade people to show their arses in public if they thought it was for the telly. In fact, I believe if you're tuned to the right satellite, you can see it happening already.

My advertisement appeared that very same evening. I read it with a certain complacent pride.

HAVE YOU COMMITTED THE PERFECT MURDER?

If so, you've probably felt the frustration of not being able to tell anyone about it. But relax! Your troubles are over. A new organisation has been formed to exchange information on method and technique. To complete your job satisfaction and enjoy at last the applause which is your due, contact:

THE PERFECT MURDER CLUB
Confidentiality guaranteed. Ring now.
You won't regret it!

After some debate I'd given my home number. It was pointless running the ad unless people could get in touch. I knew it also opened access to undesirables like the police and the usual pranksters and cranks. But not having committed any crime myself (yet!) I had nothing to fear from the law. And as for the rest, I was pretty sure I could sort out the wheat from the chaff with a few pertinent questions.

The first call came within half an hour of the evening edition hitting the streets.

The caller was male, slightly adenoidal, and, I soon deduced, not very bright.

"Hello," I said.

"Hello." Pause. "Is that the . . . er . . . Perfect Murder Club?"

"Depends," I said. "How can I help you?"

"I dunno." Another pause. "Look, I saw your advert. . . . What's it all about?"

"It's about what it says it's about."

"Yeah . . . well . . ."

I could almost smell his desire to strut his stuff.

"Are you interested in becoming a member?" I asked, very businesslike.

"Yeah . . . well, maybe . . . it depends . . ."

"It does indeed," I said. "It depends on whether you are qualified. You're not a time-waster, I hope? Ringing up out of curiosity or for a giggle?"

"No!" he replied indignantly.

"Okay. How about a few facts then, just to establish you qualify for membership. No names, of course. Nothing to give yourself away. Just an outline."

"Yeah? Well, all right. It was my wife. She fell down a cliff. Everyone thought it was an accident. It wasn't. I pushed her."

"I see. And where was this?"

"Scar . . . on holiday!"

What a twit!

"And that's it, is it?" I said.

"Yeah. Why? What's wrong with it?"

"It's not exactly perfect, is it?"

"What do you mean? She's dead. I'm married to a woman I really love. I got a hundred thou insurance. If that's not perfect, what is?"

"I'm glad things worked out so well for you," I said patiently. "But there was no guarantee she was going to die when you pushed her, was there?"

"It was a hundred-foot drop onto rocks!"

"So? There was a Yank fell five thousand feet when his parachute didn't open. Landed on a hypermarket roof in Detroit. Only injury was he sprained his ankle climbing down the fire escape. No, your wife could easily have survived to give evidence against you. Was it daylight? Good weather?"

"Of course. You don't go walking along that path in the dark when it's raining!"

"Right. Then suppose a birdwatcher had spotted you through his binoculars? Or another walker? Or maybe a farmer? Where would you have been then?"

"But that's the point! Nobody did!"

He was getting very agitated. Time to close.

"No," I said. "The point is this, Mr. . . . . sorry, I didn't catch your name?"

"Jenkinson . . . oh shit!"

"Precisely, Mr. Jenkinson," I said. "You are clearly not a perfect murderer, merely an extremely lucky murderer. Word of advice, Mr. Jenkinson. Use some of that insurance money to have a mouth bypass or you could end up in real trouble. Bye now."

I chuckled as I replaced the receiver. Poor sod. Preening himself on being the undetected Maxwell of murder when all the time he was merely its John Major, in the right place at the right time and probably too wimpish for anyone to suspect he could have given the monstrous woman in his life a fatal shove.

I settled down to wait for more calls.

They came steadily over the next couple of hours. There were two clear cranks, one confessing to the murder of Marilyn Monroe, the other claiming to be Lord Lucan, plus a few pranksters, sadly unimaginative in their tall stories. I was entertained by an indignant lady who told me I was a symbol of the moral corruption of our society and invited me to repent at a charismatic pray-in she was holding in her house later that evening. I excused myself, but compensated a little later by sending along a couple of men who'd mistaken my advert for a coded signal for the next meeting of their sadomasochist group.

And as anticipated I heard from the police. Of course the mastermind who called didn't say he was police but pretended to be a punter. It was like listening to some village thespian stumbling through *Hamlet*. I let him ramble on, till finally, thinking he'd got me fooled, he said, "Look, I'm sure I've got something that would interest you, but I'd rather not discuss it on the phone."

"Perfectly understandable," I said. "Do drop in any time you like. I'm sure you've traced my address by now."

Pity we don't have video phones. I would have liked to see the expression on his face as I rang off.

Now all this was good fun, but as yet there'd been nothing to help me in my serious research. Then finally, just as I was giving up hope, I got a call which sounded like it might be genuinely useful.

It was a woman's voice, youngish, rather nervous, but with an underpinning of determination that made me feel this wasn't just a time-waster.

Not that she gave anything away. I liked her caution. The urge to share a triumph is one thing, the kind of stupid gabbiness displayed by the idiot Jenkinson quite another.

For a long time we just walked around the subject, but I soon became aware that I wasn't doing all the leading. In the end I felt myself being steered into the first steps to openness.

I said, "So what is it I can do for you, Miss . . . er . . . ?"

Not even acknowledging this clumsy attempt to get her name, she said, "I would like to be able to talk in safety."

"The Samaritans are said to be very discreet," I said, trying to regain the initiative. "And sympathetic."

She fell silent for a while, then said softly, "It's not sympathy I want. It's empathy. And appreciation."

Gotcha! I thought.

"I think the Club can guarantee both of those," I said in my strong, serious voice. "If you could perhaps just give a flavour of what you would be bringing . . ."

Another silence. Then speaking very carefully she said, "It's to do with a person who had the power to injure me. I was not able to continue under this threat. So I worked out a method for disposing of this person without leaving any clue to link the death to myself."

"A method?" I said, perhaps too eagerly. "Poison? Accident? Can't you give a hint?"

"I think I've said enough," she said, her nervousness returning. "Perhaps too much. The compulsion to talk is strong, but the instinct of self-preservation is stronger."

I was terrified I'd lost her. This was the genuine article, there was no doubt in my mind. This was someone who had the brains to work out what had to be done and the will to do it.

I said, "I understand, believe me. You who have already had to extricate yourself from someone's power will be more reluctant than any of us to risk re-creating that situation. This is precisely why the Club has been formed. Nobody will hear your story who has not a similar story to tell in return. When secrets are exchanged, their power is cancelled. Believe me, any confession made here is as safe as any ever heard by priest in the confessional."

I stopped myself from saying more. I could feel her being tempted, but it was her own desire which would bring her to me, not anything further I could say.

She said, "I would need to see you face-to-face before I could decide whether to trust you."

"No problem," I said. I could still sense her hesitancy. This was no time for making rendezvous with copies of the *Times* and white carnations. To bring her into the open I had to put myself there first.

"My name," I said, "is Hulbert. I live at Bullivant House, Flat Thirty-six. I shall be here all evening."

"Alone?" she said, suspicious still.

"I promise. And of course you may check before you as much as open your mouth."

"I will, be assured. If I come."

The phone went dead.

After that it was a case of sitting and waiting and hoping. The phone rang again a couple of times. One was a pushy young fellow who said he hadn't committed a murder but would really like to try. I told him it was like a good golf club, you needed an official handicap before you could join. The other was my ex-wife, one of whose ferrety friends had recognised my number in the ad and passed the information on. She pretended concern for my mental health, but I knew that all she was really worried about was whether I'd hit upon some moneymaking scheme I wasn't revealing to her solicitor.

I knew better than to offer a simple denial but told her, yes, I was collecting material for a book and all I needed to get lift-off was a little financial backing to help me hire a top PR firm and could she see her way . . .

She'd rung off by now, so I turned to my list and promoted her from number four to number three, above my ex-mistress. Equal first remained my ex-accountant who'd mishandled my finances and run off with my ex-wife, and my ex-boss who'd made me redundant and shacked up with my ex-mistress.

I was debating further revision when the doorbell rang. She'd come! I dropped the list onto the coffee table and hurried to let her in before she could change her mind.

A man stood there, square jawed, red haired, and built like a rugby-league forward. I'd never seen him before but I recognised his voice as soon as he spoke.

"Evening, Mr. Hulbert. You were right. No problem tracing your address."

It was the cop I'd spoken to earlier. With my nervous murderess on the way, this was a nuisance.

Deciding the quickest way to get rid of him was to cut through the crap, I said, "Good evening, Inspector."

"Sergeant, actually," he said, producing his warrant card. "Sergeant Peacock. All right if I come in?"

He pushed by me as he spoke. Hamlet he might not be, but when it came to acting the heavy, he was clearly well rehearsed.

He said, "It's about this advert of yours, sir. We found it . . . intriguing."

"But not illegal," I said confidently.

"Not in itself maybe. But it could be a channel to illegality."

"I'm sorry?"

"Taken at its face value, this ad invited people who've committed murder to confide in you. If anyone did confess murder to you and you didn't pass on the information to us, that might be an offense. If after making that confession, this person or any persons privy to the confession went on to commit a similar offense, that too might make your advert an offense. Or if . . ."

"All right," I said impatiently. "I get the picture. All I can do is assure you that I placed the ad on a frivolous impulse, nothing more. It's a joke, a mere squib. Naturally, which I much doubt, if any of those replying should rouse my suspicions in any way, I would of course immediately contact the police."

He wasn't so easily satisfied.

He said, "So you've had replies?"

"A few. Cranks, mostly. Nutters. Nothing to worry you with."

"We worry quite a lot about nutters, sir," he said significantly, his gaze drifting down to the coffee table.

Too late I recalled that my death list lay upon it, difficult but not impossible to read upside down. This put paid to any immediate implementation. Even if my nervous murderess did turn up with the perfect method,

I'd be mad to start knocking off people whose names might have registered on Peacock's suspicious mind.

I said, "There we are then, Sergeant. Now unless there's anything else, I have a heavy day tomorrow and would really like an early night."

"Of course, sir," he said. "Work, is it?"

"Indirectly," I said. "Looking for it. I'm one of the three million, I'm afraid."

He didn't look surprised. He probably knew already. Once he'd got my name and address from the telephone company, it must have been easy to check everything else, from my health record to my credit rating. I could feel all my *exes* getting safer by the second.

"Good luck, sir," he said. "A job's important. I've seen what not having one can do to the most sensible of people. Leads them into all kinds of stupidities. Like putting silly ads in the paper."

"Yes, I'm sorry. And if anything in the least suspicious turns up . . ."

The doorbell rang.

I suppose in that brief moment my expression must have flickered from faintly-embarrassed-honest-citizen to guilty-thing-surprised and back, for he was onto me like a claims clerk.

"Expecting someone, sir?"

"No . . . well, not exactly . . ."

"Wouldn't be someone who answered your ad, would it, sir?"

I could only shrug helplessly. I mean, I was sorry for my nervous murderess, if that's who it was, but after all, I had still committed no crime.

Peacock said, "I think maybe I should deal with this. What's through that door?"

"The kitchen," I said.

"Right. You duck in there and don't come out till I tell you," he said.

What could I do but obey? I went through, leaving the door just a fraction open behind me so I could hear what was going on.

I heard his footsteps cross the tiny hall, then the front door open.

"Yes?"

"Mr. Hulbert?"

I recognised the voice instantly as belonging to my nervous murderess.

"Yes."

"We spoke on the phone earlier."

"Oh yes."

He really was a terrible actor. He couldn't hope to get by on monosyllables forever!

"You are the Mr. Hulbert who spoke to me on the phone?" insisted the woman. "About the Club?"

"Yes I am," declared Peacock, at last getting some conviction into his voice. "And what might your name be?"

I strained my ears for her reply, but all I heard was a noise like a kitchen knife cutting through an iceberg lettuce followed by a sort of bubbly sigh and a gentle thud.

Then silence. Broken by a man's voice—not Peacock's—saying thickly, "Oh my God."

"Shut that door," said the woman. "You want everyone looking in?"

"No. Let's get out of here! What are you doing?" The voice was spiralling into panic.

"Just checking in case he made any notes."

The woman's voice was unexpectedly close. She must have moved silently into the living room. Fortunately when startled I tend to freeze rather than jump. I held my breath as I listened to her rustling through the pad on the telephone table and searching through its single drawer.

"Nothing," she said.

"Sylvie, please hurry," pleaded the man in vaguely familiar tones. "God knows who else he's got coming round here!"

"You reckon the world's full of idiots like you who want to shoot their mouths off to strangers?"

Her tone was tinged with affectionate exasperation rather than real scorn and her words triggered the memory which the man's voice had primed. This was Jenkinson, who'd pushed his wife off a cliff at Scarborough. Sylvie must be the lover he'd referred to. And perhaps his accomplice? No. That wasn't likely. In the first place from what he'd said, the murder sounded more like a sudden impulse than a thought-out plan, and in the second place, if he'd confided in Sylvie even after the event, he wouldn't have felt the urge to ring the Perfect Murder Club.

Her next words confirmed this.

"If only you'd told me what happened, there'd have been no need for this."

"It didn't seem right to tell you somehow," said Jenkinson unhappily.

I could see his point. When proposing marriage it can't strengthen your case to reveal that you pushed your last wife off a cliff. But once it dawned on him that he'd been stupid enough to give a complete stranger the means to identify him, he'd gone running to her.

How marvellous to have a woman whose reaction to such a revelation was neither outrage nor recrimination, but direct action to clear up the mess. I felt quite envious. Dim wimp he might be, but Jenkinson must have something I didn't to inspire such loyalty, even if it was only a hundred thousand quids' worth of insurance money!

"Right," said Sylvie. "Nothing here. You haven't touched anything? Okay. Let's go."

I stood with my ear pinned to the kitchen door till I was sure they had left. Then I waited another five minutes to be absolutely certain.

My relief at not being discovered had been so great that it didn't leave much of my mind to speculate on the possible connection between Sergeant Peacock and the noise of a kitchen knife slicing through a lettuce, so when at last I peeped through the door into the hallway, I could still pretend I wasn't sure what I was going to find.

I saw at once that I'd been right about the kitchen knife but wrong about Peacock not getting away with monosyllables forever. They'd seen him into eternity, no bother. He looked quite peaceful slumped against the wall with the knife sticking out of his throat. His eyes were still open and seemed to be staring straight at me. Suddenly I felt a surge of hope that perhaps after all he wasn't dead. I stooped over him, took the knife handle in my fingers, and with infinite care drew it out of the wound.

That was how his driver, coming up to tell the sergeant he was wanted on the car radio, found me.

At my trial he testified he'd seen no one either entering or leaving the building after Peacock went in. But of course he wouldn't have been able to see the side door I'm sure my careful little murderess used. Naturally I told both the police and my lawyer about the man called Jenkinson who'd pushed his wife off a cliff at Scarborough. They both checked independently and both discovered there was no record of anyone of that name dying of any cause in that area in the past ten years.

Only later did it occur to me that I'd deduced Scarborough from a single syllable. It might have been Scafell in the Lakes, or the Isle of Scarba in the Inner Hebrides, or Mount Scaraben in Caithness, or simply Scar in the Orkneys.

But by then it was all over. I was sure that once Sylvie Jenkinson realised what had happened, she had set about covering their tracks too deep for pursuit. Besides, I found I didn't really want to pursue them. If a perfect murder is one you get away with, they've managed one each. That's a record you've got to respect. If they have kids, we may yet see something really spectacular.

And really spectacular is what it will have to be to make the headlines. I still watch the news every night. Life in here isn't all that different from life outside, not if you've been unemployed for a year or two. And life out there hasn't changed much either.

Starvation in Africa. Floods in Asia. War in Central Europe. And queues for hospital beds in Britain.

Now they've gone over to *Today in Parliament* where they are all bawling and yelling and bickering about whether kids today spell better or worse than kids twenty years ago. Suddenly as I watch this spectacle I get a surprising revelation, like Huggable Henry's *Thought for Today*.

A man who sets his sights too low can't win even if he hits his bull.

The headline roundup running across the screen confirms it.

The EEC are making farmers pour milk away because they have exceeded their quota.

Fifty kids an hour are dying of starvation in Somalia.

Some prat of a politician may have to resign because he's been humping his secretary.

Twenty thousand Bosnian women may have been raped in the past six months.

An England striker has been flown home from Italy for treatment to a strained tendon.

In Sarajevo they're so short of medical supplies, they are amputating limbs without anaesthetic.

Suddenly everything's clear to me. No wonder I ended up in here. I was fighting out of my league. I set up business in competition with the multinationals. Westminster, Brussels, Washington, the UN—God is always on the side of the big guns. And now it's too late even to join, as they tell me convicted criminals aren't eligible for election to Parliament.

I suppose it's only fair really. They've got to be choosy.

I mean, innocent or guilty, if you've been stupid enough to get caught, how can you possibly hope to qualify for membership in the Perfect Murder Club?

James Grady has written eleven novels, including *Six Days of the Condor*, which was made into the film starring Robert Redford. A prolific writer for Hollywood, he recently edited the crime anthology *Unusual Suspects*. "Kiss the Sky," another Edgar Award–nominated story, takes a brutal look at life behind bars, where a good day is one you live through, and nothing is taken for granted.

Kiss the Sky
JAMES GRADY

Flat on his back at night when the TV and radio whispers and the coughs and sobs faded away, Lucus felt like he could kiss the sky.

Then Lucus would let his arm float up. Press his fingers against the concrete above him that told him where he was.

Grounded, man: Got to maintain. All day. All night.

Night only meant the Admin killed the cells' overheads and dudes with desk lamps had to snap them off. Unblinking walkway bulbs still ate shadows on the tiers and cast their shimmer into the cells. And unless a lockdown was on, anybody who'd saved enough to buy a TV could leave its screen flickering in his cell.

Same as ever, cell lights snapped on at 7 A.M.

From the bunk under his, Lucus heard H. L. S. whisper: "Think they's gonna go for it today?"

Lucus said nothing.

Jackster lay on the cot an arm's length from H. L. S.'s bunk, waiting to take his cue from the two gray men the Admin had sardined him with, waiting before putting his feet on the floor and figurin' on whether to take his meal card, make for breakfast.

"Maybe it's all cool," said Jackster, careful about carving his words in stone but still, like, reminding the older guys he was there. That he counted. "Maybe it's chilled."

"They been rocking the cradle," said H. L. S. "Put a dude to sleep with *it's-forgot's*, put steel in him when he's dreaming.

171

"They thinks they got a beef," added H. L. S., "they got a beef, and it don't blow away in the wind. Hard luck."

"I know what you're saying," said Jackster, not backing down like a punk but not pushing like a fool: "What you gonna do, Lucus?"

Silence answered those whispers in cell 47, tier 3, Administrative Building 3, Central facility.

Then from down the tier came the buzz of a cell door as Officers called a D-Dude out, the tinkle of chains as they strapped him in full restraints—hands linked to a chain belt in front, ankle hobbles, a lead line and row of tail links chained to the next guy in line.

D-Designate Residents were linked up to be marched to and from the mess hall, the first cons for breakfast and last for dinner; lunch got carted to them in their cells, a universally unpopular feeding system negotiated between Eighth Amendment court rulings and the Administration.

When they moved the D-Dudes to the mess hall, other cons were supposed to stay in their cells. Their gates might be locked, but often it was easier for the guards to yell the corridors clear and march the D-Dudes past open cells as fast as the shackled men could shuffle. The D-Dudes shuffled fast: in full restraints, you were a soft mark to get tore up. The guards weren't much protection: they kept their distance from D-Dudes to avoid a blade or whack from one of those angry boys.

Two years into his stretch, Lucus became a D Designate after he and Marcus jumped the hospital bus guards, stole the bus and damn near made it to the freeway before the troopers threw up a roadblock. Lucus shot a trooper in the leg with a bus guard's pistol. When SWAT sharpshooters cracked Marcus's head open from three hundred yards, Lucus was able to press the guard's revolver in Marcus's dead hand, then surrender unharmed. The trooper who got shot couldn't make a positive I.D. on which blue-jumpsuited convict had pulled his trigger, so dead Marcus ate that beef. Lucus only got tabbed for an escape.

That adventure added five onto his forty, kept him in chains for the next seven years.

Chains tinkled past the cell. Lucus drilled his eyes into the chipped white concrete ceiling.

H. L. S. swung out from under Lucus's upper bunk, went to the seatless toilet, urinated.

"Man," he said, shivering in the cold dank air, "hard luck, my plumbin's so creaky, can't go but half the night without hitting porcelain and I still got's to go first thing in the A.M.!"

"I hear that," said Lucus.

A rhythm worked its way down the tier, squeaky shoes followed by a loud clunk, then the rhythm replayed, coming closer: the Guard Rawlins, musclebound and faceless, unlocking the manuals on each cell door. Rawlins threw their bolt, squeaked down the line.

Jackster whispered: "What *are* you going to do, Lucus?"

Respectful. Wary. But pushing. Maybe checking if his ass was on the line, too.

The warning Klaxon echoed through the five tiers of Building 3, then came the sledgehammer clang of all the cells unlocking electronically.

Lucus sat up.

Cell doors across the way were slid open by their residents. Lucus wore prison blue sweats, a white T-shirt, a denim prison shirt. The seven-inch shank slid along his right forearm inside the shirt. The knife pricked his wrist, but the blade stayed up his sleeve, hidden by how Lucus held his arm and by a fuzzy red wristband like the iron-pumpers sported. Two winters before, a fish with a machine-shop job thought he could wolf out Lucus with the shiv he'd made right under the Jerks' eyes. Lucus broke both the fish's arms and one of his knees, kept the blade and left the fish to gimp around the walls like a billboard.

At their cell sink, H. L. S. splashed water on his face.

"I'm hungry," said Lucus. He slid to the floor, slipped into his sneakers. Glanced to the man at the sink whose hair was white: "You hungry, Sam?"

H. L. S.—Hard Luck Sam.

"Hell, yes," he answered. "If it's gonna keep running out, got to put more in."

"Want to stroll, Darnell?" said Lucus. *Darnell*, not *Jackster*: deliberately not using the dude's street name. Not dissin' the younger man, but underlining who was who.

"Think I'll hang here for a while," answered Darnell.

The Jackster, thought Lucus: you keepin' safe distance?

"I ain't that hungry," added the young man.

Justifying, thought Lucus: which means he's wanting to be sure I bought what he sold.

"What's hunger got to do with it?" Sam put on his shoes.

Could have been just H. L. S. running off at the mouth again.

But Lucus knew better.

And the flicker in Darnell's eyes said that he *wondered*.

Central Facility's dining hall could hold all 2,953 of its residents, but by the time Lucus and Hard Luck Sam made their way through the checkpoints out of their cellblock, then through the chain-link fence tunnel to the Dining Hall, half of the bolted-down, picnic-style tables were empty.

Lucus recognized several crews of younger inmates clustered at their usual tables, a politicization of geography that mirrored neighborhoods from which those men drew their identity. Here and there sat old timers like Sam and him, neither apart from nor a part of any group. Tattoos from a biker gang filled a corner table; they were laughing. Spanish babbled from three tables. Two Aryan Brotherhood bloods sat close to the main doors—close to the Control Station where two guards sat. Two more guards punched out inmates' meal passes as they moved into the food line. Three guards strolled the aisles, their faces as flat as the steel tables.

The dining hall smelled of burned coffee and grease. Breakfast was yellow and brown and sticky, though the cornbread from the prison bakery was fresh.

Sam carried his tray behind Lucus, sat with him at the table that emptied of other convicts as soon as Lucus arrived. The exodus might have been coincidental, Lucus couldn't be sure. He was grateful for Sam's company, for the man staying where he didn't have to be.

"You lookin' good this morning," Lucus said.

"Hard luck is, I look like myself."

"Looking good," said Lucus. "Looking good to me."

Five tables away, Lucus spotted the Twitch 6' 3" of too-tight piano wire, a guy with kinky hair like the man who kinda thought up the atomic bomb—Lucus couldn't be sure, he'd seen the picture in the prison library encyclopedia before he'd started The Program and learned to read real good. The Twitch bunked four cells down from Lucus. Twitch lifted a spoonful of yellow toward his grim mouth—the spoon jerked, and yellow glopped down to the tray. Nobody laughed or dissed Twitch: he was a straight-arrow postal worker who'd bought his ticket here when he beat a man to death who'd complained about slow mail service.

Twitch met Lucus's eyes.

Hope you taking your medication, thought Lucus. Twitch's lawyers lost the insanity plea, so their client bussed it to the prison population instead of a loony bin, but the courts let Admin make sure Twitch took pills to keep him rational.

Crazy, thought Lucus. What's that?

In the chessboard of tables, two men occupied steel slabs to themselves. One was thin and coughed; the other looked fine. The Word was they had Ultimate Virus, and once that was the word, those men were stuck where they were.

Someone snickered to the right.

Easy, casual, Lucus drifted his eyes to the laughter.

Two tables over, sitting by himself, bald bullet head on top of three hundred pounds of barbell muscle and sweet-tooth fat: Cooley, pig blue eyes and thick lips. In the world, Cooley cruised for hitchhikers and lone walkers, made Page One when the police tied him to three corpses.

Why ain't you a D Designate? Lucus asked himself, knowing the answer, knowing that Cooley played model prisoner, 'cept for maybe once or twice a year when that hunger burned in his eyes and he found some unconnected sheep where the Admin wasn't watching. Cooley left 'em alive, which kept the heat off, and always washed his hands.

The Twitch heard Cooley snicker, jerked his head toward that mountain of flesh.

Don't do it, Twitch, thought Lucus. He made his mind a magnet for Twitch's eyes. Don't be a fool today. Crazy as you are, Cooley'll eat you alive and love the memories in his lockdown. Ride your pills. Keep it cool.

Magic worked: Twitch's eyes found Lucus; blinked. The piano wire man bused his tray and left.

Cooley snickered, but nobody rose to his bait.

"Hard luck," muttered Sam. "The Twitch losing a cushy government job like that."

Lucus smiled.

Sam lowered his voice and talked with tight lips: "Ears?"

Lucus shook his head. Sam told him his back was empty, too, then said: "So what are you going to do?"

"I'm in the flow of events," said Lucus.

"Just you?"

"Gotta be who it's gotta be, and it's gotta be just me."

Sam said: "Believe I can—"

"You can't help me enough," said Lucus. "That'd just be one more body in the beef. That'd force it up to big time, but it's not enough to back it down. I won't let you stand on that line and get slaughtered if we both know it ain't gonna do no good no how.

"But Bro," finished Lucus, "I hear you. And thanks."

"Hard luck." The older man sighed. Lucus wasn't sure if it was with sorrow or relief. Sam said: "So you're in the flow."

"There it is."

"I be on the river banks." Sam shrugged. "Never know."

Then, for all the room to see, he held out his hand, and slapped five with Lucus.

Sam said: "What about the Jackster?"

"Yeah," said Lucus. "What about our Darnell?"

Darnell had folded the cot, leaned it next to the toilet. His footlocker was jammed up against the wall facing the bunkbeds. With the small desk, the sink, the rust-stained toilet and built-in footlockers for the two planned-for prisoners in this Resident Containment Unit, enough space remained for him to pace eight steps along the front of the cell bars.

"You getting your exercise, Jackster?" asked Lucus as he and Hard Luck Sam came back home.

"No, man, I'm working on my tan," answered Darnell.

H. L. S. stretched out on his bunk—feet facing the front of the cell. "Why didn't you take it to the Rec? They got three new Ping-Pong balls and you loves to watch that talk show lady strut her stuff."

"Figured I'd just hang here," said Darnell. "Wait for you."

"Wait for us to what?" Lucus kept his voice flat, easy. He perched on top of the desk, the open front of the cell and the pacing Darnell filling his eyes.

"Shit, man, I don't know!" said Darnell, pacing, staring out across the walkway, across the yawning fifty-foot canyon between their wall of tiered cells and the identical scene facing it. "We're partnered here, I figured—"

"Partnered?" said Lucus. "Don't recall signing on with anybody when they signed me in here. You remember anything like that, Sam?"

"I disremember nothing and I don't remember that," came the words from the lower bunk.

"Shit, man," said Darnell. Not turning around.

"Course, we do have to live together," said Lucus.

"Yeah," said Darnell: "That's what I'm talking about."

"I mean," said Lucus, "we all gots the same cell number."

Darnell humphed.

"Numbers, man," chimed in Sam from the lower bunk, "they can be hard luck for a dude."

"What you mean?" snapped Darnell.

"Why, nothing, Jackster," said Sam, flat on his back, hard to see. "Just talking about numbers. Luck.

"Like when I went to that sporting house outside of Vegas," continued Sam. "Man, they trot the women out in a line, I'm gassed, blow and booze and riding a hell of a score, squinting at them long legs, them firm—"

"Stop it, man!" hissed Darnell. "Don't kill me like that!"

"How do you want us to kill you?" said Lucus, sweet and low.

Jackster didn't reply.

"Just a story!" came the words from the lower bunk. "It ain't about women, it's about numbers. Them ladies all had these number tags on 'em, kind of like our designations, only you couldn't tell as much from reading theirs, just their number. Some of 'em were dog meat, but I spot Number 9 and she's so fine—"

"I heard this shit already," said Jackster. Leaning against the wall now, watching nothing real deliberately.

"And I choose her, tells the Man the hit parade bullet I want, pays him, go to the room and skin down—and who strolls in all what-the-Hell-for-you look on her face but the skaggiest bowser in the line! I find out my girl, she's so untogether, she's Number 6 but she ain't tumbled to her number's on upside down!"

"Hard luck," said Lucus, rolling out Sam's punch line.

"Yeah," spit out the Jackster, "kind of like when old H. L. S. here, him already a two-time fall man, cases his apartment rip so bad that the lady done showed up coming home—"

"She got sick at work," said Sam. "She wasn't supposed to."

If the Jackster knew what he was hearing, he didn't show it.

"Yeah," he said, "and it was hard luck when that lamp you whomped her upside the head with—"

"She wasn't supposed to be there screaming—getting in the way of me getting clear to—"

"And hard luck when you dropped out her window and the alley Dumpster lid caved in on you, and hard luck it was empty so's you hit steel bottom and busted your foot instead of bouncing off a pile of dirty Pampers, and—"

"You talking about *my* crime."

Even Darnell heard solid cement in the man on the bottom bunk.

Can't let this shit roll down today, thought Lucus. He said: "Enough hard luck out there to fill our happy home."

Zero the score so H. L. S. won't need to, thought Lucus. He said: "Kind of like when somebody sells three bags of rock to a roller wearing a beard over his badge, deal going down just in time to catch the Man's new mandatory sentencing guidelines."

Darnell's eyes risked flicking from the lower bunk to Lucus.

Lucus smiled: "Some guys just ain't cut out for the spy game."

"I don't play no games," said Darnell. But his edge was jagged, backing away.

"Hard luck. There it is."

"Should have been thinking about that *then*," muttered Darnell, not ready to give it up, not certain who he was talking about.

"I wasn't thinking about now *then*," answered Sam, softer, sadder. "*Then* I was thinking about doing what was in my face. Scratching itches. Cool schemes that had to work for sure."

The air inside the room eased out the open cell door, whirled into the cacophony of shouts and radios and sweat in the cell-block.

"The point of the story," said Sam, his words round and smooth again, "is numbers. Some people get their number wrong, and look what hard luck that brings."

"I got my number," mumbled Darnell, "don't worry about it."

"I won't," said H. L. S. "I be glad for you."

"What about you, Lucus?" said Darnell.

"What about me what?" answered the man sitting on the desk.

"You gotta be working on your number," said Darnell. He met Lucus eye for eye. "Like you said, we live together, choose or no. That means your number's chained to mine, we on the line together."

"I know about chains," said Lucus.

"Me, too," said the Jackster. "And ain't nobody here don't know your number's up. Us being linked, it's righteous I should get to know what's what and figure my score around your play."

Jackster shrugged: "Ain't saying I'll throw with you, but I gots to do the stand-up thing by the guys I'm bunking with—"

"The right thing," interrupted H. L. S.

"Time for me to hit the shower." Lucus snagged his towel, stepped past Darnell saying: "You boys play nice while I'm gone."

Then Lucus was on the walkway, strolling down the tier, his towel looped in his left hand. Inside his right sleeve waited steel.

Split the walkway toward the right, stay closer to the rail than the cells. Not so close it's an easy bull-charge to push you over, but better close to the rail with its long drop-off than walking next to the bars where you were an easy push into a cell for a pile-on of badasses and blades. Ripping it up on the walkway meant that the tussle might get seen by the Tier Monitor in the bulletproof tower. The Tier Monitor could punch the horn, maybe get Nightsticks there while you still had some pieces left. In the cells, you'd fall into a setup so savage it'd be history before the Man got there, even if the Monitor saw you snatched.

Usually when Lucus walked the tiers, dudes sang out to him, gave him a nod or even strolled up to jazz. That morning, the guys hanging outside the open cells and doin' their busies inside sent him no words. Guys in his path rolled away.

"Hey, Sir," Lucus told the fat guard behind the desk at the cage entrance to the shower rooms, "OK if I catch a shower so's I won't stink up the Boss's office today?"

Architectural plans for the Central Facility called for two Corrections Officers to be on front desk duty at the Cleansing Units' facility entrance, and for one Officer to be stationed "in visual range" of the actual showers in each of the five locker rooms. The architectural plans took the "custody and care" charge of the incarceration laws seriously. Under the latest budget plan, enough Cleansing Units manpower existed for one front desk officer.

The fat guard had seven years left to his pension-out of the prison. When this guard found a dollar bill on a walkway, he'd been known not to smell homebrew being cooked anywhere in a three-state area.

Not a bad Jerk, thought Lucus as the guard skimmed the clipboard of demerit denials and didn't find this inmate's name or designation.

"Everybody likes clean residents," said the fat guard.

"I hear that."

"Number 2 and 4 are busted out."

"Believe I'll try 3," said Lucus, signing his name and number on the second line of the logbook.

The fat guard frowned, spun the logbook around and double-checked the scrawl on the line above Lucus's name.

"I thought you could read, boy."

Keep it level—Hell, slam joke it straight back at the fat son of a bitch: "Do my numbers, too."

"You know who's in there?"

"I don't care."

Flat out, the power mantra.

The guard shook his head, scrawled his initials in the OK column. Said: "Never figured you for that scene, Lucus."

Like all its counterparts, Unit 3's locker room had no lockers. Wooden benches were bolted to the floor. A set of prison clothes and a Day-Glo undershirt were neatly stacked against the deserted dressing room when Lucus walked in. From inside the tiled shower area came the sound of rushing water and billowing steam.

Lucus stripped to his skin, stacked his clothes on the wall opposite the other pile. A scar snaked around his left ribs where he'd been too slow seven years before.

The shiv he held pressed against his forearm, his other hand swung open and free, fanning a path through the warm fog.

There, against the far wall, under the last of the twenty spraying shower spigots, shoulder-length permed tresses protected by a flowered shower cap, watching Lucus emerge from the steam, saying: "And lo, it is the man himself."

"Who you expecting, Barry?" Lucus walked down the line of lead-heavy rain.

Barry was six feet three inches of rippling muscles. Long, sinewy legs that let him fly across the stage of the city ballet or lightspeed kick the teeth out of dudes inside who were dumb enough to think Barry's style equaled weakness. The showers' steam made mascara over Barry's right eye trickle down his cheek like a midnight tear.

"Expecting?" Barry turned his bare shoulder toward Lucus, flashed his floodlight smile and swung his arms out from his sides, up above his head, hands meeting in a point as Barry stretched to his tiptoes, eyes closed in ecstasy. He held position for a full count, then fluttered his arms down, cupped his hands shyly above his groin and lowered his chin, eyes closed: a sleeping angel scarred by a midnight tear.

One heartbeat.

Barry's eyes popped open and he beat his lashes toward the man with a shiv.

"Why I've been waiting for only you." Barry cocked poses with each beat as he sang: "Just *you*, indeed, it's *you*, only *you*, yes it's *true* . . ."

Whirling around, dancing, singing: ". . . no-body bu-ah-ut—"

Cobra coiled, shrinking back on one cocked leg, both pointing fingers aimed right at Lucus's heart: *"Yooou."*

"Good thing you came," said Lucus.

"What else is a girl supposed to do?" Barry leered: "My pleasure."

"No, man," said Lucus: "My payoff."

"Oh my yes," said Barry, washing. "Lucus to Mouser to Dancer—why, you'd think we were playing *baseball!*"

"We ain't playing shit."

"Certainly not, manchild." Barry smiled. "And right you were. The play's been called, the sign is on for a hit."

"When?"

"Well, that nervous nellie was all *denial*, you see, as if he hadn't been cruising around the yard, too scared to make a move, afraid his bros would put him down. Those savages! As if *they've* never grabbed a punk in these very tiled walls and made the poor boy weep! So since this was his first time, and since *my man* wasn't really doing it, you understand, just accepting this evening of sin I'd thrown at his feet as evidence of what a *stud* he is—"

"When?"

"Let a girl tell her story or you'll never get anywhere with her!"

"We're where we are and where we're going. You been paid, you come across."

"Always." Barry savored the moment. "What did Mouser owe you that he swapped my debt to him for?"

"Enough," said Lucus. "Now give me what I bought: when?"

"Why, *today*, Dear Man."

Lucus showed nothing.

"Probably in afternoon exercise."

Yard time, thought Lucus. Starts at 3:30. About five hours away.

Barry washed his armpits.

"My simple little use-to-be-a-virgin's crew has traded around and rigged flooding the stage and done the diplomacy and even *rehearsed* wolf-packing. They have a huge enough chorus to smother any friends of their featured star who try to crimp the show and make it more than a solo death song."

Water beat down on the two men.

"What else?" said Lucus.

"Nothing you'd want. He cried. I think he actually feels guilty. That's the only charming thing about him—though he does have nice thighs. Not as nice as yours."

"Does he got any notions that he was set up with you or that he ran his mouth too much?"

"He's mere ego and asshole," said Barry. "He can't conceive that's he's been bought and sold and suckered clean."

"How about his bros? By now, they might know about you two."

"Not from him. He's too scared of getting stigmatized to confess, and he's cagey enough to not let it slip out—for a while. If they do know, no worry: Like you said, I used to middleman powder for upscale customers from a boy tied to their crew. That makes *moi* acceptable."

"We're square." Lucus stepped back, his eyes staying on Barry as he made toward the shower room door.

"How about a little something for the road?" Barry smiled. "It'll calm your nerves. For free. For you, from me."

"I got what I need for the road."

"Oh, if only that were true for all of us!" Barry shook his head. "If only we could all *believe* that!"

Fifteen steps away, Lucus turned, disappeared in the steam.

"Good luck!" cried Barry.

Lucus dressed. Don't run. Don't show one bead of sweat.

"You'll get what you was after?" asked the fat guard as he signed Lucus out.

"Guess I did."

"Guess I did—*Sir*."

"YEAH." LUCUS SAW HIS REFLECTION in the fat guard's eyes, saw how it shrank because of what that guard thought happened in the shower.

That's his problem, thought Lucus. He went back to the cell.

Spent the morning on his cot, like he had nothing to do.

Jackster and H. L. S. puttered about, neither one leaving Lucus.

"Lunchtime," announced Lucus, swinging off his bunk. "Come on, Jackster. Today you eating with the men."

"I eat where I want," snapped Darnell.

"Why wouldn't you want to eat with us?" asked Lucus.

Darnell mumbled—then obeyed Lucus's gesture to lead the way.

A table emptied when Lucus and his cellmates sat at it.

Lunch was brown and brown and gray, with coffee.

Jackster kept sneaking looks to other tables, locking eyes with bros from his old neighborhood.

H. L. S. ran down "chumps I have known."

Like Dozer, a Valium freak who bypassed a pharmacy's alarm system, peeled its narco safe, then overindulged in booty and nodded off in the Pampers aisle. The cops woke him.

And Two Times Shorty, a midget who took it to the Stroll to bully an indy whore into being his bottom lady. She chased him through horn-honking curbside shoppers and lost tourists, pinned him on the hood of a Dodge, and pounded about a hundred dents in him with her red high-heeled shoe. Tossed him buck naked into a Dumpster. Climbing out, pizza parts stuck to his naked torso, Shorty grabbed the offered hand of a fine-looking woman. What the hell, he figured, second time's the charm, and he reeled off his be-mine pimp spiel. She slapped policewoman bracelets on him.

Then there was Paul the Spike, who tested heroin on street dogs. While he was slicing and dicing a batch of Mexican he had to keep stepping on and then retesting, Paul got the knock on the door. Because of the 'scl-usionary rule, he beat the narco charges but drew ninety days for cruelty to animals.

"Hard luck can bite anybody's ass," said Sam, "but it always eats up chumps."

"I ain't no chump," said the Jackster.

Sergeant Wendell appeared at the mess hall door, scanned the mostly empty rows of tables.

"Who said you were a chump?" said Lucus, his eyes leaving the sergeant to settle on Darnell.

"No fool better!"

Sergeant Wendell started toward them.

"Trouble with young punks today," said Sam, "they got no *finesse*. Our day, needed to smoke a guy, you caught him in private, did your business and everything's cool. These days, you young punks let fly on street corners and wing out some poor girl comin' home from kindergarten. No respect for nothing, no style or—"

"Style?" snapped the Jackster. "That what that 'finesse' bullshit means? You got no idea, man, no *idea* what style is!"

Corner of his eye, Lucus saw Sergeant Wendell, coming closer. Lucus said: "Why don't you explain style to us, Darnell?"

"Ellicott!" yelled Sergeant Wendell.

"Yes Sir?" answered Lucus.

"What the hell are you doing?"

"I was just—"

"You know your damn schedule as well as I do! Your ass belongs in Administrator Higgins's office as of ten minutes ago!"

"On my way, Sir!" said Lucus, standing.

H. L. S. pulled Lucus's tray so Lucus wouldn't need to bus it.

"Why'd you make me have to come fetch you?" Wendell command marched Lucus to visit the Administrator in front of a dozen sets of eyes; in front of Darnell.

"Just guess I ain't so smart," said Lucus.

"Don't give me that shit," said Wendell, who was no fool and a good Jerk, though no con had ever been able to buy him. "Move!"

"Yes Sir."

Assistant Administrator Higgins kept his office *almost* regulation. Sunlight streaming through the steel mesh grille over his lone window fell on a government low-bid desk positioned in line with the file cabinets and the Official Calendar on the wall next to Facility Authority and Shift Assignment charts. But Higgins had taken out the regulation two visitors' steel chairs bolted to the floor in front of his desk and risked replacing them with more inviting, freestanding wooden fold-up chairs that a strong man could use to batter you to death.

Higgins was a bantamweight in chain-store suits and plain ties. He wore metal frame glasses that hooked around his ears. Glasses on or off, his dark eyes locked on who he was talking to. That afternoon, he slowly unhooked his glasses, set them on the typed report in the middle of his otherwise blank desk, and fixed those eyes on the man sitting in the visitor's chair.

"So you have no questions or comments about this report?" Higgins asked Lucus.

"Figure it's written, I can read now, so that ain't what I gots to talk to you about."

"That was on our schedule." Higgins leaned back in his chair.

"The Administration," started Lucus, "they got to like what I been doing. They been catching hell on the news, in the TV ads from those two citizens running for Senator. I heard the Warden—"

"Chief Administrator," corrected Higgins.

"Oh yeah, I forgot. Change the names and everything's OK. Long as there's no trouble."

"What do you mean, 'trouble'?"

"There's some that say the understaffing helps you guys, 'cause it'll inspire something to happen, and then you all can say, 'See? We need more budget. Jobs.'"

"I don't see it that way."

"Maybe some of the guards do."

"The Officers are paid to watch inmates, not make policy. I need to be told about any of them who act differently."

"I ain't the telling kind," said Lucus. "I just sensitive to your problems about image and keeping up the good show so the Warden don't get bad press and take heat from his buddy the Governor and every politician looking to get elected."

"What's this got to do with anything?"

"I just glad to help out—with things like that charity program on your desk."

"You've done good work, Lucus."

"What will it get me?"

Higgins frowned. "You knew that wasn't the way this program would be when you signed on."

Lucus shrugged. "Things change."

"Don't go con on me now, Resident."

"Sir, you was the one who showed me about attitude, about getting out from behind it and how nothing would change if I didn't. So I been workin' on my attitude, what's behind it, what I do. But where's it getting me? Still right here."

"You're down for Murder One, five counts. Plus. Where do you expect to be?"

"Oh I'm a criminal," said Lucus. "No question about that. I can do the time for what I did, but man, let my crime justify my punishment."

"Five murders," said Higgins. "Plus."

"I already done my plus in chains." Keep it calm, rational. "But I never did no murders."

"The law—"

"Sir, I know *the law*. We were sticking up gamblers. The law made them crooks, which made them marks. *The law* did that—not me. Figure, heist a crook, he can't holler for cops. Rodney, he had the gun, had them fools lined up against that wall, told me check out the basement. We agreed before we went in there: in and out with cash, nobody hurt, nobody can do shit about us. I'm in the basement, looking for whatnot, I hears those *pop-pop-pops*. . . . Man, Rodney done me just as much as he done them dudes!"

"Not quite," said Higgins.

"Yeah, well, what's done is done, but I didn't kill nobody. It's the law and Rodney that made me guilty."

"You chose to rob, you chose to go with a trigger-happy partner, you chose your juvie record, your prior theft and assault rec—"

"Yes Sir," said Lucus, interrupting with police formality: Got to hurry Higgins on. "I admit I'm guilty, but fitting my crimes with two twenty-year stretches, back to back, no parole—no right man can do that kind of jus-tifying."

"It's a done deal, Lucus. I didn't think you were fighting that anymore."

"I got a lot of time to mess with it. Nineteen years more."

"Might just be enough to make yourself a new life."

"Yeah. Starting when I'm sixty-two."

"Starting every time you breathe." Higgins's dark eyes blinked. "You want something."

"This new attitude you helped me get," said Lucus. "Working with the programs—with my Program in my head. Not getting in any beefs since I got out of chains—"

"At least," said Higgins, "caught for none in your jacket."

"I been doing good time—"

"The law isn't about doing good time. That's what you're supposed to do as a minimum. No matter what you do in here, every day is on the payback clock, and you gotta get to zero before you can claim you're owed."

"Maybe yes, maybe no. Maybe not always."

Higgins shrugged. "What do you want?"

"A transfer," said Lucus.

"What?"

"Out of here. Right now. Not a parole, you couldn't pull that off. But you could take a paper out of that desk, sign it, and there it is, a transfer out of the walls to the Minimum Security unit downstate. Effective soon as the ink is dry. Call the Duty Sergeant and—"

"You're down for hard time, Lucus. You're a five-count killer with one escape and one shot-up officer—don't tell me where that gun was found—plus a jacket full of incidents—"

"All before I changed my attitude."

"Never happen. I never bullshitted you it would. You've got to deal with that in the most pos—"

"The transfer ain't for me. It's for my son."

Higgins blinked.

Blinked again, and in the Administrator's dark eyes, Lucus saw mental file cabinet drawers slide open.

"Kevin," said Higgins. "Kevin Ellicott, down for . : ."

"Last year, a nickel tour for what they could get him on instead of big dope. He's done angel time for thirteen months."

"Your boy runs with the Q Street Rockers," said Higgins. "They're not a church choir."

"I didn't say he was a genius. What he is, Sir, is a juicer. Just about to become a full-bore alcoholic, if he stays in here much longer. And what's that gonna solve? How's that gonna make life easier for the Warden? What justice is—"

"Doesn't add up," said Higgins. "He can get pruno as easy at the Farm as here."

"Maybe if he gets into the Farm's Step program—"

"It's *his* maybes," said Higgins. "Not yours. Why isn't he asking? Why are you doing this?"

"He's my son. I wasn't there to bring him up. Hell, if I had been around before I got my Attitude Program, probably wouldn't have done him much good. Maybe he could have learned better street smarts, but . . . He stays in here, he dies in here."

"Of alcoholism?" said Higgins.

"Dead is dead," said Lucus.

They watched each other for a dozen heartbeats.

"And you think a transfer to the Farm will keep him alive."

"It'll give him a chance."

"What aren't you telling me?" said Higgins.

"I'm telling you everything I can," answered Lucus.

"That you *can?*" said Higgins. "You got to learn that we create most of our own *cans* and *can'ts.*"

"We do?" Lucus waited, then said: "Thought you always said that we pay for them, too."

"That's right."

"Yeah," said Lucus. "That's right. So if somebody's already paid, then he deserves a *can.*"

Softly, Higgins said: "Don't blow it, Lucus. Whatever's going down, don't you blow everything you've accomplished."

"What's that, huh—*Sir?* Any way I cut it, I still got nineteen years to go. What could I blow?"

"The way you get to look at yourself in the mirror."

"I see a man there now. I'll see a man there tomorrow."

"If you won't help me," said Higgins, "I can't help you."

"I been helping you—Sir. Look at the report on your desk. Let the Warden take credit for it, keep his image shiny. I ain't asking nothing for me. Who I am, what I've done—what I can do, one way or the other, all that should be worth something."

Higgins shook his head: "You can't bargain for your son."

"Then what the hell can I do?"

"Let him do his own life."

"You telling me, no transfer for him?"

"That's the way it has to be."

"Thought we defined our own possibilities," said Lucus. "Are you through with me—Sir?"

"We're through, Resident."

Lucus walked to the door, turned back. "Answer me one question, Sir?"

"Maybe."

"Why you do what you do? Every day, come in here, locked up just like us, with us. Bucking the Administration and the Rules and the Law and the Word and the Attitudes: Why you do it?"

"I got kids, too."

Lucus nodded, and as he opened the door, said: "Too bad."

Clock in the sunshine on the wall facing the sergeant's desk: 1:57. Hour and a half to go.

Close that door behind you, thought Lucus. He said: "Hey, Sergeant, got some book work to do now. Can you cut me a library pass? It ain't my regular day till tomorrow."

Sergeant Wendell wrote the pass without bothering his boss behind the closed door. Wendell knew all about Lucus and his Help the Homeless Project and the grants and the reports.

The library filled the second floor of the Recreation Complex. Lucus shivered as he hurried through the open-air fenced tunnel from the Admin Building to the Rec. His exhales floated through the chain-link fence. The blade pressed against his arm was slick with sweat.

Inside the Rec, Lucus glanced at the standing-room-only crowd of blue jumpsuits watching a soap on the prison's big-screen TV that the Feds had confiscated in a drug bust. Cons laughed and joked, but soaked up the story about a beautiful blonde in slinky dresses and jewels who didn't know yet that the bearded dude she'd been banging was setting her up, secretly paying back a beef his father had with her father. With his glance, Lucus couldn't spot the face in the crowd, but he knew he was there.

The guard at the library door blinked at Lucus's pass with eyes that coveted first-floor duty where he could watch TV, too.

The A-Designate con working as librarian stood by the checkout desk, stacking books on a delivery cart to be rolled along the tiers. Another A-Designate replaced books on a shelf. Three Residents sat at tables by themselves, surrounded by lawbooks and yellow legal pads.

Over in the corner, reading at his Thursday table, Sir James Clawson.

A blue tent loomed in front of Lucus's view: Manster, the only creature in the Institution bigger than Cooley. Manster stayed out of chains because whatever he wanted from another con, the other con gave up. Outside, Manster pistol-whipped a cop to death.

"I'm here to see the Man," Lucus told Manster.

"Maybe." Manster held out a shovel-sized hand, not touching Lucus, but pinning the dude to the floor while Manster coughed to get Sir James's attention. Manster kept his eyes on Lucus, who everybody knew was one treacherous mother.

The three other ironmen between Sir James's table and the world made a space for their ruler to check out the petitioner. Sir James read to the end of the paragraph, glanced through the blue jumpsuits and let Lucus fall into his eyes.

"How you doin', J. C.?" said Lucus.

Manster exhaled a blimp of foul air: only Sir James's friends got to call him J. C.

Unless the mood was right.

"Lucus the lone wolf," said Sir James. "Join me."

So Lucus walked through the gauntlet of hard cons, sat in the chair across the table from the Man.

Sir James picked up some chump's pink Commissary Pass, used it as a bookmark for the page he was reading, then closed the volume. He turned the book so Lucus could see the cover: a picture of a suit-and-tie dude with a cocked sword in one hand and a briefcase in the other. The book's title read: *CORPORATE SAMURAI—Classic Japanese Combat Principles for the Twenty-First Century's Global Business Economy.*

"Are you still reading, Lucus?"

"Some. When I got time."

"You know what the underlying fallacy of this book is?" asked J. C., who was working on his MBA, correspondence and good-faith-in-your-prison-jacket style.

"Ain't read it."

"You don't' need to. Look at the cover."

The suit with a briefcase and sword and going-places face.

"Give a twelve-year-old a dime and a nine," said J. C., "and he'll punch a dozen red holes in Mr. Global Business Corporate Samurai before that classic sword even gets close."

A national gang once sent a crew from Angel Town to "negotiate" Sir James's Outfit into their fold. A freezer truck carted the five gangbangers back to L.A., dumped their meat in their 'hood.

"Business ain't my thing," said Lucus.

"It's the wave of the future," counseled J. C., who was down on a drug kingpin sentence until well into the twenty-first century.

"I've got something for you," said Lucus.

"Ah."

"But I need something, too," said Lucus.

"Of course you do. Or you wouldn't be here. Respect and such, you've been smart about it. But it's always been Lone Wolf Lucus."

"I've had bad luck at partnering."

"Perhaps prison has taught you something."

"Oh yeah.

"Deal is," continued Lucus, "there's trouble coming down. You run most of what moves inside here."

Sir James shrugged.

"Trouble comes down," said Lucus, "all the politics buzzing outside, the Admin will tighten the screws, and that'll crimp your business, be bad for you."

"The innocent always suffer," said J. C. "What 'trouble' has made you its prophet?"

"There's a hit on, likely for this afternoon. The guarantee is it won't be quick and clean, and you don't need any out-of-hand mess tightening the screws on your machine."

"What's the 'guarantee'?"

"I am." Risk it. Maybe he knows, maybe not. Maybe he gave the nod, maybe he just heard the Word and let it melt in his eyes.

"The hit's on my boy—Kevin. He got drunk, got in a stupid beef over a basketball game in the yard. Trash flew, couple pushes before the Man walked by and chilled it down. Dude named Jerome's claimed the beef with my boy, and Jerome and his Orchard Terrace Projects crew gonna make it a pack hit."

"This just a beef? Not turf or trade?"

"Nothing ever stays clean, J. C. You know that. The Orchard Terrace crew does my boy, it'll make them heavy—balance of power shifts don't do you no good."

"Unless the teeter-totter dips my way," said J. C.

"Far as I know, you ain't in this."

Gotta be that way! Or . . .

J. C. sent his eyes to one of his lieutenants.

"Lucus's punk runs with the Q Street Rockers," said the man whose job it was to know. "Wild boys. Orchard Terrace crew, they been proper, smart."

J. C. sat for a moment. Closed his eyes and enjoyed the sunshine streaming through the grilled window.

"You're in a hard place," he told Lucus.

"Life story."

"What do you want from me?" asked J. C.

"Quash the hit—you could do it, no cost."

"Everything costs. What's in that play for me?"

"Your profits stay cool," said Lucus.

"Your concern for my profits is touching."

"We got the same problem here."

"No," sighed J. C., "we don't.

"If I squash the hit," he said, "then I tilt the teeter-totter. Even if you're right and the hit will cause trouble, unintended adverse consequences of my indifference, there'll be trouble no matter what. Why should I become the cause of trouble instead of just one of its bystanders?

"Your boy picked his crew—"

"It's a neighborhood thing, he didn't pick—"

"He didn't grow up," said J. C. "Now, if he runs to me out of fear, wants to join up . . . I'd be signing on a weak link. I'd gain more if I fed him back to the Orchard Terrace boys—then they'd owe me. Better to be owed by lions than to own one jackrabbit."

"I figured that already."

"What else is in your column of calculations?"

Fast, everything rushing so fast, too fast.

"You quash the hit," said Lucus, drawing the bottom line, "I'll owe you one."

"Well," said J. C. "Well, well.

"What would you owe me?" asked the man with a wallet full of souls.

"Eye for eye. One for one."

"Eye for eye *plus* interest." J. C. smiled. His teeth were white and even. "You really aren't a businessman, Lucus."

"I am who I am."

"Yes. You were a gray legend when I walked in here. Lone wolf and wicked. You mind your step, never push but never walk away. Smart. Smarter than smart—schooled."

"I'm worth it."

"You ever kill anybody, Lucus?"

"I'm down for five counts of murder—plus."

"My question is," said the man whose eyes punished lies, "have your hands ever drained the blood themselves?"

"Nobody ever quite died," confessed Lucus.

"Quite is a lot." J. C.'s smile was soft. "I know you're stand-up. You'd keep your word, wear my collar. But the fit would be too tight. And down the line, who knows what problems that would mean?"

Lucus felt his stomach fall away. His face never changed.

"So . . . I can't help you. Your boy's beef is none of my business—either way, I promise you that. He makes it clean, I'm not in his shadow. But his future is his future."

Lucus nodded. Pushed his chair back from the table slowly and felt the meats close in by his sides, ready.

"Whatever happens," said Lucus, "remember I gave you heads-up, fair warning. Nothing headed your way from me. Or my boy."

"We'll see." J. C. shrugged. "If we're square on that, we're square."

On his way out the library door, Lucus checked the clock: 2:01. Less than ninety minutes until the turn-out in the Yard.

What was left was the hardest thing.

Lucus found them in the TV room, backs to the wall, street cool, running their mouths and eyeing beautiful people in the tube.

"Well, what's up here," said one of them as Lucus rolled up.

Brush past that fool like December wind.

Look at yesterday's mirror—a young man against a wall, thick hair with no gray, taller and flatter muscles, no scar cross the bridge of the nose, but *damn*: a mirror.

"We gotta talk," Lucus told the apparition.

"Say what?" said the young man. Lucus smelled pruno on the boy's breath. Fear in his sweat.

Use your fear, telepathed Lucus. If you can't kill it, use it and ride it smart! But he said: "Say, *now*."

"Old man," said his son, "anything you got to say, you say it right here, right *now*, in front of my bros."

"I thought you grew up to be enough of a man you didn't need nobody to protect you from facing your lone old man."

Catcalls and laughs bounced off Lucus—bounced off him and hit his son. Lucus knew they were all measuring Kevin, seeing how he'd handle this. Wondering if maybe Lucus could wolf their bro down. And if the old man could do it . . .

Kevin knows all that, too, sensed Lucus, and he felt proud that his son wasn't all fool.

"Well, shit!" said Kevin. "You been worrying 'bout talking to me for nineteen years, you might as well get it off your back now."

Kevin swaggered out of his crew, headed toward an empty corner by the moth-eaten pool table whose cues and balls hadn't been replaced after the last riot. Pressed his back against the wall, made Lucus turn his eyes from the distant crowd.

Good move! thought Lucus; he said: "We haven't got much time."

"You never did have the time, did you?"

"I never had much choice. Your Grandma didn't want to be bringing you down to no lockup and get you thinking that was just another part of family life, and your mother—"

"She'd have sold me for a nickel bag."

"She did what she could by you, got you to her mother. Gave up the one thing she ever loved all-out."

"I should drop by the cemetery, scrawl a thank-you on her stone."

"Don't throw your shit on her grave."

The chill in Lucus's voice touched his son.

"Why'd you two go and have me anyway?"

"Wasn't what we were thinking of," answered his father.

"Yeah, I know. A little under-the-blanket action sitting in chairs in Minimum's visitor hall, 'fore you got popped big time."

"Least you know who your father is."

"Hell of a family that gives me." Kevin shook his head. "I don't know who the hell you are. You're the big Never There."

"Nothing kept you from catching a bus out here when you turned eighteen, signing the visitors' log and calling me out."

Kevin shrugged: "I figured I'd make it here soon enough."

There it is, thought Lucus.

"Just like I could bust out in the hospital bus to see you when you was learning to walk and nobody was there to hold your hands but junkies and badasses and your spaced-out mama."

"You should have been smarter," muttered Kevin.

"Yeah," said his father. "I should have."

Got to tend to business!

But Lucus said: "Outside . . . You got a woman?"

Kevin looked away, said: "They's all bitches or whores."

"Thinkin' and talkin' like that," said his father, "no wonder you're in prison. No woman who's worth it will stick around you when you got that attitude."

"Yeah, well . . . No ladies no how was beating down my crib door." Kevin looked at his father; looked away, said: "That woman Emma, works in the dry cleaners. She calls herself your wife."

"We ain't got no law on it." Lucus shrugged, prayed for the clock not to tick. "Her old man died in a bustout, I got to know her through that. Phone calls, letters. We understand each other."

"You don't even have Minimum Security visiting privileges, the glass stays up when she visits you. What's she see in it?"

Lucus shrugged: "Safe sex."

Made his son laugh!

"We got no time," said Lucus. "The hit's on you today. Probably in the yard. They miss, they'll pick it up first chance."

Kevin blinked: "Jerome said—"

"Words are weapons! Ain't you learned that!"

"You ain't been my teacher, you can't give me grades!"

"If I'd been learning you, you wouldn't have gotten drunk and gotten in a beef over chump Yard basketball! And if you *had* run up against it, you would have done it right!"

"Yeah? Like how?"

"Like you'd have kept it *personal!* Man to man. Walked into Jerome's crew and called him out—put him on the spot. Then you'd have had a chance!"

"What chance did I ever have for anything!" hissed Kevin. "You think I'm chump enough to ask him—"

"You don't 'ask' for anything from anybody!"

"Force a throw-down, strap our arms together, toss the blade on the floor and—"

"And you got an even chance! You let it buck up to you dissin' him and his whole crew, you got a war, not a battle."

"I got my own crew!"

"Yeah, right. There's more of the other dudes, and the guys on your side would never sell anybody out—or miss getting cut up on accidental purpose. They gonna *die* for you."

"That's the way it is."

"If that's the way it was, this wouldn't be plea-bargain city."

"So what do you want me to do, Mr. Smart Time Con?"

"You got one chance. Go to the Admin. Feed them a pruno still—Robinson, Building 2, Tier 2, in the bus the auto mechanics practice on. Trade that bust for a crash transfer to—"

"You want me to rat? You a fool? That's evil! And suicide!"

"No, that's smart. Robinson wants to kick the juice—like you need to. He knows lockdown cold turkey is his only way.

"I already dealt it out with him," said Lucus. "You just gotta make your move—and right now."

"You're one treacherous mother," said Kevin.

"Believe it."

"But I go to the Farm, the Orchard Terrace guys—"

"They got no crew there."

"They will."

"That's tomorrow. You're scheduled to die today. With the time you done, keep your jacket clean and when the courts make the Admin thin the herd, you're a prime candidate for early release. Could be outta here in a year. Besides, we'll fix tomorrow when—"

"The Farm boys would know I ratted—"

"Not if Robinson puts out the Word how you two tricked the Admin."

"My crew would cut me loose."

"No loss."

"They're all I got!"

"Not anymore."

Lucus heard the babble behind him; knew a hundred eyes was checking them out. Knew the clock was ticking.

"You just don't understand," said Kevin. "If I run from—"

"You're not running *from*, you're running *towards*. And don't tell me I don't understand."

"I gotta do what I gotta do. If what's gonna happen's got to happen, that's just the way it's gotta be."

"Kevin?"

"Yeah?"

"Don't hand me bullshit street jive. That's all hollow words you stack in front of your face to keep from seeing you're too lazy or too stupid or too scared to fight so you can walk your own way. 'What's gotta be, gotta be' *shit:* you sit like a lame where the 'be'-shit is, you ain't being stand-up strong, you making yourself the most powerless chump in the world."

"You don't get it, do you, old man?"

"Yes, yes I do."

"Why you doing this?" asked Kevin.

"Just because I done a lot of wrongs doesn't mean I can't do one right."

"Why this? Why me?"

"You're what I got," whispered Lucus.

Kevin pushed off the wall. "See you."

"I can save your life!"

"No, you can't," said his son. Nineteen-year-old Kevin spread his arms out like Jesus: "Besides, what's it worth?"

And he walked away. Strutted toward his *bros.*

Nowhere to run, nowhere to hide. Lucus went back to his cell.

Jackster and H. L. S. were there, waiting out the last few minutes before Yard time.

Nobody said anything.

Soon as Kevin got sent to the Institution, Lucus put the few pictures the boy's grandmother had grudgingly sent him in a paperback book where, like now, he could flip through them without a ritualized search that might betray his heart. With those childhood snapshots were pictures that somehow Emma had scissored from high school yearbooks for both years Kevin had attended.

Lucus glanced at his cell walls. Pictures of wide outdoors. Pictures of Emma—she sent him a new one every three months. *Who says we can't grow old together?* she once told him through the phone and glass in the Maximum Designates' Visitation Room.

Couple minutes to go, Lucus leaned on the bars. Stared nowhere.

"What you doing?" asked the Jackster.

"Nothing," mumbled Lucus.

"What you gonna do?" asked Jackster.

Lucus stood wordless until the Klaxon blared the "all out" for those Residents with permission to choose whether they wanted the ninety-minute Exterior Exercise, General Population Period.

The blade rode fine inside his sleeve, even when Lucus slipped into his blue cloth prison jacket.

As his cellmates grabbed their jackets, Lucus said: "Nice day out there."

The Yard.

Inside the big wall, chop a couple football fields and box them in a square with three mammoth cellblocks, double chain-link fences topped with razor and barbed wire. Put guard towers on two adjoining sides for right-angled sniper crossfire. Lay down a running track that circles inside the fence, a couple steps from the Dead Zone trip wire. Pave a dozen basketball half-courts in one corner, stick some rusted barbells and concrete benches beside them, draw some lines on a cellblock and call them handball courts. Smack in the center, throw up a water tower, run a chain-link fence around it like a dog-protector around a hydrant. Build four chain-link fence funnels from the cellblocks and Admin Building.

Loose the animals down those funnels.

The D-Designates clink out there with their chains for thirty minutes after breakfast. General Population gets ninety minutes in the afternoon. A-Designates have unlimited lunch to dinner access.

Institution Procedures assign twelve pairs of Corrections Officers to Roaming Yard Patrol during General Population Period. The budget that day sent five pairs of Jerks out amongst *them* in the Yard.

Several hundred inmates funneled through the tunnels.

Go to the core, thought Lucus. Go to the center of the Yard, where you can watch and be ready to move any which way.

H. L. S., casually strolling along a step behind Lucus's right.

No matter how the Jackster shuffled, the old dudes hung behind him a half step and herded him where they wanted at the same time.

Sir James and a squad paraded toward the concrete chess tables in the best sun. J. C. showed his empty face to Lucus; Manster sent the lone wolf a sneer.

As inmates walked into the air, Lucus thought: They'll take their time, make sure the play is set.

Kevin and a handful of his crew hit the yard, laughing loud.

Count six, thought Lucus: Q Street Rockers supposed to be a dozen strong.

Barry strolled by with three attentive supplicants under his protection. Barry's eyes never pointed toward Lucus.

The blue sea of inmates parted for Cooley. The hulk's beady eyes jumped around the Yard, seeking a fish.

"Yo, Jackster!" called a voice. An inmate Darnell's age popped out of the crowd twenty feet away, a worn brown basketball spinning in his hands. "We shooting hoops or what?"

"Ah . . ." Darnell looked to his cellmates: "I got a game."

"Better win," said Lucus. And he smiled.

Darnell got an empty stare from Hard Luck Sam.

Jackster followed the man with the ball to a court.

The Twitch stood by the water tower fence, alone, an invisible wind roaring around him. His gloves were gone, strips of an old blue shirt were wrapped around his hands. Twitch's eyes bored through Lucus.

Lucus used both hands to rub his temples, like to rub the pain away.

Jerome and a posse of his Orchard Terrace crew, a dozen dudes, strolled into the yard, headed for turf opposite Kevin and his bros. Like nothing was on.

Looking once at Jerome, the world couldn't tell him apart from Kevin.

There, in the crowd on Kevin's flank, positioning by the Dead Zone wire: one—no, two, three Orchard Terrace boys, the O.T.'s fanning out and holding, waiting.

Making the box, thought Lucus. No need to check the other flank, O.T.'s would be there, too.

Inside his shirt, the blade burned Lucus's forearm.

Across the Yard, a b-ball game filled a court, the ball clinking through the hoops' chains, wonging off the backboards.

Jackster caught a pass, made a fast break to the hoop and laid up an air ball. A teammate tipped it in. Dude on the other team slapped the Jackster five and jogged down the court with him, mouths a-working. Time out, and the five-slapper waved a sub in for himself. Time in. Standing on the sidelines, a spectator got the word on the game from the five-slapper. Dunk shot. Ball in play. Spectator got bored, strolled away from the courts, through the crowd, cut left, cut right, materialized alongside the O.T. posse. Whispered in the main man's ear. Got a nod. The main man put his arm around Jerome, leaned to his ear.

Standing beside Lucus, H. L. S. said: "Catch that?"

"Oh yeah," said Lucus. "The Jackster."

Two tan uniformed Jerks picked their way through the blue-clothed crowd: Adkins and Tate, a too-short and too-lean combo who always got stuck with Yard duty and always walked the same beat. They headed for their shake-the-water-tower-fence-gate check, after which they would angle toward the barbells.

Lucus saw the O.T. posse adjust their cluster, the flankers anticipating the two guards' patrol, not hiding, but not letting anybody use the guards' presence to outmaneuver the game plan.

Adkins, the lean guard, swung keys retracto-chained to his belt. Shorty Tate kept his eyes on the ground, like he was looking for something. Everybody knew his eyes were in the dust so the cons wouldn't see the fear.

As if they needed to see it. Fear hung like smoke over the small guard who wished Yard Duty Officers were armed and he didn't have to rely on the Wall Snipers to protect him.

Adkins swung his keys and complained about the Union and the World Series, Tate locked his eyes in the dust, thinking about how after checking the gate to the water tower, they'd only need to—

The Twitch kicked smack between Tate's shoulder blades.

The small guard crashed into the dirt.

Adkins dropped his keys and the retracto-chain snapped them back to his belt.

But before Adkins could whirl around, Twitch was on his back, looping a thick strip of old shirt around the guard's neck. One end of the strip was tied to Twitch's wrist. He looped the strip around his hand, cinched it tight so the knife in his fist was locked point-digging into the guard's neck.

"Nobody move!" screamed Twitch. "Anybody moves, I cut this head off and let the mice run out! Nobody moves!"

The cons cared zero about Adkins, but Twitch's play stunned them into stillness.

On the ground, Tate gasped, but managed to push the button on his belt radio.

Twitch backed toward the water tower, the guard Adkins hugged in front of him, pinned by the knife at the base of his skull.

Two pairs of Yard guards ran through the blue crowd, yelling into their radios.

"Nobody come any closer! Nobody move!" Twitch yelled to the charging guards: "Don't you clear the Yard! You clear the Yard, I cut off his head and let the mice run out! Swear to Jesus, you clear the Yard, you come at me, he's dead! Dead! Mice! Ain't gonna let you clear the Yard! No Attica! No clean shots!"

The guard captain, reaching the inner ring of spectators not far from Lucus, yelled: "Everybody hold your positions! Everybody! No prisoner moves! Officers stay back!

"It's OK, Sidney!" the captain yelled to the Twitch as he backed toward the water tower fence. The captain's words flew over Guard Tate, who stayed facedown in the dust and prayed that the snipers' aim was true. "You're—"

"Nobody move! You shoot me, you'll kill him or falling on my knife will!"

A ReAct Squad of guards charged out of the Admin Building. Shotguns, man, buckshot loads bouncing on SWAT belts. They formed a picket line around the cons to be sure nobody tried to cop a point in this psycho play.

On the Wall, snipers ran to position. Lucus saw sunlight glint off a scope.

Twitch backed against the water tower wall as the Captain told him *it's OK, don't do anything stupid.* Twitch kept yelling *nobody move;* he made Adkins unlock the water tower gate and stayed pressed against the guard.

The Klaxon blared.

Higgins, radio in hand, panting, moved next to the guard captain as Twitch maneuvered himself and his hostage up the spiral steel staircase along the outside of the water tower.

"What the hell is he doing?" asked Higgins.

"We can't get a clean shot," said the captain, "Not without probably killing Adkins, too."

"Nobody move down there!" yelled Twitch. "Nobody move or we'll all die!"

Higgins radioed a report to the Warden.

In his mind, Lucus saw the State Police cars in the town a mile beyond the Wall, cops choking down donuts and slurping coffee as they turn on the party lights and race to the Pen.

Somewhere, Lucus knew, a TV news camera crew was running toward its helicopter.

Standing on the edge of a metal ledge fifty feet above the Yard, knife tied against the guard's spine, Twitch yelled down, *Don't move! Kill 'im if you do! Mice!*

Radios crackled.

The dudes started to buzz, whisper, but stood still 'cause the Admin had turned out shotguns and snipers.

Higgins's radio squawked, the Warden: "What does he want?"

Cool and careful, Lucus stepped forward.

"Administrator Higgins!" yelled Lucus, going for the man truly in charge. "I can do it!"

"Freeze and stow it!" yelled the guard captain. One of his men behind him swung a shotgun bore toward Lucus.

"I can do it!" pleaded Lucus.

"Do what?" said Higgins.

"Get your man down from there alive. Twitch, he thinks I'm like, one of him. You know I'm the only guy in here he believes."

Captain said: "What the—"

"He's crazy, Sir," said Lucus. "But he ain't stupid."

"He's a dead man!" snapped the captain.

"Drop him, your guy falls, too," said Lucus, adding: "Sir. Hell to pay for that. Hell to pay even if you just kill Twitch.

"TV cameras coming. Ask the Warden what he wants on the six o'clock news."

"Resident," snapped the captain, "you're ass—"

"How will you do it?" said Higgins.

"Careful, Sir. Real careful. I can do it, promise you that.

"But," added Lucus, "I'm gonna need something from you."

"We don't—" started the captain.

"What?" interrupted Higgins, who knew the true priorities.

"I can't bargain Twitch down off of there with just be-nice bullshit. He flat out don't care, plus he's seeing things—"

"Man's crazy!" said the captain.

"Dead on, Sir. And there's nothing you can threaten him with he don't do to himself in his cell.

"But," said Lucus, "you let me tell him he can get transferred to the state hospital—"

"The courts put him here as sane," said Higgins.

"Wasn't that a smart move." Lucus jerked his thumb toward the men on the tower. "You can administratively transfer him to the state hospital for a ninety-day evaluation. Hell, they get him in there, 'less you or his lawyer squawks, they'll keep him on an Indefinite Treatment Term. No doctor gonna risk his state job turning loose a man with a knife talking about mice!"

"Why would that work?" said Higgins.

" 'Cause I'll sell Twitch the truth. Hospital is co-ed. Even violents see women. Better drugs, better beds, more sun, people who treat him like he is: he might be crazy, but he ain't no fool.

"Course," added Lucus, "there is one more problem."

"What?" said the captain and Higgins.

"Why risk my ass to do that? Long climb up that tower."

"You get my man back," ordered the captain, "or—"

"Or what—Sir? My lockup order don't make me a hostage negotiator. I get punished for being only a model, no-volunteer prisoner, some lawyer will make the Admin eat it big time."

"What do you want?" said Higgins.

"Nothing much," said Lucus. "A righteous deal—Admin breaks its word on this, it'll get brutal in here, and real soon, Admin will need credibility with us Residents to save something else."

"What do you want?" repeated Higgins.

"That little matter we talked about earlier today will do."

The captain said: "What?"

Higgins pushed his steel eyes against Lucus. Lucus didn't fold. Higgins bargained in the radio with the Warden.

"That a helicopter I hear chopping close?" said Lucus.

Higgins lowered his radio: "Go."

Hard Luck Sam, Kevin, and Darnell, Cooley and Sir James and Manster, Jerome and the O.T. posse, Barry, Higgins and the Admin—everybody watched Lucus. Heard him yell to Twitch that he was coming up. Heard him talking about deals, making it cool. Watched him climb that spiral staircase as his words faded into the wind.

Watched three men on a platform. Watched them with cold eyes and sniper scopes.

Maybe ten, maybe nine minutes: nobody took their eyes off the three men just to read a watch.

A helicopter chopped the air above the Institution.

Movement on the ledge—a sliver of glistening steel tumbled through the sky to the Yard.

Guard Adkins scurried down the steps.

Higgins, into the radio: "No fire! Repeat, no fire!"

Half a dozen guards grabbed Twitch when he reached the bottom, hand-cuffed him and led him away. Everybody knew the guards would use the hoses on him inside, but even the mean Jerks knew the deal had to stand.

Lucus walked toward Higgins and H. L. S.

Higgins said something to the captain, who frowned, but nodded when the message was repeated as a command.

Guard captain and two of his shotgun boys marched through the crowd of prisoners. Marched up to Kevin.

"You!" yelled the captain: "Let's go!"

"Me!" said Kevin as the shotguns swung his way. "Hey! What's this shit! I didn't do anything! I didn't do anything!"

And as the guards hustled him away to pack his personal gear, the whole Yard watched.

Higgins nodded to Lucus, went home to his family.

The Klaxon sounded the return to cells. Shotguns on the Yard watched everybody shuffling back inside.

Sir James was lost in the crowd.

For a heartbeat, Lucus saw Jerome and the O.T. posse.

Roll up on that boy next Yard time, thought Lucus. Brace him, but let him back down. His posse won't be so hot to dance with him, and he'll know it. The Word will advise him to keep his cool: the sucker he wanted ain't there no more, the beef is over, and a respected, evil dude like Lucus . . . Don't mess with Lucus.

Walking beside Lucus, like he was reading his mind H. L. S. said: "What about our spy boy Darnell?"

"Oh, I'll think of something for the Jackster."

"Hard luck," said Sam.

As they strolled toward the tunnel, the other dudes kept a safe and puzzled respectful distance.

Sam said: "I gots to know—just exactly what did you tell Twitch to make him drop the blade and climb down from there?"

Lucus whispered: "Same thing I said to make him grab the guard in the first place."

Monica Quill is the pseudonym of Ralph McInerny, who, when he's not writing mysteries, is a professor at Notre Dame University. Whether writing under a pen name, or as himself, his novels, such as *Law and Ardor* and *Half Past Nun*, are always entertaining. In the next story, he shows what can happen when one tries to plot the perfect crime, only to be tripped up by something beyond even a murderer's control.

Intent to Kill
MONICA QUILL

He had often thought of killing Maud, in dreams and imagination, approaching the task with cold logic, carefully covering his tracks, getting it over with and then feigning inconsolable grief at the loss of his wife. Who would ever suspect him of being responsible for what would appear to be a quite natural, if tragic, occurrence?

Doing the deed in real life proved somewhat more taxing. For one thing, there was the fear that turned his body clammy and made it difficult to recall the steps of the plan, even caused him to imagine that a dozen pairs of suspicious eyes were on him at all times.

Nonsense, of course, and he fought against the fear. After all, he had a double motive now. The longing to be rid of Maud had become so habitual that it seemed to concern himself alone, only his freedom, the shrugging off of the weight of her hateful presence and walking the earth a free man again.

He had long since given up the notion that others would understand his desire to be rid of his wife. She was beautiful, with others she was charming, even witty. Charles had watched men fall victim to her charms as she effortlessly enchanted them. It was all an act, of course. Once she had acted in the same way with him, but in those days neither of them realized that she was not serious, could not be serious, about such matters. Men were toys to play with, and it would have been against her nature not to lure them.

Annoying but innocent. And, in its way, beneficial to him. Women sympathized with him as they fumed over Maud's triumphant domination of the room.

"She's so friendly," their next-door neighbor had said when he came upon her in the kitchen, dabbing at her eyes. In the living room, Maud was putting the woman's husband Fred through her ringmaster's hoops.

"Only in public."

"Oh?"

"She's very good at parlor games."

"Just so they remain in the parlor."

"They always have."

"Are you sure?"

"Would we be talking like this if I weren't?"

It brought them together, Catherine Willis and himself, but of course that was only a little parlor game of their own. Sometimes he and Maud and the Willises made a foursome at golf, and when Maud pleaded with Fred to show her how to hold the club, how to swing it properly, just help her, please, Charles would drive away with Catherine in the golf cart they shared, sparing them both the spectacle. Just for fun they would mimic the antics Maud and Fred were engaged in. Standing behind Catherine while she putted, his arms around her, his hands gripping hers on the club, Charles felt a sudden dizziness and stepped back.

"Isn't this right?" Catherine asked saucily, looking back at him over her shoulder.

"Too right."

"Oh."

Small wonder that his fantasies about ridding himself of Maud sometimes included a sequel in which he and Catherine, side by side in a golf cart, rode into the sunset together. He dismissed the thought. He did not intend to regain his freedom only to throw it away again before he had enjoyed it.

Enjoying it meant solitary global trips, alone in foreign cities, waiting for some unplanned adventure to happen. The point of freedom was that it be unpredictable.

Catherine called him at the office and asked him to take her to lunch. What could he do? He suggested they meet at the club.

"I'm calling from town. We don't want to go all the way out there."

"Where would you like me to take you?"

"Horners."

Horners was a saloon overlooking the river. It had a very limited luncheon menu, was frequented by college kids, and sounded like lots of fun, a real break from routine. He said he'd meet her there.

"Oh no you won't. I took a cab downtown. Shall we meet in the lobby of your building?"

He suggested they meet in the garage where he parked his car.

"Were you afraid we'd be seen together?" she asked him at the garage.

"Who suggested Horners?"

She laughed, then stopped abruptly. "Why am I laughing? It's not funny."

"What?"

"You lied to me."

"About what?"

"About Maud. About it being only a parlor game with her."

She gave him the gory details while they drank beer and plucked greasy goodies from the plastic baskets they had ordered. A hamburger, dripping with number thirty oil, french fries ditto, bock beer. The lunch might have been a suicide pact.

"I have proof that they have gone to motels at least three times."

"Proof?"

"Credit-card bills."

He looked at her. "Do your bills tell you who he was with?"

Catherine put the tip of a french fry between her sharp little teeth and nibbled it to death. After licking her fingers, she said, "I followed them."

He wanted to deny that this could be true, not to protect Maud's reputation, but to stave off the silly feeling Catherine's charges brought. Angry as he had been with Maud, hating her so much he wanted her dead, he had been complacent about her morals. Flirt, yes, she couldn't help it. But actually go off to a motel with another man? He felt the sharp sting reserved for the cuckold, a pain that does not require that the husband really give a damn about his wife. Maud had made a fool of him. It was an extra reason to kill her.

And so finally he laid his plans, moving the project from dream and fantasy into the real world, feeling, as a result, terror and fear of being apprehended, but feeling excitement, too. It was a game played for great stakes. Success would mean either of two things—freedom, if he carried out his plan to perfection, or a far more definitive loss of freedom if he were suspected, charged, convicted, imprisoned. An emotion keener than fear came over him. He felt like a god, holding both Maud's fate and his own in his hands.

Her death must seem an accident, of course, but simply as a matter of insurance, a plausible suspect must be provided. Charles himself would be miles from the scene, of course, so far as anyone knew or could come to know. Fred would be on the scene and, given Maud's liaison with him, available as suspect if suspicion was indeed aroused. Fred seemed even more perfect as a target of suspicion in the light of Catherine's later information.

"It's over," she told him as they danced one evening at the club. "And no credit to Fred."

"Oh."

"Maud dumped him."

"He told you that?"

"I heard them on the phone."

"You eavesdropped?"

"Of course. Don't you?"

"Apparently there's no longer any reason to."

There was certainly no visible sign of a breach between Maud and Fred Willis. They had made a foursome for the club Mardi Gras dance, and Charles could look over Catherine's shoulder at his wife dancing with Fred, apparently having the time of her life.

But soon he had reason to think that Catherine was lying to him. He had Gorman, an investigator his law firm often employed, check out the motels Catherine claimed Maud and Fred had dallied in. It seemed it had never happened.

"Of course they wouldn't have used real names," Gorman reported with the certainty of a longtime student of infidelity. "But no one recognized their photographs either."

"Do you trust your informants?"

"No. I buy them."

Gorman was a longtime student of informers as well. Charles believed him and decided that Catherine was either flat-out lying or imagining things. In any case, she now had conveniently removed what might have appeared to be his motivation for killing Maud. The imagined affair was over, they were all just friends again.

And it was time for Maud to die.

He arranged to be out of town. His secretary bought tickets well in advance of the Easter holiday. He arrived in Chicago to find O'Hare teeming with college kids and service personnel. The portion of his ticket to Chicago would be recorded as used; he had to insure the same for the Denver leg. A year ago at this time, he had been grateful that his ticket had been bought well in advance. All around him in the oversold flight were kids destined to spend hours waiting for the next flight, maybe even spend the night in the terminal.

Charles checked in, took a seat, and waited. This was a crucial part of his plan, yet it depended on something outside his control. Would this year be like the last? His doubts disappeared as the waiting area filled up and kids began sprawling on the floor when there was nowhere else to wait. Eventually the announcement came. The flight was overbooked, anyone willing to surrender his seat would be given a credit toward a future flight within the continental United States. A groan greeted the announcement.

Across from Charles, a young man looked wildly about. He wore a baseball cap backwards on his head and had a bright blue and gold muffler wrapped around his neck.

"And I'm standby. I got to get home."

His remark was met with a minimum of sympathy, although solidarity among the passengers grew as the offer was renewed. The boy with the backwards baseball cap went up to the counter to urge his case, but after several minutes wandered away. Charles got up and caught up with the young man.

"I heard you say you had to get on this flight."

"There's no hope. They can't even promise me I'll get on the next one." There was genuine anguish in his voice.

"An emergency?"

He opened his mouth, then closed it. He grinned. "It is to me."

"How so?"

"My girl wants to break our engagement."

Charles would have preferred a more compelling emergency, but he didn't have time to seek a substitute.

"Look, I'll give you my seat assignment. I can stay over here. While waiting for the flight, I've been tempted by the thought of checking into the Hilton and getting a good night's rest."

"But what will you do tomorrow?"

"We'll just trade tickets."

"Can you just give me your assignment?" He looked anxiously back at the counter.

Charles smiled. He got out his ticket wallet. "Just use this. Go as me. You'll have to sit in first class though."

"First class!" The kid's eyes bugged.

"Shh. Take it." He handed the ticket wallet to the kid, who almost immediately gave it back to him.

"I can't do that."

"I thought you had to get to Denver."

"I do."

"All right then."

His crisis of conscience was soon over. He took Charles's ticket and seat assignment, and handed over his own ticket. Charles suppressed a yawn, picked up his bag, and told the kid he was headed for the O'Hare Hilton.

But when he came out of the concourse, he went down to the street floor and bought a ticket on the shuttle back to Indiana. As he rode through the night, heading homeward to rid himself of Maud forever, he smiled at the thought that it would be a matter of record that he had taken the flight to Denver. Belatedly it occurred to him that checking into the Hilton would have certified his being away equally well. He could have gone to his room, messed up the bed, and left the hotel and hopped onto this shuttle bus. He would have been out some money, but less than for the plane ticket. Ah well. Next time. His smile was reflected in the window beside him.

The shuttle arrived at the airport of his hometown. Charles's car was in the parking lot. He drove to the twenty-four hour supermarket three blocks from his house, left his car in the parking lot, and continued on foot. His house was dark when he approached it but there was still a light on next-door at the Willises'. He went around to the back of his house and let himself in quietly. Later he would create the appearance of a break-in. For now it was more important not to wake Maud.

He waited inside the back door and, when his eyes had adjusted to the darkness, moved swiftly through the house toward the stairway. Before he reached it, he tripped over something, and went sprawling across the room, off balance. He crashed into a chair, overturning it, taking down a lamp as well. It fell onto the coffee table, scattering the gewgaws Maud kept on it. Charles struck his head against something, and when he got to his feet and touched his forehead his hand came away sticky with blood. He went to the wall switch and turned it on. What he had stumbled over was the body of Maud.

Her eyes stared sightlessly at him from her discolored face. He stared at her for a full minute in the stark glare of the overhead light. Then he knelt beside her. She was definitely dead. A great wave of relief rolled through his mind, bringing with it an indecent desire to shout for joy. He was innocently rid of Maud. She was dead and he hadn't killed her. He looked up the stairs, wondering if she had fallen, but then he saw the scarf twisted terribly around her throat. It looked to be one of his own.

He unwound it carefully and was standing with it in his hands when headlights swept in the drive and there was the sound of running toward the house. Someone pounded on the door. What the hell. He went to answer it. Hardly had he unlocked it, when a policeman pushed his way in and was followed by another. Charles was slammed against the wall and rapidly searched for weapons. Anger boiled up in him.

"What the hell are you doing? I live here."

"What's this?"

The second cop was looking down at Maud's body. He picked up the phone and made a call. In the still-open doorway, Catherine appeared, wearing a robe, her eyes like saucers.

"Charlie! What are you doing home?"

"Would you tell these maniacs that I live here?"

But Catherine was looking past him at Maud. Her mouth rounded in surprised horror. She looked at him.

"Oh, Charles. What have you done?"

His memory of what happened next was blurred, and try as he would to recall it accurately during the months he awaited trial, it never quite came into focus. When he was indicted for the murder of Maud, he hired Gilligan, the best trial lawyer in town, a man whose knack for getting acquittals or risible sentences for clients that everyone knew were guilty as charged had hitherto excited Charles's disdain. But he needed Gilligan now, as became increasingly clear.

"We got to come up with a story to counter the facts they've dug up, Charles."

The kid to whom he'd given his ticket had happily told investigators what had happened in O'Hare. He had kept what was left of Charles's ticket as proof of the way he had conned a man out of a first-class ticket with a story about his threatened engagement.

"You acted out of compassion," Gilligan said, trying it out. "But why did you take the shuttle back here?"

Several people on the shuttle had identified him; so much for his unrecorded return. Gilligan listened impassively while Charles told him again what had happened when he got home. He closed his eyes in thought and tried a possible reconstruction.

"Out of consideration for your wife, you didn't turn on any lights. You didn't want to wake her. We'll keep the part about stumbling too, that accounts for the furniture that was smashed up during the struggle."

"What struggle?"

Gilligan held up his hand. "Hey, I'm your lawyer. No bullshit, okay?"

Gilligan assumed he was guilty. His fate was sealed when Catherine decided to take the blame for what had happened. Charles was insanely jealous, she testified, and she and Fred had conspired to tease him. Fred had pretended to be having an affair with Maud.

"I told Charles I knew they had been going to motels together."

Under oath, Gorman reluctantly admitted checking out motels for Charles. He had also taken around photos of Maud and Fred.

"And?"

"Nothing."

"When I saw what it was doing to Charles," Catherine went on, looking tragically toward the jury, "I told Fred we had to stop. So I told Charles the big affair was all over. Maud had dismissed Fred."

Catherine burst into tears and Charles noted the sympathetic looks of the jurors. "It's all our fault. We drove him to it."

Despite Gilligan's best efforts, using what Catherine had said to play on the sympathy of the jurors, Charles got the maximum sentence from the woman judge, who insisted in her instruction to the jury that when all was said and done this was a case of the cold-blooded murder of a wife by a calculating, cruel husband who had no claim on their mercy.

"Fortunately he was stupid enough to leave unmistakable evidence of his foul deed. And he had the murder weapon in his hands when the police arrived."

Charles turned and looked at Fred Willis and his lying wife, who was seated beside him. The gleam in Fred's eye before he turned away was that of guilt. Catherine had the look of a woman whose husband would be eternally in her debt. Charles was led away. He had lost both Maud and his freedom and there wasn't a soul in the world who would believe he was innocent. A more philosophical man might have considered that he was being punished for what he had intended to do. But, if he had been philosophical, he might have gotten used to Maud.

Robert J. Randisi has had over 300 novels published in the mystery, western, men's adventure, historical, and spy genres since 1982. The creator of both the Nick Delvecchio and Miles Jacoby series, he's another author who edits anthologies, with fourteen to his credit. A founder of the Private Eye Writers of America, he is also the organization's Executive Director. In "The Girl Who Talked to Horses," his popular short story character, private investigator Henry Po, goes to the races, only to find out that crossing the finish line comes in second place to staying alive.

The Girl who Talked to Horses
ROBERT J. RANDISI

The trainer's name was Carlucci and everybody said he had an edge. What was it? Well, they said he was a whiz with horses, but he liked them better than people, and that's why they performed for him.

I don't know how many people believed it, but Anthony Carlucci had been having a hell of a career in New York for the past four years, but if he had an edge it had run out today.

Today Carlucci was lying in a stall at Belmont Park, out on Elmont, Long Island, and he didn't have an edge anymore because he was dead.

When Carlucci's body had been discovered by his assistant trainer that morning, I'd been called in because I was in charge of security for the New York State Racing Club. That is, I was in charge when there was some investigating to be done. There were uniformed guards working the track who worked for another outfit. They didn't have to report to me, but we had an understanding.

So, to get the sequence of events right, the assistant trainer, Dick Dermott, found Carlucci's body when he arrived on the backstretch at five-thirty A.M. He immediately called for a uniformed guard, who then called his boss, who then called me. Being the fair-minded man I am, since we were all up, I figured I might as well call my boss and wake him up, too.

"This better be good," J. Howard Biel said when I identified myself on the phone.

"Murder," I said.

"Murder?"

"Well," I said, "somebody's dead, let's put it that way. I don't know if it's murder, but—"

"Who's dead?"

"Apparently," I said, breaking it to him gently, "Anthony Carlucci."

"What?"

He had a right to be upset. One of the hottest young trainers to come down the pike had chosen the Belmont/Aqueduct/Saratoga/Staten Island Downs circuit to ply his trade. That was good, that was a feather in the N.Y.S.R.C.'s hat. Having him turn up dead was . . . well, bad.

Biel agreed to meet me at the track, but I arrived before he did and identified myself to the guard on duty. His name tag identified him by his last name, Mattingly.

"Anybody call the cops yet?" I asked.

"I don't know," Mattingly said. "I called my boss, and he told me to stand guard and not let anyone in until you got here."

"Okay," I said. There was nobody else around. "Where's Mr. Dermott? You didn't let him leave, did you?"

"No, sir," the guard said. "He's in Mr. Carlucci's office."

"Good."

"Do you want me to get him, Mr Po?"

"No, no," I said, "leave him there. I'll take a look at the body first, and then talk to Dermott. Since we don't know if the police have been called, if they do show up let them in, all right?"

"Yes, sir."

"Also, Mr. Biel is on his way, so let him through, too."

"Yes, sir."

That settled, I went into the barn to take a look at Anthony Carlucci. He was lying on the floor of one of the stalls, and had obviously been kicked to death by a horse. His head was bleeding, and the blood had soaked into the straw and dirt around him. I went into the stall and bent over him, but there was nothing for me to do. I didn't touch him, or move him. I got out of there, feeling slightly sick. It's not every day you see somebody's brains scattered about.

Outside I asked the guard, "Who moved the horse?"

"Mr. Dermott."

"What horse was it?"

"I'm not sure, sir," the man said, "but it might have been Tobasco Boy."

That didn't surprise me. Tobasco Boy was the crown jewel of Carlucci's barn. He was supposed to run in the Kentucky Derby in three weeks. Last year's two-year-old champ, he was going into the Derby undefeated in five starts last year, and three starts as a three year old.

As brilliant as the horse was on the track, though, his comportment off the track was legendarily bad. He had taken a piece out of more people—his trainer, assistant trainer, groom, hot walker—than any other horse, and he made the newspapers for it. It would come as no surprise to any reader of any of the racing newspapers that he had stomped someone to death.

The question I had was, what was Carlucci doing alone in the stall of such a notorious horse?

"I'm going into the office to talk to Mr. Dermott now. Watch for the cops, and Mr. Biel."

"Yes, sir."

I walked to the end of the shed row and found Anthony Carlucci's office. I knocked and entered and found Dick Dermott sitting behind his boss' desk, like he belonged there. There were photos on the walls, as well as various pieces of racing equipment, like whips and bridles, and, on one wall, a saddle. The office smelled of leather, and the creams used to soften and preserve it.

"Mr. Dermott?" I asked, even though I recognized him. I didn't know if he knew me, though.

"That's right."

He was in his mid-thirties, a bit younger than Carlucci himself, who I thought I recalled as being in his early forties. They were considered to be a good team, each a fine trainer in his own right, but the barn was Carlucci's and so was the reputation.

"My name is Henry Po," I said, "I work for the Board—"

"I know who you are, Mr. Po," Dermott said, cutting off my introduction. "I've seen you on the grounds. Are the police here?"

"No," I said. "Uh, did you call them?"

The man looked surprised. "No, I thought you had."

"I will, if I can use that phone," I said, "but afterward I'd like to ask you some questions."

"Shouldn't we wait for the police?" Dermott asked.

"We could," I said, "and we will, but we might as well talk while we're waiting, don't you think?"

"I don't know," Dermott said. I found his eyes and his state of mind remarkably clear for someone who had found his colleague, and for all I knew his friend, dead. This had never happened to me before, but I was suddenly very certain that he had something to do with Anthony Carlucci's death.

"Mr. Po?"

"Yes?"

"You wanted to use the phone?"

"Oh, yes, thank you."

That was when I knew I was staring at him, and maybe he did, too, because he was watching me, now, as I dialed 911 and reported the incident.

"It'll be a while before detectives get here," I said, as I hung up. "First they'll send a uniformed patrol, and then they'll send for a supervisor, and finally they'll call for the detectives."

"I see," Dermott said, "then this is going to go on for a while."

"Yes."

"I'd better let my people know."

His people? They were his people, already?

"Your staff, you mean?"

"Yes."

"Can you do that by phone?"

"Why?"

"Well . . . I really can't let you leave the area, Mr. Dermott. After all, you did find the body, and . . ."

"And I'm a suspect?" Dermott asked. "Is that what you mean?"

Suddenly, I felt like Columbo, playing cat-and-mouse games with a famous guest star, only I wasn't a brilliant-yet-rumpled cop, and Dermott was not a famous star.

"I thought it was an accident," I said. "At least, it looks like an accident."

Dermott surprised me by shaking his head, violently. "It couldn't be."

"Why not?"

"Tony would never have gone into Tobasco Boy's stall alone. I'm sure you're aware of the horse's violent nature."

"I've read about it, yes."

"Then you understand," Dermott said. "We agreed that no one would ever try to handle him alone."

"Who usually handled the horse?"

"His groom, and his hot walker."

"Who are they?"

"Oh, sorry," Dermott said. "The groom's name is Hennessy, and the hot walker is Amanda Ellis."

I didn't know either one of them, but then, there was no reason I should. I did spend time at the various tracks, but there was no way I could know the personnel of each individual stable, unless they had been there as long as I had, and Carlucci's Canyon Valley Stable had only been in New York four years.

"The police will want to talk to them."

"They're probably around," Dermott said. "They're usually here even before me and Tony."

There was only one guard outside, and I needed him to keep people out of the stable. I didn't have anyone to send looking for Hennessy or Ellis.

As if on cue, there was a knock at the door.

"May I?" I asked.

"Please."

I walked to the door and opened it. There was a girl standing there, about five-five, slender and attractive, wearing a sleeveless T-shirt, exposing the powerful forearms and upper arms of someone who worked with horses for a living. She was not muscle-bound, but well-toned, like Linda Hamilton was in *The Terminator II*. When your job was controlling an animal who weighed over a thousand pounds, you tended to be in shape. It was the case with jockeys, exercise riders, hot walkers and grooms.

Also, if you watch racing on television you've probably noticed how many of the people who hold these jobs—especially the hot walkers—are women, and attractive young women. I don't mean that they could be models, but they're usually wearing T-shirts and jeans, and they're almost always in fabulous shape, as this woman was. She appeared to be in her early twenties.

"What's going on?" she demanded. "Who are you? Why can't I get into the stable? Where are—"

I held up my hand and said, "I can answer your questions, Miss, but they have to come one at a time."

"Amanda?"

She looked past me to Dermott, who had called her name.

"Dick? What's going on?"

"Mr. Po, that's Amanda Ellis. Would you let her in please?"

"Of course," I said, backing away. "Miss Ellis?"

She came in, giving me a sideways glance, and walked right to the desk. "Dick?"

"There's been an accident," Dermott said, without standing up. I thought he looked extremely comfortable behind the desk.

"What kind of accident?" she asked. "One of the horses?"

"Not exactly," Dermott said. "It's Tony. He's dead."

"What?" Her back was to me, so I couldn't see her face, but she lifted her hands to her mouth.

"Tobasco Boy stomped him to death this morning."

"What?" This time her tone was more strident. "What will they do to him?"

Dermott shook his head and shrugged helplessly.

"I don't know," he said. "This is Mr. Po. He works for the Board—"

She turned quickly to stare at me. She was not the most beautiful woman I had ever seen, but at that moment she was certainly the most attractive.

She was magnificent, muscles tense, nostrils flaring . . . why did I think she was more concerned about the horse than the poor, dead trainer?

I ANSWERED HONESTLY.

"I have no idea what will happen to the horse," I said, "*if* he did, in fact, stomp Mr. Carlucci to death."

"If?" she asked. She turned on Dermott. "You said he did it."

"Mr. Dermott," I said, "found Mr. Carlucci in the stall this morning, dead."

Dermott nodded.

"Tobasco Boy's stall, and the horse was standing over him."

"So then you don't know for sure that Toby did it?" she asked.

"Toby?" I asked.

"My nickname for Tobasco Boy."

"We don't know for sure that the horse did it," I said, "no. The police are on their way, Miss Ellis. They'll want to talk to you."

"About what?"

"About the horse, about Mr. Carlucci—"

"Does Sam know?"

"Sam?"

"Hennessy," Dermott said. "I told you about him."

"The groom."

"Does he know?"

"Not yet."

"Someone has to tell him."

"Why don't you do that, if you don't mind?" I asked.

"No," she said, "I don't mind. I—I'd like to tell him."

"Fine," I said, "you can also tell him the police will want to talk to him, too."

"Are you some sort of a detective?" she asked.

"As a matter of fact, I am," I said. "I have a private detective's license, but I work primarily for the racing board. I report directly to Howard Biel."

She looked impressed. "Does he know about this?"

"Yes," I said, "in fact, it's a toss-up as to who will get here first, him or the police."

"I'll want to talk to him."

"About what?"

"Toby—Tobasco Boy," she said. "If he did it he'll need someone to plead his case, won't he?"

"Probably," I said, "but who will plead Tony Carlucci's?"

She and Dermott exchanged a glance and then she left, promising to get Hennessy and stay around.

"Why do I get the feeling she and Carlucci didn't get along?"

"They didn't."

"Why not?"

Dermott shrugged. "Who knows?"

I turned and faced him squarely. "I think you do." In fact, I thought he knew a lot more than he was saying.

"All right," he said, "Tony was something of a chauvinist. He treated Amanda like he'd treat a girl, woman . . . do you know what I mean?"

"I think I do."

"He'd pat her on the ass, send her on menial errands, like getting coffee, you know. She finally had enough one day and told him off. Since then. . . ." He shrugged.

"Why'd she stay?" I asked. "Why didn't he fire her?"

"For the same reason."

"Which was?"

"She was the only one who could handle Tobasco Boy."

"I thought nobody could handle him."

"Except Amanda," Dermott said. "She's uncanny with horses. She— well, this will sound silly . . ."

"Go ahead."

"She claims that the horses talk to her."

"I'm sorry?"

"She says that she can communicate with the horses," Dermott explained. "It sounds odd, I know, but she gets along with them like no one I've ever seen. Often she's able to figure out what's wrong with them when they're not training right in the morning, or not running right in the afternoon."

"How?"

"She says that . . . they tell her."

"And you believed her?" I asked. "You and Carlucci?"

"We didn't care," he said. "She worked wonders with them and we didn't care if she was goddamned Doctor Dolittle, as long as she was right."

"Great," I said, "maybe she can get Tobasco Boy to tell us what happened here this morning."

"Who knows?" Dermott asked. "Maybe she can, at that."

THE NEXT FEW HOURS WERE hectic, and confused. Howard Biel arrived just ahead of the police. As I'd predicted, we ended up with cops, supervisors and then plainclothes detectives. Not only that, but the man who was in charge of the uniformed guards at the track, Patrick Lukas, also arrived, ready to kick some ass. He regarded the "incident" as a black mark against himself and his crew.

The detective in charge of the case was a man named Zeke Tomachek, a tall, gray-bearded, dignified-looking man who stood over six feet tall, but seemed to stoop a bit to hide it.

Biel had a talk with Tomachek first thing and managed to arrange for me to remain on the scene as his representative.

"Henry," he said to me, "I have to go to my office and make some calls. I've got to try to keep the lid on this. Keep an eye on things, all right?"

"All right, Howard."

Tomachek asked that Carlucci's "employees," Dermott, Hennessy and Amanda Ellis, wait in the office to be questioned. Dermott agreed to do so, but complained about being called Carlucci's employee.

"I'm sorry," Tomachek said, "I'm not up on my racetrack terminology. What is it you do, Mr. Dermott?"

"I'm the assistant trainer."

"Very well," Tomachek said, "I'll refer to you that way from now on."

"Thank you."

As Dermott walked away, Tomachek asked me, "Who paid his salary?"

"Carlucci."

He nodded. "That's what I thought: He worked for the guy."

"Right."

"Then why does it upset him to hear it?"

"Because he liked to think he worked *with* Carlucci, not *for* him."

"Hmm," Tomachek said, "looks to me like somebody's not satisfied with his lot in life."

Tomachek also had an altercation with Lukas about his men. He wanted the private security people off the premises—except for me.

"My men belong here, Detective," Lukas complained.

Lukas was ex-military. You could tell it by looking at him. He might also have been an ex-mercenary. His demeanor exhibited all of the worst attributes of both.

In other words, he was an asshole.

"Mr. Lukas," Tomachek said, "I've asked you nicely to remove yourself and your men from the scene. They are free to maintain their posts in another area of the track, but I want them—and you—gone from here."

"But—"

"Please leave willingly; don't make me have you removed."

They stared at each other and, in the end, Lukas blinked.

He and his men were gone by the time the coroner and his men arrived, or else we would have really had a crowd. I never heard the coroner's name. They only called him "Doctor."

Tomachek and I entered the stable area with the coroner and watched while he examined Carlucci's body.

"What do you say, Doctor?" Tomachek asked.

The doctor—in his fifties, with steel-gray hair and goatee—crouched next to the body and shook his head.

"What a mess."

"Is that your professional opinion?" Tomachek asked.

The man ignored Tomachek's attempt at humor, the first indication that he had no sense of humor—or maybe he just didn't have one when it came to death.

"This man has been bludgeoned about the head, very possibly beaten to death. I won't say more until the autopsy."

"Just tell me this, Doctor," Tomachek said. "Did the horse do it?"

The doctor stood up and scowled. "How could I possibly say that with a certainty?"

"Then just tell me if it *could* have done it. I just want to know if I can rule it out or not."

"Of course you can't rule it out," the doctor said, "not until I've autopsied the body—and if I can get out of here, I can do that."

"All right," Tomachek said, wearily, "take him away." He turned to me and asked, "I don't suppose there's someplace we can get some coffee."

"There's a backstretch cafe," I said. "I can have somebody—wait, you chased all the track security away."

"I'll have an officer get it," Tomachek said, "Just give him directions—"

"All right."

"—and tell him what you want."

He brought a man over and I did as he asked, asking for a black coffee for myself.

We watched as the coroner's men bagged the body and removed it. That left the stall empty, except of blood. The coroner's people had also picked up whatever minute pieces of bone and brain matter might have been left behind.

"Where's the horse?" Tomachek asked me.

"He's in a stall farther down."

"Who moved him?"

"Dermott."

"I thought one person couldn't handle him?"

"The first guard on the scene, Mattingly, helped him. He, uh, just followed Dermott's instructions and they got Tobasco Boy moved."

"I don't know anything about racing," Tomachek said. "Is this a good horse?"

"One of the best in training."

"Too bad."

"Why?"

"If he did it," Tomachek said, "what will happen to him?"

"I'm not sure."

"If it was a dog they'd put him to sleep."

"A thoroughbred is not a dog," I said. "There are investors, and insurance premiums . . ."

"Hmm," Tomachek said, "insurance . . ."

We walked into the stall together.

"Did you examine him?" Tomachek asked.

"I didn't touch him," I said. "I just wanted to be sure he was dead."

He started moving bloody straw around with his foot, whether idly or with purpose, I didn't know, but I saw something.

"Wait," I said, "don't move."

"What?" he asked, freezing.

"Just back away a minute."

He did. I stepped outside the stall and looked around until I found a pitchfork. I came back in the stall and used the tool to move the straw until I had cleared it away.

"See?"

He stepped forward and looked down.

"I see," he said, and we both stared at the twin marks in the ground that could only have been made by the bootheels of a man being dragged.

"Look here," I said, pointing to the front of the stall. "There were marks, but they were wiped out."

"We've got a murder here," Tomachek said.

"And the killer missed the bootheel marks that were hidden by the straw."

"Now the question is," Tomachek said, "was he dead when he was dragged in, or was he unconscious and helpless while the horse stomped him to death?"

"Maybe," I said, "we should ask the horse."

Naturally, I had to explain that.

TOMACHEK DIDN'T KNOW WHETHER OR not to take me seriously. Frankly, I didn't know either.

"Do you believe this stuff?" he asked.

"I don't know," I said, "but Dermott believes it, and that may be what's important."

"What do you mean?"

Tomachek and I were inside, while everyone else was outside. I decided to tell him what I'd been thinking.

"Have you had many feelings like this in the past?" he asked when I was done.

"No."

"Worked on many murders?"

"No."

He regarded me curiously.

"Why should I go along with this?"

I shrugged. "What have you got to lose?" I asked.

"Okay," he said, "then tell me how you see it."

"I see it done all of a sudden," I said. "It's too sloppy to have been planned. Those heel marks showing that he'd been dragged into the stall, that's amateur stuff."

"So you're saying it's a crime of passion?" Tomachek asked. "He was killed by someone he knew?"

"I'm just telling you what I feel," I said, "and what I think. I think that horse stomped an already-dead man. Maybe the coroner can tell the difference between a hoof print and some other kind of blow, but maybe he hasn't got enough skill to be able to. If this happened the way I think then the murder weapon is still around."

Tomachek regarded me for a few more moments and then said, "I'll have a thorough search done. Meanwhile, what do you want to do?"

"I want to talk to Amanda Ellis."

"What if she's the murderer?"

"Then she'll jump at the chance to implicate someone else, won't she?"

"Maybe."

"Again," I asked, "what have you got to lose? Maybe you've got a chance to solve this thing before another hour goes by. What'll that do to your statistics?"

I was talking about the statistic that said if a murder wasn't solved in the first forty-eight hours—or twenty-four, or seventy-two, whatever it was—then it wouldn't be solved at all.

"It would knock it to hell," Tomachek said. "Okay, I'm gonna go along with you on this, only because I don't have any feeling at all for the people, and you seem to."

I didn't bother telling him that I had only just met these people about an hour ago myself—but he was right about one thing. I had a feeling, and he didn't.

"I'll get the girl and have her brought in here," Tomachek said.

"Thanks."

While he went to arrange for the search and to have Amanda Ellis join me, I studied Tobasco Boy in his new stall. He stood very still, seemingly totally relaxed, and stared at me balefully.

"What have you got to say about all this, Toby?" I asked. "Are you getting a bum rap here?"

He didn't bother answering me. Maybe he'd tell Amanda Ellis.

*   *   *

WHEN AMANDA ELLIS APPEARED SHE approached me tentatively.

"Miss Ellis," I said. "Would you like to see Tobasco Boy?"

She brightened and quickened her step. "Yes, I would."

"Here he is."

I stepped aside as she approached the stall and reached her hand out to him. He came over to her immediately and nuzzled her hand.

"That's amazing," I said. "That horse is supposed to be to be as ornery as—"

"He's not ornery with me," she said.

"Because you can communicate with him?"

She turned and looked at me. "You're not like the others."

"In what way?"

"You refer to the horse as 'him' and not 'it,' like most of the others do."

"Like Dermott?"

She snorted. "Him, especially. I suppose he told you about me talking to the animals?"

"He mentioned it."

"Did he make the Doctor Dolittle reference?"

"He did."

"Asshole."

"*Can* you talk to the horses?"

"I don't exactly talk to them," she said, "but they are able to make their feelings known to me. There is a woman, though, out in California who says she can actually talk back and forth with the horses."

"How do the people around here feel about what you can do?"

"Most of them don't believe it," she said, "but they do listen when I tell them when a change of diet, or training regimen, might improve the horse's performance."

"And then it does?"

"Most of the time, yes."

"Amanda—may I call you Amanda?"

"Sure."

"Can you tell if Tobasco Boy, uh, stomped Mr. Carlucci?"

"I can look at his hooves."

"Would you do that for me?" I asked. "You're not afraid to go into the stall with him, are you?"

"Of course not."

She opened the door, slipped in and closed it behind her. She talked gently to the horse while lifting his hooves and examining them, then rubbed his neck lovingly and came back out.

"Well?"

"He's got blood on his hooves."

"He could have walked in the blood, though," I said. "He didn't have to stomp Carlucci to get the blood on him."

"You don't believe he did it?"

"No, I don't," I said. "Even if he did stomp the man, I think he was already dead."

"Who do you think killed him?"

"I was hoping you'd be able to tell me that."

"Me? How?"

"By asking the horse."

"What are you talking about?" she demanded, annoyed. "I just told you I can't really *talk* to the horses."

"But there are people who think you can," I said.

She frowned. "What are you asking me to do?"

WHEN DETECTIVE TOMACHEK RETURNED HE was shaking his head.

"What?"

"No murder weapon," he said, "but we'll keep looking."

"It's got to be here."

"If it happened like you figure," Tomachek reminded me, "on the spur of the moment." He looked at Amanda. "Is Miss Ellis being helpful?"

"Very."

Tomachek gave her a long look.

"Am I under suspicion?" she asked him.

"At this point," he said, "everyone is. That's standard procedure."

"I'd like to talk to the others now, Detective," I said.

Tomachek showed me a warning finger. "I'm only going to give you so much leeway, Mr. Po," he said. "If your plan is not working I'm going to call it quits."

"Fine," I said "if that happens it will fall to you, anyway. I'll be out of it."

"Agreed."

We left the stable and went to Carlucci's office, where a uniformed policeman was at his post outside the door.

"Are they inside?" Tomachek asked.

"Yes, sir."

Tomachek knocked, then entered. Dermott was still behind the desk. Another man who I assumed to be Sam Hennessy was sitting in another chair, shoulders slumped. He must have been a jockey at one time, given his size and makeup. He looked to be in his late forties.

"It's about time," Dermott said. "How long are we going to be kept here? We've got work to do, you know."

"What sort of work, Mr. Dermott?" I asked.

Dermott looked from me to Tomachek in some confusion, then settled on me. "We've got a stable to run," he said. "The horses have to be tended to."

"You expect to continue to run the stable?"

"The owners will expect it," he said, "and who else will do it?"

"Well, I'd expect at least one day of mourning . . ." I said, letting it trail off.

"Don't think for one minute that we won't mourn Tony, Mr. Po," Dermott said, "but as a trainer, not as a person."

"He wasn't a . . . nice man, then?"

Hennessy snorted.

"Mr. Hennessy, is it?"

"That's right."

"You didn't like Mr. Carlucci?"

"Nobody did," Hennessy said, "not even the horses. I'm not surprised one of them killed him."

"Oh, Mr. Carlucci wasn't killed by the horse, Mr. Hennessy."

The smaller man looked confused, and tossed Dermott a long glance, which I found interesting.

"What do you mean?" he asked. "Mr. Dermott said—"

"Mr. Dermott said a lot of things," I said, looking at the assistant trainer.

"What are you talking about?" Dermott demanded. He looked at Tomachek. "Aren't you in charge?"

"Mr. Po has the floor right now, Mr. Dermott."

"You claim you found Carlucci in the stall," I said to Dermott. "You didn't."

"How dare you—"

"He was dragged into the stall," I continued. "The softer ground inside the stall still shows the drag marks made by his heels. You neglected to wipe out the marks beneath the straw."

This time it was Dermott who threw Hennessy a look. Things were becoming clearer.

"Let's get right to it, Mr. Dermott," I said. "On top of everything else, you're a bad actor."

"What . . . what do you mean, everything else?"

"The coroner's report will show that Mr. Carlucci was not killed by blows from the horse, but that he was already dead when the horse stomped him. You killed him, then put him in the stall and agitated the horse so he would stomp the dead body. Then you hid the murder weapon, which will be found, eventually."

"Y-you can't prove any of this."

"No," I said, "I can't, but the horse can."

Now Dermott looked confused and, for the first time, shaken. "What?"

"Yes," I said, "you were right about Miss Ellis being able to communicate with the horses."

"What?" he said, again.

"The horse didn't do it, Mr. Dermott," I said. "He told Miss Ellis he didn't do it."

Dermott stared at Amanda for a few moments and she kept quiet. I'd asked her to play along, and she was, silently.

"Th-that's impossible."

"No, it's not," I said. "Every living thing can communicate, Mr. Dermott. Maybe the horse doesn't talk to Miss Ellis, but he communicates with her, and what he communicated was that he didn't kill Carlucci—you did."

Dermott looked at Tomachek for help. "This is preposterous," he said. "You can't honestly believe—"

"Mr. Dermott," Tomachek said, playing his part, "I think we better go downtown."

"Am I under a-arrest?"

"I think we'll just hold onto you until we get the coroner's report," Tomachek said. "At that time I'd say yes, you will be under arrest."

"But, I didn't—"

"Yes?"

Dermott looked at Hennessy, who was looking around the room, as if seeking an avenue of escape.

"What's wrong, Mr. Hennessy?" I asked.

"Huh? Nothin's wrong . . . I just . . ."

"Do you believe that Mr. Dermott killed Carlucci?" I asked.

"I—I don't know—I—"

"What was your part, Hennessy?"

"What?"

"Did you kill him, or just help drag him into the stall?" I asked.

"Po—" Tomachek said. He was confused now, but the looks Hennessy and Dermott had been passing back and forth were—for me, anyway—remarkably easy to read.

"They both did it, Tomachek," I said. "Both of them."

They looked at each other again.

"I didn't—" Hennessy finally said.

"Shut up!" Dermott shouted.

"Hennessy?" I said. "You want to wait until Dermott goes downtown and gives you up?"

"I didn't kill him!" Hennessy shouted. "He did. He got into an argument and . . . and hit him."

"He wasn't dead!" Dermott said. "I—I hit him, but it was your idea to put him into the stall with the horse, your idea to let Tobasco Boy finish him." Dermott looked at us. "He helped me drag him into the stall." Then he looked at Hennessy again. "You were supposed to clean away the heel marks!"

"I did!"

"Not good enough," I said. "Detective?"

Tomachek went to the door, opened it and called in the uniformed officer. "I'm going to need your cuffs," he said.

LATER, AMANDA ELLIS CAME WITH me to Howard Biel's office. She was upset, and I told her we'd talk, but I had to check in with my boss first. She stayed in the outer office while I went inside.

"So who killed him?" Biel asked, after I relayed the story to him. "Was it them? Or the horse? Did the horse stomp a dead man?"

"They killed him, all right," I said. "Whether or not he was dead when they dragged him in there, they're responsible for his death."

"But if the horse—"

"If the horse did it he was their weapon, Howard," I said. "Their other weapon, aside from the one Dermott hit him with, which still hasn't been found. To tell you the truth, I don't think they even know if he was dead when they dragged him into the stall or not. The coroner will have to come up with that answer."

Biel frowned. "What do we do with the horse?" he asked. "Can we let it continue to race if . . . if it killed a man?"

"Howard," I said, "even if he did put the finishing touches on Carlucci, how can you blame the animal?"

"I'll . . . have to talk to some people—think about this very carefully."

"I've got Amanda Ellis outside," I said. "She's real upset, and I told her we'd talk a while."

"Tell me something."

"What?"

"Did you ever suspect her?"

I hesitated, then said, "Briefly."

"What changed your mind?"

"Oh, I still think she could have killed Carlucci," I said. "She didn't like him, and maybe hated him."

"So why . . ."

"The horse," I said.

"What about it?"

"She loves him, Howard," I said. "Even if she'd killed him, or been in on it with Dermott and Hennessy, she never would have tried to frame Tobasco Boy for it."

Susan B. Kelly is an accomplished writer who can get to the point of her story so subtly a reader will finish it and be on to the next before the truth sets in. Her most recent novel is *Kid Stuff*. In this tale of double crosses and deals in London, we find out just what a life is worth nowadays—and what the payment can cost as well.

Stalking Horse

SUSAN B. KELLY

I've never understood why it has to be the roughest pubs in London. Surely you can set up a hit in comfort. I suppose the clients expect it—graffitied benches, sawdust on the floor, ashtrays that were last emptied for the royal wedding—not the sort of place they will be seen by anyone they know. Just the sort of place you can get someone killed for the price of three weeks in the Seychelles in the high season.

Accidents, I tell them, are my speciality, along with burglaries/muggings-gone-horribly-wrong. They don't seem to mind that I'm a woman, after the initial surprise. Well and good: Women are less visible, less likely to arouse suspicion. We are also the less sentimental sex. If you want a job done right, get a woman to do it.

Amateurs, all of them. One chap even offered to pay me by cheque. It will come, mind you. One day—soon—they will brandish garish plastic and ask, "American Express?"

"Cash," I told him, "used notes; don't take it all out of your savings account at once. If the police suspect you, they can and will examine your bank accounts and five grand in cash is not easy to explain away. Yes, they will suspect you. You have motive. You must have. You wouldn't be here otherwise. Sell something that won't be missed; swap the Rolex for a fake. Half up front, half on delivery."

They have to justify themselves, these amateurs. One man told me at length that he had nothing against his wife, was even quite fond of her, his childhood sweetheart. But she was middle-aged now and thickening round the waist, greying round the hair. She had not kept up as he climbed the greasy pole, talking too much and too loudly at cocktail parties about her garden and the price of carpets. His Gucci mistress was getting restless, turning thirty and looking for a ring on her finger. They expect more sympathy from me than from a man—women are harder on their own sex.

"Divorce? Are you serious? The business is half hers—on paper, anyway, and that's what will matter in court. Do you know what divorce would cost me?"

Five grand to arrange a little accident: so much more economical and you get to keep the kids. Death: so much quicker, cleaner, more final. Besides, she's sagging, wrinkled; she won't find anyone else. She'll be sad and lonely. It's kinder this way. She's being killed with kindness.

I tell them, "Meet me by the canal (in the tearoom at Fortnum's, in front of the Elgin Marbles in the British Museum) two days from now. Bring the money, the name and address of the hit, details of the car she drives, and a recent photo. Keep busy: not with something that shrieks 'alibi' at the police but not just, 'I was at home watching TV on my own all evening, Inspector,' either."

They usually turn up. That's when I show them my warrant card and arrest them for conspiracy to murder.

SOME OF THEM THINK THAT since the murder has never happened, they haven't done anything wrong. They are soon disabused. Expensive lawyers squeal entrapment, but in vain. The putative victim—usually the wife—stands in court with ice in her veins and watches him go down for a long stretch. I often think, perhaps fancifully, that something in her has indeed died.

Do you read the papers? We crop up surprisingly often in trials in cozy suburbs like Isleworth and Enfield. The prosecution alleges that Mr. Norris approached an undercover police officer and offered to pay him five thousand pounds to dispose of his wife, Dorothy. They tend to be called Dorothy or Daphne or Phyllis—something slightly prewar like that. Mr. Norris denies all charges. Deny away, Mr. Norris. I have you on tape—your nice, educated, middle-class voice. The case continues. Pictures, page nine.

Pictures of Mr. Norris, that is, and the wounded, outraged Mrs. Norris, carefully made-up and wearing a hat. One picture you never see is of the undercover police officer, who doesn't use his real name in the pub and will be back there next week waiting for a new fish to bite.

I check in with my inspector by phone. I always have backup waiting round the corner when I make the arrest, in case he turns nasty; otherwise, it's a lonely job. Most policemen aren't loners—they're aggressive, gregarious, sporty types—but there's a place for everyone in the Metropolitan Police: handling dogs, backing horses into demonstrators, patrolling the river by boat; or smiling at a vicarious murderer across the unpolished brass of a saloon bar table.

They come by word of mouth. I don't exactly advertise in the local paper. What would I put? Rubbish cleared? Pubs are the arteries of any English town, where you go to make instant friends or enemies, to pick up a lover for one night, to buy drugs, or a gun, or a hit.

SHE WAS VERY NERVOUS. THEY always were, but this one's eyes were everywhere. I was to call her Rachel and she was to call me Sally. We were talking about a man we agreed to call John. At first, of course, I assumed he was her husband, but then a very different tale began to unfold and I listened with increasing interest, seeing her beginning to trust me as if I was just a girlfriend she had run into and was pouring out her troubles to.

There was instant empathy. I found, disconcertingly, that I liked her and I had never liked a punter before, never warmed to those greedy weasel eyes where pound signs clock up like in a cartoon, putting a paltry price on the head of someone they once looked at with love, sometimes haggling over the fee.

Rachel was a single mother, she explained, a divorcée with two children aged eight and six, both girls. The father had long since dropped out of sight and the Child Support Agency didn't bother looking for him since Rachel was not on welfare but supported her little family with her job in a bank.

I judged her to be about my own age, which is thirty-two. She was smart in her work clothes, belted into a raincoat on that wet October evening, looking out of place in the seedy bar. She was thin, too thin, her neck rising gauntly out of the bank clerk's white shirt and the navy scarf which matched her stiff skirt. Her damp brown hair fell loose over her tired eyes, and her lipstick had bled into the worry lines about her mouth.

I know desperation when I see it.

Fifteen months earlier she had met John, a customer at the bank, when she had discussed different types of mortgage with him. He had returned twice more for clarification and she had been amused and a little flattered to realise that he understood perfectly the distinction between endowment and repayment and just wanted an excuse to talk to her again.

By the time he had plucked up courage to ask her out for a drink, it had seemed churlish to refuse. Besides, he was attractive enough, if a little young for his declared age of twenty-eight, personable if a little shy, and she was often lonely.

A drink had led on to dinner a few days later, a walk in the country that weekend. He got on well with the children, bribing them with too-expensive presents. He seemed perfect, too good to be true. Something was wrong. She didn't fancy him and suspected that his own desires were not the simple orthodoxy she might have anticipated, a sharing of warmth and intimacy. The first time he tried to kiss her, his lips were cold and repellent and her thighs instinctively clamped together. Meanwhile, his hand trembled on her breasts as if he found the rise of flesh distasteful. One or two of his remarks made her unaccountably nervous. Regretfully, she ended the relationship before it went any further.

Or tried to.

For more than a year now she had been cruelly and unusually punished for her attempted flight from loneliness. John had rented a flat opposite her own little house and spied on her continuously. He rang her at three in the morning to give her a detailed account of who had been in and out of her home that day, what she and the children had been wearing, what they had eaten for supper. Now she kept her curtains drawn day and night—the house a prison of shadows and fear.

The cat—the girls' much-loved Sparkle—went out one day and was never seen again. Two casual men friends had been scared off by slashed tyres and scratched paintwork. Obscene letters were delivered at home and at work.

"He—" She hesitated and sucked at her lower lip, willing back tears. "He put an announcement in the *Gazette*, in the Births and Marriages, you know, saying that I had died suddenly at home that weekend—*Rachel, much-missed mother of Tess and Emma. . . .* You can imagine."

The police? I said, imagining.

So hard to prove. No one actually saw him slashing and gouging; cats *did* stray; there was no law against his taking a flat across the road, standing at his front window for hours without end. The announcement had been placed at a busy time and paid for in cash, and the girl at the newspaper couldn't identify him.

It wasn't that the local police weren't sympathetic, they were; they were just powerless. When he did something concrete—when he attacked her, raped her, burnt her and her children alive in their beds one night—then they could act. Until then, it was her word against his and he had rights too.

She had considered disappearing, but good jobs were hard to come by now and the girls were settled in their school. What if she went through all that upheaval and he simply found her again? People were gullible and he was plausible in his neat suit and tidy haircut, with his polite if colourless voice. It took only one innocent colleague, one other mum at the school gate, to say, "Rachel? Oh yes, she's gone to Peterborough."

She must be, I suggested, at the end of her tether. She mimed dissent, gulping at her glass of bad white wine.

"I would have put up with it, hoping he would get tired of it, fixate on someone else, but he rang me a week ago today, half-past four in the morning. I shall never forget his voice as long as I live, the banal matter-of-factness of it."

He hadn't identified himself, knew that she knew who it was.

" 'Rachel, darling. I know what it is—what's keeping us apart. It's the children, isn't it? But for them you would be free to love me and we could go away together and nothing would ever come between us. It's no problem, darling. I'll get rid of them for you. Permanently. They'll never come between us again.' "

My glass broke in my hand where I was squeezing it. There was blood on my fingers, thinned and paled with wine.

Rachel had screamed and slammed the phone down. The next morning she had taken the children to her sister's in Beckenham, the three of them climbing over the fence in the back garden and running for the tube, their heads down, like criminals.

A stranger, this man, a total *stranger*, demanding satisfaction, exerting power, ruining a carefully balanced life.

"Five thousand?" she said. "That's what they told me." I nodded. "It's all the money I have in the world—rainy-day money—but it'll be worth it."

I explained about not taking it all out of the bank at once. She said she would get a cheap loan from her employer, say she wanted to buy a new car.

"Meet me at the foot of Nelson's Column on Tuesday," I instructed. "Bring half the cash and all the details I need to target him. Then go away for a few days, somewhere where people can see you and remember you."

WE LEFT SEPARATELY.

I rang the inspector that night.

"Brian? It's me, Sally."

I couldn't bring myself to call him sir, not since he used to grope me and squeeze my tits when we did car surveillance together in CID, ignoring my wriggling protests with "You know you want it, really."

"What joy this week, love?"

"Not a nibble. Sudden outbreak of law-abidingness in Hounslow."

"Time to change your patch, would you say?"

"Yeah," I said. "How about the Savoy this time—better class of psychopath?"

He laughed. "Find somewhere down Acton way. Put out the usual feelers. Talk to you soon."

I grunted assent and hung up.

For the sake of two little girls and the sanity of a nice ordinary woman—a woman who might have been me if things had worked out differently—I had an accident to arrange for a man called John, a burglary gone tragically wrong. I fingered the wrought and torn tape from my dictaphone on the desk before me, then watched its brief, evil-smelling flare in the fire.

Simon Brett works in all aspects of the mystery genre with equal skill. His suspense novels have been well-received, with *A Shock to the System* having been recently made into a movie starring Michael Caine. He also has two series going as well, the Charles Paris theater mysteries and a more farcical line of books starring the elderly sleuth Mrs. Pargeter. Here he is at his comic best, with the protagonist of "A Good Thing" having to learn the hard way that he should quit while he's behind.

A Good Thing
SIMON BRETT

Generally speaking, it has to be said I'm quite good with money. I mean, I think about it, I don't just rush out and do daft things; I'm careful about whose advice I listen to. I can always spot a good thing.

Obviously, having been born to it helps. I mean, I have got this kind of genetic aptitude. You know, some ancestor of mine back in the seventeenth century or whenever caught on to the idea that there was money to be made in this new slave-trade business, and he went for it. Then subsequent generations chose their moment to go into coffee, or rubber, or railways, or armaments, or whatever it happened to be and, generally speaking, they got it right. Money breeds money, as the saying goes, though my view is more that breeding breeds money.

And it has to be said, we Foulkeses have got the breeding. Obviously we didn't have it when we started, but then who did? Mind you, once one of my distant ancestors had saved up enough to buy a peerage from James I of England—and VI of Scotland, don't let us forget—well, we were up and away.

And haven't really looked back since. Entrepreneurial we've always been—that's the word—entrepreneurial. We haven't just let our money sit and vegetate—good heavens, no—we've been out there watching it work for us. I mean, I've got a lot of chums who caught nasty colds over the Lloyd's insurance debacle, and though I feel sorry as hell for the poor buggers—and particularly for their wives—I have to say they had it coming to them.

I'd never get involved in something like that—just salting the money away and sitting quietly at home, waiting for the divvies to come in. No, I invest in things I can see. And let me tell you, I'm pretty damned sharp about recognising the kind of guy who's going to point me in the direction of the right sort of investments. I'm an extremely good judge of character. I know a good thing when I see it.

Which is why I was so delighted when I first met Roland Puissant.

It was in my club, actually. Blake's. The Foulkeses have been members there virtually since the place started, back in the—what?—1830s, some time round then. Roland himself isn't a member—came as the guest of a friend. He told me frankly when we met at the bar that Blake's wasn't really his scene. Didn't like the idea of being anywhere where he had to wear a suit and tie. Wasn't that he hadn't *got* suits and ties—he was wearing a very nice pinstriped number and the old Harrovian colours that day, actually—but he didn't like being *forced* to conform by club regulations. Said he thought it was an infringement of the rights of the individual.

And I respected him for that. Respected him for coming out with his opinion right there, at the bar in Blake's, surrounded by all those crusty old members. As I discovered later, there's never any pretence about Roland. If he thinks something, he says it. Would rather run the risk of offending someone than compromising his opinions and values.

Good thing, so far as I'm concerned. There are so many bullshitters around these days, who'll contort themselves into knots agreeing with everything you say to them, that a direct approach like Roland's is very refreshing.

Anyway, we got talking at the bar. His friend had nipped off to make a phone call—though Roland secretly suspected that the phone call would quickly lead to a nearby hotel where the friend had set up an assignation with a rather dishy little thing from a public relations company. Roland had a nasty feeling that he was being used simply as an alibi for the chap's wife.

Well, the bloke I was meant to be meeting hadn't shown, either. Can't say I was too disappointed. Some fellow I'd apparently known from Eton, though the name didn't ring a bell. Phoned up saying he'd been out of the country for some years and was dead keen to meet up with old chums like Nicky Foulkes. This already made me a bit leery; so many times that sort of introduction leads to someone trying to sell you insurance. Even been known for people in that world to lie about having been at school with you. Buy a tie and invent some rigmarole about having been three years below you in a different house and always looking up to you, soften you up a bit, then wham, in with the "I don't know if you'd ever stopped to consider what your family would stand to receive if—and heaven forbid—but *if* something were to happen to you . . ."

So, basically, I was standing at the bar wondering why the hell I'd agreed to meet this bloke, and getting chirpier with every passing minute that he didn't show up. I was beginning to feel confident that the danger had passed, reconciling myself quite cheerfully to an evening's drinking, assuming I could find someone congenial to drink with ... when—lo and behold—Roland Puissant turned up.

Answer to a maiden's prayer, eh? The other members I was surrounded with in the bar were of the crotchety nothing's-been-the-same-since-we-lost-me-Empire persuasion, so it was a relief simply to see someone round my own age, apart from anything else.

And, once we got talking, it pretty soon became clear that Roland hadn't just got age going for him. Oh no, he was very definitely an all-round good bloke.

Could put back the sauce too. I'm no mean performer in the tincture stakes, but he was more than matching me glass for glass. We were on the malt. Lagavulin from Islay's my favourite. Turned out Roland loved the stuff too. Clearly a man of taste.

Well, after an hour or so on the blessed nectar, I suggested eating something by way of blotting paper. And since the food at Blake's is indistinguishable from blotting paper, I said we should eat in the club dining room. Roland said fine, so long as it was his treat—he insisted on that. I said, your treat next time, old lad. Nonmembers aren't allowed to pay at Blake's.

At first he wasn't keen on being in my debt, but he came round graciously enough. So we got stuck into the club claret. Long experience has taught me that the only way to deal with Blake's food is to anaesthetise the old tastebuds with alcohol. Always works for me—I can never remember what I've ordered and don't notice what it is while I'm eating the stuff. Perfect.

We were into the second bottle before we got talking about money. Roland just let something slip by mistake. He tried to cover it up, but I'm pretty Lagavulin- and claret-resistant, so I leapt on it straight away.

All he actually said was "... and you know that wonderful feeling of confidence when you're onto an absolute copper-bottomed cert of a good thing."

He could have been talking in purely general terms, but the way he hastily moved the conversation on told me he was dealing with specifics. I'm pretty sharp about that kind of stuff. Something of an amateur psychologist, actually. Well, you need to be in the kind of circles I move in. Stuffed full of shysters trying to put one over on you—particularly if you happen to have a bit of the old inherited.

So I pounced. " 'Good thing,' Roland?" I said. "And what particular 'good thing' are you talking about at the moment?"

"Oh, nothing."

But I stuck at it. "Horse?"

"No, not a horse in this instance."

I was rather pleased with myself: My line of questioning had made him admit that he was talking about something specific rather than general.

"Investment opportunity?" I pressed on.

He was embarrassed that I'd seen through him so quickly, but nodded.

"Tell me more," I said. "Always like to hear the details of any investment opportunity. We Foulkeses have traditionally had a nose for this kind of thing."

Still Roland prevaricated. "Oh, I don't think it'd interest you."

"Let me be the judge of that. Go on, tell me—unless of course you've got the whole thing sewn up yourself and don't want to let anyone else in on it."

"No, for heaven's sake," he protested. "I wouldn't do that. It's just I do hate giving tips to friends. It's like selling them a car—hellish embarrassing if the thing breaks down."

"Listen," I said. "I'm a grownup. I'm quite capable of making my own decisions. I don't get taken in by anything iffy. Don't forget, my surname's Foulkes, and we Foulkeses have had quite a reputation over the years for making some pretty damned good business decisions. Come on, Roland, you bloody well tell me what this is all about!"

That little barrage broke down his resistance. He sighed, shrugged, and told me what it was all about.

Basically, like most financial projects, it was buying and selling. Buying cheap and selling expensive—the principle on which the British Empire was built. And the principle by which the Foulkeses had done so well out of the British Empire.

Like the slave trade on which the family fortune had been built, Roland's investment scheme was not illegal. Some people might perhaps go a bit wobbly about its ethics, but it was undoubtedly within the law. Sounded just the sort of "good thing" a member of the Foulkes family should get involved in.

In fact the project's parallels with the slave trade didn't stop at its legality. The commodities being bought and sold were domestic servants. Men and women from the Caribbean were offered a complete service—flight to London, job found, work permit sorted out. The investment required was to pay for these services. The profit came from the fee the clients paid to the agency which handled their cases.

When Roland mentioned this, I shrewdly asked whether the word "fee" was appropriate. Wasn't "bribe" nearer the mark? He just gave me a charming grin and said we didn't want to get bogged down in semantics.

But wasn't it hellish difficult to arrange work permits for foreigners? was my next question. Roland agreed it was. "This is the beauty of the scheme, though," he went on. "My contact has an 'in' with the Home Office."

It was the first time he'd mentioned a "contact." Felicia Rushworth, she was called. She had had the idea for the business and needed capital. Roland Puissant had backed her to the tune of fifty grand six months before. The return on his stake had quadrupled since then. People from the Caribbean definitely did want to get jobs in England.

I didn't ask how much the "fee" they paid for this privilege was. Nor did I ask the rates they were paid once they started working in London. When you're investing in something, there are some details you just don't need to know about.

By the end of the evening—rather late, as it happened, because we'd moved on to a little drinking club I know round the back of Bond Street—Roland had agreed that the next week he'd introduce me to Felicia Rushworth.

IT HAS TO BE SAID—she was bloody stunning. I mean, I've known a lot of girls, but Felicia Rushworth definitely took the Best of Show rosette. Generally speaking, I keep girls at arm's length. Of course I go around with a good few—everyone needs sex—but I don't let them get close. Always have to be on the lookout if you've come into a bit—lots of voracious females out there with their beady eyes fixed solely on the old inherited. So I've never even got near marriage. Never wanted to. Mind you, the sight of a creation like Felicia Rushworth could go a long way towards making a chap change his mind about that kind of thing.

She had this long blond hair that looked natural. I don't know much about that stuff, but if it wasn't natural it was damned cleverly done. Come to that, if it *was* natural, it was damned cleverly done.

Shrewd blue eyes. Intelligent. Normally, I don't look for that in a girl, but then what I'm looking for in most of them isn't a business partnership. Anyway, in Felicia's case, the intelligence in the eyes wasn't so overpowering they stopped being pretty.

And beautifully tanned skin. I suppose that's one of the perks of doing business with the Caribbean. Slender brown arms and endless brown legs, of whose unseen presence beneath the table I was aware right through that lunch at Nico at Ninety.

I'd suggested the venue. One of my regular bread-and-watering-holes. Sort of place that can impress clients when they need impressing. Mind you, Felicia Rushworth looked cool enough to take anything in her stride.

Roland was kind of formal with her. Don't know why I thought that odd. I'd probably assumed he knew her better than he did. After all, she was just someone he was doing business with. He was done up to the nines again, old Harrovian tie neatly in place. I think he was probably trying to impress her.

Felicia had a no-nonsense approach to the reason for our meeting. "Let's get the serious bit out of the way first," she said firmly. "Then we can enjoy the rest of our lunch."

And she spelled it all out to me. The more she said, the better I felt about the whole picture. That old Foulkes nose for a "good thing" was twitching like a ruddy dowsing rod. Felicia's long-term plan was to run the business completely on her own with her own savings, but in the short term she needed start-up capital. The experimental six months with Roland's fifty grand had worked so well that now she wanted to expand the operation— set up offices in London and Kingston, Jamaica, take on staff, put the whole affair on a more permanent footing.

"One thing I should ask at this point . . ." I said, "is about the legality of what's going on. Roland's told me it's kosher, and obviously I believe him, but in my experience you don't get the kind of profits we're talking about here without the odd rule being ever so slightly bent."

Felicia turned the full beam of those shrewd blue eyes on me. "You're not stupid, are you, Mr. Foulkes?"

I gave her a lazy grin back. "No. And please call me Nicky. Everybody does."

"All right, Nicky. Well, you've probably worked out that the area where the rules are being bent a little is round the work permits." I nodded, confirming her assumption that I was way ahead of her. "And yes, people involved in that area of the business are running risks. They're being well paid to run risks, but I suppose in a worst-case scenario they might get found out. In that eventuality, no blame could possibly be attached to the investors in the company . . . although, of course, trouble of that sort could cut down the kind of returns they'd get." Once again she fixed those unnerving blue eyes on mine. "But I'm looking for the kind of investor who likes risks."

"I like risks." Then I added, "In all areas of my life."

She didn't give me anything so rude as a wink, but I could see she'd salted the message away. There was now a kind of private bond between us, something that excluded Roland.

I moved briskly on. "So what size of investment are you looking for at the moment?"

"Over the next year I need a quarter of a million," she replied coolly. "Immediately a hundred thousand. Roland's supplying most of that, so I'm just looking for top-up funds at the moment."

"Top-up to the tune of how much?"

"Ten grand."

"What, Roland, you're already committed for the ninety?"

He nodded. "Seeing the return I got on fifty, can you blame me?"

"No." I was silent for a moment. "Pity I came in so late on the deal, isn't it?"

"What do you mean?"

"Well, ten grand's not much of a stake for a real *risk-taker*, is it?" As I said the word, I fixed Felicia with my eye. She gave an almost imperceptible acknowledgement of the secret between us.

"There'll be more opportunities," she said soothingly. "Better for you to start small. See how it goes. I mean, the next six months may not go as well as the first. I don't want you to be out of pocket."

"Not much danger of that, is there?"

She shook her head firmly and, with a little smile, said, "No."

"So are you going in for the ten grand, Nicky?" asked Roland.

"You try and stop me." I took a sip of wine. "You sure I can't go in for more, Felicia?"

"Absolutely positive."

"But look, if you're after a quarter of a million over the next year, surely I could—"

The blue eyes turned to steel. "Mr. Foulkes, I am offering you a stake of ten thousand pounds in my business. That is the offer. Ten grand—no more. Take it or leave it."

Felicia Rushworth was quite daunting in that mode. I left it there for the rest of the lunch. But I was a bit miffed. She'd opened up this glowing prospect to me, and then severely limited my access to it. Ten grand's nothing to an entrepreneur like me. I knew this was a really good thing, and I wanted to be into it a lot deeper than that.

Still, we didn't talk about it further, just enjoyed Nico Ladenis's cooking. Bloody good. Makes you realise just how bad the garbage is you get dished up at places like Blake's. We got through a couple of rather decent bottles of Pouilly Fumé too.

Which inevitably led to Roland and me needing an excursion to the Gents. It was there that I moved on to the next stage of the plan I'd been forming during the lunch.

"Any chance of my getting in for more, do you reckon?" I asked casually.

"Mm?" Roland was preoccupied with his zip.

"More than ten grand . . . in Felicia's little scheme . . . I mean, ten grand's nothing. . . . I want to be a serious player."

Roland grimaced. "Hm . . . Felicia's a strong-willed lady. She says she'd let you in for ten grand, that's what she means. Probably just protecting herself. I mean, she doesn't know much about you—only what I've told her. I know you're the genuine article, but you can't blame her for being cautious. There's a lot of villains about, you know."

"You don't need to tell me that. Do you think it's worth my having another go—asking Felicia straight out if I can invest more?"

He jutted out a dubious lower lip. "Like I say, when she's decided something . . ." He turned thoughtfully to wash his hands in the basin. "Tell you what," he said after a moment, ". . . I could cut you in on a bit of mine."

"How do you mean?"

"Well, so long as I give Felicia the ninety grand, she's not going to know where it comes from. If you give me another ten, your stake goes up to twenty, doesn't it?"

"Yes, but that's cutting down your profits, isn't it?"

Roland Puissant shrugged. "I did all right first time round. Got a few other good things I could divert the spare into."

"What are they?"

"Hm?" He shook the water off his hands and reached for a towel.

"The other good things?"

He grinned at me and shook his head. "Have to keep some secrets, you know, Nicky."

"Okay. Point taken." I straightened my old Etonian tie in the mirror. "You wouldn't consider letting me in for more than another ten. . . . ?"

We haggled a bit, but basically I got what I was after. I'd pay ten grand to Felicia and forty to Roland. She'd get the promised ninety from him, and not know that I'd contributed nearly half of it. Then Roland would account the profits back to me.

I felt pretty pleased with my day's work. Though I say it myself, I'm a bloody good negotiator. And I had achieved a fifty-grand stake in one of the most lucrative little projects I'd ever heard of: Lunch for three at Nico at Ninety was a small price to pay.

Struck me as I was walking down Park Lane from the restaurant that in fact I was almost going into the family business. The Foulkes fortune had been built up by ferrying Africans across the Atlantic. What I was now involved in was ferrying them back the other way. Rather neat, I thought.

"I JUST FEEL SO DREADFUL about this."

Roland Puissant looked pretty dreadful too. We were at dell'Ugo, noisy as ever but smashing nosh. "Tell me about it," I said.

"I'm almost embarrassed to."

"Come on, you don't have to be embarrassed with me. I'm unembarrassable. Anyway, I'm a mate, aren't I? Not to mention a business partner. You, me, and Felicia, eh?"

"That's it. Felicia," he said glumly.

"Come on, me old kipper. Pour it all out."

And he did. It was bad.

Basically we'd been had. Felicia Rushworth had calmly taken our money and gone off to Jamaica with it. Whether there actually was any employment agency business seemed doubtful. Whether there was some useful contact at the Home Office who could fix work permits for Caribbean visitors seemed even more doubtful. Roland and I had fallen for the oldest ploy in the book—a pretty girl with a convincing line of patter.

"And I just feel so guilty towards you," Roland concluded. "I should never have mentioned the project to you."

"Oh, now come on. I have to take my share of the blame too. You never volunteered anything. You never wanted to talk about it. Every detail I got out of you was like drawing a tooth."

"Yes, but I shouldn't have got you involved. Or I should have seen to it that your stake stayed at ten grand."

"Well, you didn't. You were bloody generous to me about that, Roland. At the time you were taking a considerable potential loss just to give me a chance."

"A chance I bet you wish now you hadn't taken?"

"Look, it's done. I did it. Maybe I was bloody stupid but I did it. If you take risks, some of them are going to pay off and some aren't. Anyway we're in the same boat—both of us fifty grand to the bad . . ." My words trailed off at the sight of his face. "You mean more than fifty . . . ?"

Roland Puissant nodded wretchedly. "Practically cleaned me out, I'm afraid."

"But I thought you said you'd got a lot of other good things going?"

"Yes, I did. Trouble is, all of those were recommended by Felicia. She generously took care of those investments too."

"Oh. So she's walked off with the whole caboodle?"

"About one point two million in all," he confessed.

I whistled. "Bloody hell. That is a lot."

"Yes. God, I'm stupid. I suppose . . . someone who looks like that . . . someone who's as intelligent as that . . . it just never occurs to you that they'd . . . I was putty in her hands. Is there anything more ridiculous than a man of my age playing the fool because of a pretty face? Some of us just never learn, eh?"

I didn't tell him how closely I identified with what he was saying. Instead, I moved the conversation on. "Question is . . . what're we going to do about it?"

"Bloody well get revenge!" Roland spat the words out. I'd never seen him so angry.

"How?"

"I don't know." He shook his head hopelessly. "No idea. Mind you, if I was out in Jamaica, I could do something. . . ."

"Like what?"

"I know people out there. People who could put pressure on Felicia. Reckon they could persuade her to return our money."

"Are you talking about criminals?"

He shrugged. "Often hard to say where legitimate business practice stops and criminality starts, wouldn't you say? But yes, this lot's means of persuasion are perhaps more direct than traditional negotiations."

"Would she get hurt?" The words came out instinctively. Whatever Felicia might have done to us, the idea of injury to that fragile beauty was appalling.

"She's a shrewd cookie. I think she'd assess the options and come across with the goods before they started hurting her."

"So you think we'd get the money back?"

"Oh yes. I mean, obviously we'd have to pay something for the . . . er, hired help . . . so we wouldn't get everything back . . . but we wouldn't be that much out of pocket."

"Well, then, for God's sake, let's do it."

Roland Puissant gave me a lacklustre look. "Yeah, great. How? I told you, she's cleaned me out."

"Couldn't I go to Jamaica and organise it?"

"Wish you could." He shook his head slowly. "Unfortunately, the people whose help we need are a bit wary of strangers. They know me, they've dealt with me before. But the last unfamiliar bloke who tried to make contact with them . . . ended up with his throat cut."

"Ah."

"No, I'm sorry. It'd have to be me or no one. But . . ." He spread his hands despairingly wide. ". . . I don't currently have the means to fly to Jamaica—let alone bribe the local villains. At the moment I'd be pushed to raise the bus fare to Piccadilly Circus."

"Well, look, let me sub you, Roland."

"Now don't be ridiculous, Nicky. You're already down fifty grand. I absolutely refuse to let you lose any more."

"Look, it's an investment for me. It's my only chance of getting my fifty grand back."

He still looked dubious. "I don't like the idea of you . . ."

"Roland," I said, "I insist."

IT WAS NEARLY A MONTH later when Roland next rang me. He was calling from Heathrow. "I wanted to get through to you as soon as possible. I've had one hell of a time over in Jamaica, I'm afraid."

"Any success?"

"Not immediately, no. I was just beginning to get somewhere, but then the money ran out and—"

"You got through the whole ten grand I subbed you?"

"Yes. As I said, the kind of help I was enlisting doesn't come cheap."

"But why didn't they come up with the goods? I thought you said they'd just put the frighteners on Felicia and she'd stump up the cash."

"That's how it should have worked, yes. But I'm afraid she was a step ahead of us."

"In what way?"

"She'd hired some muscle of her own. I'm afraid what I got into was like full-scale gang warfare. Bloody nasty at times, let me tell you. This time last week I didn't reckon I'd ever see Heathrow again."

"Really? What, you mean your life was at—"

"You don't want to hear all this, Nicky. It's not very interesting. Main point is, I've let you down. I said I'd go over there and get your money back and I haven't. And I've spent your extra ten grand. In fact, you're now sixty grand down, thanks to me."

"Listen, Roland, I walked into it quite knowingly. If you want to blame anyone, blame me. Blame my judgement."

"That's very sporting of you to put it like that, but I can't buy it, I'm afraid. You're out of pocket and it's my fault. But don't worry, I'll see you get your money back."

"How? You've lost one point two million."

"I know, but there's stuff I can do. There's something I'm trying to set up right now, actually. And if that doesn't work out, I'll take another mortgage on the house. Anything to stop this awful guilt. I can't stand going round with the permanent feeling that I've let an old chum down."

"Roland, you're getting things out of proportion. I won't hear of you mortgaging your house just for my sake. We can sort this thing out. Best thing you can do is get a good night's sleep and we'll meet up in the morning. See where we stand then, eh?"

"Well, if you . . ."

"I insist."

"Where're we going to meet?"

"Roland, you don't by any chance play Real Tennis, do you?"

DON'T KNOW IF YOU KNOW the Harbour Club. Chelsea, right on the river. Converted old power station, actually, but they've done it bloody well. Very high spec. Pricey, of course, but then you have to pay for class. And the clientele is, it has to be said, pretty damn classy.

Anyway, I try to play Real Tennis down there at least once a week. Enjoy the game, and it stops the body seizing up totally. Good way of sweating out a hangover too, so I tend to go for a morning court.

I thought it'd be just the thing to sort out old Roland. He'd sounded frankly a bit stressed on the phone, but I reckoned a quick canter round the court might be just the thing to sort him out. I was glad to hear he knew the game—not many people do—but surprised when he said he'd played it for the school. I didn't know Harrow had a Real Tennis court.

Still, Roland was at the place and I wasn't, so I guess he knew what he was talking about.

I said we should play the game first, to kind of flush out the old system, and then talk over a drink. Roland wasn't so keen on this—his guilt hadn't gone away and he wanted to get straight down to the schemes he had for replacing my money—but I insisted and won the day. I can be quite forceful when I need to be.

I must say his game was pretty rusty. He said he hadn't played since school but in the interim he seemed to have forgotten most of the rules. I mean, granted they are pretty complicated—if you don't know them, I haven't got time to explain all about penthouses and galleries and tambours and grilles and things now—but I thought for anyone who had played a bit, they'd come back pretty quickly. Not to poor old Roland Puissant, though. Acted like he'd never been on a Real Tennis court in his life.

Still, I suppose he was preoccupied with money worries. Though, bless his heart, he seemed to be much more concerned about my sixty grand than his own one point two million. I think he was just an old-fashioned gentleman who hated the idea of being in debt to anyone—particularly a friend of long-standing. The idea really gnawed away at him.

The game seemed to come back to him a bit more by the end of the booking and, when our time was up, we'd got into quite a decent knock-up. Enough to work up a good sweat, anyway, and dictate that we had showers before we got stuck into the sauce.

It was when Roland was stripped off that I noticed how tanned he was. Except for the dead white strip where his swimming shorts had been, he was a deep, even brown all over.

"I say," I joked as he moved into the shower, "you been spending all my money lying about sunbathing, have you, Roland?"

He turned on me a look of surprising intensity. "Damn, I didn't want you to see that," he hissed.

"Why? My suggestion true then, is it?" I still maintained the joshing tone, but for the first time a little trickle of suspicion seeped into my mind.

"No, of course not," Roland replied impatiently. "This happened when I got captured."

"You got captured? You didn't tell me."

"No, well, I . . . No point in your knowing, really—nothing you could do about it now. And I . . . well, I'd rather not think about it." He looked genuinely upset now. I'd stirred up some deeply unpleasant memories.

"What did they do to you, Roland?" I asked gently.

"Oh, they . . . Well, they stripped me off down to my boxer shorts and left me strapped out in the sun for three days."

"Good God."

He gave me a brave, wry grin. "One way to get a suntan, eh? Though there are more comfortable ones."

"But if you were strapped down . . ." I began logically ". . . wouldn't you just be tanned on your front *or* your back? . . . unless of course your captors came and turned you over every few hours." I chuckled.

Roland's eyes glowed painfully with the memory as he hissed, "Yes, they did. That's exactly what they did. So that I'd have to have the pressure of my body bearing down on my sunburnt skin."

"Good heavens! And those scratches on your back—were they part of the torture too?"

"Scratches?"

I pointed to a few scrapes that looked as if they might have been made by clutching fingernails.

"Oh yes," said Roland. "Yes, that was when they . . ." He coloured and shook his head. "I'm sorry, I'd really rather not talk about it."

"I fully understand, old man." I patted him on the shoulder. "Still, you escaped with your life."

"Yes." He gritted his teeth. "Touch and go on a few occasions, but I escaped with my life. . . ." He sighed mournfully. "Though sadly not with your money."

"Don't worry. We'll have another go. We'll get our revenge on Felicia Rushworth one way or the other."

"Hope so," said Roland ruefully as he ducked in under the spray of his shower.

At that moment his mobile phone rang. It was in the clothes locker he had just opened. "Shall I get it?" I asked.

"Well, perhaps I should—"

I pressed the button to establish contact. The caller spoke immediately. It was a voice I recognised.

I held the receiver across to Roland, who had emerged from the shower rubbing his eyes with a towel. "Felicia Rushworth," I said.

He looked shocked as he took the phone. He held his hand over the receiver. "Probably better if I handle this privately," he said, and moved swiftly from the changing room area to the corridor outside.

I sat down on the wooden bench, deep in thought. The words Felicia Rushworth spoke before she realised the wrong person had answered had been: "Roland, is the idiot still buying the story?"

Now I'm a pretty shrewd guy, and I smelled a rat. For a start, Felicia's tone of voice had sounded intimate, like she and Roland were on the same side rather than ferocious adversaries. Also, if one was looking round for someone to cast in the role of the "idiot" who was hopefully "buying the story" . . . well, there weren't that many candidates.

Roland's wallet was in the back pocket of his trousers, hanging in the locker. Normally I wouldn't pry into a chap's private possessions, but, if the ugly scenario slowly taking shape in my brain was true, then these weren't normal circumstances.

Nothing in the wallet had the name "Roland Puissant" on it. All the credit cards were imprinted with "R. J. D. Rushworth." In the jacket pocket I found a book of matches from the Sunshine Strand Luxury Hotel, Montego Bay, Jamaica.

I heard the door to the changing room clatter closed and looked up. "Roland" was holding the phone, and had a towel wrapped round his waist.

"God, she's got a nerve, that woman—bloody ringing me up to taunt me about what she's done."

"Oh yes?"

He must've caught something in my tone, because he looked at me sharply. "What's up, old man?"

"The game, I would say, 'Roland Puissant.' "

He looked genuinely puzzled. "Look, I'm sorry. I told you I haven't played for a while, bit rusty on the old—"

"Not that game. You know exactly what I mean."

"Do I?"

I hadn't moved from the bench. I'd curbed my anger, not even raised my voice while I assessed how I was going to play the scene.

I still didn't raise my voice as I said, "I've just looked in your wallet. All your credit cards are in the name of 'R. J. D. Rushworth.' "

"Yes," he replied in a matter-of-fact way. "I only got back last night. I haven't got round to changing them yet."

"What do you mean? Aren't you R. J. D. Rushworth?"

He looked at me incredulously. "Of course I'm not, Nicky. For God's sake—you know I'm Roland Puissant, don't you? But you surely never thought I was going to travel to Jamaica under my own name, did you? I didn't want to advertise to Felicia what I was up to."

For a second I was almost convinced, until another discordant detail struck me. "But why, of all the names in the world, did you choose her name—'Rushworth'?"

"Well, I had to get to see her, didn't I? Felicia's got her security pretty well sorted out. I had to pretend to be her husband, so that they'd let me through *to* her."

"But the minute she saw you, your cover'd be blown."

"That was a risk I was prepared to take." He winced. "An ill-advised one, as it turned out."

"What do you mean?"

"I'd been hoping that I'd get to see her on her own, but a couple of her heavies took me in. Well, I had no chance then, had I?"

"That's when the torturing started?"

He nodded, then shook his head. "I'd rather not talk about it, if you don't mind."

My heart went out to him. Poor bugger, not only had he lost all his money and been tortured by Caribbean thugs, now one of his best friends was suspecting him of . . .

Just a minute. Just a minute, I said to myself, hold your horses there, old man. The way he'd accounted for the credit cards was maybe feasible, but it didn't explain the words with which Felicia had opened her telephone call.

"When I answered your phone," I began coolly, "Felicia, presumably thinking she'd got through to you, said: 'Roland, is the idiot still buying the story?' . . ."

"Yes," he agreed, totally unfazed.

"Well, would you like to explain to me what she meant by that, because I'm not much enjoying the only explanation my mind's offering."

Roland looked torn. At last he sighed and said, "Well, all right. I suppose I'll have to tell you. I wanted to keep it a secret, but . . ." He sighed again. "Nicky, you've heard of Jeffrey Archer?"

"Hm? Yes, of course I have, but what the hell's he got to do with what we're talking about?"

"Well, you may know that he lost a lot of money in an investment that went wrong . . ."

"Yes. I've heard the story."

". . . and then he fixed the situation by writing his way out of it."

"Mm."

"He sold books and ideas for books and made another huge fortune from that."

"Yes, I still don't see—"

"That's what I've been trying to do, Nicky. I've felt so absolutely lousy about the way you've lost money over this—and all because of me—that I've been trying to sell a book idea so that I can pay you back."

"Really?"

"Yes. I've worked out a synopsis for this story about a conman and—touch wood—it's looking good. There's a publisher who's expressing interest—strong interest. Trouble is, I was stupid enough to mention this to Felicia when I was in Jamaica, and now of course she'll never let me hear the end of it. She's tickled to death that she's driven me to try and make money as a writer."

"So what she said . . . ?"

"Exactly. She was talking about this publisher . . . for whom she doesn't have a lot of respect. That's why she said, 'Roland, is the idiot still buying the story?' "

I couldn't think of anything to say.

"And the answer," Roland went on, "is—please God—yes. Because if the idiot *does* buy the story, then I have a chance of paying back at least some of the money that my foolish advice has cost one of my best mates—Nicky Foulkes."

I felt very humbled, you know, by the way Roland was taking my troubles on himself in this way. And to think of the suspicions I'd been within an ace of voicing about him. Well, thank God some instinct stopped me from putting them into words.

Even a nature as generous and loyal as Roland Puissant's might have found that kind of accusation a bit hard to take. Sort of thing that could ruin a really good friendship.

ROLAND'S BACK IN THE COUNTRY again. Called me a couple of days ago. He's been having a dreadful time. Well, we'd both agreed after Felicia managed to escape him in Jamaica, he should have another go to try and retrieve our money. He went on again about mortgaging his house, but I said, don't be daft, we're in this together, and stumped up a bit of ante for his expenses.

Trouble was, when he got to Jamaica, he found Felicia's moved on. To Acapulco. So he's had to spend the last month down there trying to find her and put the pressure on. Poor bugger, rather him than me, I must say. But one can't but admire his dedication. I'm lucky to have someone like him out there rooting away on my behalf.

Anyway, we've fixed to get together next week. Roland's a bit busy at the moment. But he's making time to meet up with me. Letting me take him out for dinner at Bibendum. Expensive, I know, but it'll be a small price to pay. Roland never stops, you know. Always grafting away on some new scheme or other. He's got a whole lot of new investment opportunities he's going to put my way. If I play my cards right, you know, I think I could be on to another good thing.

The mean streets of the Bronx play a prominent part in S. J. Rozan's story, "Hoops." A native of New York City, she works for an architectural firm when not plotting mysteries. She recently won the Shamus Award for Best Novel, and this story made the final ballot for the Edgar Award. Her latest novel is titled *Mandarin Plaid*. Here she shows how integral the setting of a story can be, as her detective uncovers broken dreams among inner-city basketball games.

Hoops

S. J. ROZAN

A cold wind was pulling sharp waves from the Hudson as I drove north, out of town. The waves would strain for height, pushing forward, reaching; but then they'd fall back with small, violent crashes, never high enough, never breaking free.

I was heading to Yonkers, a tired, shabby city caught between New York and the real suburbs. I'd been there over the years as cases had taken me, but I'd never had a client from there before. I'd never had a client who was just eighteen, either. But it was a week since I'd closed my last case. Money was a little tight, I was getting antsy, and working was better than not working, always.

Even working for a relative of Curtis's. I'd been surprised when he'd called me. The ring of the telephone had burst into a practice session where a Beethoven sonata I'd thought I had in my fingers was falling apart, where rhythm, color, texture, everything was off. I usually don't like being interrupted at the piano, but this time I jumped at it.

Until I heard who it was, and what he wanted.

"A nephew of yours?" I said into the phone. "I didn't know scum like you had relatives, Curtis."

"Now, you got no call to be insulting," Curtis's smooth voice gave back. "Though it ain't surprising. I told the boy I could get him a investigator do a good job for him, but he gonna have to put up with a lot of attitude."

"What's he done?" I asked shortly.

"Ain't done nothing. A friend of his got hisself killed. Raymond think someone should be paying attention."

"When people get killed the cops usually pay attention."

"Unless you some black kid drug dealer in Yonkers, and you the suicide half of a murder-suicide."

He had a point. "Tell me about it."

He told me. An eighteen-year-old high school senior named Charles Lomax had been found in a park where the kids go at night. His pregnant girlfriend, beside him, had a bullet in her heart. Lomax had a bullet through his head and the gun in his hand.

The bodies had been discovered by the basketball coach, who said he'd gone out looking after Lomax hadn't shown up for practice. He hadn't shown up for class, either, but apparently that wasn't unusual enough for his classroom teachers to be bothered about. Lomax had been a point guard with a C average. He'd been expected to graduate, which distinguished him from about half the kids at Yonkers West. He'd been in trouble with the police all his life, which distinguished him from nobody. There was nothing else interesting about him, except that he'd been a friend of Raymond Coe, and Raymond wasn't happy with the official verdict: murder-suicide, case closed.

"What's Raymond's theory?" I asked Curtis, shouldering the phone so I could close the piano and stack my music.

"Let me put it to you this way," Curtis oozed. "I ain't suggested the boy hire hisself a honky detective because I admire the way you people dance."

I PULLED SLOWLY AROUND THE corner, coasted past the cracked asphalt playground I'd been told to find. The late-day air was mean with the wind's cold edge, but six black kids in sweats and high-tech sneakers crowded the concrete half-court. Their game was fast, loud, and physical, elbows thrown and no fouls called. One kid, tall and meaty, had a game on a level the others couldn't match: Faster and smarter both, he muscled his man when he couldn't finesse him. But it didn't stop the rest. No one hung back, no one gave in. Slam dunks and three-pointers flew through the netless rim. They didn't seem to be keeping score.

A kid fell, rolled, jumped up shaking his hand against the sting of a scrape. Without missing a beat he was back in the game. I parked across the street and watched. One of those kids was Raymond; I didn't know which. Right now I knew nothing about any of them, except for what I could see: strength, focus, a wild joy in pushing themselves. I finished a cigarette. In a minute I'd become part of their world. This moment of possibility would end. Knowledge can't be shaken off. And knowledge is always limiting.

The game faltered and then stopped as I walked to the break in the chain-link fence. They all watched me approach, silent. A chunky kid in a hooded sweatshirt shifted the ball from one hand to the other. To the one who'd fallen he said, "Yo, Ray. This your man?"

"Don't know." Raising his voice as though he suspected I spoke a different language, the kid said, "You Smith?"

I nodded. "Raymond Coe?"

"Yeah." He jerked his head at the others. "These my homeboys."

I glanced at the tight, silent group. "They in on this?"

"You got a problem with that?"

"Should I?"

"Maybe you don't like working for a bunch of niggers."

I stared into his dark eyes. It seemed to me they were softer than he might have wanted them to be. "Maybe I don't like having to pass an exam to get a case." I shrugged, turned to go.

"Yo," Raymond said, behind me.

I turned back.

"Curtis say you good."

"I don't like Curtis," I told him. "He doesn't like me. But we're useful to each other from time to time."

Surprisingly, he grinned. His face seemed, for a moment, to fit with what I'd seen in his eyes. "Curtis tell me you was gonna say that."

"What else did he tell you?"

"That you the man could find out about my man C."

"What's in it for you?"

A couple of the other kids scowled at that, and one started to speak, but Raymond silenced him with a look. "Nothing in it for me," he said.

"I cost money," I pressed. "Forty an hour, plus expenses. Two days up front. Why's it worth it to you?"

The chunky kid slammed the ball to the pavement, snatched it back. "Come on, Ray. You don't need this bull."

Raymond ignored him, looked steadily at me. "C was my main man, my homie. No way he done what they say he done. Somebody burned him. I ain't gonna let that pass."

"Why me?" I asked. "Curtis knows every piece of black slime that ever walked the earth, but he sent you a white detective. Why?"

" 'Cause the slime we looking for," Raymond said steadily, "I don't believe they black."

RAYMOND, HIS HOMIES, AND I made our way to the end of the block, to the pizza place. The day had gone and a tired gray evening was coming in, studded with yellow streetlights and blinking neon. The homies gave me their names: Ash, Caesar, Skin. Tyrell, the one who could really play. The chunky one, Halftime. None of them offered to shake my hand.

Inside, where the air swirled with garlic and oregano, we crowded around a booth, hauling chairs to the end of the table. Halftime went to order a pizza. He came back distributing Cokes and Sprites, and he brought me coffee. Across the room, from the jukebox, a rap song began, complicated rhythm under complex rhyme, music with no melody. I drank some coffee. "Well?"

Everyone glanced at everyone else, but they all came back to Raymond. Raymond looked only at me. "My man C," he started. "Someone done him, make it look like suicide."

"People kill themselves," I said.

Some heads shook; Tyrell muttered, "Damn."

"You don't know him," Raymond said. "C don't never give up on nothing. And he had no reason. He was gonna graduate, he was gonna have a kid. The season was just starting."

"The season?" I left the rest for later.

"Hoops," Raymond told me, though it was clear I was straining the patience of the others. "My man a guard. Tyrell, Ash, and me, we on the squad too." Tyrell and Ash, a round-faced quiet kid, nodded in acknowledgment. "The rest of them," Raymond's sudden, unexpected grin flashed again, "they keep us on our game."

"So you're telling me if Lomax was going to kill himself he would have waited until after the season?" I lit a cigarette, shook the match into the tin ashtray.

"Man, I am telling you no way he did that." Raymond's voice was emphatic. "C don't have no reason to want out. Plus, Ayisha. Ain't no way he gonna do her like that, the mother of his baby."

"He wanted the baby?"

Halftime grinned, poked at something on the table. Raymond said, "He already buying it things. Toys and stuff. Bought one of them fuzzy baby basketballs, you know? It was gonna be a boy."

"How was he planning to support a family?"

Raymond shrugged. "Some way. Ayisha, she bragging like he gonna get tapped to play for some big school and they gonna be rich, but she don't believe it neither."

"It wasn't true?"

"Nah." Raymond shook his head. "Only dude around here got that kind of chance be my man Tyrell. He gonna make us famous. Put us on the map."

I turned to Tyrell, who was polishing off his second Coke in the corner of the booth. "I watched you play," I told him. "You're smart and fast . . . You have offers?"

Tyrell stared at me for a moment before he answered. "Coach say scouts coming this season." His voice was deep, resonant, and slow. "He been talking to them."

Halftime's name rang out; he went to the counter for the pizza. I looked around at the others, at their hard faces and at their eyes. Seventeen, eighteen: They should have been on the verge of something, at the beginning. But these boys had no futures and they knew it; and I could see it, in their eyes.

I didn't ask where the money was coming from to pay me. I didn't want to know. I didn't ask what would happen to Tyrell if he didn't get a college offer, or whether the others, the ones who weren't on the squad, were still in school. So what if they were? Where would it get them?

I asked a more practical question. "Who'd want to kill Lomax?"

Raymond shrugged, looked at his homeboys. "Everybody got enemies."

"Who were his?"

"Nobody I know about," he said. "Except the cops."

"Cops?" I looked at Raymond, at the other grim faces. "That's what this is about? You think this was a cop job?"

Halftime came back, with a pizza and a pile of paper plates. Everyone reached for a slice but me; Raymond made the offer but I shook my head.

Raymond didn't answer my question, gave Tyrell a look. Tyrell's deep voice picked it up. "C and me was in a little trouble last year. Gas-station holdup. It was bull. Charges was dropped."

"But them mothers didn't let up," Raymond said impatiently. "Tyrell, nobody care, but C been a pain in the cops' butt for years. You know, up in their face, trash-talking. I tell him, man, back off, you leave them alone and they leave you alone. But he don't never stop. C like to win. Also he like to make sure you know you lose. Cops was all over him after he get out."

"And?"

"And nothing. They couldn't get nothing else on him."

"And?" I said again, knowing what was coming.

"I figure they get tired waiting for him to make a mistake and make it for him."

I pulled on my cigarette. There was nothing left; I stubbed it out. I wanted to tell them they were wrong, they were crazy, that kind of stuff doesn't really go on. But that would be pointless. They might be wrong, in this case, but they weren't crazy and we all knew it.

"Anyone in particular?" I asked.

Raymond shook his head. "Cops around here, they run in packs," he said. "Could be anyone."

Two slices were left on the tray. Without discussion, and seemingly by general consent, Raymond and Tyrell reached for them.

"Okay," I said. "Tell me about her."

Tyrell looked away, as though other things in the room were more interesting than I was.

"Ayisha?" Raymond asked. He seemed to think about my question as he ate. "He can't get enough of her," he finally said.

"But you didn't like her?"

"Nah, she okay." He flipped a piece of crust onto the tray, sat back, and popped the top of a Sprite. "She sorta—you know. She got a smart mouth. And she been around."

A couple of the other guys snickered. I wondered whom she'd been around with.

"She have enemies?"

"I don't know. But like I say, everybody got them. Can't always tell what you done to get them, but everybody got them."

I LEFT, TRADING PHONE NUMBERS with Raymond. I took the homies' numbers too, though I was less than certain that getting in touch with any of them would be as easy as a phone call. But I might want to talk to some of them, separately, later. Now, I wanted to talk to a few other people.

The first, from a phone booth down the street, was Lewis Farlow, the basketball coach who'd found the bodies. I called him at the high school, to find a time he'd be available. Half an hour, he told me. He knew about me; he'd been expecting my call.

Next I called the Yonkers PD, to find the detective on the Lomax case. Might as well get the party line.

He was a high-voiced Irish sergeant named Sweeney. He wasn't impressed with my name or my mission, and he wasn't helpful.

"What's to investigate?" he wanted to know. "That case has already been investigated. By real detectives."

"My client's not sure it was suicide," I said calmly.

"Yeah? Who are you working for?"

"Friend of the family."

"Don't be cute, Smith."

"I'm just asking for the results of the official investigation, Sweeney."

The grim pleasure in Sweeney's voice was palpable. "The official results are, the kid killed the girlfriend. Blam! Then he blew his own brains out. Happy?"

Start out with an easy one. "Whose was the gun?"

"The Pope's."

"You couldn't trace it?"

"No, Smith, we couldn't trace it. Numbers were filed off, inside and out. That a new one on you?"

"Seems like a lot of trouble to go to for a suicide weapon."

"Maybe suicide wasn't on his mind when he got it."

"Why'd he do it?"

"How the hell do I know why he did it? You suppose it had anything to do with her being pregnant?"

"And what, his reputation would be ruined? Anyway, his friends say he wanted the baby."

"Yeah, sure. Da-da." Sweeney made baby noises into the phone.

"Sweeney—"

"Yeah. So maybe he did. And then maybe he finds out it isn't his. You like that for a motive? It's yours."

"You have any proof of that?"

"No. Matter of fact, I just thought it up. I'll let you in on something, Smith. I got better things to do than bust my hump to prove a kid with his brains in the dirt and the gun in his hand pulled the trigger."

"I understand you guys knew this kid."

"We know them all. Most of them have been our guests for short stays in our spacious accommodations."

"I hear you couldn't hold onto this one."

"What, for that gas-station job?" He didn't rise to the bait. "Way I look at it, it's just as well. If we could hold them all as long as they deserve, the streets would be clean and I'd be out of a job."

"Come on, Sweeney. Didn't it steam you just a little when the kid walked? I hear it wasn't the first time."

"Matter of fact, it wasn't."

"Matter of fact, I hear there were cops who had this kid on a special list. Was he on your list, Sweeney?"

"Now just hold it, Smith. What are you getting at? I killed him because I couldn't keep his ass in jail where it belonged?"

I'd made him mad. Good; angry men make mistakes.

"Not necessarily you, Sweeney. It's just that I'll bet there weren't a lot of tears in the department when Lomax bought it."

"Oh," he said slowly, his voice dangerously soft. "I get it. You're looking for a lawsuit, right?"

"Wrong."

"Crap. The family wants to milk it. You find a hole in the police work, they sue the department. The city settles out of court; it's got no backbone with these people. You drive off in your Porsche and I get pushed out early on half my stinking pension. That's it, right?"

"No, Sweeney, that's not it. I'm interested in what really happened to this kid. That's what any good cop would be interested in, too."

"You know what, Smith? You're lucky I don't know your face. Here's some advice for free: Don't let me see it."

The phone slammed down; that was that.

*   *   *

YONKERS WEST HIGH SCHOOL FILLED the entire block, a sulking brick-and-concrete monster whose windows were covered with a tight wire mesh. I asked the security guard at the door the way to the gym. "I'm here to see Coach Farlow," I said.

"You a scout?" he asked after me, as I started down the hall.

"No. You have something worth scouting?"

The guard grinned. "Come back tomorrow, at practice," he said. "You'll see."

I found Lewis Farlow behind his desk in his Athletic Department office, a windowless, cramped, concrete-block space that smelled of liniment, mildew, and sweat. Dusty trophies shared the top of the filing cabinets with papers and old coffee cups. Here and there a towel huddled on the floor, as though too exhausted to make it back through the connecting door to the locker room.

I knocked, checked Farlow out while I waited for him to look up from his paperwork. He was a thin white man, smaller than his players, with deep creases in the sagging skin of his face and sparse, colorless hair that might once have been red.

"Yeah." Farlow lifted his head, glanced over me swiftly with blue eyes that were bright and sharp.

"Smith," I said.

"Oh, yeah. About Lomax, right? Sit down." He gestured to a chair.

"The guard at the door asked me if I was a scout," I said as I moved into the room, trying to avoid the boxes of ropes and balls that should have been somewhere else, if there'd been somewhere else for them to be. "He meant that big guy? Tyrell?"

Farlow nodded. "Tyrell Drum," he said. "Best thing we've had here in years. Everybody's just waiting for him to catch fire. You seen him play?" He looked at me quizzically.

"He was with Raymond Coe just now," I explained. "You have scouts coming down?"

"I already had some stringers early last season. Liked what they saw, but the big guns didn't get a chance to get here while Drum was still playing."

"He didn't play the whole season?"

"Sat it out." One corner of Farlow's mouth turned up in a smile that wasn't a smile.

"Hurt?"

"In jail."

"Oh," I said. "The gas-station job?"

"You heard about that?"

"He told me. It was him and Lomax, right?"

"They say it wasn't either of them. Charges were eventually dropped, but the season was over by then."

"Did he do it?"

"Who the hell knows? If he didn't, he will soon. Or something like it. Unless he gets an offer. Unless he gets out of here. Look, Smith: about this Lomax thing."

Farlow stopped, turned a pencil over in his fingers as though looking for a way to say what he wanted. I waited.

"The guys are pretty upset," Farlow said. "Especially Coe; he and Lomax were pretty tight. Coe's got this half-assed idea that the cops killed Lomax. He's sold it to the rest of them. They told me they were going to hire a private eye to prove it."

"How come they told you?"

"I'm the coach. High school, that's like a father confessor. Wasn't it that way when you were there?"

"The high school I went to, all the kids were white."

"You surprised they talk to me? They gotta talk to someone." He shrugged. "I'm on their side and they know it. I go to bat for them when they're in trouble. I bully them into staying in school. Coe wouldn't be graduating if it weren't for me."

He threw the pencil down on the desk, slumped back in his chair. "Not that I know why I bother. They stay in school, so what? They end up fry cooks at McDonald's." Farlow paused, rubbed a hand across his square chin; I got the feeling he was only half talking to me. "Eighteen years in this hole," he went on, "watching kids go down the drain. No way out. Except every now and then, a kid like Drum comes along. Someone you could actually do something for. Someone with a chance. And the stupid sonuvabitch spends half his junior year in jail."

He looked at me. The half-grin came back. "Sorry, Smith. I get like this. The old coach, feeling sorry for himself. Let's get back to Lomax. Where the hell was I?"

"The guys came to you," I said. "They told you they wanted a P.I."

"Yeah. So I told them to go ahead. Coe's like Lomax was, a stubborn bastard. Easier to agree with than to cross. So I said go ahead, call you. He probably thinks I think he's right, that there's something fishy here. But I don't."

"What do you think?"

"I think the simple answer is the best. Sometimes it's hard, but it's the best. Lomax killed the girl and he killed himself."

"Why?"

"Some beef, I don't know. Old days, he'd have knocked her around, then gone someplace to cool off. Today, they all have guns. You get mad, someone's dead before you know it. By the time he realizes what he's done it's over. Then? She's dead, the baby's dead, what's he gonna do? He's still got the gun."

He reached for the pencil again, turned it in his hand, and watched it turn.

"A guy's best friend turns up dead," he said in a quiet voice, "he wants to do something. Hiring you makes them feel better. Okay." He looked up. "So what I'm asking you is, go through the motions. You gotta do that; they're gonna pay you for it. But try to wrap it up fast. The sooner they put this behind them the better off they'll be."

I had my own doubts about how easy it ever was to put a friend's death behind you, but that didn't make Farlow wrong.

"If there's nothing to find, I'll know that soon enough," I said.

Farlow nodded, as though we'd reached an agreement. I asked him, "You found the bodies?"

"Yeah." He threw the pencil down again.

"What did it look like?"

"Look like?"

"Tell me what you saw."

Farlow's bright eyes fixed me. He paused, but if he had a question he didn't ask it.

"She's lying on her back. Just this little spot of blood on her chest; but God, her eyes are open." He stopped, licked his dry lips. "Him, he's maybe six feet away. Side of his head blown off. Right side; gun's in his right hand. What do you need this for?"

"It's the motions," I said. "What kind of gun?"

"Automatic. Didn't the police report tell you?"

"They won't let me see it."

"Jesus, don't tell Coe that. Is that normal?"

"Actually, yes. Usually you can get someone to tell you what's in it, but I rubbed the detective on the case the wrong way."

"Jim Sweeney? Everything rubs him the wrong way."

"How about Lomax?"

"You mean, Coe's theory? There's not a cop in Yonkers who wouldn't have thrown a party if they could make something stick to Lomax. Backing off wasn't something he knew how to do. They all hated him. But I don't think Sweeney any more than anyone else."

"Tell me about Lomax. Was he good?"

"Good?" Farlow looked puzzled; then he caught on. "Basketball, you mean? He was okay. He could wear better guys out, is what he could do. He'd get up for balls he couldn't reach and shoot shots he couldn't make, even after the bell. He was everywhere, both ends of the floor. Bastard never gave up."

"Did he have a future in the game?"

"Lomax? No." There was no doubt in Farlow's voice. "Eighteen years in this place, I've only seen two or three that could. Drum is the best. An NCAA school could make something out of him. Right school could get him to the NBA. Even the wrong school would get him out of here." I thought back to the concrete playground, to the eyes of the boys around the pizza-parlor table. Here, I had to admit, was a good place to get out of. "But Lomax? No."

"About the girlfriend," I said. "Had you heard anything about trouble between them?"

"No. She had a rep, you know. But all the guys seemed to think she'd quieted down since she took up with Lomax."

"Who'd she been with before?"

"Don't know."

"Do you know anyone with a reason to kill Lomax, or the girl?"

He sighed. "Look," he said. "These kids, they talk big, look bad, but these are the ones who're trying. Coe, Drum, even Lomax—still in school, still trying. Like something could work out for them." He spread his hands wide, showing me the shabby office, the defeated building, the dead-end lives. "But me, all my life I've been a sucker. My job, the way I figure, is to do my damndest to help, whenever it looks like something might. That's your job too, Smith. You're here because it makes Coe feel like a man, avenging his buddy. That helps. But you're not going to find anything. There's nothing to find."

"Okay." I stood. I was warm; the air felt stuffy, old. I wanted to be outside, where the air moved, even with a cold edge. I wanted to be where everything wasn't already over. "Thanks. I'll come back if I need anything else."

"Sure," he answered. "And come see Drum play Saturday."

SEEING THE FAMILY IS ALWAYS hard. People have a thousand different ways of responding to loss, of adjusting to their grief and the sudden new pattern of their lives. A prying stranger on a questionable mission is never welcome; there's no reason he should be.

Charles Lomax's family lived in a tan concrete project about half a mile from the high school. There were no corridors. The elevators went to outdoor walkways; the apartments opened off them. The door downstairs should have been locked, but the lock was broken, so I rode up to the third floor, picked my way through kids' bikes and folding beach chairs to the apartment at the end.

The wind and the air were cold as I waited for someone to answer my ring, but the view was good, and the apartments' front doors were painted cheerful colors. Here and there beyond the doors I could hear kids' voices yelling and the thump of music.

"Yes, can I help you?" The woman who opened the door was thin, tired-looking. She wore no makeup, and her wrists and collarbone were knobby under her shapeless sweater. Her hair, pulled back into a knot, was streaked with gray. It wasn't until I heard her clear soft voice that I realized she was probably younger than I was.

Electronic sirens came from the TV in the room behind her. She turned her head, raised her voice. "Darian, you turn that down."

The noise dropped a notch. The woman's eyes came back to me.

"Mrs. Lomax?" I said. "I'm Smith. Raymond Coe said you'd be expecting me."

"Raymond." She nodded slightly. "Come in."

She closed the door behind me. Warm cooking smells replaced the cold wind as we moved into the living room, where a boy of maybe ten and a girl a few years older were flopped on the sofa in front of the TV. An open door to the left led into a darkened bedroom. On the wall I glimpsed a basketball poster, Magic Johnson calling the play.

Charles Lomax's mother led me to a paper-strewn table in one corner of the living room, offered me a chair. "Claudine," she called to the girl on the sofa, "come and get your homework. Don't you leave your things around like that." The girl pushed herself reluctantly off the pillows. She looked me over with the dispassionate curiosity of children; then, fanning herself with her papers, she flopped onto the floor in front of the TV.

Sitting, Mrs. Lomax turned to me and waited, with the tired patience of a woman who's used to waiting.

"I'm sorry to bother you," I began. "But Raymond said you might answer some questions for me."

"What kind of questions?"

I looked over at the children, trying to judge whether the TV was loud enough to keep this discussion private. "Raymond doesn't think Charles killed himself, Mrs. Lomax."

"I know," she said simply. "He told me that. I think he just don't want to think it."

"Then you don't agree with him?"

She also looked to the children before she answered. "Raymond knew my boy better than I did. If he says someone else had more reason to kill Charles than Charles had, might be he's right. But I don't know." She shook her head slowly.

"Mrs. Lomax, did Charles have a gun?"

"I never saw one. I guess that don't mean he didn't have one."

A sudden sense of being watched made me glance toward the sofa again. My eyes caught the boy's; the girl was intent on the TV. The boy turned quickly back to the set, but not before Mrs. Lomax lifted her chin, straightened her shoulders. "Darian!" The boy didn't respond. "Darian," she said again, "you come over here."

Darian sullenly slipped off the sofa, came over, eyes watching the floor. His sister remained intent on the car chase on TV.

"Darian," his mother said, "Mr. Smith asked a question. Did you hear him?"

Hands in the pockets of his oversized jeans, the boy scowled and shrugged.

"He asked did your brother have a gun."

The boy shrugged again.

"Darian, if you know something you ain't saying, you're about to be in some serious kind of trouble. Did you ever see your brother with a gun?"

Darian kicked at a stray pencil, sent it rolling across the floor. "Yeah, I seen him."

I looked at Mrs. Lomax, then back to the boy. "Darian," I said, "do you know where he kept it?"

Without looking at me, Darian shook his head.

"You sure?" said his mother sharply.

" 'Course I'm sure."

Mrs. Lomax looked closely at him. "Darian, you know anything else you ain't saying?"

"No, 'course not," Darian growled.

"If I find you do . . ." she warned. "Okay, you go back and sit down."

Darian spun around, deposited himself on the sofa, arms hugging his knees.

I turned back to Mrs. Lomax. "Can I ask you about Ayisha?"

She shrugged.

"Did you like her?"

"Started out I did. She was smart to her friends, but she was polite to me. I remember her when she was small, too. Bright little thing. . . . But after I found out what she did, no, I didn't like her no more."

"Do you mean getting pregnant?" I asked.

She frowned, as though I were speaking a foreign language she was having trouble following. "Not the baby," she said. "The baby wasn't the problem. Though she didn't have no right to go and do that, after she knew. You got to see I blame her. She killed my son."

"Mrs. Lomax, I don't understand. According to the police, your son killed *her*, and himself."

"Oh, well, he pulled the trigger. But they was both already dead. And that innocent baby, too."

"I don't get it."

"Raymond didn't tell you?" Her eyes, fixed on mine, hardened with sudden understanding, and the realization that she was going to have to tell me herself. "She gave him AIDS."

Back on the winter street, I dropped a quarter in a pay phone, watched a newspaper skid down the walk, and waited for Raymond.

"Your buddy Charles was HIV positive," I said when he came on. "Did you know that?"

A short pause, then Raymond's voice, belligerent around the edges. "Yeah, I knew it."

"And his girlfriend, too."

"Uh-huh."

"Why didn't you tell me?"

"What difference do it make?"

"Sounds like a motive to me."

"What you talking about?"

"Hopelessness," I told him. "Fear. Not wanting to wait around to die. Not wanting to watch his son die."

"Oh, man!" Raymond snorted a laugh. "C didn't care. He say he never feel better. He tell me it gonna be years before he get sick. Not even gonna stop playing or nothing, even if it do piss Coach off. Just 'cause you got the virus don't mean you sick, you know," he pointed out with a touch of contempt. "You as ignorant as some of them 'round here."

"What does that mean?"

"Some of the homies, they nervous 'round C when they find out he got the virus. Talking about he shouldn't be coming 'round. Like Ash, don't want to play if C stay on the squad. I had to talk to that brother. But C just laugh. Say, some people ignorant. Don't pay them no mind, do what you be doing. Maybe someday I get sick, he say, but by then they have a cure."

"Goddamn, Raymond," I breathed. I stuck a cigarette in my mouth, lit it to keep from saying all the angry things I was thinking, things about youth, strength, arrogance not lasting, about consequences, about decisions closing doors behind you. I took a deep drag; it cleared my head. Not your business, Smith. Stick to what Raymond hired you for. "All right: Ayisha," I said. "Who else was she with?"

"Ayisha? She been with a lot of guys." Raymond paused. "You thinking some jealous dude gonna come after C and Ayisha 'cause they together?"

"It happens."

"Oh, man! Ain't no homie done this. Black man do it, it be straight up. Coming with this suicide bull, this some crazy white man. That why you here. See," he said, unexpectedly patient, trying to explain something to me, "C and me and the crew, we tight. Like . . ." He paused, reaching for an analogy I'd understand. "Like, you on a squad, maybe you don't like a brother, but you ain't gonna trip him when he got the ball. You got something to say to him, you go up in his face. You do what you gotta do, and you take what you gotta take."

Uh-huh, I thought. If life were like that.

"Okay, Raymond. I'll call you."

"Yeah, man. Later."

I TURNED UP THE COLLAR of my jacket; the wind was blowing harder now, off the river. You could smell the water here, the openness of it, the movement and the distance. To me there had always been an offer in that, and a promise: Elsewhere, things are different. Somewhere, not here, lives are better; and the water connects that place and this.

That offer, that promise, probably didn't mean much to Raymond and his buddies. This was what they had, and, with a clear-eyed understanding I couldn't argue with, they knew what it meant.

Except Tyrell Drum, of course. "Offer" meant something different to him, but maybe not all that different: a chance to start again, to climb out of this and be somewhere else.

I started back to my car. I was cold and hungry, and down. I'd been buying into Raymond's theory. A conspiracy, the Power bringing down a black kid because they couldn't get him legally and they knew they could get away with it. I'd bought into it because I'd wanted to. Wanted to what, Smith? Be the righteous white man, the one on their side? The part of the Power working for them? Offering them justice, this once, so the world wouldn't look so bad to them? Or so it wouldn't look so bad to you? So you could sleep at night, having done your bit for the oppressed. Terrific.

But now it was different. Lomax had a motive, and a good one, if you asked me. Teenage swagger can plunge into despair fast. One bad blood test, one scarey story about how it feels to die of AIDS: Something like that could have been enough. Especially if he really loved Ayisha. Especially if he already loved his son.

Running footsteps on the pavement behind me made me spin around, ready. The electricity in my skin subsided when I saw who it was.

"Mister, wait." The voice was small and breathless. Jacket open, pink backpack heavy over her arm, Claudine Lomax stopped on the sidewalk, caught her breath. She regarded me with suspicion.

"Zip your jacket," I said. "You'll freeze."

She glanced down, then did as she was told, pulling up her hood and tucking in her braids. She narrowed her eyes at me. "Mister, you a cop?"

"No," I said. "I'm a private detective."

"Why you come around asking questions like that?"

I thought for a moment. "Raymond asked me to. There were some things about Charles he wanted to know."

She bit her lower lip. "You know Raymond?"

"I'm working for him."

"Raymond was Charles friend."

"I know."

She nodded; that seemed to decide something for her. Looking me in the eye, she said, "You was asking Mama about Charles gun."

"That's right. I was asking where he kept it. Do you know?"

"Yeah. And so do Darian. He gonna kill me when he find out it gone. But he just a *kid*. I been crazy worried about this ever since Charles . . ." She trailed off, looking away; then she lifted her head and straightened her shoulders, her mother's gesture. Putting her backpack on the ground with exaggerated care, she pulled a paper bag from it, thrust it at me. "Here."

"What's this?" It was heavy and hard and before I looked inside I knew the answer.

"I don't want it in the house. Mama don't know nothing about it. I don't want it where Darian can get it. He think he stepping like a man, gonna take care of business. Make me laugh, but he got this. Boys like that all the time, huh?"

"Yeah," I said. "Boys are like that all the time."

"I thought Charles took it with him. Meeting some guy at night like that. But he must have—he must have had another one, huh?"

"Maybe," I said carefully. "Claudine, what do you mean, 'meeting some guy at night'?"

"Charles don't like to go do his business without his piece. But maybe it wasn't business," she said thoughtfully. " 'Cause usually he tell Ayisha stay home when he taking care of business."

I asked her, "What guy was Charles meeting? Do you know?"

"Uh-uh. He just say he gotta go meet some guy, and Ayisha say she want to come. So Charles say okay, she could keep him company. Then he tell me I better be in bed when he get back, 'cause I got a math test the next day and he gonna beat my butt if I don't pass." In a small voice she added, "I passed, too."

I opened the bag, looked without taking the gun out. It was a long-barreled .32. "Claudine, how long had Charles had this?"

"About a year."

"How did you know he had it?"

"I hear him and Tyrell hiking on each other when he got it. Tyrell say it a old-fashioned, dumb kind of piece, slow as shit. Oh." She covered her mouth with her hand. "Sorry. But that what Tyrell say."

"It's okay, Claudine. What did Charles say?"

"He laugh. He say, by the time Tyrell get his fancy piece working, he gonna find out some guy with a old-fashioned dumb piece already blowed his head off, every time."

She stared at me under the yellow streetlights, a skinny twelve-year-old kid in a jacket not warm enough for a night like this.

"Claudine," I said, "did Charles and Tyrell argue a lot?"

"I hear them trash-talking all the time," she answered. "But I don't think nothing of it. Boys do that, don't they?"

"Yeah," I said. "They do."

TYRELL, THEN. CLAUDINE TOLD ME where to go; I drove over. Tyrell Drum lived with his family in a run-down wood-frame house with a view of the river in the distance and the abandoned GM plant closer in. Towels were stuffed around the places where the warped windows wouldn't shut. The peeling paint had faded to a dull gray.

My knock was answered by a young boy with hooded eyes who left me to shut the door behind myself as I followed him in. From the room to the left I heard the canned laughter of a TV game show; from upstairs, the floor-shaking boom of a stereo. "Tyrell be in the basement," the boy told me, pointing without interest to a door under the stairs.

"Who's that?" a woman's voice called from above as I opened that door, headed down.

"Man to see Tyrell," the boy answered, and the household went about its business.

The basement was a weight room. The boiler and hot-water tank had been partitioned off into dimness. On this side of the partition were bright fluorescent lights, mats, weights, jump ropes. The smell of damp concrete mixed with the smell of sweat; the hum of the water heater was punctuated by grunts. Tyrell was on the bench, working his left biceps with what looked like sixty pounds. He lifted his eyes to me when I came down, but he didn't move his head out of position, and he finished his set. He was shirtless. His muscles were mounds under his glinting skin.

When he was done, he clanked the weights to the floor, ran a towel over his face.

"Yeah?" he said. He took in air in deep, controlled breaths.

"I want to talk about Ayisha," I said. "And Lomax."

"Go ahead." He kept his eyes on me for a few moments. Then, straightening, he picked up the weights with the other hand, started pumping. "Talk."

"She was your girl once, wasn't she?"

He smiled, didn't break his rhythm. "She been everyone's girl once."

"Maybe everyone didn't care."

"Maybe not." Nineteen, twenty. He put the weights down, left the bench, moved over to a Universal machine. He loaded it to 210, positioned himself, started working the big muscles in his thighs.

"But you did."

He stopped, looked at me. He held the weights in position while he spoke. "Yeah. I cared. I was so glad get rid of her and C at the same time I coulda went to Disney World." Slowly, in total control, he released the weights. He relaxed but didn't leave the seat, getting ready for his next set.

"What does that mean, get rid of them?"

Either he really had no idea what I was getting at, or he was a terrific actor. "Didn't have no time for her." Pump, breathe. "For him neither. C always got something going, some idea." Hold. Release, relax. "Always talking at you. Get me confused. Lost my whole last season because of him."

"The gas-station job was his idea?"

He gave me a sly grin. "Charges was dropped." He strained against the weights again. "C talking about, only way to make it be stealin' and dealin'." Pump, release, pump. "I try that, ain't no good at it. Now Coach be telling me—" pump, breathe "—say, I got a chance, a real chance. But I ain't got all the time in the world. Got to do it now, you understand?"

He looked at me. I didn't respond.

"C, he don't never shut up. Don't give a man no chance to think." Hold, release, relax. He swung his legs off the machine, picked up the towel again, wiped his face. "C don't like to think. Don't like it quiet. Dude get nervous if horns ain't honking and sirens going by." He laughed. "Surprise me him and Ayisha end up where they do."

"Meaning?"

"C don't never go to the park. They got nothing there but trees and birds, he say. What I'm gonna do with them?"

"His sister says he was going to meet someone that night."

Tyrell shrugged. He put his legs back in position, started another set.

"And that was it?" I said. "You were through with Lomax and his ideas? You weren't helping him take care of business anymore?"

This time he ran the set straight through before he answered. When he was done, he looked at me, breathing deeply.

"Coach be talking at me, I'm seeing college, the NBA, hotels and honeys and dudes carrying my suitcase. C up in my face, I'm looking at the inside of Rikers. Now what you think I'm gonna do?"

"And that was what you thought of when Lomax took up with Ayisha?"

"Damn sure. They both out my face now, I can take care my business."

"Your business," I mused. "You have a gun, right? An automatic. Can I see it?"

"What the hell for?"

"Lomax was a revolver man, wasn't he?" I asked conversationally. "He had a .32."

Tyrell shook his head in mild disbelief. "Man, Wyatt Earp coulda carried that piece."

"Why do you carry yours, Tyrell?"

"Now why the hell you think I carry mine?" He scowled. "You some kind of detective, can't figure out why a man got to be strapped 'round here?"

"Is it like that around here?" I asked softly. "A man has to have a gun?"

"God*damn*!" Tyrell exploded. "You think I like that? Watching my back just whenever I'm walking? Can't be going here, can't be going there, you got beef or your homies got beef and someone out to get you for it, go to school, everybody packing, just in case. You think I like that?" A sharp pulse throbbed in his temples; his eyes were shining and bitter. "Man, you can forget about it! I'm gonna make it, man. I'm gonna be all that. C, he got this idea, that idea, don't never think about what come next, what gonna happen 'cause of what he do. I tell him, you got Ayisha, now get out my face, leave me be. I got things to do."

His hard eyes locked on mine. The stereo, two floors up, sent down a pounding, recurring shudder that surrounded us.

"Tyrell," I said, "I'd like to see your gun."

For a moment, no reaction. Then a slow smile. He sauntered over to a padlocked steel box on the other side of the room. He ran the combination, creaked the top open, lifted out a .357 Coonan automatic. Wordlessly he handed it to me.

"How long have you had this?" I asked.

"Maybe a year."

"You sure you didn't just get it?"

He looked at me without an answer. Then, climbing the stairs to where he could reach the door, he opened it and yelled, "Shaun!" He paused; then again, "Shaun! Haul your ragged ass down here!"

The boy with the hooded eyes appeared in the doorway. "You calling me, Tyrell?" he asked tentatively.

Tyrell moved aside, motioned him downstairs. The boy, with an unsure look at me, started down. He walked like someone trying not to take up too much room.

"Shaun, this my piece?"

The boy looked at the gun I held out. "Yeah," he said. "I guess."

"Don't be guessing," Tyrell said. "This my piece, or ain't it?"

The boy gave Tyrell a nervous look, then peered more closely at the gun, still without touching it. "Yeah," he said. "It got that thing, here."

"What thing?" I asked. I looked where the boy pointed. A wide scrape marred the shiny stock.

Tyrell said, "Shaun, where that come from?"

Shaun answered without looking at Tyrell. "I dropped it."

"When?"

"Day you got it."

"What happen?"

"You mean, what you do?"

"Yeah."

The kid swallowed. "You be cursing at me and you smack me."

"Broke your nose, didn't I?"

The kid nodded.

"So you remember that day pretty good, huh?"

"Yeah."

"When was that?"

"About last year."

"You touched it since?"

"No, Tyrell." The kid looked up quickly.

"Good. Now get the hell out of here."

Shaun scuttled up the stairs and closed the door behind him.

"See?" Tyrell, smiling, took the gun from me. "My heat. Had it a year. How about that?"

"That's great, Tyrell," I said. "It must be great to be so tough. Two more questions. Where were you the night Lomax and Ayisha died?"

"Me?" Tyrell answered, still smiling, looking at the gun in his hand. "I was here."

"Can you prove that?"

"Depends. You could see if my two cousins remember. I went to bed early. Coach say discipline make the difference. You got to be able to do what need to be done, whether you want to or not."

"Uh-huh. You're a model citizen, Tyrell. One more thing. Did you know Lomax was HIV positive?"

Tyrell shrugged, locked his gun back in the box.

"Did it bother you? Friend of yours, with a disease like that?"

"Uh-uh," he said. "Don't got no time to worry about C. He got his troubles, I got mine."

I DROVE SOUTH, FOUND BROADWAY, stopped at a tavern near the Bronx line. It was a half-empty place, the kind where dispirited old-timers nurse watery drinks and old grudges. In a scarred booth I lit a cigarette, worked on a Bud. I thought about Raymond, about the simple desire to do something, to try to help. About wanting justice, wanting what's right.

Of course, that meant so many things. To Sweeney it could mean taking a taunting, slippery drug dealer out of the picture. To Tyrell Drum it could mean getting rid of a smooth-talking, dangerous distraction. To Lomax himself, it might have meant having the last laugh: not cheating death, but choosing it, choosing your time and your way and your pain. None of these kids had ever had a lot of choices. This was one Lomax could have given himself.

But I didn't like it.

I had a couple of reasons, but the biggest was what Raymond had instinctively felt: Lomax wasn't the type.

I hadn't known Lomax, but the picture I'd gotten of him was consistent, no matter where it came from. Suicide is for when you give up. Lomax never gave up. Taunting cops. Trying to fast-talk Tyrell into his kind of life. Going up for balls he couldn't reach and shooting shots he couldn't make. That's what the coach said.

Even after the bell.

I lit another cigarette, seeing in my mind the asphalt playground in the fading light, watching the kids charge and jump, hearing the sound of the pounding ball and of their shouts. I saw one fall—I knew now it was Raymond—roll to his feet, try to shake off the sting of the scrape on his hand. Then, immediately, he was back in the game.

Even after the bell.

Suddenly I was cold. Suddenly I knew.

Wanting justice, wanting to help.

There was something else that could mean.

THE NEXT DAY, LATE AFTERNOON again. The same gray river, the same cold wind.

It would have been pointless to go earlier. I would have been guessing, then, where to look; at this hour, I knew.

I'd made one phone call, to Sweeney, just to check what I already was sure of. He gave me what I wanted, and then he gave me a warning.

"I'm giving you this because I know you'll get it one way or another. But listen to me, Smith: Whatever road you're heading down, it's a dead end. The first complaint I hear, you'll get a look up close and personal at the smallest cell I can find. Do I make myself clear?"

I thanked him. The rest of the day, I worked on the Beethoven. It was getting better, slowly, slowly.

Yonkers West loomed darker, bigger, more hostile than before. At the front door I greeted the guard.

"You were here yesterday." He grinned. "Go on, tell me you're not a scout."

"Practice in session?" I asked.

"Uh-huh. Go on ahead. I'm sure Coach won't mind."

I wasn't. But I went.

The gym echoed with the thump of the basketball on the maple. The whole team, starters and bench, was out on the floor, practicing a complicated high-low post play. They were rotating through it, changing roles so that each man would understand it in his gut, know how each position felt; but in play, the point would be to get the ball to the big man. To Tyrell. As many times as the play was called, that's how it would end up. Tyrell shooting, Tyrell carrying the team's chances, carrying everyone's hopes.

Coach Farlow was standing on the sideline. He watched the play as they practiced it, following everyone's moves, but especially Tyrell's. I walked the short aisle between the bleachers, came and stood next to him.

He glanced at me, then turned his eyes back to his players. "Hi," he said. "Come to watch practice?"

"No," I said. "I came to talk."

He looked over at me again, then blew the whistle hanging around his neck. "All right, you guys!" The sweating players stopped, stood wiping their faces with their shirts, catching their breath. He rattled off two lists of names. Four guys headed for the sidelines; two teams formed on the court. Raymond, on one end of the floor, caught my eye. I nodded non-committally. The others looked my way, curious, but snapped their attention back to Farlow when he shouted again.

"Okay, let's go," he called. "Hawkins, take the tip. You and Ford call it."

One of the guys who'd been on his way off the court chased down the ball. Another trotted over to take the coach's whistle. The ball was tossed up in the center of the circle; the game began.

"You let them call games often?" I asked Farlow, as he stood beside me, following their movements with his sharp blue eyes.

"It's good for them. Forces them to see what's going on. Makes them take responsibility. Most of them get pretty good at it."

I said, "I'll bet Lomax wasn't."

"Lomax? He used to tick them all off. He'd call fouls on everyone, right and left. Just to throw his weight around."

"Did you stop him?"

Farlow watched Raymond go for a lay-up and miss it. Tyrell snatched the rebound, sank it easily. Farlow said, "The point is for them to find out what they're made of. What each other's made of. Doesn't help if I stop them."

"Besides," I said, "you couldn't stop Lomax, could you?"

This time his attention turned to me, stayed there. "What do you mean?"

"No one could ever stop Lomax from doing whatever he wanted. No matter how dangerous it was, to him or anyone else. He wouldn't stop playing, would he?"

"What?"

"That was it, wasn't it? He had AIDS and he wouldn't stop playing."

A whistle blew. Silence, then the slap of sneakers on wood, the thump of the ball as the game went on. Farlow's eyes stayed on me.

"You couldn't talk him out of it," I said. "You couldn't drop him, because he was too good. You'd have had to explain why, and the law protects people from that kind of thing. He'd have been back on the court and you'd have been out of a job.

"But you couldn't let him keep playing. That could have ruined everything."

Shouts came from the far end of the court as Tyrell stole a pass, broke down the floor, and dunked it before anyone from either team got near him.

"Could have ruined what?" Farlow asked in a tight, quiet voice.

"You're going through the motions," I said. "You know I have it. But all right, if you want to do that."

I watched the game, not Farlow, as I continued. "If Lomax had stayed on the team there might have been no season. Some of his own buddies didn't want to play with him. Guys get hurt in this game. They bleed, they spit, they sweat. The other guys were afraid.

"That's what happened to Magic Johnson: He couldn't keep playing after everyone knew he had AIDS because guys on other teams were afraid to play against him. Magic had class. He didn't force it. He retired.

"But that wasn't Lomax's way, was it? Lomax felt fine and he was going to play. And if it got out he had AIDS his own teammates might have rebelled. So would the teams you play against. The whole season would have collapsed.

"That's what you were afraid of. Losing the season. Losing Drum's last chance."

We stared together down the court, to where a kid was getting set to take a foul shot.

"Lomax killed himself," Farlow said, harshly and slowly. "He took his gun and shot his girl and shot himself."

I said, "I have his gun."

"He had more than one. He bragged about it."

"Maybe," I said. "Maybe not. But the one I have is a revolver. Guys who like revolvers—I'm one—like them because they're dependable. You can bury a revolver in the mud for a month and it'll fire when you pull it out. Lomax was like that about this gun. There've been times when I've had to carry an automatic, and it always makes me nervous. Even if I owned one, it's not the gun I'd take if I were going out to shoot myself."

Farlow said nothing, watching his kids, watching the game.

"Then there are the guys who like automatics," I said. "They're fast. They're powerful. That's what you have, isn't it?"

"Me?" Farlow tried to laugh. "You're kidding. A gun?"

"An automatic," I said. "Same make and model as the one that killed Lomax and Ayisha. Drum got me thinking about it. He said everyone around here was packing. I started to wonder who 'everyone' was. I checked your permit with Sweeney. He told me about it, and said if I harassed you he'd throw me in jail. Does he know?"

The ball was knocked out of bounds, near us. The officials and players organized themselves, resumed the game. The ball flew out again almost immediately. Another whistle blew, play began again.

"No," Farlow said quietly.

We watched together in silence for a while. Some of the ball handling was sloppy, but the plays were smart, and every player played flat out, giving the game everything he had.

"Not every coach can get this from his players," I said.

Farlow asked, "How did you know?"

"Little things. They all clicked together. The gun. The fact that Lomax didn't like the park."

"Didn't like the park?" Farlow said. "A guy might pick a place he doesn't like, to die in."

"Sure. But his coach wouldn't think to go looking for him there, unless he had some reason to think he might be there."

Farlow didn't answer. He glanced at the clock on the gym wall; then he stepped onto the court, clapped his hands, and bellowed, "All right, you guys! Looking good. Showers! Stay and wait. I'll talk to you afterwards."

The kid with the whistle brought it back to the coach; the kid with the ball sent it Farlow's way with a bounce pass. Raymond raised his eyebrows as he went by on his way to the locker room. I shook my head.

Farlow watched them go. When the door swung shut behind them he stayed unmoving, as though he were still watching, still seeing something.

"One kid," he said, not talking to me. "One chance. Year after year, you tear your heart out for these kids and they end up in the gutter. Then you get one kid with a way out, one chance. Drum's ready, but he's weak. Not physically. But he can't keep his head in the game. If he loses this season too, there'll be nothing left. He'll hold up another damn gas station, or something. It has to be now."

"Lomax was eighteen," I said. "Ayisha was seventeen. She was pregnant."

"They were dead!" The coach's eyes flashed. "They were dead already. How many years do you think they were going to have? Baby born with AIDS, it wouldn't live through Drum's pro career."

"You did them a favor?"

He flinched. "No." His voice dropped. "That's not what I mean. But Drum—so many people are waiting for this, Smith. And they were already dead."

I needed a cigarette. I lit one up; the coach didn't try to stop me.

"You asked him to meet you at the park?"

He nodded. "In this weather, there's no one there. I knew he didn't like it there, but . . ." He didn't finish.

"But you were the coach."

"I knew Lomax. He'd never let me see he was nervous. Afraid. It never occurred to me he'd bring her along."

"For company," I told him. "That's what his little sister said."

"I almost didn't—didn't do it, when I saw she was there. I tried one more time to talk him out of it. Told him I'd get his academic grades raised so he'd be sure to graduate. Told him I'd get him a job. Told him Drum needed him to quit."

"What did he say?"

The coach looked across the gym. "He said if scouts were coming down to look at Drum, maybe they were interested in point guards, too."

He brought his eyes back to me. "It was the only way, Smith."

"No," I said.

I smoked my cigarette. Farlow looked down at his hands, tough with years of balls and blackboards.

"What are you going to do?" he asked. "Will you tell Sweeney?"

"Sweeney won't hear it. I have no hard evidence. To him this case is closed."

"Then what?" he asked. His eyes lit faintly with something like hope.

I looked toward the door the players had disappeared through. "I have a client," I said.

"You'll tell Coe?"

I crushed the cigarette against the stands, dropped the butt back in the pack. "Or you will."

We stood together, wordless. "You know what's the worst part?" he finally said.

"What?"

"Coe's twice the man the rest of them are. Drum's a bully, Lomax was a creep. Ash is a coward. But Coe, he's tough but not mean. He can tell right from wrong and he doesn't let his ego get in the way. But there's nothing I can do for him. I can't help him, Smith. But I can help Drum."

"Yesterday," I said, "you told me I was here because avenging his buddy made Raymond feel like a man. And that that helped."

He stared at me. He made a motion toward the door where the players had gone, but he stopped.

"I'll wait for Raymond to call me," I said. "I'll give him a few days. Then I'll call him."

I looked once more around the gym, then walked the short aisle between the stands, leaving the coach behind.

*   *   *

I WAS AT THE PIANO the next afternoon when Raymond called. No small talk: "Coach told me," he said.

I shut the keyboard, pulled a cigarette from my pocket. "What did you do?"

"First, I couldn't believe it. Stared at him like an idiot. Coach, man! You know?"

I did know; I said nothing.

"Then I feel like killing him."

I held my breath. "But?"

"But I hear C in my head," Raymond said. "Laughing. 'What so damn funny, homey?' I ask him. 'This the guy burned you.' C keep laughing, in my head. He say, 'For Tyrell, brother? This about the funniest thing ever.' Just laughing and laughing."

"What did you do?"

"Slammed out of there, to go and think. See, I was stuck. What you gonna do, Ray, I be asking myself. Go to the cops? Give me a break."

"If you want to do that," I said, "I'll see it through with you."

"No," he said. "Ain't my way. Another thing, I could do Coach myself; but that ain't my way neither. So what I'm gonna do, just let him walk away? He done my main man; got to pay for that. Got to pay. But in my head, C just laughing. 'For Tyrell, man?' And then I know what he mean. And I know I don't got to do nothing."

"Why not?" I asked.

" 'Cause Tyrell, he been with Ayisha before C."

It took a second, then it hit.

"Jesus," I said.

"Yeah," Raymond agreed. "What Coach done, he done to get Tyrell his shot. But Tyrell ain't gonna have no shot."

No shot. No pro career, no college years. Two murders. A lifetime of hard-won trust, everything thrown away for nothing. Tyrell might be able to avoid going public, might be able to keep his mouth shut the way Lomax hadn't; people might not know, at first. But the virus was inexorable. It would get Tyrell before Tyrell had a chance to make everyone's dreams come true.

"Raymond," I said, "I'm sorry."

"Man," he said, "so am I."

There wasn't anything more. I told Raymond to keep in touch; he laughed shortly and we both knew why. When we hung up I stood at the window for a while. After the sky turned from purple to gray, after the promise faded, I pulled on my jacket, went over to the 4th Street courts, and watched the kids play basketball under the lights.

Sarah Shankman started writing mystery fiction under the pen name Alice Storey, to distinguish those books from her more mainstream work. However, those novels proved so successful that she now writes all of her fiction under her own name. Her series character is Samantha Adams, an investigative reporter in Atlanta and the subject of six novels so far. Currently she has started another series, this one based in Nashville. Her latest book is *I Still Miss My Man, But My Aim Is Getting Better*. In "Real Life" she puts an excellent twist on the saying, "truth is stranger than fiction."

Real Life
SARAH SHANKMAN

If there were a space more deadly than Room 1517, 100 Centre Street, New York, New York, Clare Meacham didn't want to know about it.

She'd been sitting in the dreadful room for two hours, and her bones were overdone linguine. Her neck could barely support her curly head. The room had sucked off what energy she'd packed in with her—which had been precious little, God knows, on this steamy rotten morning. A month into the heat wave of the century, Manhattan had all the appeal of an overripe dinosaur carcass.

Besides which, since David dumped her, Clare had been mightily depressed and hadn't been sleeping worth a damn. She yawned now, and Room 1517 seemed to open its jaws in answer around her. The giant municipal maw filled with long rows of dark blue cushioned armchairs. Cream-colored walls, splotched as an adolescent's complexion. Cheap particle-board wainscoting. White acoustic ceiling tile mushed whispers into a slow steady hiss. On the floor, patched beige linoleum squares cheated at hopscotch.

Dust motes floated in the refrigerated air, recycled, no doubt, thought Clare, through the dead dinosaur's respiratory system. Yes, the very air itself was dank and dangerously gelatinous. Teeming, one felt, with tuberculosis, cholera, hantavirus, Ebola. (Good. Maybe she'd contract one of those and die a spectacular lingering death, and then David would be sorry.) God knows, the fluorescent lighting, which cast a greenish pallor over the room's captives, gave them the look of disease.

273

The two hundred and seventy-five prospective jurors slumped and lumped in the blue armchairs.

Oh, God, could it be borne, their faces asked, that this was only the first, the number one, the maidenhead of their ten endless days of jury duty? Ten, that is, if an actual trial didn't glue them even longer into some angry crouch of deliberation.

Clare shifted in her seat, careful not to upset the notebook computer perched on her lap. Thirty-nine, a tall, languorously attractive brunette despite the dark circles of despair beneath her eyes, Clare wore brown woven leather loafers, a short khaki skirt, a red-and-white striped shirt, and gold hoop earrings. Her long, dark, curly hair was pulled back off her face with a tortoise barrette. She was as presentable as she could bring herself to be under the circumstances.

The circumstances being (a) a broken heart and (b) the fact that this little trip down the lane of civic responsibility was most certainly going to cost her her livelihood. Her inevitable financial ruin and bankruptcy proceedings could later be traced back to this precise and fetid A.M. Not only was she not in the mood, but Clare could not, goddammit, *afford* to be on jury duty.

Try telling that to Norman O. Goodman, New York county clerk of court. Or any of his stiff-necked minions. Did they care? Ho ho. *That* was a good one.

The freshly blondined woman in the appalling gold-braided fuchsia suit behind the desk in Room 105 or 106 or whatever it was downstairs, where Clare had gone two weeks earlier to beg for just one more reprieve from her civic responsibility, had said, "Forget it, Ms. Meacham. No more excuses, no more deferments. We, the puffed-up jealous, self-righteous, civilly employed we, hereby sentence you to jury duty. Or else."

That had been the peroxided bitch's final word. On the exact same day that Arnie, Clare's producer, had called her in and said, "The ratings go up, Clare. Or else."

It was the O. J. trial that had set in motion the avalanche of the viewer share of *Real Life*, the soap opera on which Clare was head writer.

"Court TV is a fucking vampire," Arnie had said. "We've got to jazz *Real Life* way up, Clare. Pick up the pace. Add some sizzle. Give those sofa tuberettes some blood and guts along with their romance. *Real Life's* gotta be more like real life. Grittier. Sexier. Meaner. Hotter."

Then his terrible last words. "The whole story line has to be in overdrive in the next three weeks—even if you have to write ninety-six hours a day."

That had been two weeks ago, and Clare, bleak and blue, hadn't written a word. Now, with one week left to save her ass, here she was locked in Room 1517. Squashed cheek-by-jowl with almost three hundred of her fellow Gothamites of every race, nationality, and socioeconomic category.

Earlier this morning, in the long line behind the security check, the sticky crowd had made nervous jokes about knives and guns and bombs, all the while sussing one another out with the quick once-over that is second nature to every New Yorker: assessing caste, class, tailoring, and degree of homicidal impulse in a millisecond. Then, after they'd received their guides to restaurants in neighboring Chinatown and Little Italy and had watched the video on the ins and outs of jury duty, they'd filed into Room 1517 and the sea of dark blue chairs.

But inevitably, the stew of strangers had settled into the reality of their task.

It was theirs to wait.

And wait.

And wait.

They'd looked around, then, okay, damn it, with a collective sigh they'd opened their briefcases, backpacks, purses, and bags and unearthed newspapers, magazines, books they'd been meaning to read, find-a-word puzzles, needlework, the paperwork that had long been shoved aside. They'd clamped on Walkmen. Clare spotted two other people, both Wall Street types, bent over laptop computers. A young Hispanic woman in the last row, next to the windows, fiddled with the antenna of a tiny television. Here and there, a couple of people talked quietly. And fully a third of the room lurched and listed and snored and snuffled through mid-morning naps.

Clare stared accusingly at her computer's blank screen. Her brain was frozen. It was totally quiet in there. Except for a constant interior refrain. *Nobody loves you. Never will again.* That was the main melody.

Then, winding in around it, a wailing glissando: *Why is it my job to turn the tide of thirty-odd years of sappy story lines about soggy romance, all slow as molasses? Why do I have to make the shift from slow-rising yeast to Pop Tarts? Horse-and-buggy to the Concorde? Whalebone corsets to Madonna and her jet-nose tits?*

Because they said so, that's why. Because they paid her the big bucks to swallow what "art" she might have once fancied herself possessed of, zip her lip, and deliver whatever crap they demanded. On time and in the flavor of the moment. No matter what her personal problems. Who gave a shit about them?

The cursor on the small green screen before her blinked. *Write, Clare. Suck it up. Get your ass in gear. Take a deep breath. Push some oxygen in and out. Get the old gray matter moving.*

Could she do that? Maybe.

It wasn't as if she didn't know these characters. These silly people, most of whom she'd inherited from her predecessor, who had, incidentally, hanged herself in the bathroom of her East Hampton beach house one fine morning two summers earlier. Just down the lane from Martha Stewart's house. Her death had made the six o'clock local news. Clare wondered, would *her* suicide play as well?

But she digressed. Well, Christ, who wouldn't? What the hell else was there to do with Dirk and Carol and Josh and Trish and Richard and Paula, the three main couples of *Real Life*? They were such stupid people with such stupid problems. *Slow* stupid problems. Problems that moved at the pace of a banana slug (or a soap) and were about as fascinating.

No, actually, a banana slug was a hell of a lot more interesting than the ailing marriage of Trish, played by a busty brunette with the voice of a mosquito, and Josh, the simpering nephew of Arnie the producer, who couldn't act his way out of a damp Kleenex.

Clare couldn't even *think* about Richard and Paula, her whiny preppie couple.

So she'd have to start with Carol and Dirk—C for Clare and D for David, get it? Ms. Clare Meacham Herself and her erstwhile lover, Dr. David Teller. Yes, Carol and Dirk were loosely based on her own pathetic life.

"Excuse me."

Clare jumped. It was the woman to her left. An attractive middle-aged black woman in a navy business suit, good pumps, substantial gold jewelry. "Do you have change for a dollar? I need to call my office."

Clare checked her wallet, handed the woman three quarters and two dimes. "I'll have to owe you a nickel."

The woman's smile was warm. "Nope, I owe you." And she headed off to the phone room.

She'd be a while. Clare had already checked it out: three machines vending poisonous substances, a water fountain, and more of those damned blue chairs in which to wait for the four phones. Four phones for nearly three hundred New Yorkers, and no cellulars allowed? You might as well have cut off their oxygen.

Clare stared back at the blank screen. Okay. Dirk and Carol, step up, please, front and center. In *Real Life*, they'd weathered many problems, such as the time when Dirk, who was a plastic surgeon, had been called away to Wisconsin for two months to reconstruct the faces of an entire family of protected witnesses (as had David) and had strayed with a Scandinavian scrub nurse (which Clare had suspected). Then there'd been Carol's automobile accident and the coma and the long while after she'd come out of it when she thought Dirk was an extraterrestrial.

Now, lagging about six weeks behind Clare's real life, Dirk had just leaned over a table in an Italian restaurant and told Carol he was calling off their engagement. Because, well, he was marrying someone else. Carol had burst into tears and bolted out of the restaurant. (As had Clare.)

"What are you writing?"

Again, Clare started. This time, her interrogator was to her left, a very short man sitting two chairs over. About her age, late thirties, he was nicely turned out in fine fawn-colored trousers, a T-shirt in chocolate, a handsome blue, brown, and beige jacket. Armani probably. His dark, clean profile reminded her of David.

David. Clare's stomach flip-flopped.

Meanwhile, the gorgeous little babe was waiting.

What was she writing?

Nothing. Not a word. She was simply staring at her screen. Listening to the computer's tiny hum, much quieter than the terror gnawing at her intestines. The hideous, bright yellow fear that she couldn't do it. Couldn't, couldn't, couldn't revamp *Real Life*. They'd fire her ass, she'd be a bag lady within a year. Reeking of urine. Scratching at herself. Begging for alms, from real people, with real jobs, like she used to be. And then, for sure, no one would ever love her again. She'd die all alone, her grave in a potter's field dug by inmates from Riker's Island.

"A script," she finally said.

"A screenplay?" The dapper little man slipped one chair closer.

"No." She shook her head.

What did this guy want? This was New York, for Christ's sake, where strangers might ask you where you bought your shoes—and how much you paid for them. But your business? They stayed out of it.

He smiled brightly and extended a hand. "I'm Vinnie. I'm in the restaurant business, but I'm starting to write screenplays on the side. I figure, hey, everybody else is."

"I write for a soap."

Usually, when she said that, eyebrows rose. Wasn't she prostituting herself? Why didn't she write novels? Publish arty stories in little magazines? She'd done both. She wasn't cut out for the life of the starving artist.

But Vinnie said, "Cool." Then he said, "Could I borrow a quarter till after lunch? I don't have any change, and I need to make a phone call."

What did she look like, a bank? "I think I gave all my change to somebody else a few minutes ago," she said. But then she dug in her purse and came up with a shiny new quarter that had been hiding in a corner.

But before Vinnie could make his call, an officer of the court sauntered from behind the tall wide desk at the front of the room and began calling names from the summons slips he pulled at random from a bingolike contraption. They were to answer to their names, then follow him to a courtroom where *they* would be judged on their worthiness to judge another.

Juan Reyes. Kashonda Smallwood. Gillian Holch. Duncan McKenzie III. Ellen Bradley. Yolanda Ramirez. Estelle Krim. Angela Wong. Jacqi Albano. Rita Sitnick. Vincent Gallo.

"That's me." Vinnie waved at the clerk.

Clare Meacham.

Clare groaned and raised a hand. She *couldn't* get stuck on a jury. Not now. Please, God.

The woman Clare had given change to reentered the room just as the last of the forty names was being called. *Wilma Paris.* "Oh, Lord," she cried. "Wouldn't you know? And my boss just said he's going to kill me if I don't get my butt back to the office."

BEHIND THE JUDGE, HUGE LETTERS spelled out "IN OD WE TRUST."

Vinnie pointed at the words, whispered to Clare, "Kind of makes you wonder, doesn't it?" They were two of the twelve seated in the juror's box, the remainder of their panel of forty spread across the spectators' seats.

Frowsy-haired Judge Rabinowitz frowned over her horn rims at Vinnie. Their instructions had been to listen up, no eating, no sleeping, no talking. The judge had just finished introducing the prosecution, the defense, and the defendant, and outlining the bare bones of the case.

The defendant—a big handsome black kid, about twenty—was charged with attempting to hold up a Korean grocer. He'd purportedly used a gun: the plaintiff, a short but muscular man, had answered with a whirling baseball bat.

This was the stuff of real life, thought Clare. *This* was material. How would it work? Dirk follows Carol out of the restaurant. She runs into the Korean store. They're caught smack in the middle of the holdup. Carol grabs up a tray of hot sweet-and-sour pork from the steam table, heaves it at the robber . . .

The judge had chosen to conduct the voir dire herself, questioning the twelve citizens in the box:

Do any of you know me, the defendant, the plaintiff, either of the prosecution or the defense attorneys, or any of the witnesses I've just named?

How?

Do you know the area, Broadway between Bleecker and Third, where the incident took place?

What is your knowledge of that site?

Are you related to any law enforcement officers, and, if so, how?

What is the nature of your employment?

What magazines do you subscribe to?

Have you ever been the victim of a street crime?

Have you ever been the victim of a crime involving a gun?

Wilma Paris, the advertising account exec to whom Clare had given change, had a brother who was a cop, and she said it was her belief that cops lied as much as anybody else.

Vinnie Gallo said he himself, as a customer, had been held up at gunpoint in a Korean store. By a kid. With a gun. (Clare wasn't sure she believed him.)

Clare declared that she herself didn't know anyone in the courtroom. She lived in the Village and had walked by the crime scene many times but wasn't certain if she'd ever stopped in. She was not related to any police officers, nor did she know any personally. She was the head writer on *Real Life*. She subscribed to the *New Yorker*. *New York, Saveur, Soap Digest*, and *Conde Nast Traveler*. She had lived in Manhattan eighteen years and had never been the victim of any crime whatsoever.

(Unless you counted having her heart run over and squashed flat by one Dr. David Teller, who was not a defendant here today.)

At the end of the questioning, Clare was excused with no explanation, along with Vinnie and Wilma. Thank you. Good-bye.

BACK IN ROOM 1517, THE CHAIRS where Clare, Vinnie, and Wilma were sitting had been taken. Clare scanned the room. There was an empty bloc of seats back toward the windows, near the young Hispanic woman watching TV. She headed for them. She *had* to get to work.

But Vinnie and Wilma were close on her heels.

"I can't believe they didn't take you," said Vinnie. "Me, that's one thing, but you? You're perfect, except for that part about living in Manhattan for years and never even having your purse snatched. That made you sound like a liar."

Wilma leaned across him, interrupting. "*I* want to ask you about *Real Life*. My mom is a *huge* fan. She'll be so excited when I tell her I met you. You really make up all those stories?"

"I'm afraid so." Clare grimaced. *When I can. When I don't have writer's block. When I'm not scared to death. Depressed. Sleep-deprived. On jury duty.*

"She's writing right here." Vinnie pointed at the computer in Clare's hand.

"I don't know how you do it," said Wilma. "I'm an account exec. Not a creative bone in my body."

"Mine, either," said Clare.

"Come on." Vinnie laughed. "You're just being modest."

"No, I'm not." And then it just spilled out, the whole nine yards of her pathetic tale. How she was upset about her personal life and hadn't been sleeping well. How she had only a week left to revamp *Real Life*, to make it hotter than O. J., bigger than real life. How she didn't have a clue.

"You can do it," said Vinnie. "I know you can."

"I don't think so." Clare shook her head.

Just then, an officer stood from behind the long desk. "Lunch break," he announced. "Be back at two-thirty. Did anyone not get a list of restaurants in Chinatown and Little Italy?"

The whole room stampeded for the door.

Except Julia, the young Hispanic woman in the row behind them, who was plugged into the earphones of her little TV. "Jesus!" she screamed. "I can't believe it! Shoot the fucker!"

Mid-flight, people stopped and stared.

"Shoot him! Don't let him get away with that!"

The officer started toward her.

"*Kill* the son of a bitch!" Julia shouted.

"Miss?" The clerk tapped her arm. "You're going to have to quiet down. And you can't use that kind of language in here."

"What?" Julia jumped and jerked out her earphones. "Was I loud? I'm sorry. But I get so excited at my program. That Dirk! He's such a . . ." She caught herself. ". . . bad person. I can't believe Carol lets him get away with that . . . stuff!"

"Oh, Christ!" Clare slapped a hand to her mouth. "She's talking about *Real Life*."

Vinnie grabbed both Clare and Wilma, then leaned over Julia. "Miss? You wanna go to lunch with us? My treat."

VINNIE TOOK THEM TO A restaurant where he was obviously known, Luigi's on Mulberry Street. Restaurants were the only thing that remained Italian about Little Italy. The old families had long since moved to Staten Island, and the real estate was being swallowed up by the Chinese. But that didn't stop the tourists, especially the ones who imagined gangland hits over every plate of meatballs and spaghetti.

The food at Luigi's, old-fashioned red-sauce Italian, was good enough to please the most demanding mobster. Vinnie had ordered a giant antipasto platter for the table. "Have some more ooppa," he urged, pouring the Chianti. "And peppers. These mushrooms Luigi said he smuggled in from Italy last week. Finish them up. Then we'll get down to work."

"Work?" asked Julia, her eyes big as she looked up from her plate. It was clear this meal was a special treat for her. She was very impressed by Luigi's. Not to mention Vinnie.

"Sure," said Vinnie. "We're going to write Clare's story. *Real Life* is getting itself fixed right here. Right now. At this table."

Clare almost choked. Just as the food and the wine and the company were beginning to make her feel a little human, Vinnie had to bring *that* up.

"You think we can't?" Vinnie reared back in his chair. " 'Cause we ain't professional writers? I'm telling you, we can, and we will. We are the people. The people who *know* about real life. We are your friggin' audience you don't ever give no respect."

Clare raised her glass. "Hear, hear."

"I DON'T LIKE THE IDEA of using the stickup in the Korean store," said Julia, sipping her coffee.

"Why not?" Wilma asked.

"The stickup is real," insisted Clare.

"It'd be more real if somebody got killed. In my neighborhood, every time there's a stickup, somebody gets killed."

"So who do you pick to die?" Vinnie signaled for more grappa. "You got the black kid. You got the Korean. You got Carol and Dirk."

"Carol," said Julia.

Clare put down her glass. "Why Carol?"

" 'Cause she's a wimp," Julia said. "Take today's show. Dirk tells her he's marrying another woman, what does she do? She just leaves the table. Carol makes me sick."

"Oh, really?" said Clare, a little defensive. "What do you want her to do? Kill him, like you were saying back upstairs?" Clare pointed a thumb in the direction of 100 Centre Street and the courthouse. At least she thought it was in that direction. She was getting pretty loaded.

"Yeah," said Julia. "Kill him."

"How? When? Where?" asked Wilma.

"How? Pick up a knife from the table and stab the sucker. When? As soon as he said he was dumping her for another chick. Where? In the gut."

Clare thought about that. How would that have gone down, the two of them in Bar Pitti having dinner when David had made his announcement. He had ordered the veal. There was a sharp knife at his place. It certainly would have been possible. Of course, she'd be in Riker's now. Or wherever it was they locked up female murderers. The Tombs, maybe, right next door to 100 Centre.

"If she'd killed him in the restaurant," said Wilma, "then they wouldn't be in the Korean store together."

"Screw the Korean store," said Julia.

Clare said, "Look, folks, we can't go back to the scene in the restaurant and do it differently. It aired today, remember? Then there are three more weeks of shows already in the can. That's where we have to pick up."

"Okay, so what happened after Carol ran out of the restaurant?" asked Julia.

Clare could tell from Julia's tone that she was thinking, *I bet not much*.

And she was right. "But it's not my fault," Clare insisted. "This was before they wanted the show to pick up speed. To be more like real life."

"Let's hear it," said Wilma.

"Dirk's ex-wife, Molly, who has always hoped that Dirk would come back to her, is shattered when she hears that Dirk is marrying yet *another* woman. She flips out and has to be institutionalized. She ends up in the hospital where David does most of his cosmetic surgery, and she rages in while he's in the middle of doing somebody's face. The patient, who is Richard of Richard and Paula, has been in a terrible skiing accident and ended up with no nose."

"Now, *that's* interesting," said Vinnie.

"Who's David?" asked Wilma. "You said David was performing the surgery."

Clare blushed. "I meant Dirk. David's my real ex-boyfriend. The real plastic surgeon."

"And did David dump you like Dirk dumped Carol?" Wilma asked.

Clare nodded.

"Then forget what I said," said Julia. "Let's get him back in that Korean store and shoot that sucker full of holes."

"I like the Korean store, too," said Vinnie, knocking back the last of his grappa. "But now it's two-fifteen, and we've got to scoot back over to Centre Street."

BACK IN ROOM 1517, THE FOUR of them clustered in a corner. They were picking up speed. Dirk lay dead in the grocery store, and they were arguing over whether or not the Korean grocer or Carol subdued the shooter, when the court officer stepped from behind the desk and called their names once more and they had to file into another courtroom.

This time, the defendant, as Judge O'Banion explained, was a twenty-two-year-old man who, when his girlfriend jilted him, had thrown her in front of a subway train which cut her to ribbons.

The four cowriters stared at one another. *Dirk*, mouthed Julia. *It's even better. It's perfect.*

They couldn't wait to get out of that courtroom and back to *Real Life*.

Vinnie had said that he thought the jiltee was justified. Wilma had said that her eighty-six-year-old mother was once dragged by a train and she just couldn't listen to the testimony. Julia's lie was that she had gone to high school with the victim. Clare said that she was obsessed with this case, had followed every smidgen of news about it, and thought the defendant should be strung up. They were all excused.

"Okay," said Vinnie, back in Room 1517, "I take it that you like running David, I mean Dirk, over with a subway train?"

"I love it," said Wilma. "Carol pushes him, and the train runs over his gorgeous face."

"Oh, yeah," said Julia.

"Absolutely," said Clare. "It's perfect. It's poetic justice."

"And does Clare, I mean Carol, get caught?" asked Vinnie.

"No way," said Julia. "She doesn't do it herself. Somebody else does it."

"Somebody she paid?" asked Vinnie.

"Probably," said Wilma.

"How much?" asked Vinnie. Then he reached in a pocket of his lovely fawn slacks and pulled out the quarter Clare had loaned him for the phone earlier that morning. He flipped it a couple of times and gave her a wink.

"Not in real life." Clare laughed. "Not nearly enough."

BUT IT WAS.

Shortly after that conversation, the prospective jurors of Room 1517 were dismissed for the day. Clare, energized for the first time in weeks, went straight home and wrote like a crazy person. As the four of them had plotted, Dirk died, his pretty face mangled beyond recognition, and Carol got away with it. Then Dirk's long-lost twin brother, Dylan, a pediatrician, comes to New York, and the two of them fall madly in love. But then a child in his care dies mysteriously, and an autopsy discovers that the child's heart is missing. It turns out that Dylan, whose only child drowned ten years ago, has snapped. He's become a kind of Frankenstein, and there's a terrible trial . . .

Involved in the narrative, Clare had lost track of time. Even though she hadn't slept in weeks, she was alive with energy. It was almost eleven when her phone rang.

"Turn on the TV," said a familiar voice. One she'd heard recently but couldn't quite place. "The news."

"Who is this?"

"Vinnie."

"What . . . ?"

"Just turn on the TV, okay?"

Clare did as he said, and there was blond Chuck Scarborough looking deadly serious as he reported a horrible accident that evening at the 79th Street station of the IRT. "The victim, Dr. David Teller, a prominent plastic surgeon, was waiting for a train about 8 P.M. this evening when he seemed to fall onto the tracks and was dragged by the head and killed. There were no immediate witnesses to the accident. No one noticed him standing at the far end of the platform. At this point, there's no indication of foul play . . ."

"Vinnie!" Clare shrieked. "You killed him."

"What makes you say that?"

"I didn't mean for you to really kill him! He was a son of a bitch, but I didn't mean . . . we can't be judge and jury . . ."

"What makes you think you had anything to do with this little incident? How do you know Dr. Teller wasn't just an accident waiting to happen?"

"What are you talking about?"

"Let's just pretend . . ." And then Vinnie chuckled softly. "You know, pretend, like we were writing a story, that Dr. Teller had really pissed off some important people by giving new faces to some reprehensible characters in the feds' witness protection program. Like on *Real Life*, but in real life, too."

"Oh, my God," Clare breathed.

"And let's say that these very important people wanted to deliver a very strong message to Dr. Teller. Well, more than a message. They wanted to make damned sure that he cease and desist these practices. Immediately. And permanently."

"Oh, Vinnie," said Clare. She could feel something rising in her chest. Something like relief. Could that be? Something like joy? Delight? Something that tasted like sweet revenge?

"And let's say that a friend of these very important people was asked to take care of this Dr. Teller who was causing them so much grief. And this friend had set out to do that very thing when he, by a piece of great coincidence, ran into the former girlfriend of said Dr. Teller in a jury room. And she was having a problem with *Real Life*. And so he and some other people helped her with her problem."

"With *Real Life*?"

"Yeah," said Vinnie. "And this guy, he liked their story so much he rolled it over into little r, little l real life."

The feeling in Clare's chest bubbled over into laughter. And once she started, she couldn't stop.

"Good night, Clare," said Vinnie. She could hear his grin. "Sweet dreams. And good luck with *Real Life*. If I was you, I'd use this, babe. Use *this* material. We *like* this poetic justice business out in the real world."

Clare did. She used it all. And when *Real Life* became number one in its time slot, and the Emmies and the money started pouring in, Arnie, Clare's producer, raised a glass of champagne to her. "How sweet," he said, "real life is."

Nancy Pickard is the creator of the Jenny Cain series of mysteries, thoughtful explorations of life and crime in a small New England town. Her novels have won the Anthony, Agatha, and Macavity Awards, and have been nominated for the Edgar. Her short fiction is just as impressive, appearing in such anthologies as *Vengeance Is Hers* and *A Woman's Eye*. She has also edited anthologies, most notably *Women on the Edge*. In "A Rock and a Hard Place," her main character is markedly different from her series detective. But both get their respective jobs done with equal skill.

A Rock and a Hard Place
NANCY PICKARD

I'm not a hard woman; I'm only a private investigator.

You see me, you think I'm an athlete, a tough girl, even at my age, which is fifty-one. You hear my voice, my language sometimes, you think, she's a rough one. But I'm college educated, with two degrees, one of them in English lit, believe it or not. Besides, lifting weights never built up muscles between a person's ears, if you see what I mean. I work out on computers more than I do at the gym, that's the nature of this job.

It's fairly respectable, my profession.

I'm fairly respectable, is what I'm saying, even if I do carry weapons and use them, even if I did serve in Vietnam for six months that are supposed to be top secret, even now, and even if I have witnessed sordid scenes and participated in violent acts. I still maintain I am basically a respectable and mostly law-abiding person, or I was, until recently. Now, I don't know what I am. Except that one thing I am for sure is dying. Yeah, right, aren't we all? No, I mean, specifically me, specifically now, from breast cancer. My doctors claim they excised it with one of those "partials," but I don't believe them. I hear it growing, infinitesimal and stealthy, escaping their means of detection, but not mine. The saving grace is: I'm good at guns. Things get bad, too painful, I always have my stockpile of large and little friends, the ones with the long noses and the short ones, the loud voices and the soft. Dying definitely does not scare me; I would not move one foot off the sidewalk to get out of its way.

Are we clear on all this, so far?

I was already all of those things I have just described—except the part about not knowing any longer what I am—at the moment when Grace Kairn (not her real name) applied her knuckles to a tentative knock on my office door. I looked up from my Macintosh Quadra, where I was trying to hack my way into a database I wasn't supposed to be able to get into, and saw her: late thirties, really short blond hair, Audrey Hepburn bones, one of those women who makes a woman like me feel big and bulky and clumsy, like we're all muscle and cuss words and she's all lace and fragrance.

"Hello?" she said, from my doorway. "Angela Fopeano?"

Immediately, I was awkward, not at my best, barking back at her like I was an MP and she was a private caught off base.

"Yeah!" I said.

Yeah. As if my mother hadn't raised me to say "yes," or to be polite, to be a nice girl. *Yeah. Duh. I'm Angie.*

"Who are you?" I asked her, point-blank, like that.

God, sometimes I make myself cringe.

"I'm Grace Kairn, may I talk to you, do you have time?"

No appointment. I hate that. Who do people think they are, expecting me to drop everything for them? I always do, though, because one of my failings is curiosity. God knows, I would hesitate to call it intellectual. Still, I want to *know*, even when I'm pissed at people—who they are, what they want. People in general were starting to bore me, though, with their repetitive stories about infidelity and fraud and deception and greed. Big deal. Did they think that made them different? It was all starting to feel banal and sordid. My own clients were beginning to bore me. Bad sign for a working gal. What did I think I was going to do if I didn't solve crimes? *Crimes*, hah. Misdemeanors of the ego, was more like it, that was what I investigated. Who was sleeping with whom. Who cooked the books. Who stole the paper clips. Who the hell cared. Not me anymore.

Man, I sound angry, don't I? Even I can hear it.

At least this woman asked if I had the time.

I waved her into a chair, and she looked across my desk at me with the gentlest smile I ever saw in anybody's blue eyes. In a humble kind of way, definitely not boasting, she said, "What I have to say is . . . maybe . . . unusual."

"Uh huh."

Yeah right, I thought, tell me a new one, or better yet give me a cure for cancer.

"I want to hire you," she said, concisely, gently, "to prevent three murders."

"You have my attention," I said, wryly. "I'm taping this."

"All right." Her voice was a sweet, melodic breeze across my desk, and

I couldn't imagine she could have anything so very "unusual" to tell me. In fact, her first words were ordinary, to my jaded ears. "Five years ago, before Christmas of that year, I was held up at gunpoint in a parking lot of the Oberlin South Mall."

She was surprisingly direct, for someone so soft.

I sat back and listened.

"It was one man, with a gun, and he pushed me into the car and made me drive him out of town to a riverbank. And he raped me and shot me and left me there, thinking I was dead."

Jesus, I thought, and was surprised to feel tears in my eyes.

I cleared my throat. "I guess you weren't dead."

"No." She smiled, a wonderful, calming, gentle expression of serenity that I instantly coveted. "I *was* dead."

"Okay."

"To be specific, I was still alive when he left me, but I was bleeding to death and I was in shock and I was starting to be hypothermic, it was winter, after all, and I was lying in the snow."

Dear God, I thought. I hated this story already, and I didn't want to hear any more of it, but at least it had a happy ending. Didn't it? I mean, she was there, telling me her terrible tale, wasn't she?

Raped. Shot. Lying in snow.

I stared at the gentle, delicate woman seated across from me, and tried very hard *not* to allow a picture of the warlike scene to come into my mind.

Sweet Mother Mary.

And I'm not even Catholic.

"I was still alive when the paramedics arrived," Grace Kairn told me, while my stomach knotted as she spoke, "because a passing driver with a phone in his car found me pretty quickly. But I died in the ambulance on the way back into town. I was dead for ten minutes. No heartbeat, No brain activity. No respiration. They said I was absolutely, clinically dead."

"Yeah? One of those near-death experiences?"

I sat up, interested for obvious reasons. It's always good to meet a tourist who has already visited your next destination. They can clue you in as to the weather, what to wear. I'd heard plenty of those tales in 'Nam, but that was a long time ago, and these days I have a more personal interest in collecting any available data. As she told the familiar tale of the tunnel, the light, the love at the end of it, her face was—aren't they all—glowing with happiness. She almost, but not quite, made me want some of it.

But I was still waiting to hear anything "unusual."

"While I was dead," Grace Kairn said, predictably, "I felt loved in a way that I can never fully describe to anyone who hasn't felt it. And I learned some things from that love . . ."

I couldn't help it, I had to ask: "Like, what?"

She smiled, almost a grin, catching me in my curiosity. Before she could reply, I realized we'd better skip the fantasies and cut to the chase. "So who do you want me to keep from getting killed?" I asked her.

But she would tell it at her pace, not mine.

"The man who attacked me was captured and tried and convicted of armed robbery and put into prison."

"Just armed robbery? Was it a plea bargain?"

"Yes. He served four years of his sentence."

"Four . . . you mean he's out now?"

"Yes," she said, gently, "he is."

I felt a chill for her sake.

At that moment, I also experienced a strange, physical sense of a compression of time; it seemed to cast my office in shadow, as if the day were drawing too quickly to a close. All in all, I had a sudden and unaccountable feeling of urgency, which I tried to quell within me, because it was weirdly close to panic.

I couldn't remember the last time I'd felt panic.

"And you're afraid?" I asked her.

Or was I talking to myself?

She glanced out my window, smiling a little to herself, before she looked back at me. "I'll tell you the truth, the answer to that is yes and no. I'm not afraid of anything for myself, certainly not of dying, not anymore. But yes, I'm . . . afraid . . . for other people."

"Who?"

"My husband." The expression in her eyes made me envy any person who occasioned such affection. "Rick absolutely believes that I really died. In Rick's eyes, the man who . . . killed me . . . is a murderer. Not an attempted murderer. A *murderer* who should have been convicted of premeditated homicide."

"But you're alive," I pointed out.

"But I was dead," she countered, quite firmly. "He did kill me."

I let out a whistle. "Try telling that to the law."

"We did—to the police, to the prosecutors, to the judge, to the jury, to anybody who would listen, but they laughed at us. Not openly, they weren't that unkind, but they didn't take us seriously, because, as you yourself said . . ." Grace Kairn touched her blouse above her heart. "I'm alive." Then she added the kicker: "Rick says he'll kill the man who murdered me."

"Murdered you."

"I was dead."

"And you want me to keep Rick from doing that?"

"Oh, yes!"

"You want me to protect the man who assaulted you?"

I heard my own voice rise in disbelief and protest at the idea of it, and yet, I understood the logic of her plea: She didn't want her husband to commit a murder—a real one—and go to jail for it. And he would, because—trust me—the law is an ass, and so are many of the men and women who administer it. It wouldn't matter that he killed a very bad guy, or that he was acting out of perfectly understandable rage at the man and the system. He'd still get the very sentence the true bad guy didn't get. Grace Kairn was correct to fear for her husband. Not to mention the fact that he could, instead, get himself killed by the bad guy, and then what would become of *her*, left alone in the universe with a monster?

Her thoughts were way ahead of mine. "Yes," she affirmed, "I want you to protect that man and I also want you to protect Rick, so he doesn't get himself killed."

"Who's the third person?" I asked her.

She had said she wanted me to prevent three murders.

"Well, it's me." She smiled that gentle smile. "The man who killed me—his name is Jerry Heckler—has friends who have sent me threatening letters and phone calls, all of them saying that Heckler will 'get me' when he gets out." She blushed at the phrase, "get me," as if she were embarrassed to be uttering such a cliché, but that's about as disturbed as she seemed to be. The fact that this vicious bastard—this Jerry Heckler (also not his real name)—was once again free to hurt her seemed not to perturb her peace of mind. I, on the other hand, felt a quickening of horror on her behalf and a heavy dose of rage. I utterly sympathized with her husband's vendetta. Like I always say, where's the goddamned death penalty when you really need it?

"Okay," I said, "so you want me to protect Jerry Heckler so your husband won't do something stupid and get arrested for it. And you want me to protect Rick, so Heckler doesn't kill him for trying. And you want me to protect you, so Heckler can't kill you. Again."

"No," she said, gently correcting me. "I want you to protect all of us, because killing is . . . wrong. Under any circumstances, for any reason, it's a . . . mistake." That weird look of serenity—the one I coveted—came over her face again. "That's one of the things I learned."

"Just a mistake?"

"An error."

"Mistakes can be corrected," I pointed out. "But if I kill somebody, he's never coming back."

She smiled at me. "I'm back."

I agreed to take the case. Not for her reason. I didn't believe her reason. I accepted her advance money for *my* reason: That bastard Heckler was not going to hurt this nice woman again—or any other woman—if I could prevent it, and he was also not going to lure her husband into making a stupid, possibly fatal mistake.

"Will you agree to do what I tell you?" I asked her, and then when she said she would, I asked her to give me a few minutes to think about what that was going to be.

BECAUSE I FELT SUCH URGENCY for her sake, I sent Grace Kairn immediately out of town to stay with my mother, figuring Heckler would never know to look there. I didn't even let her go home to pack. I told her not even to call home until I okayed it; I'd inform and deal with her husband—that was part of what she was paying me for.

Maybe you think I was wrong to take a chance on endangering my own mother, but then you've never met Mom. Her only child grew up to be in the military, and then became a private investigator. Think about it: This is probably a mother who can take care of herself. Anyway, who do you think first taught me to shoot? Not Dad, he'd have been the one she shot if he'd ever come back to the rotten neighborhood he left us in. She'd have told the cops she thought he was a prowler, and I'd have backed up her story, even while I was privately thinking, is this any kind of woman for a man to marry? My mother cracks me up; I think she's great, but I can see how she looks from Dad's point of view.

Anyway, once I had Grace safe, the next three steps on my list were: visits, of varying degrees of cordiality, to Rick Kairn, Lt. Janet Randolph, and Mr. Jerry Heckler.

IN DESCENDING ORDER OF CORDIALITY, I started with the cop.

"On a scale of clear water to cesspool, Janet," I said to her in her office, "where does this Heckler fall?"

"Close your mouth *and* hold your nose."

"That bad?"

"You can't be too careful with this one, Angie." The lieutenant, no beauty queen to begin with, hiked an eyebrow, which gave her the appearance of a quizzical rottweiler: black hair, brown skin, pugnacious face, aggressive nature. "What *are* you going to do?"

"Take a look at him."

"That's all?"

I grinned at her. "Somebody's got to be able to identify the body."

Her answering smile was grim. "We were all hoping some other prisoner would kill him."

"It's not too late for that. The world is full of ex-prisoners."

"Don't I know it."

"Can I see a picture of him?"

"You don't need to. He's not real hard to spot. He's a carrottop."

I had to laugh. "You're kidding."

"No. If I had carrot hair, I would never be a criminal. Criminals are so stupid."

"He's out after only four years. So who's stupid? Him or us?"

She handed me the address of the halfway house where he was residing. I wanted to say, "Good dog." Janet had been in Vietnam, too, but in spite of the fact that we were coffee friends, she didn't know I had been there, and there was no way she could look it up, because those files don't exist. Hardly anybody now living does know. It's not too difficult, pretending innocence. People don't expect a woman veteran, not even other women. When Janet or some other 'Nam vet starts in on their war stories or trauma tales, I know how to widen my eyes and look awed and sympathetic.

She doesn't know about the cancer, either.

I'm good at disguise, so I went home and put one together.

I PUT ON MY BLACK wig that is long enough to make a ponytail and that has bangs down to my eyelashes . . . and I put in my false bridgework that gives me an overbite . . . and my green contacts and plain glasses . . . and from out of my Goodwill clothing pile I selected a soiled white waitress uniform and dirty white waitress shoes. But my best trick is probably the only one I ever really need: I increased my bust size dramatically enough to draw a man's eyes away from my face. I added makeup, which I usually don't wear, or dangly earrings, either, and I offered a silent apology to all of the legitimate, hardworking waitresses in the world.

One good thing about a DD cup is that you can snug a pistol right down in there between the pads, and nobody suspects a thing unless they try to hug you. If you ever see a buxom waitress reaching in to adjust her bra strap—duck.

THUS CAMOUFLAGED, I SET OFF to find Jerry Heckler.

Do not assume I took that visit lightly.

There's a writer, Andrew Vachss, who wrote a short story I read one time that I'll never forget, because he was so right. In the story, which was called "The White Crocodile," Vachss compares certain kinds of people to crocodiles. He says baby crocodiles get abandoned by their mothers, so they have to fend for themselves, and if they live to be adults, they spend the rest of their lives getting even.

I figured Jerry Heckler was one of the world's crocodiles.

It didn't matter how much theoretical pity I might feel for whatever abuse he might have suffered as a child, the fact remained he was a man now and he would rend other people limb from limb and eat them if they got within striking distance of him, as proved by what he did to Grace Kairn.

I don't mess around with the Jerry Hecklers of the world; there's no talking to them, no reasoning with them, no sympathy to be got from them, they have no conscience, they are the most dangerous kind of human being that exists, the crocodiles of the human kingdom, and they have—quoting Vachss again—no natural enemies. If I have to deal with them at all, I do the only thing you can do, what I was taught first by my mother and then in 'Nam: strike first.

I MADE HIM WITHIN HALF an hour of waiting at a bus stop across from the halfway house. Suppertime. Carrottop came out of the halfway house and walked two doors down to a deli.

While he ate, I made use of the time by getting on the pay phone across the street and calling Grace Kairn's husband, Rick. There was no need for me to go see him personally, not when I had only one basic message to deliver, which was: Don't do it, you'll get caught. According to the schedule Grace had given me, her husband should be home from work now, and only just beginning to wonder where his wife could be.

"Rick? My name is Angela Fopeano, and I'm a private investigator that your wife hired today. She wants me to keep you from trying to kill Jerry Heckler."

I couldn't mince words; Heckler might eat fast.

Kairn was incoherent, indignant, frightened, on the other end of the line, but I could tell he really did love his wife, because he verbally took his frustrations out on me, not on her at what she'd done that day to knock his pins out from under him.

I interrupted Kairn to tell him, "Here's how I'm going to stop you from making a dead man or a prisoner out of yourself, Rick. I have been to see Lt. Janet Randolph today and I have informed her of your intention to kill Heckler."

Dead silence from Kairn.

So often the simple way is the best way.

There was nothing he could do now, without getting himself—and by extension, his wife—in a hell of a mess. And if he loved her—which she believed, and I did too—he just wouldn't do that. It was one thing for him to rant in private; another thing entirely for those rantings to become police knowledge. Whether Grace knew it or not, this is why she had come to me—she couldn't be the traitor who betrayed her husband to the police in order to protect him, but I could be.

"He deserves to die," Rick said, sounding furious, paralyzed, sad.

"You bet," I agreed. "But you don't, and Grace doesn't deserve to be left alone if Heckler gets you first, or you get arrested."

"I can't get arrested, can I, just for wanting to kill him?"

"No, Rick, there's no law against that, yet."

"But this leaves him free to hurt Grace again!"

"It's my job to see that he doesn't."

Rick Kairn didn't sound convinced that I could do that, but then why should he, he didn't know me. I felt for him. When he asked me where Grace was, I said I couldn't tell him until I was absolutely sure that Jerry Heckler would never bother her again, no matter where she was. Kairn didn't like the mystery, probably half suspected me of kidnapping Grace, but he could see the point. If he didn't know where his wife was, he couldn't accidentally—or as the result of force—give that information away to Heckler. I wasn't worried about Heckler's friends, the ones who'd terrorized Grace and Rick with their messages that Heckler would "get her" when he got out; if they were going to do the job on her, they would have done it by now. No, Heckler sounded to me like a man who wants to take his pleasures for himself.

I assured Rick that I'd relay messages between Grace and him.

And then I got off the phone fast when I saw Jerry Heckler in the deli start to dig in his pants pockets for cash to pay for his supper.

WHEN HECKLER CAME BACK OUTSIDE, I called out to him.

"Oh, sir!"

He turned, a beefy, red-haired, suspicious-faced man in his thirties, bumpy-skinned and heavy-lidded as a croc.

I advanced, holding a man's wallet out so he could see it.

"Did you leave this—"

"That ain't mine."

By then, I was close enough.

Strike first, but know your enemy.

"Grace," I said, low and clear. He looked startled, but then a corner of his mouth ticked, as if in amusement. "If anything happens to her or to her husband or to anybody she has ever met in her life, I will find you and I will kill you."

He laughed, at my appearance, at my threat.

"Yeah? What if something happens, and it's not my fault?"

He was having fun now, playing with his food.

"If I were you, I would work under the assumption that everything is your fault, Heckler."

He told me what to do with myself, his eyes on my chest, and then walked off, in no hurry to escape from me. But now I knew him: he was arrogant, unobservant, and careless, the kind of guy who never, never learns that he will get caught, which means he will not only do the time, he will do the crime.

What I said to him wasn't a warning.

Guys like that, they don't take warnings, because they have no restraint.

The shrinks call it "low impulse control." No, what I was doing was making a positive identification and scouting behind the lines to protect my own rear.

I have high impulse control. I am very careful, at least I always have been. Now, with this cancer thing, something's coming loose.

I SPENT THE SUBWAY RIDE home considering my choices and the consequences of them. When I was in the military, they took intelligent advantage of my best skill, which is exactly that—the ability to observe multiple opportunities and to foresee the consequences of all of them, quickly. It was a rare example of the armed services actually matching ability to assignment.

I spent only ten minutes at home setting up my plan.

First, I called Lt. Randolph.

"I talked to the husband, Janet. How about if I set up an appointment for him to go to your office?"

"Sure."

"When? You say."

"Tomorrow morning, ten-fifteen."

"I'll send him in."

Next, I called Grace's husband back, and told him.

"But I'll be at work—"

"Tell them something. You gotta be there, Rick. You have to convince her you won't harm a strand of Heckler's red hair."

He cursed me, but he agreed to do it.

I could have asked the lieutenant to call him to set up the appointment, but I had to hear his acquiescence, had to be sure he'd really make the appointment. Without mercy, I said to him, "Rick, I want to be able to tell your wife that Lt. Randolph actually saw you at ten-fifteen tomorrow morning."

That got him. "All right!" he said, shouting at me.

Last, I called Mom.

She said things were cool, and she said, "Grace is a nice woman."

"Absolutely. You taking her grocery shopping with you tomorrow morning, Mom?"

"Grocery—?" She stopped herself. "Am I?"

"Big sale on at ten-fifteen. I'd get there before that, and then hang around a while afterward, introduce her to folks, let her see what a friendly little town you have up there."

"She'll want to move here, by the time I finish."

"That's fine."

"You take care, Daughter."

"Yes, ma'am."

My mother didn't know what I was up to, she rarely did anymore, but she was quick to *understand*, and you don't need facts for that. She used to tell me a story, drilled it into me, really, her favorite story from mythology. Where other girls heard about Snow White, I heard the one about Daphne and Apollo. Apollo's a god, Daphne's a wood nymph, and he wants her, but she runs away. Just when he's about to catch her, and she's desperate, she prays to her father, a river-god, for help. Her daddy, thinking he's doing a good thing, saves her by turning her into a tree. Thanks a lot, Dad. You couldn't turn Apollo into a tree, instead, and let your daughter run free? My mother always said the moral of this story is: Don't trust the fathers. Never ask the fathers for help. They will freeze you where you stand, always, to protect their precious status quo.

The inference was: When I need help, ask Mom.

I WASN'T CRAZY ABOUT MY own plan.

It was all more complicated than I liked, but I had a lot of alibis to arrange, my own included. I also had to work fast, because I couldn't stall Grace out of town forever. What I was planning to do was take Heckler out. Just like that. No farting around. Strike first. Set him up and take him out, in a way that protected Grace, Rick, and me from any suspicion. I was crossing a line here, a line I hadn't crossed since Vietnam.

The rest of the setup was easy, even enjoyable, requiring a couple of hours of scouting near the halfway house for a good shooting gallery, and a few hours of rehearsal with my clothing changes and with my equipment, to develop certain ambidextrous skills.

I went to sleep thinking about Vietnam. Bad move, resulting in weird dreams. By now, most everybody knows we had assassination squads working in country, but hardly anyone knows—and no one would believe it even if you showed them photographs, which I could—there were women involved. Let me put it this way: Not every peacenik who traveled to Hanoi was a pacifist, not every girl with a cross on her uniform was a nurse, not every female with a pencil was a journalist. This all happened, you understand, before I realized—it was a man vet who bitterly told me this—that all soldiers, especially draftees, are prisoners of their government. You don't believe me? Name one other job you can get shot for leaving.

I didn't dream about 'Nam, though.

I dreamed about my mother. She was coming toward me, smiling with determination, a bottle of almond-and-strawberry-scented shampoo in her hand. She was going to wash my hair. I really didn't want her to use that stuff on me, and I really didn't want her to get hold of my head.

I woke up screaming.

Then I lay there thinking—what a dramatic response to such a nothing little dream. My heart was thudding with fear and my upper body was slick with sweat. I put my hands on my chest right above where the X rays had shown the shadow, and I thought: Weird.

After that, I slept like a baby.

A cancerous baby.

WHEN I AWOKE, I REALIZED that being trained as an assassin is like knowing how to type: it's a skill you can always fall back on. Ever since I sensed what I was going to do about Jerry Heckler, I'd been thinking about him, but also about a certain child molester I read about who was released on a technicality, and about a terrorist who has somehow finagled his way into a minimum security prison.

I have debts from 'Nam.

And I'd been thinking, maybe I could pay them off—*pick* them off—one by one, starting with Heckler. Then I could write up my stories—like this one—and get them published anonymously to scare some of the bad guys. Let them start looking over their shoulders and wondering if they could be next. I was getting real excited about this plan. Like Mom always said: Angie, try to leave this world a better place than you found it.

Yes, ma'am.

I was almost laughing as I dressed, turning myself into a plain little wren of a woman. My equipment—sniper's rifle, telescopic scope, silencer, ammo, tripod, cellular telephone—disassembled quickly and fit perfectly into an ordinary straw bag that I had reinforced for strength. Over my first layer of camouflage, I slipped on thin plastic gloves, then put on coveralls, a well-padded jacket with a hood, a baseball cap with a long bill, and men's work shoes over my thin ladies' slippers. I'd already stashed a tool chest in my car after my practice sessions the night before.

As the old song advised: Walk like a man.

I would go up on the roof of a building across from the halfway house dressed as a workman with a tool chest. I would come down as a little wren with a straw bag, a woman so plain as to be nearly invisible.

It was a gorgeous day, chilly, sunny, no clouds.

And it was 9:45 A.M.

UP ON THE ROOF, AT ten-fifteen, I called the halfway house on my cellular phone and told the man who answered that I was from the gas company and that we had a major gas leak on the block.

"Evacuate. Get everybody out now."

"Right!" he agreed. People can be so gullible.

Then I called the lieutenant and asked her if Rick Kairn was there yet.

"Sitting right here," she announced, sounding smug.

At that moment, Jerry Heckler walked out the front door of the halfway house. He was a big man, with a lovely large chest for aiming at, and I had ammo that would take down a grizzly, no mistake. I had to fire a cannonball, because silencers dissipate power.

"Tell me what you're telling him," I suggested to Janet.

As she did, I placed one finger of my left hand on the Mute button on my telephone and eased the trigger of the rifle with my right forefinger. Ambidextrous, for sure! And right then—at the worst possible moment in terms of the job—my memory kicked in.

It wasn't a Vietnam flashback.

What I remembered was that fear resides in an almond-shaped organ deep in the brain, the amygdala. Trigger that, and you trigger terror.

Terror. Heart pounding. Cold sweats.

Like my dream. Mom and the shampoo. The almond-and-strawberry-scented shampoo. I didn't know what the strawberry meant, but I knew the almond meant: fear.

Mom?

Shit! I didn't want to think about this now!

As she had warned me, I had never gone to "the fathers" for advice. Thousands of my male contemporaries had and they'd ended up in 'Nam. I had only gone to "the mothers." And here I was with a gun in my hand anyway.

I felt confused, paralyzed.

In that moment, with one finger on the Mute button . . . and Janet talking into my ear . . . and one eye on Jerry Heckler's chest . . . and another finger on a trigger, I felt empty as a jar.

Then I resighted, and fired the rifle.

When what noise there was subsided, I released the Mute button. And all the while, the lieutenant was telling me what she was telling Rick Kairn, who was seated right there in her office while his wife was being introduced to a dozen people fifty miles away. If the cops got suspicious enough of me to go to the trouble of tracking this cellular call, I was in deep shit. But, hey, I was already in deep shit according to several doctors, so what was a little more? Especially if I kept a crocodile from eating people?

Some days, everything works.

It all went perfectly.

LAST WEEK, I HAD LUNCH with Grace.

"We're safe, aren't we?" she asked me.

"Yes, at least from Heckler, I can't say about the rest of your life."

She smiled at me. "Thank you, however you did it."

"You're welcome. Now will you tell me what else you learned while you were dead?"

"I learned that we're already forgiven."

"Well, that is good news."

She laughed. "I learned that every evil act is actually a cry from the heart for healing, it is a plea to be reunited with God."

"Okay," I said, while she smiled at the skepticism on my face. "Then tell me this, who's God?"

She laughed again. "There's no 'who.' There's nothing—no thing—out there. It's all in here." Grace pointed to her chest, right about where my tumor is. "God is a name we give to love."

"Great bumper sticker," said I, tactless as ever.

But it seemed Grace wasn't defensive and I couldn't offend her. I decided not to mention that some scientists would say her near-death experience was merely a release of endorphins in the brain.

As usual, she was way ahead of me.

"You don't have to believe me, Angie."

"Okay, then if you don't mind, I won't."

We laughed, both of us, while I wondered why in the world I was resisting the idea that I could be forgiven for every bad thing I had ever done. And then I knew why: because that would mean the Jerry Hecklers of the world were forgiven too.

I HAD CALLED HIM, THE evening after the morning when my shot had missed him by an inch. I had meant to kill him, had gone up on the roof to blast him. But in that instant when I stood empty—with the voices of both the mothers and the fathers silenced in my head—I changed my mind. I think that may have been the first truly independent act of my life, and I wish I could say I felt good about it.

"I told you not to mess with Grace," I said to him.

"I didn't do anything!" he protested. I knew he'd been frightened; I'd seen it in his face after my shot nearly hit him, after I'd purposely aimed off target.

"I know that," I told him. "That shot was for thinking about hurting her. Now consider what's going to happen if you *do* hurt her."

Maybe crocodiles don't take warnings, but they're not complete imbeciles. Even crocs will swim away to another swamp if they hear the sound of gunfire.

I was still worried about those other swamps, though.

"Jerry?" I said. "I'll be keeping tabs on you. If I hear that you are under suspicion for injuring any woman, not just Grace, I will come after you again."

"Who *are* you?"

"A good shot," I said, and hung up.

Who was I? A good question. I was no daddy's girl, and never had been.

And now perhaps I was no longer my mother's girl, either. Who was I? A woman, empty, but for something shadowy growing in my breast. For once in my life, I can't foresee the consequences. But I know this natural law: Shadows cannot be cast in total darkness; where there is a shadow, there must be light.

Donald E. Westlake's series characters are as different as night and day. Parker is a hard-boiled professional thief who's making a well-deserved return after almost twenty years in the novel *Comeback*. Dortmunder is a bumbling burglar whose capers inevitably fall apart, the only question being how much damage he causes to himself and others along the way. The short story "Too Many Crooks" garnered Dortmunder's author an Edgar Award, proving that it's not always the hard-boiled or serious mystery stories that deserve recognition. Once again, though, we find no series character here, just a thief who thinks he's discovered the perfect setup, until he runs into the one flaw in his plan, a flaw he could have never thought of in a hundred years.

The Burglar and the Whatsit
DONALD E. WESTLAKE

"Hey, Sanity Clause," shouted the drunk from up the hall. "Wait up. C'mere."

The man in the red Santa Claus suit, with the big white beard on his face and the big heavy red sack on his shoulder, did not wait up, and did not come here, but instead continued to plod on down the hall in this high floor of a Manhattan apartment building in the middle of a cold evening in the middle of December.

"Hey, Sanity! Wait *up*, will ya?"

The man in the Santa Claus suit did not at all want to wait up, but on the other hand he also did not at all want a lot of shouting in this hall here, because in fact he was not your normal Santa Claus but was something else entirely, which was a burglar, named Jack. This Jack was a burglar who had learned some time ago that if he were to enter apartment buildings costumed like the sort of person who in the normal course of events would carry on himself some sort of large bag or box or reticule or sack, he could probably fill that sack or whatever with any number of valuable items without much risk of his being challenged, questioned or— in the worst case—arrested.

Often, therefore, this Jack would roam the corridors of the cliff dwellers garbed as, for instance, a mailman or other parcel delivery person, or as a supermarket clerk pushing a cart full of grocery bags (paper, because you can see through plastic, and plastic bags don't stand up). Just once he'd been a doctor, with a stethoscope and a doctor's black bag, but that time he'd been snagged at once, for everybody knows doctors don't make house calls. A master of disguise, Jack even occasionally appeared as a Chinese restaurant delivery guy. The bicycle clip around his right ankle, to protect his pants leg from the putative bicycle's supposed chain, was the masterstroke of that particular impersonation.

But the best was Santa Claus. First of all, the disguise was so complete, with the false stomach and the beard and the hat and the gloves. Also, the Santa sack was more capacious than almost anything else he could carry. And finally, people *liked* Santa Claus, and it made the situation more humane, somehow, gentler and nicer, to be smiled upon by the people he'd just robbed.

The downside of Santa was that his season was so short. There was only about a three-week period in December when the appearance of a Santa Claus in an apartment building's public areas would not raise more questions than it would answer. But those three weeks were the peak of the year for Jack, when he could move in warmth and safety and utter anonymity, his sack full of gifts—not for the nearby residents but from them. And all in peace and quiet, because people leave Santa Claus alone, when they see him they know he's on his way somewhere, to a party or a chimney or something.

So they leave Santa *alone*. Except for this drunk here, shouting in the hallway. Jack the burglar didn't need a lot of shouting in the hallway, and he didn't want a lot of shouting in the hallway, so with some reluctance he turned around at last and waited up, gazing at the approaching drunk from eyes that were the one false note in the costume: They definitely did not twinkle.

The drunk reeled closer and stared at the burglar out of his own awful eyes, like blue eggs sunny-side up. "You're just the guy I need," he announced, inaccurately, for clearly what he most urgently needed was both a 12-step program and a whole lot of large, humorless people to enforce it.

The burglar waited, and the drunk leaned against the wall to keep the building from falling over. "If anybody can get the goddamn thing to work," he said, "it's Sanity Clause. But don't talk to me about batteries. Batteries not included *is not* the problem here."

"Good," the burglar said, and then expanded on that: "Goodbye."

"Wait!" the drunk shouted as the burglar turned away.

The burglar turned back. "Don't shout," he said.

"Well, don't keep going away," the drunk told him. "I got a real problem here."

The burglar sighed through his thick white beard. One of the reasons he'd taken up this line of work in the first place was that you could do it alone. "All right," he said, hoping this would be short, at least. "What's the problem?"

"Come on, I'll show you." Risking all, the drunk pushed off from the wall and tottered away down the hall. The burglar followed him, and the drunk touched his palm to an apartment door, which clicked and swung open—*that* was cute—and they went inside. The door swung shut, and the burglar stopped dead and stared.

Jack the burglar had seen a lot of living rooms in his business, but this one was definitely the strangest. Nothing in it looked right. All the furniture, if that's what it was, consisted of hard and soft shapes from geometry class, in a variety of pastel colors. Tall narrow things that looked like metal plants might have been lamps. Short wide things that crouched could have been chairs. Some of the stuff didn't seem to be anything in particular at all.

The drunk tottered through this abstract landscape to an inner doorway, then said, "Be right back," and disappeared.

The burglar made a circuit of the room, and to his surprise found items of interest. A small pale pyramid turned out to be a clock; into his sack it went. Also, this avocado with ears seemed to be a CD player; pop, in it went.

In a far corner, in amazing contrast to everything else, stood a Christmas tree, fat and richly green and hung with a million ornaments, the only normal object in sight. Or, wait a minute. The burglar stared and frowned, and the Christmas tree shimmered over there as though it were about to be beamed up to the starship *Enterprise*. What was wrong with that tree?

The drunk returned, aglow with happy pride. Waving at the wavering Christmas tree, he said, "Whaddya think?"

"What *is* it, that's what I think."

"A hologram," the drunk said. "You can walk all around it, see all the sides, and you never have to water it, and it never drops a needle and you can use it next year. Pretty good, huh?"

"It isn't traditional," the burglar said. He had his own sense of the fitness of things.

"Tra-*dish*-unal!" The drunk almost knocked himself over, he rocketed that word out so hard. "*I* don't need tradition, I'm an *inventor*!" Pointing at a whatsit that was just now following him into the room, he said, "See?"

The burglar saw. This whatsit was a metal box, pebbly gray, about four feet tall and a foot square, scattered all over with dials and switches and antennas, plus a smooth dome on the top and little wheels on the bottom that hummed as the thing came straight across the bare gray floor to stop in front of the burglar and go, "Chick-chick, chillick, chillick."

The burglar didn't like this artifact at all. He said, "Well, what's *this* supposed to be?"

"That's just it," the drunk said and collapsed backward onto a trapezoid that just possibly could have been a sofa. "I don't know *what* the heck it is."

"I don't like it," the burglar said. The thing buzzed and chicked as though it were a supermarket scanner and Jack the burglar were equipped with a bar code. "It's making me nervous."

"It makes *me* nervous," the drunk said. "I invented the darn thing, and I don't know what it's for. Whyn't you sit down?"

The burglar looked around. "On what?"

"Oh, anything. You want an eggnog?"

Revolted, the burglar said, "Eggnog? No!" And he sat on a nearby rhomboid, which fortunately was more comfortable than it looked.

"I just thought, you know, the uniform," the drunk said, and sat up straighter on his trapezoid and began to applaud.

What's he got to applaud about? But here came another whatsit, this one with skinny metal arms and a head shaped like a tray. The drunk told it, "I'll have the usual." To the burglar he said, "And what for you?"

"Nothing," said the burglar, "Not, uh, on duty."

"OK. Give him a seltzer with a slice of lime," he told the tray-headed whatsit, and the thing wheeled about and left as the drunk explained, "I don't like to see anybody without a glass."

"So you got a lot of these, uh, things, huh? Invented them all?"

"Used to have a lot more," the drunk said, getting mad, "but a bunch got stolen. Goddamn it, goddamn it!"

"Oh, yeah?"

"If I could get my hands on those burglars!" The drunk tried to demonstrate a pretend choke in midair, but his fingers got all tangled together, and in trying to untangle them he fell over on his side. Lying there on the trapezoid, one eye visible, he glared at the domed whatsit, hovering near the burglar and snarled, "I wish they'd steal *that* thing."

The burglar said, "How can you invent it and not know what it is?"

"Easy." The drunk, with a lot of arm and leg movements, pushed himself back to a seated position as the bartender whatsit came rolling back into the room with two drinks on its head/tray. It zipped past the drunk, who grabbed his glass from it on the fly, then paused in front of the burglar on the rhomboid, who accepted the glass of seltzer and suppressed the urge to say "Thanks."

Tray-head wheeled around the enigmatic whatsit and left. The drunk frowned at the whatsit and said, "Half the things I invent I don't remember.

I just do them. I do the drawing and fax it to my construction people, and then I go think about other things. And after a while, dingdong, United Parcel, and there it is, according to specifikah—speci—plan."

"Then how do you find out what anything's for?"

"I leave myself a note in the computer when I invent it. When the package shows up, I check back and the screen says, 'We now have a perfect vacuum cleaner.' Or, 'We now have a perfect pocket calculator.' "

"How come you didn't do that this time?"

"I did!" A growl escaped the drunk's throat and his face reddened with remembered rage. "Somebody stole the computer!"

"Ah," said the burglar.

"So here I am," the drunk went on, pointing with his free hand at himself and the whatsit and his drink and the Christmas tree and various other things, "here I am. I got this thing—for all I know it's some sorta boon to mankind, a perfect Christmas present to humanity—and I don't know what it is!"

"But what do you want from me?" the burglar asked, shifting on his rhomboid. "I don't know about inventions."

"You know about *things*," the drunk told him. "You know about *stuff*. Nobody in the world knows *stuff* like Sanity Clause. Electric pencil sharpeners. Jigsaw puzzles. *Stuff*."

"Yeah? And? So?"

"So tell me stuff," the drunk said. "Any kinda stuff that you can think of, and I'll tell you if I did one yet, and when it's something I never did we'll try out some commands on Junior here and see what happens."

"I don't know," the burglar said, as the whatsit at last wheeled away from him and out into the middle of the room. It stopped, as though poised there. "You mean, just say *products* to you?"

"S'only thing I can think of," the drunk explained, "that might help." Then he sat up even more and gaped at the whatsit. "Looka that!"

The whatsit was extruding more aerials. Little lights ran around its square body. A buzzing sound came from within. The burglar said, "It isn't gonna explode, is it?"

"I don't think so," the drunk said. "It looks like it's broadcasting. Suppose I invented something to look for intelligence on other planets?"

"Would you want something like that?"

The drunk considered, then shook his head. "No. You're right, it isn't that." Perking up, he said, "But you got the idea, right? Try me, come on, tell me stuff. We gotta get moving here. I gotta figure out what this thing's supposed to do before it starts doing it all on its own. Come on, come on."

The burglar thought. He wasn't actually Santa Claus, of course, but he was certainly familiar with stuff. "A fax machine," he said, there being three of them at the moment in his sack on the floor beside the rhomboid.

"Did one," the drunk said. "Recycles newspapers, prints on it."

"Coffee maker."

"Part of my breakfast maker."

"Rock polisher."

"Don't want one."

"Air purifier."

"I manufacture my own air in here."

They went on like that, the burglar pausing to think of more things, trying them out, bouncing them off the drunk, but none of them right, while the whatsit entertained itself with its chirruping and buzzing in the middle of the room, until at last the burglar's mind had become drained of artifacts, of ideas, of things, of *stuff*. "I'm sorry, pal," the burglar said, after their final silence. Shaking his head, he got up from the rhomboid, picked up his sack and said, "I'd like to help. But I gotta get on with my life, you know?"

"I appreciate all you done," the drunk said, trying but failing to stand. Then, getting mad all over again, he clenched his fists and shouted, "If only they didn't steal my computer!" He pointed an angry fist toward a keypad beside the front door. "You see that pad? That's the building's so-called burglar alarm! Ha! Burglars laugh at it!"

They did. Jack himself had laughed at several of them just tonight. "Hard to find a really good burglar al——" he said, and stopped.

They both stared at the whatsit, still buzzing away at itself like a drum machine with the mute on. "By golly," breathed the drunk, "you got it."

The burglar frowned. "It's a burglar alarm? That thing?"

"It's the perfect burglar alarm," the drunk said, and bounced around with new confidence on his trapezoid. "You know what's wrong with regular burglar alarms?" he demanded.

"They aren't very good," the burglar said.

"They trap the innocent," the drunk told him, "and they're too stupid to catch the guilty."

"That's pretty much true," the burglar agreed.

"A *perfect* burglar alarm would sense burglars, know them by a thousand tiny indications, too subtle for you and me, and call the cops before they could pull the job!"

Behind his big white Santa Claus beard, Jack the burglar's chin felt itchy all of a sudden. The big round fake stomach beneath his red costume was heavier than before. Giving the whatsit a sickly smile, he said, "A machine that can *sense* burglars? Impossible."

"No, sir," said the drunk. "Heavier-than-air flight is impossible. Sensing guilt is a snap, for the right machine." Contemplating his invention, frowning in thought, the drunk said, "But it was broadcasting. Practicing, do you suppose? Telling me it's ready to go to work?"

"Me, too," the burglar said, moving toward the door.

"Go to work. Nice to——"

The doorbell rang. "Huh," the drunk said. "Who do you suppose that is at this hour?"

Sara Paretsky is an award-winning author and editor who's won awards in both fields. She and her series detective V. I. Warshawski both reside in the city of Chicago. The subject of eight novels, Warshawski is currently on vacation, but that hasn't stopped her best work from appearing in the short story collection *Windy City Blues*. The story "Publicity Stunts" appeared in *Women on the Case*, another anthology of crime fiction written by women only and edited by Sara Paretsky.

Publicity Stunts
SARA PARETSKY

"I need a bodyguard. I was told you were good." Lisa Macauley crossed her legs and leaned back in my client chair as if expecting me to slobber in gratitude.

"If you were told I was a good bodyguard someone didn't know my operation: I never do protection."

"I'm prepared to pay you well."

"You can offer me a million dollars a day and I still won't take the job. Protection is a special skill. You need lots of people to do it right. I have a one-person operation. I'm not going to abandon my other clients to look after you."

"I'm not asking you to give up your precious clients forever, just for a few days next week while I'm doing publicity here in Chicago."

Judging by her expression, Macauley thought she was a household word, but I'd been on the run the two days since she'd made the appointment and hadn't had time to do any research on her. Whatever she publicized made her rich: wealth oozed all the way from her dark cloud of carefully cut curls through the sable protecting her from February's chill winds and on down to her Stephane Kelian three-inch platforms.

When I didn't say anything she added, "For my new book, of course."

"That sounds like a job for your publisher. Or your handlers."

I had vague memories of going to see Andre Dawson when he was doing some kind of baseball promotion at Marshall Field. He'd been on a dais, under lights, with several heavies keeping the adoring fans away from him.

307

No matter what Macauley wrote she surely wasn't any more at risk than a sports hero.

She made an impatient gesture. "They always send some useless person from their publicity department. They refuse to believe my life is in danger. Of course, this is the last book I'll do with Gaudy: my new contract with Della Destra Press calls for a personal bodyguard whenever I'm on the road. But right now, while I'm promoting the new one, I need protection."

I ignored her contract woes. "Your life is in danger? What have you written that's so controversial? An attack on Mother Teresa?"

"I write crime novels. Don't you read?"

"Not crime fiction: I get enough of the real stuff walking out my door in the morning."

Macauley gave a self-conscious little laugh. "I thought mine might appeal to a woman detective like yourself. That's why I chose you to begin with. My heroine is a woman talk-show host who gets involved in cases through members of her listening audience. The issues she takes on are extremely controversial: abortion, rape, the Greens. In one of them she protects a man whose university appointment is attacked by the feminists on campus. She's nearly murdered when she uncovers the brainwashing operation the feminists are running on campus."

"I can't believe that would put you in danger—feminist-bashing is about as controversial as apple pie these days. Sounds like your hero is a female Claud Barnett."

Barnett broadcast his attacks on the atheistic, family-destroying feminists and liberals five days a week from Chicago's WKLN radio tower. The term he'd coined for progressive women—femmunists—had become a much-loved buzzword on the radical right. Claud had become so popular that his show was syndicated in almost every state, and rerun at night and on weekends in his hometown.

Macauley didn't like being thought derivative, even of reality. She bristled as she explained that her detective, Nan Carruthers, had a totally unique personality and slant on public affairs.

"But because she goes against all the popular positions that feminists have persuaded the media to support I get an unbelievable amount of hate mail."

"And now someone's threatening your life?" I tried to sound more interested than hopeful.

Her blue eyes flashing in triumph, Macauley pulled a letter from her handbag and handed it to me. It was the product of a computer, printed on some kind of cheap white stock. In all caps it proclaimed, YOU'LL BE SORRY, BITCH, BUT BY THEN IT WILL BE TOO LATE.

"If this is a serious threat you're already too late," I snapped. "You should have taken it to the forensics lab before you fondled it. Unless you sent it yourself as a publicity stunt?"

Genuine crimson stained her cheeks. "How dare you? My last three books have been national best sellers—I don't need this kind of cheap publicity."

I handed the letter back. "You show it to the police?"

"They wouldn't take it seriously. They told me they could get the state's attorney to open a file, but what good would that do me?"

"Scotland Yard can identify individual laser printers based on samples of output but most U.S. police departments don't have those resources. Did you keep the envelope?"

She took out a grimy specimen. With a magnifying glass I could make out the zip code in the postmark: Chicago, the Gold Coast. That meant only one of about a hundred thousand residents, or the half-million tourists who pass through the neighborhood every day, could have mailed it. I tossed it back.

"You realize this isn't a death threat—it's just a threat, and pretty vague at that. What is it you'll be sorry for?"

"If I knew that I wouldn't be hiring a detective," she snapped.

"Have you had other threats?" It was an effort to keep my voice patient.

"I had two other letters like this one, but I didn't bring them—I didn't think they'd help you any. I've started having phone calls where they just wait, or laugh in a weird way or something. Sometimes I get the feeling someone's following me."

"Any hunches who might be doing it?" I was just going through the motions—I didn't think she was at any real risk, but she seemed the kind who couldn't believe she wasn't at the forefront of everyone else's mind.

"I *told* you." She leaned forward in her intensity. "Ever since *Take Back the Night*, my fourth book, which gives a whole different look at rape crisis centers, I've been on the top of every femmunist hitlist in the country."

I laughed, trying to picture some of my friends out taking potshots at every person in America who hated feminists. "It sounds like a nuisance, but I don't believe your life is in as much danger as, say, the average abortion provider. But if you want a bodyguard while you're on Claud Barnett's show I can recommend a couple of places. Just remember, though, that even the Secret Service couldn't protect JFK from a determined sniper."

"I suppose if I'd been some whiny feminist you'd take this more seriously. It's because of my politics you won't take the job."

"If you were a whiny feminist I'd probably tell you not to cry over this because there's a lot worse on its way. But since you're a whiny authoritarian there's not much I can do for you. I'll give you some advice for free, though: If you cry about it on the air you'll only invite a whole lot more of this kind of attention."

I didn't think contemporary clothes lent themselves to flouncing out of rooms, but Ms. Macauley certainly flounced out of mine. I wrote a brief summary of our meeting in my appointments log, then put her out of mind until the next night. I was having dinner with a friend who devours crime fiction. Sal Barthele was astounded that I hadn't heard of Lisa Macauley.

"You ever read anything besides the sports pages and the financial section, Warshawski? That girl is hot. They say her contract with Della Destra is worth twelve million, and all the guys with shiny armbands and goose-steps buy her books by the cord. I hear she's dedicating the next one to the brave folks at Operation Rescue."

After that I didn't think of Macauley at all: a case for a small suburban school district whose pension money had been turned into derivatives was taking all my energy. But a week later the writer returned forcibly to mind.

"You're in trouble now, Warshawski," Murray Ryerson said when I picked up the phone late Thursday night.

"Hi, Murray: good to hear from you, too." Murray is an investigative reporter for the *Herald-Star*, a one-time lover, sometime rival, occasional pain-in-the-butt, and even, now and then, a good friend.

"Why'd you tangle with Lisa Macauley? She's Chicago's most important artiste, behind Oprah."

"She come yammering to you with some tale of injustice? She wanted a bodyguard and I told her I didn't do that kind of work."

"Oh, Warshawski, you must have sounded ornery when you turned her down. She is not a happy camper: she got Claud Barnett all excited about how you won't work for anyone who doesn't agree with your politics. He dug up your involvement with the old abortion underground and has been blasting away at you the last two days as the worst kind of murdering femmunist. A wonderful woman came to you, trembling and scared for her life, and you turned her away just because she's against abortion. He says you investigate the politics of all your potential clients and won't take anyone who's given money to a Christian or a Republican cause and he's urging people to boycott you."

"Kind of people who listen to Claud need an investigator to find their brains. He isn't likely to hurt me."

Murray dropped his bantering tone. "He carries more weight than you, or maybe even I, want to think. You may have to do some damage control."

I felt my stomach muscles tighten: I live close to the edge of financial ruin much of the time. If I lost three or four key accounts I'd be dead.

"You think I should apply for a broadcast license and blast back? Or just have my picture taken coming out of the headquarters of the Republican National Committee?"

"You need a nineties kind of operation, Warshawski—a staff, including

a publicist. You need to have someone going around town with stories
about all the tough cases you've cracked in the last few years, showing how
wonderful you are. On account of I like hot-tempered Italian gals I might
run a piece myself if you'd buy me dinner."

"What's a nineties operation—where your self-promotion matters a
whole lot more than what kind of job you do? Come to think of it, do you
have an agent, Murray?"

The long pause at the other end told its own tale: Murray had definitely
joined the nineties. I looked in the mirror after he hung up, searching for
scales or some other visible sign of turning into a dinosaur. In the absence
of that I'd hang on to my little one-woman shop as long as possible.

I turned to the *Herald-Star*'s entertainment guide, looking to see when
WKLN ("The voice of the Klan," we'd dubbed them in my days with the
public defender) was rebroadcasting Barnett. I was in luck: he came on
again at eleven-thirty, so that night workers would have something to froth
about on their commute home.

After a few minutes from his high-end sponsors, his rich, folksy baritone
rolled through my speakers like molasses from a giant barrel. "Yeah, folks,
the femmunists are at it again. The Iron Curtain's gone down in Russia so
they want to put it up here in America. You think like they think or—
phht!—off you go to the Gulag.

"We've got one of those femmunists right here in Chicago. Private investigator. You know, in the old stories they used to call them private dicks.
Kind of makes you wonder what this gal is missing in her life that she
turned to that kind of work. Started out as a baby-killer back in the days
when she was at the Red University on the South Side of Chicago and grew
up to be a dick. Well, it takes all kinds, they say, but do we need this kind?

"We got an important writer here in Chicago. I know a lot of you read
the books this courageous woman writes. And because she's willing to take
a stand she gets death threats. So she goes to this femmunist dick, this
hermaphrodite dick, who won't help her out. 'Cause Lisa Macauley has
the guts to tell women the truth about rape and abortion, and this dick,
this V. I. Warshawski, can't take it.

"By the way, you ought to check out Lisa's new book. *Slaybells Ring*.
A great story which takes her fast-talking radio host Nan Carruthers into
the world of the ACLU and the bashing of Christmas. We carry it right
here in our bookstore. If you call in now Sheri will ship it right out to you.
Or just go out to your nearest warehouse: they're bound to stock it. Maybe
if this Warshawski read it she'd have a change of heart, but a gal like her,
you gotta wonder if she has a heart to begin with."

He went on for thirty minutes by the clock, making an easy segue from
me to the First Lady. If I was a devil, she was the Princess of Darkness.
When he finished I stared out the window for a time. I felt ill from the bile

Barnett had poured out in his molassied voice, but I was furious with Lisa Macauley. She had set me up, pure and simple. Come to see me with a spurious problem, just so she and Barnett could start trashing me on the air. But why?

MURRAY WAS RIGHT: BARNETT CARRIED more weight than I wanted to believe. He kept on at me for days, not always as the centerpiece, but often sending a few snide barbs my way. The gossip columns of all three daily papers mentioned it and the story got picked up by the wires. Between Barnett and the papers, Macauley got a load of free publicity; her sales skyrocketed. Which made me wonder again if she'd typed up that threatening note herself.

At the same time, my name getting sprinkled with mud did start having an effect on my own business: two new clients backed out mid-stream, and one of my old regulars phoned to say his company didn't have any work for me right now. No, they weren't going to cancel my contract, but they thought, in his picturesque corpo-speak, "we'd go into a holding pattern for the time being."

I called my lawyer to see what my options were; he advised me to let snarling dogs bite until they got it out of their system. "You don't have the money to take on Claud Barnett, Vic, and even if you won a slander suit against him you'd lose while the case dragged on."

On Sunday I meekly called Murray and asked if he'd be willing to repeat the deal he'd offered me earlier. After a two-hundred-dollar dinner at the Filigree he ran a nice story on me in the *Star*'s "Chicago Beat" section, recounting some of my great past successes. This succeeded in diverting some of Barnett's attention from me to Murray—my so-called stooge. Of course he wasn't going to slander Murray on the air—he could tell lies about a mere mortal like me, but not about someone with a big media operation to pay his legal fees.

I found myself trying to plan the total humiliation of both Barnett and Macauley. Let it go, I would tell myself, as I turned in the bed in the middle of the night: this is what he wants, to control my head. Turn it off. But I couldn't follow this most excellent advice.

I even did a little investigation into Macauley's life. I called a friend of mine at Channel 13 where Macauley had once worked to get the station's take on her. A native of Wisconsin, she'd moved to Chicago hoping to break into broadcast news. After skulking on the sidelines of the industry for five or six years she'd written her first Nan Carruthers book. Ironically enough, the women's movement, creating new roles for women in fiction as well as life, had fueled Macauley's literary success. When her second novel became a best seller, she divorced the man she married when they were both University of Wisconsin journalism students and started positioning herself as a celebrity. She was famous in book circles for her insistence on her personal security: opinion was divided as to whether it had started as a publicity stunt, or if she really did garner a lot of hate mail.

I found a lot of people who didn't like her—some because of her relentless self-promotion, some because of her politics, and some because they resented her success. As Sal had told me, Macauley was minting money now. Not only Claud, but the *Wall Street Journal*, the *National Review*, and all the other conservative rags hailed her as a welcome antidote to writers like Marcia Muller or Amanda Cross.

But despite my digging I couldn't find any real dirt on Macauley. Nothing I could use to embarrass her into silence. To make matters worse, someone at Channel 13 told her I'd been poking around asking questions about her. Whether by chance or design, she swept into Corona's one night when I was there with Sal. Sal and I were both enthusiastic fans of Belle Fontaine, the jazz singer who was Corona's Wednesday night regular headliner.

Lisa arrived near the end of the first set. She'd apparently found an agency willing to guard her body—she was the center of a boisterous crowd that included a couple of big men with bulges near their armpits. She flung her sable across a chair at a table near ours.

At first I assumed her arrival was just an unhappy coincidence. She didn't seem to notice me, but called loudly for champagne, asking for the most expensive brand on the menu. A couple at a neighboring table angrily shushed her. This prompted Lisa to start yelling out toasts to some of the people at her table: her *fabulous* publicist, her *awesome* attorney, and her *extraordinary* bodyguards, "Rover" and "Prince." The sullen-faced men didn't join in the raucous cheers at their nicknames, but they didn't erupt, either.

We couldn't hear the end of "Tell Me Lies" above Lisa's clamor, but Belle took a break at that point. Sal ordered another drink and started to fill me in on family news: Her lover had just landed a role in a sitcom that would take her out to the West Coast for the winter and Sal was debating hiring a manager for her own bar, the Golden Glow, so she could join Becca. She was just describing—in humorous detail—Becca's first meeting with the producer, when Lisa spoke loudly enough for everyone in the room to hear.

"I'm so glad you boys were willing to help me out. I can't believe how chicken some of the detectives in this town are. Easy to be big and bold in an abortion clinic, but they run and hide from someone their own size." She turned deliberately in her chair, faked an elaborate surprise at the sight of me, and continued at the same bellowing pitch, "Oh, V. I. Warshawski! I hope you don't take it personally."

"I don't expect eau de cologne from the sewer," I called back heartily.

The couple who'd tried to quiet Lisa down during the singing laughed at this. The star twitched, then got to her feet, champagne glass in hand, and came over to me.

"I hear you've been stalking me, Warshawski. I could sue you for harassment."

I smiled. "Sugar, I've been trying to find out why a big successful gal like you had to invent some hate mail just to have an excuse to slander me. You want to take me to court I'll be real, *real* happy to sort out your lies in public."

"In court or anywhere else I'll make you look as stupid as you do right now." Lisa tossed her champagne into my face; a camera strobe flashed just as the drink hit me.

Fury blinded me more than the champagne. I knocked over a chair as I leapt up to throttle her, but Sal got an arm around my waist and pulled me down. Behind Macauley, Prince and Rover got to their feet, ready to move: Lisa had clearly staged the whole event to give them an excuse for beating me up.

Queenie, who owns the Corona, was at my side with some towels. "Jake! I want these people out of here now. And I think some cute person's been taking pictures. Make sure she leaves the film with you, hear? Ms. Macauley, you owe me three hundred dollars for that Dom Pérignon you threw around."

Prince and Rover thought they were going to take on Queenie's bouncer, but Jake had broken up bigger fights than they could muster. He managed to lift them both and slam their heads together, then to snatch the *fabulous* publicist's bag as she was trying to sprint out the door. Jake took out her camera, pulled the film, and handed the bag back to her with smile and an insulting bow. The attorney, prompted by Jake, handed over three bills, and the whole party left to loud applause from the audience.

Queenie and Sal grew up together, which may be why I got Gold Coast treatment that night, but not even her private reserve Veuve Clicquot could take the bad taste from my mouth. If I'd beaten up Macauley I'd have looked like the brute she and Barnett were labeling me; but taking a faceful of champagne sitting down left me looking—and feeling—helpless.

"You're not going to do anything stupid, are you, Vic?" Sal said as she dropped me off around two in the morning. " 'Cause if you are I'm babysitting you, girlfriend."

"No. I'm not going to do anything rash, if that's what you mean. But I'm going to nail that prize bitch, one way or another."

Twenty-four hours later Lisa Macauley was dead. One day after that I was in jail.

ALL I KNEW ABOUT LISA'S murder was what I'd read in the papers before the cops came for me: Her personal trainer had discovered her body when he arrived Friday morning for their usual workout. She had been beaten to death in what looked like a bloody battle, which is why the state's attorney finally let me go—they couldn't find the marks on me they were looking for. And they couldn't find any evidence in my home or office.

They kept insisting, though, that I had gone to her apartment late Thursday night. They asked me about it all night long on Friday without telling me why they were so sure. When Freeman Carter, my lawyer, finally sprang me Saturday afternoon he forced them to tell him: the doorman was claiming he admitted me to Lisa's apartment just before midnight on Thursday.

Freeman taxed me with it on the ride home. "The way she was carrying on it would have been like you to demand a face-to-face with her, Vic. Don't hold out on me—I can't defend you if you were there and won't tell me about it."

"I wasn't there," I said flatly. "I am not prone to blackouts or hallucinations: there is no way I could have gone there and forgotten it. I was blamelessly watching the University of Kansas men pound Duke on national television. I even have a witness: My golden retriever shared a pizza with me. Her testimony: She threw up cheese sauce in front of my bed Friday morning."

Freeman ignored that. "Sal told me about the dust-up at Corona's. Anyway, Stacey Cleveland, Macauley's publicist, had already bared all to the police. You're the only person they can locate who had reason to be killing mad with her."

"Then they're not looking, are they? Someone either pretended to be me, or else bribed the doorman to tell the cops I was there. Get me the doorman's name and I'll sort out which it was."

"I can't do that, Vic: you're in enough trouble without suborning the state's key witness."

"You're supposed to be on my side," I snapped. "You want to go into court with evidence or not?"

"I'll talk to the doorman, Vic: you go take a bath—jail doesn't smell very good on you."

I followed Freeman's advice only because I was too tired to do anything else. After that I slept the clock around, waking just before noon on Sunday. The phone had been ringing when I walked in on Saturday. It was Murray, wanting my exclusive story. I put him off and switched the phone to my answering service. In the morning I had forty-seven messages from various reporters. When I started outside to get the Sunday papers I found a camera crew parked in front of the building. I retreated, fetched my coat and an overnight bag, and went out the back way. My car was parked right in front of the camera van, so I walked the three miles to my new office.

When the Pulteney Building went under the wrecking ball last April I'd moved my business to a warehouse on the edge of Wicker Park, at the corner of Milwaukee Avenue and North. Fringe galleries and nightspots compete with liquor stores and palm readers for air here, and there are a lot of vacant lots, but it was ten minutes—by car, bus, or L—from the heart of the financial district where most of my business lies. A sculpting friend had moved her studio into a revamped warehouse; the day after visiting her I signed a five-year lease across the hall. I had twice my old space at two-thirds the rent. Since I'd had to refurnish—from Dumpsters and auctions—I'd put in a daybed behind a partition: I could camp out here for a few days until media interest in me cooled.

I bought the Sunday papers from one of the liquor stores on my walk. The *Sun-Times* concentrated on Macauley's career, including a touching history of her childhood in Rhinelander, Wisconsin. She'd been the only child of older parents. Her father, Joseph, had died last year at the age of eighty, but her mother, Louise, still lived in the house where Lisa had grown up. The paper showed a frame bungalow with a porch swing and a minute garden, as well as a tearful Louise Macauley in front of Lisa's doll collection ("I've kept the room the way it looked when she left for college," the caption read).

Her mother never wanted her going off to the University of Wisconsin. "Even though we raised her with the right values, and sent her to church schools, the university is a terrible place. She wouldn't agree, though, and now look what's happened."

The *Tribune* had a discreet sidebar on Lisa's recent contretemps with me. In the *Herald-Star* Murray published the name of the doorman who had admitted "someone claiming to be V. I. Warshawski" to Macauley's building. It was Reggie Whitman. He'd been the doorman since the building went up in 1978, was a grandfather, a church deacon, coached a basketball team at the Henry Horner Homes, and was generally so virtuous that truth radiated from him like a beacon.

Murray also had talked with Lisa's ex-husband, Brian Gerstein, an assistant producer for one of the local network news stations. He was appropriately grief-stricken at his ex-wife's murder. The picture supplied by Gerstein's publicist showed a man in his mid-thirties with a TV smile but anxious eyes.

I called Beth Blacksin, the reporter at Channel 13 who'd filled me in on what little I'd learned about Lisa Macauley before her death.

"Vic! Where are you? We've got a camera crew lurking outside your front door hoping to talk to you!"

"I know, babycakes. And talk to me you shall, as soon as I find out who set me up to take the fall for Lisa Macauley's death. So give me some information now and it shall return to you like those famous loaves of bread."

Beth wanted to dicker but the last two weeks had case-hardened my temper. She finally agreed to talk with the promise of a reward in the indefinite future.

Brian Gerstein had once worked at Channel 13, just as he had for every other news station in town. "He's a loser, Vic: I'm not surprised Lisa dumped him when she started to get successful. He's the kind of guy who would sit around dripping into his coffee because you were out-earning him, moaning, trying to get you to feel sorry for him. People hire him because he's a good tape editor, but then they give him the shove because he gets the whole newsroom terminally depressed."

"You told me last week they met up at UW when they were students there in the eighties. Where did they go next?"

Beth had to consult her files, but she came back on the line in a few minutes with more details. Gerstein came from Long Island. He met Lisa when they were both Wisconsin juniors, campaigning for Reagan's first election in 1980. They'd married five years later, just before moving to Chicago. Politics and TV kept them together for seven years after that.

Gerstein rented an apartment in Rogers Park on the far north side of the city. "And that's typical of him," Beth added as she gave me his address. "He won't own a home since they split up: he can't afford it, his life was ruined and he doesn't feel like housekeeping, I've heard a dozen different whiny reasons from him. Not that everyone has to own, but you don't have to rent a run-down apartment in gangbanger territory when you work for the networks, either."

"So he could have been peevish enough to kill Lisa?"

"You're assuming he swathed himself in skirts and furs and told Reggie Whitman he was V. I. Warshawski? It would take more—more gumption than he's got to engineer something like that. It's not a bad theory, though: maybe we'll float it on the four o'clock news. Give us something different to talk about than all the other guys. Stay in touch, Vic. I'm willing to believe you're innocent, but it'd make a better story if you'd killed her."

"Thanks, Blacksin." I laughed as I hung up: her enthusiasm was without malice.

I took the L up to Rogers Park, the slow Sunday milk run. Despite Beth's harangue, it's an interesting part of town. Some blocks you do see dopers hanging out, some streets have depressing amounts of garbage in the yards, but most of the area harks back to the Chicago of my childhood: tidy brick two-flats, hordes of immigrants in the parks speaking every known language and along with them, delis and coffee shops for every nationality.

Gerstein lived on one of the quiet side streets. He was home, as I'd hoped: staking out an apartment without a car would have been miserable work on a cold February day. He even let me in without too much fuss. I told him I was a detective, and showed him my license, but he didn't seem to recognize my name—he must not have been editing the programs dealing with his ex-wife's murder. Or he'd been so stricken he'd edited them without registering anything.

He certainly exuded misery as he escorted me up the stairs. Whether it was grief or guilt for Lisa, or just the chronic depression Beth attributed to him, he moved as though on the verge of falling over. He was a little taller than I, but slim. Swathed in a coat and shawls he might have looked like a woman to the nightman.

Gerstein's building was clean and well maintained, but his own apartment was sparely furnished, as though he expected to move on at any second. The only pictures on the walls were a couple of framed photographs—one of himself and Lisa with Ronald Reagan, and the other with a man I didn't recognize. He had no drapes or plants or anything else to bring a bit of color to the room, and when he invited me to sit he pulled a metal folding chair from a closet for me.

"I always relied on Lisa to fix things up," he said. "She has so much vivacity and such good taste. Without her I can't seem to figure out how to do it."

"I thought you'd been divorced for years." I tossed my coat onto the card table in the middle of the room.

"Yes, but I've only been living here nine months. She let me keep our old condo, but last summer I couldn't make the payments. She said she'd come around to help me fix this up, only she's so busy . . ." His voice trailed off.

I wondered how he ever sold himself to his various employers—I found myself wanting to shake him out like a pillow and plump him up. "So you and Lisa stayed in touch?"

"Oh, sort of. She was too busy to call much, but she'd talk to me sometimes when I phoned."

"So you didn't have any hard feelings about your divorce?"

"Oh, I did. I never wanted to split up—it was all her idea. I kept hoping, but now, you know, it's too late."

"I suppose a woman as successful as Lisa met a lot of men."

"Yes, yes she certainly did." His voice was filled with admiration, not hate.

I was beginning to agree with Beth, that Gerstein couldn't possibly have killed Lisa. What really puzzled me was what had ever attracted her to him in the first place, but the person who could figure out the hows and whys of attraction would put Ann Landers out of business overnight.

I went through the motions with him—did he get a share in her royalties?—yes, on the first book, because she'd written that while they were still together. When she wanted a divorce his lawyer told him he could probably get a judgment entitling him to fifty percent of all her proceeds, even in the future, but he loved Lisa, he wanted her to come back to him, he wasn't interested in being vindictive. Did he inherit under Lisa's will? He didn't think so, I'd have to ask her attorney. Did he know who her residuary legatee was? Some conservative foundations they both admired.

I got up to go. "Who do you think killed your wife, ex-wife?"

"I thought they'd arrested someone, that dick Claud Barnett says was harassing her."

"You know Barnett? Personally, I mean?" All I wanted was to divert him from thinking about me—even in his depression he might have remembered hearing my name on the air—but he surprised me.

"Yeah. That is, Lisa does. Did. We went to a conservative media convention together right after we moved here. Barnett was the keynote speaker. She got all excited, said she'd known him growing up but his name was something different then. After that she saw him every now and then. She got him to take his picture with us a couple of years later, at another convention in Sun Valley."

He jerked his head toward the wall where the photographs hung. I went over to look at them. I knew the Gipper's famous smile pretty well by heart so I concentrated on Barnett. I was vaguely aware of his face: he was considered so influential in the nation's swing rightward that his picture kept popping up in news magazines. A man of about fifty, he was lean and well groomed, and usually smiling with affable superiority.

In Sun Valley he must have eaten something that disagreed with him. He had an arm around Lisa and her husband, stiffly, as if someone had propped plyboard limbs against his trunk. Lisa was smiling gaily, happy to be with the media darling. Brian was holding himself upright and looking close to jovial. But Claud gave you the idea that thumbscrews had been hammered under his plywood nails to get him into the photo.

"What name had Lisa known him by as a child?" I asked.

"Oh, she was mistaken about that. Once she got to see him up close she realized it was only a superficial resemblance. But Barnett took a shine to her—most people did, she was so vivacious—and gave her a lot of support in her career. He was the first big booster of her Nan Carruthers novels."

"He doesn't look very happy to be with her here, does he? Can I borrow it? It's a very good one of Lisa, and I'd like to use it in my inquiries."

Brian said in a dreary voice that he thought Lisa's publicist would have much better ones, but he was easy to persuade—or bully, to call my approach by its real name. I left with the photo carefully draped in a dish towel, and a written promise to return it as soon as possible.

I trotted to the Jarvis L stop, using the public phone there to call airlines. I found one that not only sent kiddie planes from O'Hare to Rhinelander, Wisconsin, but had a flight leaving in two hours. The state's attorney had told me not to leave the jurisdiction. Just in case they'd put a stop on me at the airport, I booked a flight under my mother's maiden name and embarked on the tedious L journey back to the Loop and out to the airport.

LISA'S NEW BOOK, *SLAYBELLS RING*, was stacked high at the airport bookstores. The black enamel cover with an embossed spray of bells in silver drew the eye. At the third stand I passed I finally gave in and bought a copy.

The flight was a long puddle-jumper, making stops in Milwaukee and Wausau on its way north. By the time we reached Rhinelander I was approaching the denouement, where the head of the American Civil Liberties Union was shown to be opposing the display of a Christmas creche at City Hall because he secretly owned a company that was trying to put the creche's manufacturer out of business. Nan Carruthers, owing to her wide and loyal band of radio fans, got the information from an employee the ACLU baddie had fired after thirty years of loyal service when the employee was found listening to Nan's show on his lunch break. The book had a three-hanky ending at midnight mass, where Nan joined the employee—now triumphantly reinstated (thanks to the enforcement of the Civil Rights Act of 1964 by the EEOC and the ACLU, but Lisa Macauley hadn't thought that worth mentioning)—along with his wife and their nine children in kneeling in front of the public creche.

I finished the book around one in the morning in the Rhinelander Holiday Inn. The best-written part treated a subplot between Nan and the man who gave her career its first important boost—the pastor of the heroine's childhood church who had become a successful televangelist. When Nan was a child he had photographed her and other children in his Sunday school class engaged in forced sex with one another and with him. Since he held an awful fear of eternal damnation over their heads they never told their parents. But when Nan started her broadcast career she persuaded him to plug her program on his Thursday night "Circle of the Saved," using covert blackmail threats to get him to do so. At the end, as she looks at the baby Jesus in the manger, she wonders what Mary would have done—forgiven the pastor, or exposed him? Certainly not collaborated with him to further her own career. The book ended on that troubled note. I went to sleep with more respect for Macauley's craft than I had expected.

IN THE MORNING I FOUND Mrs. Joseph Macauley's address in the local phone book and went off to see her. Although now in her mid-seventies she carried herself well. She didn't greet me warmly, but she accepted without demur my identification of myself as a detective trying to find Lisa's murderer. Chicago apparently was so convinced that I was the guilty party, they hadn't bothered to send anyone up to interview her.

"I am tired of all those Chicago reporters bothering me, but if you're a detective I guess I can answer your questions. What'd you want to know? I can tell you all about Lisa's childhood, but we didn't see so much of her once she moved off to Madison. We weren't too happy about some of the friends she was making. Not that we have anything against Jews personally, but we didn't want our only child marrying one and getting involved in all those dirty financial deals. Of course we were happy he was working for Ronald Reagan, but we weren't sorry they split up, even though our church frowns on divorce."

I let her talk unguided for a time before pulling out the picture of Claud Barnett. "This is someone Lisa knew as a child. Do you recognize him?"

Mrs. Macauley took the photo from me. "Do you think I'm not in possession of my faculties? That's Claud Barnett. He certainly never lived around here."

She snorted and started to hand the picture back, then took it to study more closely. "She knew I never liked to see her in pants, so she generally wore a skirt when she came up here. But she looks real cute in that outfit, real cute. You know, I guess I can see where she might have confused him with Carl Bader. Although Carl was dark-haired and didn't have a mustache, there is a little something around the forehead."

"And who was Carl Bader?"

"Oh, that's ancient history. He left town and we never heard anything more about it."

All I could get her to say about him was that he'd been connected to their church and she never did believe half the gossip some of the members engaged in. "That Mrs. Hoffer always overindulged her children, let them say anything and get away with it. We brought Lisa up to show proper respect for people in authority. Cleaned her mouth out with soap and whipped her so hard she didn't sit for a week the one time she tried taking part in some of that trashy talk."

More she wouldn't say, so I took the picture with me to the library and looked up old copies of the local newspaper. In *Slaybells Ring*, Nan Carruthers was eight when the pastor molested her, so I checked 1965 through 1967 for stories about Bader and anyone named Hoffer. All I found was a little blurb saying Bader had left the United Pentecostal Church of God in Holiness in 1967 to join a television ministry in Atlanta, and that he'd gone so suddenly that the church didn't have time to throw him a going-away party.

I spent a weary afternoon trying to find Mrs. Hoffer. There were twenty-seven Hoffers in the Rhinelander phone book; six were members of the United Pentecostal Church. The church secretary was pleasant and helpful, but it wasn't until late in the day that Mrs. Matthew Hoffer told me the woman I wanted, Mrs. Barnabas Hoffer, had quit the church over the episode about her daughter.

"Caused a lot of hard feeling in the church. Some people believed the children, and they quit. Others figured it was just mischief, children who like to make themselves look interesting. That Lisa Macauley was one. I'm sorry she got herself killed down in Chicago, but in a way I'm not surprised—seemed like she was always sort of *daring* you to smack her, the stories she made up and the way she put herself forward. Not that Louise Macauley spared the rod, mind you, but sometimes I think you can beat a child too much for its own good. Anyway, once people saw little Lisa joining in with Katie Hoffer in accusing the pastor no one took it seriously. No one except Gertrude—Katie's mom, I mean. She still bears a grudge against all of us who stood by Pastor Bader."

And finally, at nine o'clock, I was sitting on an overstuffed horsehair settee in Gertrude Hoffer's living room, looking at a cracked color photo of two unhappy children. I had to take Mrs. Hoffer's word that they were Katie and Lisa—their faces were indistinct, and at this point in the picture's age so were their actions.

"I found it when I was doing his laundry. Pastor Bader wasn't married, so all us church ladies took it in turn to look after his domestic wants. Usually he was right there to put his own clothes away, but this one time he was out and I was arranging his underwear for him and found this whole stack of pictures. I couldn't believe it at first, and then when I came on Katie's face—well—I snatched it up and ran out of there.

"At first I thought it was some evilness the children dreamed up on their own, and that he had photographed them to show us, show the parents what they got up to. That was what he told my husband when Mr. Hoffer went to talk to him about it. It took me a long time to see that a child wouldn't figure out something like that on her own, but I never could get any of the other parents to pay me any mind. And that Louise Macauley, she just started baking pies for Pastor Bader every night of the week, whipped poor little Lisa for telling me what he made her and Katie get up to. It's a judgment on her, it really is, her daughter getting herself killed like that."

IT WAS HARD FOR ME to find someone in the Chicago Police Department willing to try to connect Claud Barnett with Carl Bader. Once they'd done that, though, the story unraveled pretty fast. Lisa had recognized him in Sun Valley and put the bite on him—not for money, but for career advancement, just as her heroine did her own old pastor in *Slaybells Ring*. No one would ever be able to find out for sure, but the emotional torment she put Nan Carruthers through must have paralleled Lisa's own misery. She was a success, she'd forced her old tormentor to make her a success, but it must have galled her—as it did her heroine—to pretend to admire him, to sit in on his show, and to see a film of torment overlay his face.

When Barnett read *Slaybells*, he probably began to worry that Lisa wouldn't be able to keep his secret to herself much longer. The police did find evidence of the threatening letters in his private study. The state argued that Barnett sent Lisa the threatening letters, then persuaded her to hire me to protect her. At that point Barnett didn't have anything special against me, but I was a woman. He figured if he could start enough public conflict between a woman detective and Lisa, he'd be able to fool the nightman, Reggie Whitman, into believing he was sending a woman up to Lisa's apartment on the fatal night. It was only later that he'd learned about my progressive politics—that was just icing on his cake, to be able to denounce me on his show.

Of course, not all this came out right away—some of it didn't emerge until the trial. That's when I also learned that Whitman, besides being practically a saint, had badly failing vision. On a cold night anyone could have passed himself off as me.

Between Murray and Beth Blacksin I got a lot of public vindication, and Sal and Queenie took me to dinner with Belle Fontaine to celebrate on the day the guilty verdict came in. We were all disappointed that they only slapped him with second-degree murder. But what left me gasping for air was a public opinion poll that came out the next afternoon. Even though other examples of his child-molesting behavior had come to light during the trial, his listeners believed he was innocent of all charges.

"The femmunists made it all up trying to discredit him," one woman explained that afternoon on the air. "And then they got *The New York Times* to print their lies."

Not even Queenie's reserve Veuve Clicquot could wipe that bitter taste out of my mouth.

Bill Pronzini's creation, the Nameless Detective, is an example of mystery writing at its finest. The central character is defined through his relationships with others, his work, and his life—everything but his name. The novels and short stories are practically required reading in the genre. But, like so many other authors in this year's volume, we've chosen a nonseries story. Brief but devastating, "The Monster" is a paradigm of a modern mystery master at work.

The Monster
BILL PRONZINI

He was after the children. Meg knew it, all at once, as soon as he was inside the house. She couldn't have said exactly how she knew. He was pleasant enough on the surface, smiling, friendly. Big and shaggy-haired in his uniform, hairy all over like a bear. But behind his smile and underneath his fur there was menace, evil. She felt it, intuited it—a mother's instinct for danger. He was after Kate and Bobby. One of those monsters who preyed on little children, hurt them, did unspeakable things to them—

"Downstairs or upstairs?" he said.

". . . What?"

"The stopped-up drain. Downstairs here or upstairs?"

A feeling of desperation was growing in her, spreading toward panic. She didn't know what to do. "I think you'd better leave." The words were out before she realized what she was saying.

"Huh? I just got here, Mrs. Thompson. Your husband said you got a stopped-up drain—that's right, isn't it?"

Why did I let him in? she thought. Just because he said Philip sent him, that doesn't make it so. And even if Philip did send him . . . Oh God, why *him*, of all the plumbers in this city?

"No," she said. "No, it . . . it's all right now. It's working again, there's nothing wrong with it."

He wasn't smiling anymore. "You kidding me?"

"Why would I do that?"

324

"Yeah, why? Over at the door you said you been expecting me, come on in and fix the drain."

"I didn't—"

"You did, lady. Look, I haven't got time to play games. And it's gonna cost you sixty-five bucks whether I do any work or not so you might as well let me take a look."

"It's all right now, I tell you."

"Okay, maybe it is. But if it was stopped-up once today, it could happen again. You never know with the pipes in these old houses. So where is it, up or down?"

"Please . . ."

"Upstairs, right? Yeah, now I think of it, your husband said it was in the upstairs bathroom."

No! The word was like a scream in her mind. The upstairs bathroom was between their room, hers and Philip's, and the nursery. Baby Kate in her crib, not even a year old, and Bobby, just two, napping in his bed . . . so innocent and helpless . . . and this man, this beast—

He moved past her to the stairs, hefting his tool kit in one huge, scab-knuckled hand. "You want to show me where it is?"

"No!" She cried it aloud this time.

"Hey," he said, "you don't have to bust my eardrums." He shook his head the way Philip did sometimes when he was vexed with her. "Well, I can find it myself. Can't hide a bathroom from an old hand like me."

He started up the stairs.

She stood paralyzed, staring in horror as he climbed. She tried to shriek at him to stop, go away, don't hurt the babies, but her voice had frozen in her throat. If any harm came to Kate and Bobby, she could never forgive herself—she would shrivel up and die. So many childless years, all the doctors who'd told her and Philip that she could never conceive, and then the sudden miracle of her first pregnancy and Bobby's birth, the second miracle that was Kate. . . . If she let either of them be hurt she would be as much of a monster as the one climbing the stairs—

Stop him!

The paralysis left her as abruptly as it had come on; her legs pumped, carried her headlong into the kitchen. A knife, the big butcher knife . . . She grabbed it out of the rack, raced back to the stairs.

He was already on the second floor. She couldn't see him, but she could hear his heavy menacing tread in the hallway, going down the hallway.

Toward the nursery.

Toward Kate and Bobby.

She rushed upward, clutching the knife, her terror so immense now it felt as though her head would burst. She ran into the hallway, saw him again—and her heart skipped a beat, the fear ripped inside her like an animal trying to claw its way out of a cage.

He was standing in the nursery doorway, looking in at the children.

She lunged at him with the knife upraised. He turned just before she reached him, and his mouth shaped startled words. But the only sound he made was an explosive grunt when she plunged the knife into his chest.

His mouth flew open; his eyes bulged so wide she thought for an instant they would pop out like seeds from a squeezed orange. One scarred hand plucked at the knife handle. The other groped in her direction, as if to catch and crush her. She leapt back against the far wall, stood huddled against it as he staggered away, still grunting and plucking at the knife handle.

She saw him fall once, lurch upright again, finally reach the top of the stairs; then the grunting ended in a long heaving sigh and he sagged and toppled forward. The sounds he made rolling and bouncing down the stairs were as loud and terrible as the thunder that had terrified her as a child, that still frightened her sometimes on storm-heavy nights.

The noises stopped at last and there was silence.

Meg pushed away from the wall, hurried into the nursery. Bobby, incredibly, was still asleep; he had the face of a golden-haired angel, lying pooched on his side with his tiny arms outstretched. Kate was awake and fussing. Meg picked her up, held her tight, soothed and rocked and murmured to her until the fussing stopped and her tears dried. When the baby was tucked up asleep in her crib, Meg steeled herself and then made her way slowly out to the stairs and down.

The evil one lay crumpled and smeared with red at the bottom. His eyes still bulged, wide open and staring. Dead.

And that was good, it was *good*, because it meant that the children were safe again.

She stepped over him, shuddering, and went to the phone in the kitchen. She called the police first, then Philip at his office to ask him to please come home right away.

A DETECTIVE SERGEANT AND TWO uniformed officers arrived first. Meg explained to the detective what had happened, and he seemed very sympathetic. But he was still asking questions when Philip came.

Philip put his strong arms around her, held her; she leaned close to him as always, because he was the only person since her daddy died who had ever made her feel safe. He didn't ask her any questions. He made her sit down in the living room, went with the detective to look at what lay under the sheet at the foot of the stairs.

". . . don't understand it," Philip was saying. "He was highly recommended to me by a friend. Reliable, honest, trustworthy—the best plumber in town."

"Then you did send him over to fix a stopped-up drain."

"Yes. I told my wife I was going to. I just don't understand. Did he try to attack her? Is that why she stabbed him?"

"Not her, no. She said he was after your children. Upstairs in the nursery where they're asleep."

"Oh my God," Philip said.

He must have sensed her standing there because he turned to look at her. I had to do it, Philip, she told him with her eyes. He was a monster and I had to protect the children. Our wonderful son Bobby, sweet baby Kate . . . I'm their mother, I couldn't let them be hurt, could I?

But he didn't believe her. She saw the disbelief in his face before he turned away again, and then she heard him lie to the detective. He lied, he lied, Philip lied—

"We don't have any children," he said.

BIBLIOGRAPHY
A 1996 yearbook, compiled by Edward D. Hoch

I. COLLECTIONS AND SINGLE STORIES

Alcott, Louisa May. *Modern Magic*. New York: Modern Library. Introduction by Madeleine B. Stern. Five thrillers ranging in length from short story to novella, first published 1863–69. (1995)

————. *A Whisper in the Dark*. New York: Barnes & Noble. Twelve thrillers from previous collections. Edited by Stefan Dziemianowicz.

Barnard, Robert. *The Habit of Widowhood and Other Murderous Proclivities*. New York: Scribner. Seventeen stories, one new, mainly from *EQMM*.

Bloch, Robert. *Robert Bloch: Appreciations of the Master*. New York: Tor. Tributes to the late author from several well-known writers, together with nineteen of his best stories, both mystery and fantasy. Edited by Richard Matheson & Ricia Mainhardt.

Bradbury, Ray. *Quicker Than the Eye*. New York: Avon Books. Twenty-one stories, eight new. Mainly fantasy but a few criminous, one from *EQMM*.

Brenchley, Chaz. *Blood Waters*. Newcastle upon Tyne, England: Flambard Press. Ten crime and horror stories, three new.

Burke, Jan. *Unharmed*. Mission Viejo, CA: A.S.A.P. Publishing. Limited edition of a single award-winning short-short story from *EQMM*, mid-December 1994. Introduction by Wendy Hornsby.

Chizmar, Richard T. *Midnight Promises*. Springfield, PA: Gauntlet Publications. A limited edition of dark suspense stories. Introduction by Ed Gorman, afterword by Ray Garton.

Clark, Mary Higgins. *My Gal Sunday: Henry and Sunday Stories*. New York: Simon & Schuster. Four novelettes about a sleuthing ex-president and his wife.

Gorman, Ed. *The Dwyer Trilogy*. Baltimore: CD Publications. A limited edition containing reprints of two novels about detective Jack Dwyer plus a new Dwyer short story.

———. *Moonchasers and Other Stories*. New York: Forge/Tor. The 1993 title novelette and sixteen short stories from various sources. Afterword by Dean Koontz.

———. *Out There in the Darkness*. Burton, MI: Subterranean Press. Limited edition of a single short story. (1995)

Goulart, Ron. *Murder for Dummies*. New York: The Mysterious Bookshop. A single new short story in a booklet published as a Christmas gift by a Manhattan bookstore.

Hoch, Edward D. *Diagnosis: Impossible. The Problems of Dr. Sam Hawthorne*. Norfolk, VA: Crippen & Landru. Twelve stories from *EQMM*, 1974–78, with an introduction by the author and a chronology of the series by Marvin Lachman.

Jackson, Shirley. *Just an Ordinary Day*. New York: Bantam. Fifty-four stories, thirty-one previously unpublished. A mixed collection containing some criminous and macabre stories.

Jakubowski, Maxim. *Life in the World of Women: A Collection of Vile, Dangerous, and Loving Stories*. London: The Do-Not Press. Nine stories, three new, some criminous.

Lovisi, Gary. *Extreme Measures*. Brooklyn: Gryphon Publications. Fifteen mystery and crime stories. Introduction by Richard A. Lupoff.

Lowe, William T. *After the Summer People Leave*. Elizabethtown, NY: Pinto Press. Twelve mystery stories set in the Adirondack Mountains of New York State, seven from *AHMM*. (A thirteenth story is nonmystery.)

Lupoff, Richard A. *Before . . . 12:01 . . . and After*. Minneapolis: Fedogan & Bremer. A mixed collection of twenty-three science fiction, fantasy, and mystery stories, one new, from various sources over the past forty years.

Masur, Harold Q. *Dig My Grave & Shroud Me Not*. Brooklyn: Gryphon Publications. Reprints of a Scott Jordan novelette and a Harvey St. John novella from the pulps, 1949–53.

Moyes, Patricia. *Who Killed Father Christmas? and Other Unseasonable Demises*. Norfolk, VA: Crippen & Landru. A novella and twenty short stories from various sources. Introduction by the author.

O'Donnell, Peter. *Cobra Trap*. London: Souvenir Press. Five new novelettes of intrigue featuring Modesty Blaise.

Pronzini, Bill. *Spadework*. Norfolk, VA: Crippen & Landru. Fifteen stories about the Nameless Detective, two of them new. Introduction by Marcia Muller and afterword by the author. Includes checklist of all Nameless novels and stories to date.

Rhea, Nicholas. *Constable About the Parish*. London: Robert Hale. Ten new untitled stories in a continuing series about a British police constable.

Salisbury, Luke. *Blue Eden*. Brooklyn: The Smith. Three connected crime stories about J. Edgar Hoover and the black proprietor of a Washington diner.

Starrett, Vincent. *The Memoirs of Jimmy Lavender*. Shelburne, Ontario, Canada: The Battered Silicon Dispatch Box. Twelve stories, 1917–56, about a gentleman detective, previously uncollected.

Suter, John F. *Old Land, Dark Land, Strange Land*. Charleston, WV: University of Charleston. Nineteen stories, 1953–92, seventeen from *EQMM* and two from *AHMM*. Five of the stories are continuations of Melville Davisson Post's Uncle Abner series. Introduction by the author.

Swart, Carter. *Mysteries: Tales of Suspense*. Concord, CA: AE Press. Seven crime stories from various sources, two with detection. (1995)

Tepperman, Emile C. *Ed Race: Murder in the Spotlight*. Medford, NJ: Pulp Adventure Press. A pamphlet containing four short stories from The Spider Magazine, 1934–36.

Timlin, Mark. *Sharman and Other Filth*. London: Vista/Cassell. Eight stories about private eye Nick Sharman, and a new nonseries novella, "Filth."

II. ANTHOLOGIES

Ashley, Mike, ed. *Classical Whodunnits*. London: Robinson. Twenty stories, fifteen new, set in ancient Greek and Roman times. Preface by Steven Saylor.

Bedford, Jean, ed. *Moonlight Becomes You*. St. Leonards, Australia: Allen & Unwin. Eleven new stories by Australian mystery writers, all with a moonlight theme. The sixth of an annual "Crimes for Summer" series. (1995)

Brownworth, Victoria A. & Judith M. Redding, eds. *Out for More Blood: Tales of Malice and Retaliation by Women*. Chicago: Third Side Press. Sixteen new stories.

Bryant, Mark, ed. *Sins of the Fathers: An Anthology of Clerical Crime*. London: Gollancz. Fourteen stories by Chesterton, Christie, Doyle, and eleven mainstream writers of the 19th and early 20th centuries. Some fantasy.

Cameron, Victoria & Audrey Jessup, eds. *The Ladies' Killing Circle*. Burnstown, Ontario, Canada: General Store Publishing House. Twenty-six new stories and poems by Canadian women writers. Includes Mary Jane Moffini's "Cotton Amour," winner of the Crime Writers of Canada annual short story award. (1995)

Collins, Barbara & Robert J. Randisi, eds. *Lethal Ladies*. New York: Berkley. Sixteen stories, nine new, presented by the Private Eye Writers of America.

Cox, Michael, ed. *The Oxford Book of Spy Stories*. New York: Oxford University Press. Twenty-eight stories, 1891–1994.

Edwards, Martin, ed. *Perfectly Criminal*. Sutton, Surrey, England: Severn House. Nineteen stories, sixteen new, in an annual anthology from the Crime Writers' Association, including the winner of the 1996 CWA Gold Dagger, Ian Rankin's "Herbert in Motion." Foreword by Kate Charles.

Gorman, Ed; Larry Segriff & Martin H. Greenberg, eds. *Murder Most Irish*. New York: Barnes & Noble. Fifteen stories, eight new, plus two novels by John Brady and Ann C. Fallon.

Grady, James, ed. *Unusual Suspects*. New York: Vintage. Fifteen new stories and two reprints.

Greeenberg, Martin H., ed., *The Edgar Award Book*. New York: Barnes & Noble Books. Twenty-four stories that were MWA Edgar winners or nominees. Introduction by Edward D. Hoch.

Greenberg, Martin H., & Elizabeth Foxwell, eds. *Malice Domestic 5*. New York: Pocket Books. Introduction by Phyllis A. Whitney. Sixteen new stories in an annual anthology series.

Greenberg, Martin H., John L. Lettenberg & Carol-Lynn Waugh, eds. *Holmes for the Holidays*. New York: Berkley. Fourteen new Sherlock Holmes stories with Christmas settings.

Greenberg, Martin H., Jill M. Morgan & Robert Weinberg, eds. *Great Writers & Kids Write Mystery Stories*. New York: Random House. Thirteen new children's stories by adult mystery writers collaborating with their children or grandchildren.

Haining, Peter, ed. *Crime Movies*. New York: Severn House. Twelve stories associated with famous crime films.

———, ed. *London After Midnight*. New York: Barnes & Noble Books. Twenty-two detective and crime stories from various sources.

———, ed. *Murder on the Railways*. London: Orion. Thirty-two detective and crime stories involving trains or subways.

———, ed. *The Orion Book of Murder*. London: Orion. Forty-five stories, arranged in three groupings of fifteen stories each, covering lawbreakers, police detectives, and private eyes.

———, ed. *Pulp Frictions*. London: Souvenir. Twenty hard-boiled stories, mainly from the pulps.

Hillerman, Tony & Rosemary Herbert, eds. *The Oxford Book of American*

Detective Stories. New York: Oxford University Press. Thirty-three stories, 1841–1991.

Hopler, Jay, ed. *The Killing Spirit: An Anthology of Murder for Hire*. Woodstock, NY: The Overlook Press. Seventeen stories about hit men, including four excerpts from novels. With an appendix of hit man movies.

Hutchings, Janet, ed. *Murder Most British*. New York: St. Martin's. Twenty stories, both classic and modern, from *Ellery Queen's Mystery Magazine*.

———, ed. *Once Upon a Crime II*. New York: St. Martin's Press. Sixteen historical mysteries from *EQMM*.

Jakubowski, Maxim, ed. *The Mammoth Book of Pulp Fiction*. London: Robinson. Thirty-two stories covering seven decades, including some modern hard-boiled tales.

Kaye, Marvin, ed. *The Resurrected Holmes: New Cases From the Notes of John H. Watson, M.D.* New York: St. Martin's Press. Fifteen new Sherlockian pastiches, each written in the style of a famous author.

Manson, Cynthia, ed. *Christmas Crimes*. New York: Signet. Twelve stories from *EQMM* and *AHMM*.

——— ed. *Garden of Deadly Delights*. New York: Signet. Nineteen mysteries about flowers and gardens, mainly from *EQMM* and *AHMM*.

——— ed. *Murder at Teatime: Mysteries in the Classic Cozy Tradition*. New York: Signet. Thirteen stories from *EQMM* and *AHMM*.

——— ed. *Mysterious Menagerie*. New York: Berkley. Sixteen stories involving animals, from *EQMM* and *AHMM*.

——— & Kathleen Halligan, eds. *Murder Intercontinental*. New York: Carroll & Graf. Twenty stories from *EQMM* and *AHMM*, set in various parts of the world.

——— & Constance Scarborough, eds. *Senior Sleuths*. New York: Berkley. Sixteen stories from *EQMM* and *AHMM* involving senior citizen sleuths.

———, eds. *Win, Lose, or Die*. New York: Carroll & Graf. Twenty-six stories about games and gambling from *EQMM* and *AHMM*.

Muller, Marcia & Bill Pronzini, eds. *A Century of Mystery 1980–1989: The Greatest Stories of the Decade*. New York: MJF Books/Fine Communications. Twenty stories from various sources, in the first of a planned anthology series. Introduction and headnotes by Edward D. Hoch.

Mysterious Erotic Tales. Edison, NJ: Castle Books. Eight new erotic stories and five reprints by Rendell, Stoker, Bloch, Highsmith, and Poe. (No editor credited.)

Mystery Scene, Staff of, eds. *The Year's 25 Finest Crime & Mystery Stories*. New York: Carroll & Graf. Twenty-five of 1995's best short mysteries.

Introduction by Jon L. Breen, bibliography and necrology by Edward D. Hoch.

Oates, Joyce Carol, ed. *American Gothic Tales*. New York: Plume/Penguin. Fifty stories by forty-six authors, from various sources. Mainly fantasy but some criminous.

Olmsted, Helen Esper, ed. *Homicide Host Presents*. Aurora, CO: Write Way Publishing. Fourteen new mystery and crime stories.

Paretsky, Sara, ed. *Women on the Case*. New York: Delacorte. Twenty-six new mystery and crime stories by women writers from several countries.

Penzler, Otto, ed. *Murder For Love*. New York: Delacorte. Fourteen new stories and two poems by best-selling authors, including Michael Malone's Edgar-winner "Red Clay."

Randisi, Robert J., ed. *First Cases: First Appearances of Classic Private Eyes*. New York: Dutton. Fifteen stories of contemporary private eyes from various sources.

Ripley, Mike & Maxim Jakubowski, eds. *Fresh Blood*. London: The Do-Not Press. Twelve new stories and two reprints.

Skene-Melvin, David, ed. *Investigating Women: Female Detectives by Canadian Writers, An Eclectic Sampler*. Toronto: Simon & Pierre. Sixteen stories, six of them new, with a historical survey by the editor. (1995)

Turow, Scott, ed. *Guilty as Charged*. New York: Pocket Books. Sixteen new legal stories in an anthology from Mystery Writers of America.

Waugh, Charles G. & Martin H. Greenberg, eds. *Supernatural Sleuths*. New York: Penguin/Roc. Fourteen stories, mainly fantasy.

Westlake, Donald, ed. *Murderous Schemes: An Anthology of Classic Detective Stories*. New York: Oxford University Press. Consulting Editor: J. Madison Davis. Thirty-two stories from various sources in a volume from the International Association of Crime Writers.

Wilson, F. Paul, ed. *Diagnosis: Terminal. An Anthology of Medical Terror*. New York: Forge/St. Martin's Press. Fourteen new crime and horror stories.

III. NONFICTION

Ashley, Mike & William C. Contento. *The Supernatural Index: A Listing of Fantasy, Supernatural, Occult, Weird, and Horror Anthologies*. Westport, CT: Greenwood Press. Includes some mystery and crime anthologies. (1995)

Atkinson, Michael. *The Secret Marriage of Sherlock Holmes*. Ann Arbor: University of Michigan Press. Sherlockiana.

Beinhart, Larry. *How to Write a Mystery*. New York: Ballantine. A guide for beginning writers.

Belford, Barbara. *Bram Stoker: A Biography of the Author of* Dracula. New York: Knopf. A life of the mystery-horror-fantasy novelist.

Bounds, J. Dennis. *Perry Mason: The Authorship and Reproduction of a Popular Hero*. Westport, CT: Greenwood Press. A study of Erle Stanley Gardner's most popular creation.

Chase, Elaine Raco & Anne Wingate. *Amateur Detectives*. Cincinnati: Writer's Digest Books. A writer's guide.

Clark, Al. *Raymond Chandler in Hollywood*. Los Angeles: Silman-James Press. Updated edition of a title first published in 1982, covering Chandler's years in Hollywood and the various film versions of his novels.

Cooper, John & B. A. Pike. *Artists in Crime: An Illustrated Survey of Crime Fiction First Edition Dustwrappers 1920–1970*. Brookfield, VT: Scolar/Ashgate. Illustrations of some 350 (mainly British) dust jackets, forty-eight in color, with brief comments on the jacket artists and the relationship of their art to each book's plot. (1995)

Dale, Alzina Stone. *Mystery Reader's Walking Guide: Chicago*. Chicago: Passport Books/NTC Publishing. Walking tours of the city, spotlighting places mentioned in well-known mystery novels. (1995)

Greene, Graham. *The Quiet American: Text and Criticism*. New York: Penguin. Edited by John Clark Pratt. A volume in the Viking Critical Library containing the full text of Greene's novel plus twenty-eight essays and reviews examining it as reportage, political statement, detective story, allegory, and romance.

Haut, Woody. *Pulp Culture: Hardboiled Fiction and the Cold War*. New York: Serpent's Tail. A study of hardboiled mystery writers in the period from 1945 to 1963.

Hutchison, Don. *The Great Pulp Heroes*. Oakville, Ontario, Canada & Buffalo, NY: Mosaic Press. Chapters on The Shadow, Doc Savage, and a dozen other pulp heroes, with accounts of their authors and the magazines that published them.

Keirans, James E. *Poison and Poisoners in the Mysteries of John Dickson Carr*. South Benfleet, Essex, England: CADS. A 57-page booklet published by the popular British fanzine, containing an alphabetical annotated list of references to poisons and poisoners in Carr's works.

Kellerman, Jonathan & Faye. *Jonathan and Faye Kellerman Bibliography 1972–1996*. Mission Viejo, CA: A.S.A.P. Publishing. A 54-page chapbook listing all Kellerman books and short stories. Introduction by Faye Kellerman, afterword by Jonathan Kellerman. Includes a reprint of Faye Kellerman's story "Malibu Dog."

Mellen, Joan. *Hellman and Hammett: The Legendary Passion of Lillian Hellman and Dashiell Hammett*. New York: HarperCollins. The intertwined lives of the playwright and the mystery writer, from their meeting in 1930 until their deaths.

Miller, Ron. *Mystery! A Celebration: Stalking Public Television's Greatest Sleuths.* San Francisco: KQED Books. An illustrated history of the popular PBS television series, from its beginnings in 1980 through the 1996–97 season, describing every series and individual story, authors, actors, hosts, etc. Foreword by P. D. James.

North, John, ed. *Dishes to Die For . . .* Scarborough, Ont., Canada: Crime Writers of Canada. A cookbook with recipes contributed by Canadian mystery writers.

Page, David W., M.D. *Body Trauma.* Cincinnati: Writer's Digest Books. A writer's guide to wounds and injuries.

Pederson, Jay P., ed. *St. James Guide to Crime & Mystery Writers.* Detroit: St. James Press. Updated fourth edition of the retitled *Twentieth Century Crime & Mystery Writers.* Preface by Kathleen Gregory Klein.

Pelzer, Linda C. *Mary Higgins Clark: A Critical Companion.* Westport, CT: Greenwood Press. Introduction by Kathleen Gregory Klein. An academic study of Clark's plots and characters, designed for writing students. Includes interviews, reviews, and bibliography. (1995)

Rosenheim, Shawn James. *The Cryptographic Imagination: Secret Writing from Edgar Poe to the Internet.* Baltimore: Johns Hopkins University Press. A study of cryptography in literature, beginning with Poe.

Sayers, Dorothy L. *The Letters of Dorothy L. Sayers: 1899–1936: The Making of a Detective Novelist.* New York: St. Martin's. Edited by Barbara Reynolds, with a preface by P. D. James. Hundreds of letters covering Sayers's childhood and her career as a mystery writer. The first of two volumes.

Skene-Melvin, David. *Canadian Crime Fiction.* Shelburne, Ontario, Canada: The Battered Silicon Dispatch Box. An annotated bibliography, 1817–1996, with a biographical dictionary of Canadian crime writers.

Soitos, Stephen F. *The Blues Detective: A Study of African American Detective Fiction.* Amherst: University of Massachusetts Press. A history and critical study.

Sova, Dawn B. *Agatha Christie A to Z: The Essential Reference to Her Life and Work.* New York: Facts on File. An alphabetical guide.

Swanson, Jean & Dean James. *By a Woman's Hand: A Guide to Mystery Fiction by Women. Second Edition.* New York: Berkley. Revised and expanded edition of a book first published in 1994.

Talbot, Rob. *Brother Cadfael's Herb Garden.* London: Little Brown. Illustrated descriptions of all plants and herbs mentioned in Ellis Peters's Cadfael novels.

Thompson, Peggy & Saeko Usukawa. *Hard-boiled: Great Lines from Classic Noir Films.* San Francisco: Chronicle Books. Over 300 lines from crime films of the 1930s, '40s, and '50s, indexed and illustrated with scenes from the films. Introduction by Lee Server. (1995)

Turnbull, Malcolm J. *Elusion Aforethought: The Life and Writings of Anthony Berkeley Cox.* Bowling Green, OH: Bowling Green State University Popular Press. A critical biography of the Golden Age mystery writer best known as Anthony Berkeley and Francis Iles.

Van Hise, James. *Pulpmasters.* Yucca Valley, CA: Midnight Graffiti. Sixteen essays, many new, on pulp writers and the characters they created.

Villines, Sharon, ed. *The Deadly Directory, 1997–1998 International Edition.* New York: Deadly Serious Press. An expanded edition of a telephone and address book of the mystery, detective, and crime fiction world, listing bookstores, conventions, web sites, etc.

Walsdorf, John J., with the assistance of Bonnie J. Allen. *Julian Symons: A Bibliography.* New Castle, Delaware: Oak Knoll Press. A complete bibliography of fiction, poetry, and nonfiction, with commentaries, including a personal memoir by the late British mystery writer, a brief memoir by his wife, and a preface by H. R. F. Keating.

Necrology

Robert H. Adleman (1919–1995). Author of two crime novels, including the fact-based *The Bloody Benders* (1970).

Spiro T. Agnew (1918–1996). Former U.S. vice president who authored a single political thriller, *The Canfield Decision* (1976).

Marvin H. Albert (1924–1996). Author of more than one hundred westerns, mysteries, spy novels, and nonfiction books under his own name and as by Mike Barone, J. D. Christilian, Al Conroy, Albert Conroy, Ian MacAlister, Nick Quarry, and Anthony Rome, notably the Edgar-nominated *The Gargoyle Conspiracy* (1975).

Harrison Arnston (?–1996). Author of several original paperback mysteries beginning in 1987 with *The Warning.* Cofounder of MWA's Florida chapter.

C. C. Bergius (1910–1996). Pseudonym of Egon Maria Zimmer, author of a single crime novel, *The Noble Forger* (1962), translated from the German.

Kenneth Bernstein (1929?–1996). NBC-TV correspondent who authored two thrillers, *Intercept* and *The Senator's Ransom* (both 1971).

Caroline Blackwood (1931–1996). British author of at least two crime novels, *The Fate of Mary Rose* (1981) and *Corrigan* (1984).

William J. Caunitz (1933–1996). Former New York City police lieutenant who authored six best-selling police novels starting with *One Police Plaza* (1984).

Richard Condon (1915–1996). Well-known author of twenty-five novels, mainly crime-suspense, notably *The Manchurian Candidate* (1959) and *Prizzi's Honor* (1982).

Margaret Cousins (1905–1996). Writer and editor who authored a single crime novel *Traffic With Evil* (1962) under the pseudonym of Avery Johns.

Norman A. Daniels (1910?–1996?). Best-known pseudonym of Norman A. Danberg, pulp and paperback writer who also published as John L. Benton, William Dale, Peter Grady, Frank Johnson, G. Wayman Jones, Harrison Judd, C. K. N. Scanlon, and Robert Wallace. Author of more than sixty novels, about three dozen in the mystery-crime field, as well as some 250 stories and novelettes, many about pulp sleuths The Phantom, The Black Bat, The Masked Detective, and Dan Fowler.

William L. DeAndrea. (1952–1996). Author of more than a dozen detective novels including two Edgar winners, *Killed in the Ratings* (1978) and *The Hog Murders* (1979). He also wrote and edited an important non-fiction work, *Encyclopedia Mysteriosa* (1994) and contributed a column to *The Armchair Detective* for twelve years. He published two novels under the pseudonym of Philip DeGrave.

Gordon De Marco (1944?–1995). Author of four mystery novels in the 1980s and founder of West Coast Crime, a San Francisco publisher.

Madelaine Duke (1925–1996). British author of mainstream novels and travel books, in addition to seven mystery novels, two published first in England as by Maxim Donne. Past president of the Crime Writers Association.

Marguerite Duras (1914–1996). Well-known French author of mainstream novels, including at least two crime novels, notably *Ten-Thirty on a Summer Night* (1962).

Mignon G. Eberhart (1899–1996). Well-known author of fifty-nine suspense novels starting with *The Patient in Room 18* (1929), and several short story collections, notably *The Cases of Susan Dare* (1934). A past president of Mystery Writers of America and recipient of its Grand Master Award.

James Elward (1928–1996). Novelist who authored two mysteries in the 1970s under the pseudonym of Rebecca James and another, *Monday's Child Is Dead* (1995), under his own name.

Shusako Endo (1923–1996). Japanese Catholic novelist who authored a borderline suspense novel, *Scandal* (1988).

William K. Everson (1929–1996). Film historian who authored *The Detective in Film* (1972).

Jesse Hill Ford (1928–1996). Mainstream novelist who authored *The Liberation of Lord Byron Jones* (1965) and won an MWA Edgar for his short story "The Jail" (1975).

Leon Garfield (1921–1996). Writer of children's books who authored two crime novels, one of them a continuation of Dickens's *The Mystery of Edwin Drood*.

Paul J. Gillette (1938–1996). Author of a crime novel and two paperback novelizations of films, notably *Play Misty for Me* (1971).

S. T. Haymon (1918–1996). Professional name of British author Sylvia Theresa Haymon, who published a series of novels about Inspector Ben Jurner, notably the CWA Silver Dagger winner *Ritual Murder* (1982).

Cornelius Hirschberg, (1901–1995). Author of a single mystery novel, the Edgar-winning *Florentine Finish* (1963).

Eleanor "Betty" Inglefield (1908?–1996). British author of three short stories in *London Mystery Magazine*.

Eugene Izzi (1953–1996). Author of a dozen or more crime and suspense novels beginning with *The Take* (1987), set mainly in Chicago. He also published four novels under the name of Nick Gaitano.

Molly Keane (1904?–1996). Mainstream author whose work included at least one crime novel, *Good Behavior* (1981).

Harry Kemelman (1908–1996). Well-known author of the popular Rabbi David Small series of eleven novels, starting with *Friday the Rabbi Slept Late* (1964). He also published a classic short story collection, *The Nine Mile Walk* (1967).

Walter Kerr (1913–1996). Well-known drama critic who authored three one-act mystery plays, 1935–40.

Graham Landrum (1923?–1995). Author of *The Famous DAR Murder Mystery* (1992) and others.

Michel Lebrun (1930–1996). Best-known pseudonym of Michel Cade, French mystery writer who also edited a number of anthologies.

Ethel Lindsay (1920?–1996). British fan who authored *Here Be Mystery and Murder* (1982), a privately printed guide to nonfiction books in the mystery field.

Leo Malet (1909–1996). Well-known French mystery writer and precursor of the modern French thriller, who published a series of fifteen darkly humorous novels about private eye Nestor Burma, *The New Mysteries of Paris*, starting in 1943. The character became popular on French television, but the books remain unpublished in English.

Ernest Mandel (1923?–1995). Marxist writer who authored *Delightful Murder, A Social History of the Crime Story* (1984).

Derek Marlowe (1938–1996). British author of five spy and intrigue novels, notably *A Dandy in Aspic* (1966).

Berkley Mather (1909?-1996). Pseudonym of John E. W. Davies, British author of more than a dozen spy and adventure thrillers, starting with *The Achilles Affair* (1959).

Philip McCutchan (1920–1996). British author of some fifty mysteries and thrillers, many about Commander Shaw. Also published a dozen novels of intrigue as "Robert Conington Galway."

Thomas M. McDade (1907–1996). An FBI agent prior to World War II, he became active in MWA and the Baker Street Irregulars, publishing a story and a Sherlockian essay in *EQMM* (9/49, 2/57) and winning a special Edgar for his fact-crime bibliography *Annals of Murder* (1961).

(Edward) Shepherd Mead (1914–1994). Humorist who published a novel of industrial espionage, *How to Succeed at Business Spying by Trying* (1968).

Sam Merwin Jr. (1910–1996). Science fiction author and editor who also published nine mystery novels under his own name and other novels and stories as Elizabeth Deare Bennett, Clarke Hammond, Angela Davidson, Rebecca Noyes Winstead, and Carter Sprague. As Brett Halliday he authored ten novelets for *Mike Shayne Mystery Magazine*.

Diana Morgan (1908?–1996). British actress and playwright who authored a few mystery plays, notably a 1979 dramatization of Daphne Du Maurier's *My Cousin Rachel*.

Anton Myrer (1922–1996). Mainstream author who published one crime novel, *The Intruder* (1965).

Al Nusbaum (1934–1996). Author of numerous short stories in *EQMM* (1982–92) and elsewhere under his own name and as by Carl Martin.

Anthony Oliver (1922–1995). British author of four detective novels featuring Lizzie Thomas and Inspector Webber.

Jack Popplewell (1909?–1996). British playwright who authored at least seven mystery dramas, notably *Blind Alley* (1956).

Frank Riley (1915–1996). Science fiction author whose work included two suspense novels, *The Kocska Formula* (1971) and *Jesus II* (1972).

Samuel Rosenberg (1910–1996). Author of *Naked Is the Best Disguise* (1974), which traced the literary and sexual roots of the Sherlock Holmes canon.

Bob Shaw (1931–1996). Irish science fiction writer who published a 1973 short story collection, *Tomorrow Lies in Ambush*, containing at least two crime stories.

Stirling Silliphant (1918–1996). Oscar-winning screenwriter for his adaptation of *In the Heat of the Night* (1967), who also published four paperback crime novels.

George H. Smith (1922–1996). Science fiction writer who authored a Sherlockian novel, *The Second War of the Worlds* (1978), and also a paperback crime novel as by Hal Stryker.

Edward Stewart (1938–1996). Author of a half dozen crime and mystery novels, from *Heads* (1969) to *Jury Double* (1997).

Dan Streib (1928–1996). Author of some twenty-five mystery-adventure novels under his own name plus others as Frank Colter, Mark Cruz, Paul Richards, Paul Ross, and once as Nick Carter.

John F. Suter (1914–1996). Author of some fifty short stories, mainly in *EQMM* and *AHMM*, sixteen of which continued Melville Davisson Post's "Uncle Abner" series. Nineteen of Suter's stories are collected in *Old Land, Dark Land, Strange Land* (1996).

L. A. Taylor (1939–1996). Byline of Laurie Aylma Taylor Sparer, author of a dozen novels, mainly crime and mystery but some science fiction.

Ira Wallach (1913?–1995). Under the pseudonym of Lillian Roberts, he authored a novelization of the 1975 film *Rafferty and the Gold Dust Twins*.

Evangeline Walton (1907–1996). Professional name of Evangeline Walton Ensley, well-known fantasy writer who published one mystery-fantasy, *Witch House* (1945).

Stephen Wasylyk (1923?–1996). Author of more than one hundred short stories in *AHMM* and *EQMM*, beginning in 1968.

Collin Wilcox (1924–1996). Author of some thirty crime novels, many of them police procedurals about Lt. Frank Hastings of the San Francisco Homicide Squad. He also published a nonseries suspense novel as by Carter Wick and collaborated with Bill Pronzini on *Twospot* (1978).

Ann M. Williams (1936?–1996). Author and fan whose first mystery novel, *Flowers for the Dead*, was published in 1991. From 1986 through 1996 she edited and published *The Criminal Record*, a magazine of mystery reviews.

Drood Review's Editors' Choice list

BEST OF 1996

No Birds Sing by Jo Bannister
The Whispering Wall by Patricia Carlon
The Chatham School Affair by Thomas Cook
Kill Me Again by Terence Faherty
Hearts and Bones by Margaret Lawrence
The Mermaid's Singing by Val McDermid
Tularosa by Michael McGarrity
The Death of Friends by Michael Nava
Dance for the Dead by Thomas Perry
A Brother's Blood by Michael C. White

FIVE BEST ONGOING SERIES

Elizabeth Eyre's Sigismondo
Reginald Hill's Dalziel & Pascoe
William Marshall's Yellowthread Street
Kate Ross's Julian Kestrel
S. J. Rozan's Lydia Chin/Bill Smith

FIVE MOST UNDERAPPRECIATED WRITERS

Jo Bannister
K. C. Constantine
Peter Dickinson
Terence Faherty
Barbara Paul

341

FIVE FAVORITE MALE DETECTIVES

Michael Connelly's Harry Bosch
Robert Crais's Elvis Cole
Parnell Hall's Stanley Hastings
Peter Lovesey's Peter Diamond
William Tapply's Brady Coyne

FIVE FAVORITE FEMALE DETECTIVES

Linda Barnes's Carlotta Carlyle
Nevada Barr's Anna Pigeon
Laurie King's Mary Russell
Patricia Moyes's Emily (and Henry) Tibbett
Dana Stabenow's Kate Shugak

FIVE BOOKS WE'D LIKE TO SEE IN PRINT AGAIN

On My Honor by Malacai Black (Barbara D'Amato)
P. M. Carlson's Maggie Ryan series
Liza Cody's Anna Lee series
Murder's Out of Tune by Simon Shaw
anything by June Thomson

About *The Drood Review*:

The Drood Review of Mystery is the genre's foremost book review newsletter. Published on a bimonthly schedule and now in its sixteenth year, *The Drood Review* offers reviews of and comments about current mysteries, along with comprehensive listings of new and forthcoming titles. An annual subscription is $14 in the U.S.; a sample copy is $2.50. Contact: *The Drood Review*, Box 50267, Kalamazoo, MI 49005.